Liberalism, Diversity and Domination

This study addresses the complex and often fractious relationship between liberal political theory and difference by examining how distinctive liberalisms respond to human diversity. Drawing on published and unpublished writings, private correspondence and lecture notes, the study offers comprehensive reconstructions of Immanuel Kant's and John Stuart Mill's treatments of racial, cultural, gender-based and class-based difference to understand how two leading figures reacted to pluralism, and what contemporary readers might draw from them. The book mounts a qualified defence of Millian liberalism against Kantianism's predominance in contemporary liberal political philosophy, and resists liberalism's implicit association with imperialist domination by showing different liberalisms' divergent responses to diversity. Here are two distinctive liberal visions of moral and political life.

Inder S. Marwah is Assistant Professor of Political Science at McMaster University, Ontario. He has published articles in political theory in leading peer-reviewed journals. His research focuses on the intersection of race, empire, and political theory, both in the history of political thought and in the present.

Liberalism, Diversity and Domination

Kant, Mill and the Government of Difference

INDER S. MARWAH

McMaster University

CAMBRIDGE
UNIVERSITY PRESS

University Printing House, Cambridge CB2 8BS, United Kingdom

One Liberty Plaza, 20th Floor, New York, NY 10006, USA

477 Williamstown Road, Port Melbourne, VIC 3207, Australia

314–321, 3rd Floor, Plot 3, Splendor Forum, Jasola District Centre,
New Delhi – 110025, India

79 Anson Road, #06–04/06, Singapore 079906

Cambridge University Press is part of the University of Cambridge.

It furthers the University's mission by disseminating knowledge in the pursuit of
education, learning, and research at the highest international levels of excellence.

www.cambridge.org
Information on this title: www.cambridge.org/9781108493789
DOI: 10.1017/9781108608497

© Inder S. Marwah 2019

First published 2019

Printed and bound in Great Britain by Clays Ltd, Elcograf S.p.A.

A catalogue record for this publication is available from the British Library.

Library of Congress Cataloging-in-Publication Data
NAMES: Marwah, Inder S., 1977– author.
TITLE: Liberalism, diversity and domination : Kant, Mill, and the government of difference /
Inder S. Marwah, McMaster University, Ontario.
DESCRIPTION: New York : Cambridge University Press, [2019] | Includes bibliographical
references.
IDENTIFIERS: LCCN 2019003157 | ISBN 9781108493789
SUBJECTS: LCSH: Liberalism – Philosophy. | Pluralism – Political aspects. | Kant, Immanuel,
1724–1804. | Mill, John Stuart, 1806–1873
CLASSIFICATION: LCC JC574 .M392 2019 | DDC 320.51–dc23
LC record available at https://lccn.loc.gov/2019003157

ISBN 978-1-108-49378-9 Hardback

For Lally and Marlène Marwah

Contents

Acknowledgments

This book owes a lot of debts to a lot of people, which have only accrued over its long (too long) development. The kernel started at the University of Toronto and gained its shape from the wise counsel and steering of both peers and teachers. On the latter front, I owe special thanks to Peggy Kohn, Joe Carens and, most of all, Ronnie Beiner. All were as perceptive as they were supportive, and Ronnie in particular was endlessly generous with his time and attention, and still is. Peggy sparked a critical inclination that has only grown over time, and there are few conceptual muddles, I discovered, that can't be unriddled over a dog walk with Joe. Simone Chambers and Lisa Ellis provided invaluable feedback on this project's early phases, along with equally invaluable guidance in the intervening years. Their exemplary scholarship on Kant, along with Arthur Ripstein's seminar on his legal and political philosophy, shaped my appreciation for Kant's ethical and political thought, and whatever comprehension I might have of it is their doing (the misapprehensions remain mine). I had the good fortune to be surrounded by a vibrant group of theorists in Toronto, including Kiran Banerjee, Erica Frederiksen, Özgür Gürel, Margaret Haderer, Alex Livingston, James McKee, Mihaela Mihai, Adrian Neer, Jakeet Singh, Leah Soroko, Serdar Tekin and Mathias Thaler, many of whom remain cherished interlocutors. All have commented on, cut to pieces or otherwise improved the rough patch of ideas from which this book emerged, and I very much appreciate it. Alex and Kiran, in particular, read way more of this, at way rougher stages, than any person should have to. Their generosity as critics is exceeded only by their generosity as friends.

A second community of scholars, at the University of Chicago, were especially influential in moving this book toward its final form. Over an all-too-brief time in Chicago, I not only benefited from their rich expertise, but also came to see what political theory looks like from a different vantage point. I'm grateful to have had the opportunity to shift my sights. Daniel Nichanian kindly scheduled me into the Political Theory Workshop on short notice, where Gordon Arlen offered incisive comments. Patchen Markell graciously discussed the introduction and pushed me to clarify the project's ambitions. Sankar Muthu indulged me with many long and invariably generative discussions on Kant. My greatest debt, though, is owed to Jennifer Pitts, who drew this book's latent argument to the fore. Despite our divergences over Mill's political philosophy, Jennifer was unfailingly open and generous in her willingness to argue them with me, and in hosting me at the Department of Political Science. She is a model of scholarly capaciousness and insight, and I am profoundly grateful to her.

Thanks are also owed to audiences at conferences and workshops who provided vital feedback on various parts of various chapters. These include annual meetings of the American Political Science Association, the Western Political Science Association, the Canadian Political Science Association and, most helpfully, the Association for Political Theory, whose intellectual community has been (and continues to be) exceptionally vibrant and supportive. Workshops at Acadia University, the University of Toronto, the University of Chicago and the University of Cambridge were singularly productive, and I thank them for hosting me. Over the years, I have also profited from colleagues and friends willing to share their ideas and ameliorate mine. I would like to thank Barbara Arneil, Duncan Bell, Stefan Dolgert, Stephen Engelmann, Loren Goldman, Burke Hendrix, Jared Holley, Murad Idris, Onur Ulas Ince, Duncan Ivison, Emma Stone Mackinnon, Karuna Mantena, Ben McKean, Charles Mills, Jeanne Morefield, Menaka Philips, Phil Triadafilopoulos, Inés Valdez and Lynn Zastoupil for more or less formal or informal comments and conversations pushing me to rethink things. In addition to editing the introduction, Daniel Aureliano Newman has over a lifelong friendship quietly shaped not just what's here, but my interests and person more generally.

McMaster University is a wonderful disciplinary home, and I'm grateful to my colleagues in the Department of Political Science for their ever-present support and interest – in particular, James Ingram, whose spirited engagement and provocations have improved this book beyond measure. I'm also grateful to the graduate students I've been fortunate to know at McMaster, whose originality and inquisitiveness always change my perspective, and always for the better. One such student, Justin Ng, provided valuable editorial assistance, and I thank him for it.

Generous support in the form of a postdoctoral scholarship from the Social Sciences and Humanities Council of Canada provided the time and space to move this book forward. Various parts of it appeared earlier in several journal articles. Sections of Chapters 2 and 3 were first published in "*Elateres Motiva*: From the Good Will to the Good Human Being," *Kantian Review* 18, no. 3 (2013): 413–437; "What Nature Makes of Her: Kant's Gendered Metaphysics," *Hypatia* 28, no. 3 (2013): 551–567; and "Bridging Nature and Freedom? Kant, Culture and Cultivation," *Social Theory and Practice* 38, no. 3 (July 2012): 385–406. A section of Chapter 5 originally appeared as

"Complicating Barbarism and Civilization: Mill's Complex Sociology of Human Development," *History of Political Thought* 32, no. 2 (2011): 345–366, and a brief segment of Chapter 6 was first published in "Two Concepts of Liberal Developmentalism," *European Journal of Political Theory* 15, no. 1 (2016): 97–123. All are reprinted with permission, for which I am grateful to the journals and their presses.

I'm also grateful to Cambridge University Press, and particularly, to Robert Dreesen, who has guided this book through the editorial process with equal measures of patience and enthusiasm. Robert Judkins, Doreen Kruger and Krishna Prasath have been invaluable in transforming the manuscript into a book, and I'm especially indebted to the press's two reviewers for their attentiveness, critical acumen and generosity.

Finally, thanks are owed to my family, and to my family-in-law for their constant warmth and kindness, as well as for introducing me to Cornish pasties (they're delicious). My brother Jaspal's boundless independence of thought is inspiring, as is his willingness to hop on a plane and come explore whatever city the WPSA happens to be in on any given year. My wife Morwenna has borne the many ups and downs that accompanied this project with unwavering good-heartedness, support and love. She is the pivot around which my life revolves, and I'd be entirely lost without her. My children, Piran and Una, make anything and everything worthwhile, and have patiently (as patiently as toddlers are able) tolerated evenings and weekends sucked into the vortex of this book. My greatest thanks are for my parents. Their enduring intellectual curiosity not only remains a beacon to aspire to, but instilled in me from as early as I can remember an unquestioned faith in the value of learning. Of the innumerable goods they have graced me with, chief among them was never having to wonder whether this kind of a life was worth pursuing. This book is dedicated to them.

I

Introduction

[T]hat which remains "unrealized" by the universal constitutes it essentially.

Judith Butler, *Excitable Speech*

1.1 HATING MILL, AND A FEW QUESTIONS RAISED BY HATING MILL

The impetus for this book was cemented at a conference where I gave a paper on Kant's and Mill's philosophies of history. The presentations concluded and our discussant began: "Now, I normally absolutely hate John Stuart Mill, but..."

What other political philosopher is, today, perceived as so evidently misguided (perhaps downright malevolent) that one might comfortably assume an audience's sympathy – or at the very least, understanding – in treating his views as presumptively detestable? More striking than the strong feelings that Mill elicited was the supposition that his liberalism was so clearly wrong-headed and corrupted by his imperial entanglements that it seemed barely necessary to qualify the opening salvo. This wasn't a unique experience. John Stuart Mill's moral and political philosophy has, in recent years, fallen on hard times, as the hostility toward it has become palpable in many parts of the discipline. Recent work by Jennifer Pitts, Thomas McCarthy, Bhikhu Parekh and Uday Singh Mehta – to name only a few of the best-developed critiques in what has become a substantial literature – has persuasively drawn out his liberal imperialism, and in so doing, thrown into question the viability of his thought.

The charges against him are as varied as they are damning. Critics contend that Mill conjoined an impoverished, reductive account of the Scottish Enlightenment's "four stages" theory of development with a Benthamite utilitarianism to generate a rigid index of social advancement. The resulting civilizational hierarchy provided the theoretical justification for British imperialism, which Mill's long tenure at the East India Company certainly appears to confirm. In this, he's understood to uncritically reproduce (and even further entrench) his father James Mill's faith in a universal course of human history, carved out by Europe, through which all societies would progress. In the Mills' imagination, history charts humanity's progressive rationalization, our movement from savagery, through barbarism, and upward toward civilization. Beyond justifying despotic colonial rule, this incorporative historicism leaves little space to register the worth of non-European cultures by "assimilat[ing] all 'rude' peoples into a single category of moral and political inferiority"[1] – Europe's own past, frozen in time. John Stuart Mill's view of progress is, then, emblematic of the western tendency to treat "historical time as a measure of the cultural distance (at least in institutional development) that was assumed to exist between the West and the non-West."[2] His liberalism is by consequence taken to be internally – conceptually – bound to a racially inflected gradation of societies sustaining his ambitions as a colonial administrator.

Mill's personal history further compounds these charges. He was the son of James Mill, a principal architect of early nineteenth-century British colonialism in India and the author of *The History of British India*, the period's standard reference work on the subcontinent (proofread in its entirety by the younger Mill at the age of 11), which portrayed Indian society as backward, irrational and in desperate need of European governance. The elder Mill's sway over his son is well documented: as J. S. Mill readily acknowledges, James Mill exercised an outsized influence over his personal, intellectual and professional development. Beyond the "effect my father produced on my character,"[3] documented in his *Autobiography*, he was also drafted by James Mill into the East India Company in 1823, at the age of 17, where he rose to serve as a high-ranking functionary for 35 years. J. S. Mill's accounts of race, civilization, government and progress are as a result commonly treated as substantively similar, if not identical, to his father's.

In short, Mill's is in many critics' view an exemplary imperialist liberalism, taken to carry all of its most objectionable philosophical commitments: a stage-based account of human development blind to the value of non-European cultures; a civilizational discourse securing, in Edward Said's words, Europeans' "positional superiority";[4] a categorical and Manichean distinction between progressive, western societies and retrograde, non-western ones; a hubristic paternalism consigning colonial subjects to a permanent state of "not yet,"[5] as Dipesh Chakrabarty characterizes it; a view of historical progress as universal, inevitable and convergent; a conflation of modernization and westernization; and the list goes on. Still worse, we need only look to *On Liberty*'s restriction of self-government to peoples "in the maturity of their faculties"[6] to see that these troubling features appear central, and not merely peripheral, to his liberalism.

His views on international law and transnational relations fare no better: as Jennifer Pitts observes, Mill explicitly excluded "barbarians" from the "moral rules" governing interactions between civilized states.[7] "To be a Millian liberal," Bhikhu Parekh concludes, "is to take a condescending and paternalistic view of non-liberal societies."[8] Analysts of liberalism and empire are not alone in their criticisms. Dana Villa and Charles Larmore, for instance, find in Mill's liberalism a perfectionism particularly ill-suited to the pluralistic societies we have come to inhabit.[9] His readiness to use "laws and social arrangements"[10] to harmonize individual happiness with the social good sits as uncomfortably with late modern diversity as with liberal-democratic commitments to state neutrality. In total, then, Parekh's view exemplifies what has become the default position in liberal political theory: Mill is no longer the wellspring of moral, political, normative or institutional insight to which liberals turn in navigating ethical and political dilemmas – and still less so when those pertain to the challenges presented by present-day pluralism.

Our wellspring, today, is Kant. Since 1971, Kant's stature in liberal political theory has become virtually hegemonic. Current liberal theory is shaped by his moral and political philosophy and adopts many of its presumptions (albeit in importantly renovated ways). This is, of course, due to its operating almost entirely within the normative, methodological, vernacular and ideational space carved out by John Rawls's *A Theory of Justice*. Rawls's Kantian constructivism gave Anglo-American political philosophy the shot in the arm it so desperately needed in the early 1970s, and in so doing carved out the questions and approach steering liberal political thought that remain with us today. Since then, Kant's influence – alongside Rawls's – has only become more firmly entrenched in mainstream liberal theory, spreading far beyond Rawls, his followers and his critics. As William Galston puts it, contemporary normative theory "has rested to an extraordinary degree on Kantian foundations ... Kant [has] unexpectedly become the preeminent practical philosopher of our day."[11]

Kant also figures prominently in international and cosmopolitan political thought.[12] "In recent years," David Armitage observes, "Kant has become variously the theorist of democratic peace, the avatar of institutional internationalism and the grandfather of globalisation."[13] From Habermas's cogitations on perpetual peace to Seyla Benhabib's hospitality-based cosmopolitanism, Kant's dream of a law-governed global order continues to inform contemporary reflections on international justice, right and law.[14] A suitably chastened Kant also provides the normative direction for certain strands of recent critical theory, such as Thomas McCarthy's critical theory of global development (which I engage throughout this book, particularly in Chapter 6). Kant's "approach to the tasks of universal history," McCarthy holds, "is a more viable option today than more strongly theoretical approaches descended from Hegel, Marx, or the evolutionary theories that succeeded them."[15] Kant's credibility as an international theorist is further buttressed by his explicit and oft-cited opposition to European imperialism. Imperialism was, in his view, a fundamentally irrational mode of global intercourse, detracting not only from present and future peace, but also from commerce, a much more fruitful form of transnational relation.[16] It was also unwarranted from the perspective of right: a state's interest in interfering with an existing legal order, he argued, "can no more annul that condition of right than can the pretext of revolutionaries within a state."[17] Given this principled resistance to political expansionism, Sankar Muthu and Pauline Kleingeld take Kant's cosmopolitanism to anchor "his defence of non-European peoples' resistance against European imperial power."[18] Kant thus retains a marked currency in contemporary cosmopolitan political thought, framing the relationship between states and peoples in important ways.

Even critics of liberal political theory can't help but to engage Kant and neo-Kantianism. As James Miller observes, Michel Foucault – an exacting expositor of liberalism, neoliberalism and post-Enlightenment humanism, if there ever was one – "never ceased to consider himself a kind of Kantian."[19] That Kantianism floated to the surface in his late life, when he drew on "What is Enlightenment?" to sketch "a philosophical ethos that could be described as a permanent critique of our historical era."[20] Kant's project of radical critique, Foucault confessed, initiated the line of inquiry – driven by the question: "in what is given to us as universal, necessary, obligatory, what place is occupied by whatever is singular, contingent, and the product of arbitrary constraints?"[21] – within which he situated his own efforts. William Connolly, conversely, treats liberal theory's endemic Kantianism as its principal failing. Kant's misbegotten fantasy of isolating reason from the vagaries of the phenomenal world is reflected in the "bland intellectualism" of neo-Kantian liberalisms that "neglect [thinking's] affective sources, somatic entanglements, and effects."[22] The deficits of liberalism, Connolly tells us, are really deficits of its Kantianism. The broader deficit, you might say, is that contemporary liberalism *is* Kantian liberalism.

I want to argue that there are problems with this state of affairs that we can tease out of my erstwhile discussant's comments, and that shed light on this book's central concerns. The first is historical and exegetical: the presumption that Mill's commitments as an imperialist directly impugn his moral and political philosophy, and that they clearly reflect his views on human diversity more generally (the converse also holds true: Kant's anti-imperialism is taken to demonstrate his openness, tolerance, or benign indifference toward social, cultural and racial heterogeneity). Mill is an imperialist, his political thought is qualified by that imperialism, and as such it is constitutively closed to the claims of difference. The second problem concerns the wider issue of liberalism's relationship with pluralism. The ease with which my discussant dismissed Mill bespeaks a tendency in certain postcolonial, decolonial and critical literatures to treat liberalism, either explicitly or implicitly, as inextricable from colonial depredations and political domination. Liberalism's historicism, the argument goes, makes it structurally antipathetic to non-liberals (and more specifically to non-Europeans); its inbuilt Eurocentrism renders it ill-equipped to register human multiplicity, at best folding it awkwardly into its own conceptual horizon.[23] Finally, my discussant's comments carried an evident normative weight: Millian liberalism, specifically, cannot sustain a politics responsive to deep social, cultural, racial and gender-based diversity.

There's a lot happening here – a wide range of assumptions lying just beneath the surface. How, for instance, do seminal thinkers' biographical and personal entanglements shape the theoretical vocabularies they developed? How should we, as contemporary interlocutors, treat philosophical doctrines historically enmeshed with practices of domination and exclusion? Are given traditions of political thought such as liberalism internally bound to those historical injustices, or is the relation contingent? Given its internal variability, is liberalism amenable to such generalizations? Are Kant's and Mill's responses to the world beyond Europe's gates assimilable to one another, as distinctively liberal visions of heterogeneity and difference? Do their views on imperialism reflect their broader understandings of human diversity? Are contemporary liberals warranted in fencing off their bigotries as time-bound prejudices extricable from otherwise freestanding moral and political philosophies? Or, conversely, are contemporary critics warranted in treating liberalism as conceptually bankrupted by its historical shortcomings?

These are the questions that this book addresses and hopes to clarify. These and related questions are shrouded in confusion if they are disentangled at all, and accordingly liberalism's relationship – historical and contemporary – with human diversity is unclear. Their conceptual stakes and distinctions are often elided, conflated or simply disregarded by detractors and defenders of Kant, Mill and liberalism alike. As long as these ambiguities persist, we will be unable to understand very much about liberalism and diversity.

This book is about liberalism and pluralism – most simply, about how certain particularly influential strands of liberal political theory encounter, respond to and incorporate the fact of human diversity and difference. That liberalism's universalist pretensions have invariably exceeded their reach, both theoretically and practically, is no surprise. The boundaries of moral and political communities are demarcated by an age's norms, and – without relinquishing our critical perspective – there's little to be gained, other than charges of presentism, from faulting them for falling short of our standards. Anachronistically treating Kant, Mill or any other such historical figure as "racist" or "sexist" *tout court* doesn't answer many questions. My aim, rather, is to examine how distinctive strains of liberal political thought respond to human heterogeneity in more or less productive, capacious and receptive ways.[24] In other words, I aim to consider how these liberalisms encounter human difference – to consider not just who they might exclude, but the conceptual apparatus through which those forms of difference are incorporated (sometimes through exclusion) into given visions of moral and political life. This approach pursues the conviction that what we inherit from Kant and Mill, and what ought to concern us, is less their own prejudices than these theoretical frameworks; what's of interest is not the *fact* of those prejudices but rather where they *fit* within their philosophical systems.

I undertake this by mounting a qualified defense of Millian liberalism against the Kantian liberalism that has come to predominate in contemporary political theory.[25] I argue that Mill's liberalism is far more complex and generative than the prevailing view suggests, that it articulates a political philosophy that is in important respects preferable to Kant's, and that it is well placed to navigate a pluralistic world. Against Thomas McCarthy's contention that Kant's universal history comprises "a mode of empirically informed, practically oriented, reflective judgment which ... provides a better indication of what might still make sense today than do the more extravagant views that followed,"[26] I argue that Millian liberalism is fallibilistic, culturally sensitive (even if he was not), and responsive to late-modern social diversity. Many critics see the ambivalences in Mill's liberalism as disjunctures entailed by his attempt to square imperialism with liberty and self-government. I suggest, conversely, that the critical focus on his imperialism has over-determined the embeddedness of hierarchy and exclusion in his liberalism, obscuring his nuanced treatment of human heterogeneity. Despite his own evident chauvinisms, Mill's liberalism registers the worth of cultural difference, recognizes the contingency of social progress and understands the task of politics as enabling self-determination.

Over the course of the book, I defend a few central claims, structured around three arguments. The first is historical and exegetical. I argue that Kant's and Mill's accounts of human diversity are subject to important interpretive deficits stemming from a failure to properly situate their conceptualizations of difference – racial, cultural, gender-based, class-based – within their respective philosophical systems. These deficits have led to miscasting their liberalisms, and more particularly the place of exclusion, hierarchy and domination within them. The preponderant emphasis on both thinkers' relationship to empire, as important as it is, has overshadowed and distorted their views of human diversity more generally. By widening the analytical lens, my reconstructions challenge many of the orthodoxies that have come to surround their treatments of pluralism.

The second argument is conceptual, addressing liberalism and pluralism. By unpacking the breadth of liberalisms represented by Kant and Mill, I dispute the claim that liberalism comprises a singular, cohesive doctrine intrinsically linked to imperialism and political domination. Kantian and Millian liberalisms are substantively dissimilar: their visions of moral, social and political life are philosophically distinctive and in many ways irreconcilable. Most significantly, for my purposes, they respond to human diversity in importantly different ways, with importantly different consequences. I argue that critics charging liberalism with the "continental chauvinism and implicit and explicit racism ... inherent to the Western canon"[27] tend to obscure more than they reveal. The profound divergences in Kant's and Mill's incorporations of pluralism undermine the contention that liberalism is driven by an impulsion to dominate non-liberals that we might trace throughout its history and into the present.

Finally, I make a normative claim, drawing out the historical argument's contemporary stakes. Millian liberalism, I argue, avoids problematic dimensions of Kantian liberalism and is particularly well equipped to respond to late-modern pluralism. Properly understood, it is more receptive to diversity than is commonly recognized; it is attuned to the political import of individual and national character, treating social variation as embedded in the human condition, and anchored in a "Social Science" pushing irreducibly idiosyncratic societies to seek their own ends. Millian liberalism's distinctive features, as I elaborate them, dispose it to encountering human difference with generosity and openness. It is, then, a liberalism well worth recovering.

This is not to defend Mill's views, or liberalism more generally, root and branch. Mill's political philosophy justified imperialism, and his professional life was dedicated to its extension. In an impassioned speech before Parliament in 1858, he lauded the East India Company's achievements and lamented its demise, proudly noting its beneficence toward the subcontinent's native inhabitants.[28] Many other liberals shared in his views, and many other liberalisms bear the marks of their presumptions. He (and they) readily advanced a wide range of Eurocentrist confabulations that shaped the modern world and continue to resonate in contemporary global relations. As postcolonial scholars have demonstrated, a wide swath of western thinkers – liberals, Marxists and others – adopted historicist frameworks and civilizational hierarchies upholding injustices ranging from the dispossession and extermination of Indigenous peoples, to slavery, to imperial and colonial domination.[29] Still further, critics of neo-colonialism have drawn out their ongoing impacts, as the imperial era's structural foundations – legal, political and economic – endure, cementing the subjugation of subaltern peoples through uneven global institutions and associations.[30]

My argument does not neglect, resist or minimize these harms and inequities. It is in no way set against the spirit and ambitions of postcolonial theorists, critics of liberal imperialism or scholars of neo-colonialism, neither does it discount or devalue their efforts. On the contrary, my interests are continuous with their driving impulse: to critically examine traditions of political thought so as to shed light: (a) on their exclusions, injustices and blind spots (b) on the conceptual mechanisms through which these were operationalized and integrated into wide-ranging visions of social and political life, and (c) on their legacies, traces and ongoing implications in contemporary politics and political thought. This is, then, no reactionary defense of liberalism against postcolonial critique. Much of the book agrees with critics of liberalism about its worst impulses and tendencies.[31]

Of course, many critics will regard any defense of liberalism as a non-starter, treating it as inescapably Eurocentric, both historically and conceptually.

Duncan Bell characterizes this view as the "necessity thesis," which "asserts that imperialism is an integral feature of liberal political thought"[32] and traces an internal linkage between the philosophical tradition and the forms of domination accompanying its development. Liberalism's deficits, the claim goes, are endemic, pervasive and persistent: its rationalism, its moral universalism, its possessive (or atomistic) individualism, its embroilments with capitalism and free markets, its developmentalism, its complicity in colonial and imperialist practices – each singly, or in combination, are taken to entail its unavoidable expansionism. A non-dominating liberalism, then, isn't just a historical anomaly, but a contradiction in terms; liberalism's categories and foundational assumptions carry the taint of its provincialism.

A still-deeper issue, raised by postcolonial and comparative political theorists, concerns the narrowness of the moral and political imagination on which a project such as mine draws. From this standpoint, my turn to Kant and Mill would both reflect and reinforce the discipline's longstanding inwardness by addressing human diversity within the confines of western theory, rather than engaging non-western sources of political reflection. The problem lies in "a mode of philosophic investigation that presupposes the basic sufficiency of its own moral-intellectual resources,"[33] as David Scott puts it, and so resists the "labor of learning how to read from *within* another tradition."[34] To defend any form of liberalism, then, is to avoid the task of "*unlearning* the presumptive privilege of one's own moral-intellectual traditions, and ... *learning* something of the internal composition of questions and answers through which the relevant traditions of others have been historically shaped."[35]

Much of the criticism is undoubtedly warranted and points to important limitations in my project, and more broadly, in the field of political theory. And yet, it is also qualified by certain considerations. While entirely agreeing with Scott's injunction to widen beyond the discipline's near-total focus on western thinkers, texts and contexts, his remarks concern the imperatives of postcolonial and decolonial theory. As pressing an endeavor as it is, it is not my intention here to contribute to the decolonization of political theory.[36] While imperialism and its legacies are central to my analysis, I treat them in the service of a sustained engagement with two thinkers in the liberal tradition, in order to reflect on that tradition. I also resist the argument tying liberal epistemology to the domination of non-Europeans by showing, in Chapters 5 and 6, the incommensurability of Kantian and Millian epistemologies. None of these efforts oppose the aims of postcolonial theory (even if I am critical of certain of its presumptions): I neither defend liberalism generally, nor suggest that all societies ought to be (or aspire to be) liberal ones, nor that Millian liberalism is *the* way to think about human diversity, rather than one especially generative approach among others. My task here is to demonstrate that certain forms of liberalism *are* defensible, that distinctive liberalisms integrate pluralism in markedly different ways, and that it is worth our while, as both critics and analysts, to pull them apart. As such, I see this project as contributing to efforts in the history of political thought, postcolonial theory, and intellectual history to better understand colonialism's wide-ranging political impacts and after-effects – historical, conceptual, normative and disciplinary.

My critique of certain facets of the postcolonial literature in Chapter 6 is, then, a sympathetic one, aiming to advance these efforts while resisting the charge that liberalism is implicitly bound to imperialism. First, the contention hinges on an over-general depiction of liberalism (itself often conflated, still more generally, with Enlightenment, modernity, the West and other cognates) that obscures its variability, ideological fluidity, internal rifts and outright contradictions. This kind of flattening conceals what Amanda Anderson characterizes as "the self-critical and transformative nature of liberalism throughout its history, its responsiveness to ethical, philosophical and historical challenges." Liberalism, she observes, is "a philosophical and political orientation that has more existential density than it is often presumed to possess."[37] Second, it fails to clarify what it is within liberalism that ought to concern us. Kant, Mill and many others perceived non-Europeans in deeply problematic ways, but those problems are distinctive, and not recognizing them as such diminishes our understanding of them. The tendency to generalization also papers over liberalism's emancipatory tenors, which surface even in colonial contexts. As Christopher Bayly observes, for instance, "Indian liberal ideas were foundational to all forms of Indian nationalism,"[38] "a broad field on which Indians and other South Asians began ... to resist colonial rule."[39] Liberalism has traveled widely, undergoing wholesale transmutations along the way; to paint it with broad brushstrokes is to lose track of its utility in resisting political domination. Finally, a wide range of liberal commitments – to individual and political autonomy, to self-government and self-direction, to non-paternalist independence and to sustaining the conditions for freedom – are well aligned with the postcolonial scholarship's ambitions. I argue, still further, that particular features of Millian liberalism are congruent with many of its philosophical assumptions and concerns.

My aim here, ultimately, is to get what's wrong right, to elucidate how and why certain liberalisms are more open and receptive to human diversity than others. It's to understand precisely what, historically, sustained profound injustices in given liberalisms so that we might recognize and redress shortcomings in our own political thinking and practices. This requires an analysis attuned to the specific features of certain liberalisms, without which the nature of the problem is oversimplified. In Chapters 2–5 I show how such oversimplifications miss important distinctions in Kant's and Mill's liberalisms; Chapter 6 shows how they miss what we might draw out of them. The overall idea is not to resist the postcolonial critique of liberalism but rather to extend it by distinguishing the tradition's problematic features from those that advance its freedom-enhancing character.

1.2   WHY KANT AND MILL?

There is no shortage of contemporary political theory addressing liberalism and pluralism – since Rawls, liberalism's central preoccupation is, arguably, precisely how best to manage social, cultural and religious diversity. Why then approach the question historically? Why turn to the history of political thought rather than current debates?

Let's start by considering what the historical approach offers. To begin, the contemporary literature on liberalism and pluralism is framed almost entirely in Kantian terms. For over four decades, liberal political theory has operated in a neo-Kantian landscape that has shaped its relationship with pluralism. By turning away from it, I aim to enlarge our view of liberalism beyond Kantian strictures whose narrowness renders it singularly unreceptive to the claims of difference. Moreover, it is by turning and returning to its historical foundations that we comprehend and constitute the liberal tradition.[40] Defenders and critics of liberalism alike persistently draw on its seminal philosophers not only as rich repositories of reflection on ethics and politics, but also to assess those philosophers' impacts on current political thinking and institutions. And yet, the linkages between historical figures, ideas and texts and their contemporary uptake tend to remain murky.[41] In order to clarify this murkiness, my reconstructions of Kantian and Millian liberalisms work through what we might reasonably carry forward from bodies of political thought mired in historical injustice, recognizing their deficits and parochialisms – past and present – without over-determining them.[42] Finally, given the long shadow they cast, it's worth getting these thinkers right. Without clearly understanding the moorings of our political ideas, we're more likely to reproduce their failures.

But why focus on Kant and Mill specifically? First, they are among the liberal totems whose ties to race and empire have been most extensively addressed in the scholarship. For better or worse, their accounts of race, gender, culture, civilization, class and empire are among the most influential and widely debated by liberals and their critics. While Duncan Bell has persuasively argued in favor of widening its ambit, much of the critical literature centers on a relatively narrow cast of characters within which Kant and Mill figure prominently.[43] Second, from a methodological standpoint, I suggest that more panoramic treatments of liberalism tend of necessity toward sometimes thin and selective readings of given thinkers that skew their views of human difference (among other things).[44] By focusing closely on two theorists – rather than on liberalism's supposedly implicit proclivities, or on a wider range of its exponents – I aim to situate their conceptualizations of diversity within their respective systems of thought. Third, as noted, Kant and Mill are subject to important and now-common misinterpretations that I challenge by looking beyond their respective connections to empire. Treating Kant's anti-imperialism as symptomatic of his valuing "cultural agency"[45] or Mill's imperialism as evidence of his antipathy toward "the unfamiliar"[46] miscasts their ideas and the liberalisms descended from them.

In building my case, I argue (in Chapters 4 and 5) against the central charges leveled at Mill by critics of liberal imperialism. Mill did not reproduce or extend his father's political philosophy, moral psychology or imperialist pedagogy, but rather departed (and distanced himself) from them. He did not differentiate between civilized and non-civilized peoples in Manichean terms, or as categorically distinctive types; he did not understand societies as aggregated wholes progressing through fixed stages of social advancement; he did not treat European civilizations as unqualified goods, or as implicitly superior to non-European ones; he did not gauge democratic fitness on the simple basis of a population's cognitive capacities; he did not see European history as charting any kind of universal trajectory. While its developmentalist structure has led critics to portray Mill's liberalism as continuous with Enlightenment-era historicisms, I argue in Chapter 5 that it breaks with their presumptions and ideals, yielding an entirely different conceptualization of (and response to) social, cultural and racial difference. Properly understood, Mill's liberalism models an attractive vision of social progress, cultural diversity and democratic public life that has been misapprehended, dismissed or overlooked by criticism.

By contrast, Kant's critical, practical and political thought has generally been treated as philosophically distinct and separable from his views on race and gender, and from the writings (particularly, but not exclusively, on history and anthropology) in which they appear. While the critical system is subject to an exhaustive scholarship, its connections to Kant's accounts of the embodied facets of moral personhood have received markedly less attention, for both conceptual and historical reasons.[47]

Conceptually, Kant's ethical and political theories are predicated on attributes shared by all human beings, as rational agents.[48] As Kant understands it, public right is derived from humanity's innate right to outer freedom and so remains unaffected by such phenomenal features as gender, race and class.[49] More generally, the rigidity of Kant's theoretical distinctions – most importantly, between transcendental and anthropological enterprises treating, respectively, our nature as rational and sensible agents – enables a strict division between his (systematic) practical and political philosophies, on one hand, and (unsystematic) pragmatic expositions of humanity's corporeal character, on the other.

Historically, this diremption has led to a longstanding and widespread neglect of Kant's writings on anthropology, history, biology, geography, race, moral psychology and pedagogy – especially in the English-language scholarship in which they were until recently unavailable.[50] While the critical system has been tirelessly pored over for well over two centuries, only in the last decade or two have commentators begun to seriously examine how Kant's expansive treatments of humanity's materiality might affect it.[51] Despite a welcome and growing interest in Kant's "impure" ethics, their implications for his moral and political thought remain anything but clear. This dereliction is all the more surprising in light of Kant's own profession that "morality cannot exist without anthropology, for one must first know of the agent whether he is also in a position to accomplish what is required from him that he should do."[52] While Kant turned his attention to the phenomenality of moral agency in the 1790s, most of the scholarship in the intervening years has failed to follow suit.

Until recently, then, Kant's views on race, culture, gender and moral progress have largely been perceived as isolated from, and inconsequential for, his presumptively free-standing accounts of ethics and right. Much of the commentary either disregards or brackets his pioneering role as one of the first natural scientists to develop a systematic racial theory, a hierarchy crowned by "Whites of brunette color";[53] his pondering Amerindian and Negro races' cognitive ceilings; his belief in women's inborn and lifelong "immatur[ity] in civil matters";[54] his conviction that European civilizations alone fostered the "cultures of skill and discipline" sustaining humanity's moral progress;[55] his defense of a property qualification for the enfranchisement of poorer classes; and much more. These views do not directly or implicitly impugn Kant's ethics or politics, as some critics have suggested, but neither are they easily separated, or even separable, as I argue in Chapter 3. The effort here is to properly situate Kant's reflections on humanity's embodied character in relation to his moral and political philosophy – to try to understand how they fit together, against the common contention that they simply do not.

The tendency to favor Kant's "formal" political arguments over his anthropological ones in assessing his views of non-Europeans is particularly pronounced in the literature on his cosmopolitanism. His resistance to empire, the story goes, reflects an egalitarian ecumenism toward peoples, societies and ways of life.[56] And yet, this approaches the matter rather obliquely. From the 1750s onward, Kant wrote and lectured extensively on history, moral psychology, pedagogy, anthropology, geography and the natural sciences.[57] These were the disciplines through which he explored the intersections of phenomenality and morality; as such, they most clearly articulate his conceptualizations of human heterogeneity in relation to moral ends. I argue in Chapter 2 that Kant's full account of a properly human moral agency incorporates both formal, transcendentally derived principles of moral obligation, and an acute sensitivity to the subjective, developmental facets of moral volition; the latter remain subject to the sway of race, culture and gender. Far from being extricable aberrations from otherwise self-contained ethical doctrines, then, anthropological characteristics belong to Kant's complete view of moral personhood. In Chapter 3, I examine the challenges that this presents for the cohesiveness of his moral and political thought.

Finally, there remains a question facing any defense of Millian liberalism: didn't Rawls settle this in 1971, putting a decisive end to utilitarianism's century-long run as political philosophy's guiding light? Don't liberals have to be Kantians of some kind or another in the wake of *A Theory of Justice*?

Theory famously challenged the coherence and moral defensibility of utilitarianism, in both its classical and updated (average utility) iterations, as the basis for principles of justice governing complex, pluralistic late-modern societies. To rehearse the barest sketch of his wide-ranging and penetrating critique, Rawls charged utilitarianism with: (a) undermining the sanctity of individual rights by countenancing utility-maximizing schemes that might violate them; (b) "adopt[ing] for society as a whole the principle of rational choice for one man" and so failing to "take seriously the distinction between persons";[58] (c) maximizing social goods absolutely, rather than securing the greatest goods for the least well off (Rawls's maximin principle); (d) allowing the good to determine the right rather than the other way around, indulging the twin evils of teleology and perfectionism; (e) requiring an improbably expansive identification with the interests of others; (f) relying on inherently indeterminate interpersonal comparisons of goods; and (g) resting on unstable principles unlikely to secure wide social endorsement.[59] What, then, remains of the possibilities for Millian liberalism?

Despite the force of Rawls's critique, the problem may be less acute than it appears, for several reasons. First, a defense of certain facets of Mill's ethical and political thought does not entail a defense of utilitarianism more generally, and I don't intend to develop or advance any kind of comprehensive utilitarian doctrine of justice. Rawls himself acknowledges that Mill was no straightforward utilitarian, which is why his attack on classical utilitarianism centers on Sidgwick, who provides "its clearest and most accessible formulation."[60] As with most of his ideas, Mill's relationship to utilitarianism shifted over time, complicating any clear assessment of its place in his political thought. From his early years as faithful doctrinaire, to his post-depression rejection of its excessive scientism, to his later return to a renovated view of utility and happiness, Mill's ambivalences are familiar to the innumerable commentators seeking to reconcile his seemingly contradictory commitments to utility and to liberty. Some, such as Isaiah Berlin, go so far as to consider him "not so much an open heretic from the original utilitarian movement, as a disciple who quietly left the fold,"[61] his fallibilism running "directly counter to traditional . . . utilitarianism."[62] In Mill's mature political philosophy, Berlin concludes, "the letter remains; but the spirit . . . the true utilitarian spirit – has fled."[63]

It is precisely this ambivalent Mill whom I defend in this book, a Mill whose liberalism thus drifts rather far from Rawls's crosshairs. This Mill self-consciously avoided ideological stringency in general, and all the more so in matters of social and political life that he saw as especially poorly served by it. This Mill is no more a strict utilitarian than the libertarian he's sometimes miscast as; he is sensitive to the cultivation of social virtue, but not quite a virtue ethicist; he is as much an eighteenth-century rationalist as a nineteenth-century romantic. It's a Mill who, I argue in Chapter 4, understands democracy as sustained by both rational argument and an ethos of public-mindedness – by the right sets of ideas and feelings. The Millian liberalism that I develop in Chapter 6 quite intentionally reproduces these ambivalences, regarding them as a virtue. It resists the constraints of neo-Kantian frameworks that neglect (or exclude) ethics and affects, and is implicitly attuned to what Steven K. White describes as "the aesthetic-affective soil necessary to the flowering of central liberal virtues."[64] It sees the Rawlsian-analytic conception of politics as impoverished by its anchoring in ideal theory, particularly as regards matters of race and gender treated as either secondary to "true" principles of justice (at best), or as politically irrelevant (at worst).

As noted, my defense of Mill is a qualified one. What follows is neither a systematic appraisal nor a full-throated endorsement of Mill's political philosophy (much of Chapter 4 criticizes it directly). My interest lies, more narrowly, in the conceptual resources that Mill's liberalism offers for thinking about diversity and difference – in how as a particular vision of associational life it responds to and incorporates human plurality.

To construct a comprehensive utilitarian alternative to Rawls's theory of justice would also be to understand political thinking in terms alien to the Millian enterprise. Mill was resolutely opposed to system-building in social and political thought, as its apriorism failed to register the character of given peoples. Peoples (as much as people), he argued, fit uncomfortably with predetermined ideals of government whose universality turned on their neglect of social facts. As a mode of political analysis, Mill's "inverse deductive method" sought to avoid moving from abstraction to abstraction without every touching down – as a matter of principle, for both Kant and Rawls – on the realities of social existence. Part of my task here is thus methodological: Millian liberalism reconceives the aims of liberal political theory and resists its reduction, witnessed in recent decades, to shuffling deck chairs on the Rawlsian ship. There's no particular reason to treat liberal thought in Anglo-analytic terms; liberalism, I argue, is a more fertile ground for reflection on the human condition, social goods and political association. Millian liberalism is neither congruent nor compatible with Rawlsian ambitions, and this very much by design.

My turn to Mill, then, is not especially affected by Rawls's critique of utilitarianism: I'm defending neither utility as a general theory of value nor all of Mill's views. My project is, rather, an attempt to think ethically and politically through, with and alongside Mill on questions of human diversity and alterity. In this, I follow Kwame Anthony Appiah in treating Mill more as a traveling companion than a fixed reference point, a figure who sheds light on contemporary concerns without commanding our agreement on them. "What will make him an agreeable traveling companion – as opposed to a traveling icon, dangling from the rearview mirror," Appiah avers, "isn't that we will agree with all his analyses; it's that he cared about so many of the issues we care about, and, in a day when talk of 'identity' can sound merely modish, he reminds us that the issues it presents are scarcely alien to the high canon of political philosophy."[65]

1.3 A NOTE ON LIBERALISM(S)

Liberalism is notoriously difficult to pin down, "[t]he ambiguity of its political commitments," Duncan Ivison notes, stemming "from the very pluralism it accepts as a fact of political life."[66] It's a now-common observation that liberalism is better characterized as a family of values, ideals and principles than as a readily identifiable doctrine; we're thus unlikely to find "any single cluster of theoretical and practical propositions that might be regarded as the core or the essence of the ideology."[67] Liberal theories are inescapably diverse and mutable, crystallizing in myriad ways around commitments to individual freedom, autonomy, equality and toleration; differences in their weighting and arrangement generate a constellation of liberalisms with accordingly divergent views of its fundamental priorities.[68] Liberalism is subject to profound theoretical and historical variation, a tradition resistant to simplification and marked by disjuncture, competing and often-incompatible values, and a breadth of social, political and moral ideals – some in tension, others in outright contradiction. For this reason, I contest generalizations about its "essential" features or impulsions throughout this book, and directly confront the presumption that "[t]he mere fact that liberalism is implicated in the justification of colonialism is evidence enough ... that it is tainted beyond redemption"[69] in Chapter 6.

Liberalism, I argue, is better captured by its ruptures than by its continuities.[70] This isn't to deny the common and distinctive features of liberal political thought, which is, after all, a particular way of understanding human ends and the political structures best suited to pursuing them. It "rests on a certain view about the justification of social arrangements," Jeremy Waldron notes, and "this view helps us to understand some of the differences and some of the similarities between liberalism and other ideologies."[71] Kant and Mill undoubtedly share recognizably liberal commitments to individual freedom, self-direction, self-government and autonomy (understood, of course, very differently). And yet, the divergences setting their liberalisms apart are substantial, substantive and often obscured by coarse-grained lines of criticism. In Chapters 2–5, I explore the conceptual divisions demarcating Kant's and Mill's liberalisms and argue, against the presumption of liberalism's coherence, that they are philosophically distinct. They are importantly different kinds of liberalisms.

Referring to Kant's and Mill's liberalisms, however, raises methodological questions – one concerning anachronism (relating to Kant specifically), the other concerning terminology (relating to both Kant and Mill). Despite his retrospective incorporation into the tradition, Kant was himself no liberal – no more than was Locke, Quentin Skinner points out, despite his canonical status in contemporary liberalism's self-understanding. It would be anachronistic to treat him as such. Liberalism emerged as a self-conscious political doctrine in the early nineteenth century, and while Mill saw himself as a liberal, Kant could not have had any such self-understanding. As Skinner notes, commentators all too often conflate progenitors of "the modern ... liberal school of political thought" and liberals themselves.[72] And yet, this need not imply Kant's wholesale divorce from a tradition of thought within which he has become firmly embedded (which Skinner also recognizes, treating Locke – as we might treat Kant – as a founder of modern liberalism, without himself being a liberal). As Jennifer Pitts observes, "liberalism has been usefully evoked to describe overlapping strands of thought long prior to the term's invention at the turn of the nineteenth century."[73] Despite their historical antecedence, we can draw out "patterns of liberal belief" in thinkers such as Locke and Kant – among them, a "shared commitment to the values of equal human dignity, the rule of law, and accountable, representative government"[74] – comprising distinctively "liberal lineages."[75] My references to Kant's liberalism throughout this book thus capture his wide-ranging moral and political philosophy and its liberal substance, and not any kind of self-attributed liberal doctrine. My critique of his liberalism centers on problems and inconsistencies internal to his moral and political world; at no point do I suggest that Kant failed to live up to his own liberal commitments, as he had none to live up to.

As for terminology, my focus on Kant's and Mill's liberalisms aims to expand beyond more focused treatments of their ethical or political theories alone. The idea is to capture their broader visions of ethical, social and political life, of the interconnections between them, of their ends, of the institutions through which those ends might be realized and of the conditions enabling given people(s) to progress toward them. While both thinkers erected fences between these spheres, they also recognized their imbrication: Mill saw the task of politics as fostering citizens' "desirable qualities, moral and intellectual,"[76] and Kant's pragmatic anthropology investigates "what [man] as a free-acting being makes of himself ... as a *citizen of the world*."[77] Despite their claims to the contrary (Kant's in particular), and very much to their credit, neither stays within the strict boundaries of ethics and politics; to address their liberalisms, then, is to adopt the wider lens that they favored. By focusing on their liberalisms in this comprehensive sense, I aim to faithfully – but no less critically – reconstruct their moral and political arguments, avoiding the interpretive pitfalls incurred by narrower or more selective readings. I also hope to move past the over-determined contrast between the deontological and consequentialist streams of ethics that each has come to represent, and to which their ideas are all too often reduced. For both thinkers, ethics and politics were inseparable from surrounding fields of study – moral psychology, pedagogy, anthropology, history, biology – enabling us to understand the kinds of creatures that we are and might be.

Delving into those liberalisms also serves a larger purpose: it speaks to liberalism's relationship with domination and exclusion, which I treat in detail in Chapter 6. This relationship might be approached in three basic ways. First, we might argue that liberalism is conceptually – internally, non-contingently – bound to the exclusion of non-liberals. The historicism underpinning liberal ideals of progress sustains the West's domination over the non-West, infecting the tradition's core and carrying through into contemporary liberalisms.[78] Alternatively, we might treat liberalism as historically, and so contingently, linked to empire, violence and subjugation. Despite egregious failures of realization, liberalism's universalist pretentions are not implicitly exclusionary; on the contrary, Rawls and Habermas assure us, the historical record reveals their progressive, if bumpy, fulfilment.[79] Finally, we might understand distinctive conceptual elements in distinct liberalisms as tending toward greater or lesser receptivity to the claims of diversity. The work lies in distinguishing those impulsions, in given liberalisms, toward openness and generosity from those inclined to closure, antipathy, myopia and non-recognition. This third position is the one I defend: liberalism, I argue, is neither implicitly tied to exclusion nor entirely extricable from it.

1.4 A NOTE ON SUBJECT MATTER

This book's subject matter courts what Quentin Skinner describes as the mythology of prolepsis, "the type of mythology we are prone to generate when we are more interested in the retrospective significance of a given episode than in its meaning for the agent at the time."[80] Is an examination of Kant's and Mill's treatments of women, the uncivilized, poorer classes and non-Europeans necessarily anachronistic, decontextual or presentist? Does it draw together forms of difference that Kant and Mill would scarcely have recognized as related?

Two responses present themselves. First, as I elaborate in Chapter 6, nothing prevents us from being presentist in our concerns and contextualist in our approach. As John Zammito and Jeanne Morefield argue, well-warranted cautions regarding historical figures' intentions need not preclude reading them with an eye to our own interests.[81] It is surely not unreasonable to allow our preoccupations with race, diversity and domination to orient our thinking toward those figures, so long as we resist imputing these preoccupations and surrounding norms to them. Contextualist circumspection rightly proscribes evaluating past philosophers' ideas by contemporary measures and imputing a doctrinal coherence to them shaped by our values. Indeed, as I argue throughout, as welcome an advance as it is, the current interest in empire and political theory also distorts Kant's and Mill's conceptualizations of human diversity by projecting a cohesive attitude toward difference, based on contemporary sensibilities – a broad-ranging openness to cultural variation or an intractable hostility toward non-Europeans – onto their views of imperialism. And yet, with these cautions in mind, there is no reason why we shouldn't reconstruct their ideas – faithfully – to consider their implications for our own concerns. The aim isn't to prognosticate on what Kant or Mill *should* have thought about any given subject, or to criticize them for failing to do it as we might have liked them to. It is to excavate what they *did* say on subjects of interest to us, and to think through the repercussions of those ideas for our purposes.

The second response to the charge of presentism and anachronism is that the concerns raised in this book are not ours alone. By way of an illustration, consider the following passage from Frances Power Cobbe's article "Criminals, Idiots, Women and Minors," published in December 1868 in *Fraser's Magazine for Town and Country*:

the just and expedient treatment of women by men is one of the most obscure problems, alike of equity and of policy. Nor of women only, but of all classes and races of human beings whose condition is temporarily or permanently one of comparative weakness and dependence. In past ages, the case was simple enough. No question of right or duty disturbed the conscience of Oriental or Spartan, of Roman or Norman, in dealing with his wife, his Helot, his slave, or his serf. 'Le droit du plus fort' was unassailed in theory and undisturbed in practice. But we, in our day, are perplexed and well nigh over-whelmed with the difficulties presented to us. What ought the Americans to do with their Negroes? What ought we to do with our Hindoos? What ought all civilized people to do with their women? It is all very easy to go on driving down the 'high *a priori*' road of equal rights for all human beings, but as it is quite clear that children and idiots cannot be entrusted with full civil and political rights, the question always resolves itself into the further one, Where shall we draw the line? When has a human being fairly passed out of the stage of pupilage and attained his majority?[82]

"Criminals, Idiots, Women and Minors": four groups of citizen excluded from political and (some) civil rights in mid-Victorian England. Cobbe's tract is remarkable not only for its attentiveness to multiple registers of injustice – sociological, social, historical, political and personal – but also for its far-reaching scope. While aiming at women's disenfranchisement, Cobbe draws out the shared state of inequality suffered by all dependent classes. She targets the incongruity of a politics rooted in universalistic rights-talk while subjecting women, the poor and non-Europeans – the Helots of late modernity, as she puts it – to a joint condition of minority.

Cobbe raises concerns typically treated as explicitly contemporary – animated by present-day norms and leveled at inequities that thinkers of the era would not, we tell ourselves, have linked together. This clearly is far from being the case. Cobbe illuminates the common injustice in disparate forms of civic, political and moral marginalization, and the common cause binding disparate categories of people subject to them. The disjuncture between principled commitments to moral inclusiveness and their failures of application were as evident, and as jarring, to her in 1868 as they are to us today; she did not need our standards to recognize them. It's undoubtedly true that many of the exclusions that concern us were of little consequence, or would have been entirely inaudible (to borrow from Jacques Rancière), to the Victorians.[83] Our political languages and moral expectations have, of course, shifted.[84] And yet, despite her distance from us, Cobbe clearly perceived the generic harm in denying the rights of British women, the working classes and slaves in the American south (among others) from within her own normative horizon.[85] "So long as you allow I possess moral responsibility and sufficient intelligence to know right from wrong (a point I conclude you will concede, else why hang me for murder?)," she admonishes, "I am quite content. It is *only* as a Moral and Intelligent Being I claim my civil rights. Can you deny them to me on that ground?"[86]

These aren't just our concerns, then, anachronistically reflected backward, and neither is it the case in Victorian England alone. As Hannelore Schröder demonstrates, a number of thinkers and public figures in eighteenth-century Europe – and still closer to home, in Kant's Königsberg – were roundly critical of women's disenfranchisement.[87] In 1790, Condorcet advocated for women's accession to civil and political rights in *Sur l'admission des femmes au droit de cité*, as did Theodor Gottlieb von Hippel, mayor of Königsberg and a personal acquaintance of Kant. Hippel's point of view was hardly exceptional: as Kurt Stavenhagen notes, in Königsberg in 1758, "[q]uite properly one spoke of an emancipation of the women of the city from their hitherto narrowly cloistered world."[88] Writing contemporaneously with Kant, Christoph Martin Wieland "regard[ed] women as intellectually equal to men ... criticize[d] the racially biased aesthetics of his contemporaries" and was "more critical of sexism and racism than Kant."[89] The inconsistencies between Kant's views on race and gender and his moral egalitarianism are thus neither a matter of merely retrospective attribution, nor did they go unnoticed by his contemporaries.

My point is this: a justifiable attentiveness to historical context need not overblow the currency of the concerns addressed here; they are not ours alone. While our moral egalitarianism has gladly become more fine-tuned, more inclusive, more consistent and more sensitive, its foundations were well established in Kant's and Mill's worlds – in no small part, due to their own efforts. As Judith Butler argues, the all-encompassing reach of universalistic claims pushes us, as it did Kant and Mill, to question and contest their limitations; the failure to follow through on their promise also invites critical scrutiny, for us as for Cobbe.[90] "In this age of exquisite hermeneutic sensitivity," Jeremy Waldron observes, "*we* may be anxious to avoid the anachronism of reading the traditional texts in light of our own concerns. But the authors whose works we are handling with this sensitivity had no such scruples themselves, and I think it is fair to say that our sensitivity to their context seriously distorts our understanding of their philosophical intentions."[91]

Kant and Mill both clearly failed to recognize the civil, political and moral equality of a great many people, citizens and non-citizens alike. The question is why, exactly. What concerns stand behind Kant's view of women's civil incapacity, or Mill's barring of "barbarians" from the moral rules governing international relations? What do these exclusions do for their political theories? What are the philosophical stakes of Kant's racial theory, which appears to throw certain races' moral status into question? Or of Mill's distinguishing between societies capable "of being guided to their own improvement by conviction or persuasion" and "those backward states of society in which the race itself may be considered as in its nonage"[92]? How do these seeming contradictions fit within their respective theoretical edifices, and what are their implications for the liberalisms descended from them?

These are the questions I turn to consider. The bulk of my argument is historical, analytical and exegetical: it undertakes a systematic investigation of, as McCarthy puts it, "how putatively universalistic, inclusive, moral doctrines could so readily countenance particularistic, exclusionary practices – and, as it seems, with surprisingly little cognitive dissonance."[93] My response is developed along three related tracks. The first, elaborated in Chapters 2 and 4, is expository: I examine the ways that Kant and Mill negotiated these tensions and contradictions, rather than foreclosing the question by attributing them to age-bound prejudices. I reconstruct their respective liberalisms, paying particular attention to the kinds of persons at their center. The book's second dimension, the focus of Chapters 3 and 5, is critical: I consider how the exclusion of those at the margins of their political ideals – women, the uncivilized, non-Europeans, the unpropertied – impacts their moral and political philosophies. These chapters explore how Kant and Mill encounter human diversity and difference, situating their views within their respective liberalisms. In Chapter 6, I turn to the difficult question of inheritance – to the relationship between historical injustice and contemporary uptake – and develop my account of Millian liberalism. My goal in this chapter is to clarify the implications of Kant's and Mill's views of difference for present-day interlocutors, addressing what we might reasonably carry forward from political ideas mired in histories of inequity and exclusion. In so doing, I draw out the distinctions between Kantian and Millian liberalisms and make the case for the latter's advantages. Chapter 7 concludes the book with a brief reflection on why we should care about liberalism at all.

NOTES

1. Jennifer Pitts, *A Turn to Empire: The Rise of Imperial Liberalism in Britain and France* (Princeton: Princeton University Press, 2005), 130.
2. Dipesh Chakrabarty, *Provincializing Europe: Postcolonial Thought and Historical Difference* (Princeton, N.J.: Princeton University Press, 2000), 7.
3. John Stuart Mill, *Autobiography*, in *The Collected Works of John Stuart Mill, Volume I – Autobiography and Literary Essays*, eds. John M. Robson and Jack Stillinger (Toronto; Buffalo; London: University of Toronto Press; Routledge & Kegan Paul, 1981), 1:33.

4. Edward Said, *Orientalism* (New York: Pantheon Books, 1978), 7.

5. Chakrabarty, *Provincializing Europe*, 8.

6. John Stuart Mill, *On Liberty*, in *The Collected Works of John Stuart Mill Volume XVIII, Essays on Politics and Society, Part 1*, ed. John Robson (Toronto: University of Toronto Press, 1977), 18:224.

7. Jennifer Pitts, "Empire, Progress and the 'Savage Mind,'" in *Colonialism and Its Legacies*, eds. Jacob T. Levy and Iris Marion Young (Lanham, MD: Lexington, 2011).

8. Bhikhu Parekh, "Decolonizing Liberalism," in *The End Of "Isms"?: Reflections on the Fate of Ideological Politics after Communism's Collapse*, ed. Alexander Shtromas (Cambridge MA: Oxford University Press, 1994), 92.

9. Dana Villa, *Public Freedom* (Princeton: Princeton University Press, 2008); Charles Larmore, "Political Liberalism," *Political Theory* 18, no. 3 (1990): 339–360.

10. John Stuart Mill, *Utilitarianism*, in *The Collected Works of John Stuart Mill, Vol. X: Essays on Ethics, Religion and Society* (Toronto: University of Toronto Press, 1985), 10:218.

11. William Galston, "Moral Personality and Liberal Theory: John Rawls's 'Dewey Lectures'," *Political Theory* 10 (1982): 492. For the ubiquity of Kantian liberalism in Rawls' wake, see Charles Mills, "Racial Liberalism," *PMLA* 123 (2008): 1380–1397.

12. For an overview of Kant's influence in cosmopolitan political thought, see James Bohman and Matthias Lutz-Bachmann, eds., *Perpetual Peace: Essays on Kant's Cosmopolitan Ideal* (Cambridge: MIT Press, 1997).

13. David Armitage, "The Fifty Years' Rift: Intellectual History and International Relations," *Modern Intellectual History* 1, no. 1 (2004): 97–109.

14. Jürgen Habermas, "Kant's Idea of Perpetual Peace: At Two Hundred Years' Historical Remove," in *The Inclusion of the Other*, eds. Ciaran Cronin and Pablo de Greiff (Cambridge MA: MIT Press, 1998), 165–202; Seyla Benhabib, *Another Cosmopolitanism: Hospitality, Sovereignty and Democratic Iterations* (New York: Oxford University Press, 2006).

15. Thomas McCarthy, *Race, Empire, and the Idea of Human Development* (Cambridge: Cambridge University Press, 2009), 140. For a strong critique of McCarthy's developmentalism, see Alexander Livingston, "Moralism and its Discontents," *Humanity: An International Journal of Human Rights, Humanitarianism and Development* 7, no. 3 (2016): 499–522.

16. For the importance of commerce in eighteenth-century global relations, see Sankar Muthu, "Conquest, Commerce, and Cosmopolitanism in Enlightenment Political Thought," in *Empire and Modern Political Thought*, ed. Sankar Muthu (Cambridge: Cambridge University Press, 2012), 199–231; and Lea Ypi, "Commerce and Colonialism in Kant's Philosophy of History," in *Kant and Colonialism*, eds. Lea Ypi and Katrin Flikschuh (Oxford: Oxford University Press, 2014).

17. Immanuel Kant, *The Metaphysics of Morals*, in *Practical Philosophy*, ed. Mary J. Gregor (Cambridge: Cambridge University Press, 1999), 6:353. Given hereafter as MS.

18. Sankar Muthu, *Enlightenment against Empire* (Princeton: Princeton University Press, 2003), 172; Pauline Kleingeld, "Kant's Second Thoughts on Race,"

The Philosophical Quarterly, 57 (2007), 573–592; and Pauline Kleingeld, *Kant and Cosmopolitanism: The Philosophical Ideal of World Citizenship* (Cambridge: Cambridge University Press, 2013).

19. James Miller, *The Passion of Michel Foucault* (London: Flamingo, 1993), 138. See also Mark Olsen, "Foucault and Critique: Kant, Humanism and the Human Sciences," in *Futures of Critical Theory: Dreams of Difference*, eds. Michael Peters, Mark Olsen and Colin Lankshear (Lanham: Rowman & Littlefield, 2003).

20. Michel Foucault, "What is Enlightenment?" in *The Politics of Truth*, eds. Sylvère Lotringer and John Rajchman (Los Angeles: Semiotext(e), 2007), 109.

21. Ibid., 113.

22. William Connolly, *Neuropolitics: Thinking, Culture, Speed* (Minneapolis: University of Minnesota Press, 2002), 1. For Connolly's critique of neo-Kantian political thought, see also *Why I Am Not a Secularist* (Minneapolis: University of Minnesota Press, 1999), *The Ethos of Pluralization* (Minneapolis: University of Minnesota Press, 1995), and *Capitalism and Christianity, American-Style* (Durham: Duke University Press, 2008).

23. I treat a wide range of arguments to this effect in Chapter 6; for a good summary of the view, see Jakeet Singh, "Colonial Pasts, Decolonial Futures: Allen's *The End of Progress*," *Theory & Event* 19, no. 4 (2016).

24. This of course invokes contemporary measures of productivity, capaciousness and receptivity that, a critic might argue, lapse into presentism; I address the matter in section 1.4, and in Chapter 6.

25. There are a few important points to note here, each elaborated further throughout the book. First, there's an important distinction to be drawn between Kant's and Mill's liberalisms (their own moral and political philosophies) and Kantian and Millian liberalisms (the contemporary moral and political philosophies reconstructed on the basis of their ideas). Most of this book (Chapters 2–5) focuses on Kant's and Mill's liberalisms, which informs the Kantian and Millian liberalisms developed in Chapter 6. Second, I use the term *liberalism* intentionally, advisedly and with a clear consciousness of the anachronisms (in Kant's case) and terminological difficulties (in both cases) that it invites; I explain my usage of the term and confront these challenges in section 1.3.

26. McCarthy, *Race*, 134.

27. Brett Bowden, "The Ebb and Flow of Peoples, Ideas and Innovations: Towards a Global History of Political Thought," in *Western Political Thought in Dialogue with Asia*, eds. T. Shōgimen and C. J. Nederman (Lanham MD: Lexington Books, 2008), 93.

28. John Stuart Mill, "The Petition of the East India Company," in *The Collected Works of John Stuart Mill, Volume XXX – Writings on India*, eds. John M. Robson, Martin Moir and Zawahir Moir (Toronto: University of Toronto Press, London: Routledge & Kegan Paul, 1990), 30:75–90.

29. I engage critiques of liberalism's historicism throughout this book, paying particular attention to its most sophisticated expositors – Ashis Nandy, Dipesh Chakrabarty, Bhikhu Parekh, Jennifer Pitts, Thomas McCarthy and Uday Singh Mehta, among others. A rich tradition of decolonial scholarship, focused on colonialism in Latin America, is similarly critical of Eurocentrist developmentalism; see, for instance, Enrique Dussel, *Philosophy of Liberation* (Maryknoll: Orbis, 1985).

30. For a few critiques of neo-colonialism, see James Tully, *Public Philosophy in a New Key: Volume 2, Imperialism and Civic Freedom* (Cambridge: Cambridge University Press, 2008); Antony Anghie, *Imperialism, Sovereignty and the Making of International Law* (Cambridge: Cambridge University Press, 2004); Enrique Dussel, "Eurocentrism and Modernity," *boundary 2* 20 no. 3 (1993), 65–67.

31. For a strong critique of postcolonial theory from a Marxist standpoint, see Vivek Chibber, *Postcolonial Theory and the Specter of Capitalism* (London: Verso, 2013). For outright defenses of liberal imperialisms, past and present, see Michael Ignatieff, *Empire Lite: Nation-Building in Bosnia, Kosovo, Afghanistan* (Toronto: Penguin Canada, 2003); Michael Ignatieff, "The American Empire; The Burden," *New York Times Magazine*, January 5, 2003; and Niall Ferguson, *Empire: How Britain Made the Modern World* (London: Penguin, 2004).

32. Duncan Bell, *Reordering the World: Essays on Liberalism and Empire* (Princeton: Princeton University Press, 2016), 21.

33. David Scott, "The Traditions of Historical Others," *Symposia on Gender, Race and Philosophy* 8, no. 1 (2012): 2.

34. Ibid., 7.

35. Ibid., 3.

36. For recent efforts to decolonize political theory, see Charles W. Mills, "Decolonizing Western Political Philosophy," *New Political Science* 37, no. 1 (2015): 1–24; Amy Allen, *The End of Progress: Decolonizing the Normative Foundations of Critical Theory* (New York: Columbia University Press, 2016); Bruce Baum, "Decolonizing Critical Theory," *Constellations* 22, no. 3 (2015): 420–434; and George Ciccariello-Maher, *Decolonizing Dialectics* (Durham NC: Duke University Press, 2017).

37. Amanda Anderson, *Bleak Liberalism* (University of Chicago Press, 2017), 22.

38. C. A. Bayly, *Recovering Liberties: Indian Thought in the Age of Liberalism and Empire* (Cambridge: Cambridge University Press, 2011), 1.

39. Ibid., 343.

40. For an exposition of the mutability of these historical reconstructions, see Bell, *Reordering*, ch. 3.

41. I elaborate on the confusions pervading these linkages in Chapter 6.

42. For two recent works exploring similar questions, see McCarthy, *Race*, and Amy Allen, *The End of Progress: Decolonizing the Normative Foundations of Critical Theory* (New York: Columbia University Press, 2015). Frederick Cooper and Andrew Sartori also treat these questions with particular sensitivity; I consider their accounts in Chapter 6.

43. Bell, *Reordering*, ch. 2.

44. See, for instance, Domenico Losurdo, *Liberalism: A Counter-History*, trans. Gregory Elliott (New York: Verso, 2011).

45. Muthu, *Enlightenment*.

46. Uday Singh Mehta, *Liberalism and Empire: A Study in Nineteenth Century British Liberal Thought* (Chicago: University of Chicago Press, 1999), 104.

47. Disciplinary divisions also figure here. The weight of Kantian scholarship falls in philosophy, rather than political theory, which focuses overwhelmingly on the *Critiques*, paying little attention to Kant's philosophy of right and still less to his accounts of anthropology, history, moral education, geography, and biology.

48. Kant's moral theory is largely developed in the *Critique of Practical Reason*, the *Groundwork of the Metaphysics of Morals*, and the *Metaphysics of Morals'* "Doctrine of Virtue." His political theory is most clearly elaborated in the *Metaphysics of Morals'* "Doctrine of Right" and several essays (most importantly, "Toward Perpetual Peace," "What is Enlightenment?" and "Theory and Practice").

49. For the most sophisticated account of Kant's legal and political philosophy, see Arthur Ripstein, *Force and Freedom: Kant's Legal and Political Philosophy* (Cambridge: Harvard University Press, 2009).

50. The Cambridge editions of Kant's works are generally considered the authoritative standard in English. While I draw on a wide range of Kant's works throughout this book, certain materials were less readily available, less reliable or entirely unavailable prior to their Cambridge publication. As regards texts relevant for my case, *Anthropology, History and Education* was published in 2007, *Natural Science* in 2012, and *Religion and Rational Theology* and *Practical Ethics* in 1996. Much of the supplementary materials surrounding Kant's works – in particular, lecture notes from his students – have been invaluable in tracing the development of his views; these were published in 2001 (*Lectures on Ethics* and *Lectures on Metaphysics*), 2012 (*Lectures on Anthropology*), and 2016 (*Lectures and Drafts on Political Philosophy*).

51. For pioneering work, see Allen Wood, *Kant's Ethical Thought* (Cambridge: Cambridge University Press, 1999); Robert Louden, *Kant's Impure Ethics: From Rational Beings to Human Beings* (New York: Oxford University Press, 2000); Holly Wilson, *Kant's Pragmatic Anthropology: Its Origin, Meaning and Critical Significance* (Albany: SUNY Press, 2006); Patrick Frierson, *Freedom and Anthropology in Kant's Moral Philosophy* (Cambridge: Cambridge University Press, 2003); G. Felicitas Munzel, *Kant's Conception of Moral Character: The "Critical" Link of Morality, Anthropology, and Reflective Judgment* (Chicago: Chicago University Press, 1999); Alix Cohen, *Kant and the Human Sciences: Biology, Anthropology and History* (London: Palgrave Macmillan, 2009); and Brian Jacobs and Patrick Kain, eds., *Essays on Kant's Anthropology* (Cambridge: Cambridge University Press, 2007).

52. Immanuel Kant, *Lectures on Ethics*, eds. Peter Heath and J. B. Schneewind (New York: Cambridge University Press, 1997), 27:244. Given hereafter as VE.

53. Immanuel Kant, "Determination of the Concept of a Human Race," in *Anthropology, History, and Education*, eds. Günter Zöller and Robert B. Louden (Cambridge: Cambridge University Press, 2011), 2:441. Given hereafter as BM.

54. Immanuel Kant, *Anthropology from a Pragmatic Point of View*, ed. Robert B. Louden (Cambridge: Cambridge University Press, 2006), 7:209.

55. Immanuel Kant, *Critique of Judgment*, ed. Werner S. Pluhar (Indianapolis: Hackett Publishing Co., 1987), 5:432. Given hereafter as KU.

56. Sankar Muthu is the primary exponent of this view; see *Enlightenment*. For recent readings of Kant's understanding of non-Europeans through a colonial lens, see Katrin Flikschuh and Lea Ypi, eds., *Kant and Colonialism: Historical and Critical Perspectives* (Oxford: Oxford University Press, 2014).

57. Allen W. Wood, Introduction to *Lectures on Anthropology*, eds. Allen W. Wood and Robert B. Louden (New York: Cambridge University Press 2012), 1–10.

58. John Rawls, *A Theory of Justice: Revised Edition* (Cambridge: Harvard University Press, 1999), 24.

59. For a cursory sketch of these arguments, see Rawls, *Theory of Justice*, 19–27, 77–78, 138, 154–158, 165, 185, 439–440, 445 and 486–491. For a concise account (and refutation) of Rawls's critique of utilitarianism, see Richard J. Arneson, "Rawls versus Utilitarianism in the Light of *Political Liberalism*," in *The Idea of a Political Liberalism: Essays on Rawls*, eds. Victoria Davion and Clark Wolf (Lanham: Rowman & Littlefield, 1999), 231–252.

60. Rawls, *Theory of Justice*, 20.

61. Isaiah Berlin, "John Stuart Mill and the Ends of Life," in *J. S. Mill's On Liberty in Focus*, eds. John Gray and G. W. Smith (London: Routledge, 2015), 134.

62. Ibid., 139.

63. Ibid., 138.

64. Steven K. White, *The Ethos of a Late-Modern Citizen* (Cambridge MA: Harvard University Press, 2009), 1. For an updated version of the argument, see Steven K. White, *A Democratic Bearing: Admirable Citizens, Uneven Justice, and Critical Theory* (Cambridge: Cambridge University Press, 2017).

65. Kwame Anthony Appiah, *The Ethics of Identity* (Princeton: Princeton University Press, 2005), xiv.

66. Duncan Ivison, *Postcolonial Liberalism* (Cambridge: Cambridge University Press, 2002), 31.

67. Jeremy Waldron, "Theoretical Foundations of Liberalism," *The Philosophical Quarterly* 37, no. 147 (1987): 127.

68. For a brief overview of liberal political theory, see Inder S. Marwah, "Liberal Theory," in *The Encyclopedia of Political Thought*, eds. Michael T. Gibbons et al. (Malden: Wiley-Blackwell, 2014). For fuller treatments, see Waldron, "Theoretical Foundations of Liberalism"; Alan Ryan, *The Making of Modern Liberalism* (Princeton: Princeton University Press, 2012), ch. 1; and Gerald Gaus and Shane Cortland, "Liberalism," *Stanford Encyclopedia of Philosophy*, December 22, 2013, http://plato.stanford.edu/entries/liberalism/. For an incisive reflection on ambiguities in liberalism's self-understanding, see Duncan Bell, "What is Liberalism?" *Political Theory* 42, no. 6 (2014): 682–715.

69. Ivison, *Postcolonial Liberalism*, 34.

70. For treatments of these ruptures in liberalism, see Pitts, *Empire*; Muthu, *Enlightenment*; and Karuna Mantena, *Alibis of Empire: Henry Maine and the Ends of Liberal Imperialism* (Princeton: Princeton University Press, 2010).

71. Waldron, "Theoretical Foundations," 128.

72. Quentin Skinner, "Meaning and Understanding in the History of Ideas," *History and Theory* 8, no. 1 (1969): 24.

73. Pitts, *Turn To Empire*, 3.

74. Ibid.

75. James Meadowcroft, "The New Liberal Conception of the State," in *The New Liberalism: Reconciling Liberty and Community*, eds. A. Simonhy and D. Weinstein (Cambridge: Cambridge University Press, 2001), 133. For further reflection on liberalism's historical and conceptual makeup, see Knud Haakonssen, *Traditions of Liberalism: Essays on John Locke, Adam Smith and John Stuart Mill* (St. Leonards: Center for Independent Studies, 1988); Bell, "What is Liberalism?"; and Bell, *Reordering*.

76. John Stuart Mill, *Considerations on Representative Government*, in *The Collected Works of John Stuart Mill, Volume XIX – Essays on Politics and Society Part II*, ed.

John M. Robson, Introduction by Alexander Brady (Toronto: University of Toronto Press, London: Routledge & Kegan Paul, 1977), 19:390–391.

77. Kant, *Anthropology*, 7:119–120.

78. For arguments treating contemporary liberalisms (and in particular, liberal multiculturalism) as extending the tradition's inborn Eurocentrism, see Glen Coulthard, *Red Skin, White Masks: Rejecting the Colonial Politics of Recognition* (Minneapolis: University of Minnesota Press, 2014); Rita Dhamoon, *Identity/Difference Politics: How Difference is Produced and Why it Matters* (Vancouver: UBC Press, 2009); and Himani Bannerji, *Dark Side of the Nation: Essays on Multiculturalism, Nationalism and Gender* (Toronto: Canadian Scholars' Press, 2000).

79. Jürgen Habermas, *Between Facts and Norms: Contributions to a Discourse Theory of Law and Democracy* (Cambridge: MIT Press, 1996); Habermas, "Perpetual Peace"; and John Rawls, *Political Liberalism* (Columbia: Columbia University Press, 2005). For more radical (and triumphalist) version of the argument, see Francis Fukuyama, *The End of History and the Last Man* (New York: Free Press, 2006).

80. Skinner, "Meaning and Understanding," 73.

81. John Zammito, *Kant, Herder, and the Birth of Anthropology* (Chicago: University of Chicago Press, 2002), 13; Jeanne Morefield, *Empires without Imperialism: Anglo-American Decline and the Politics of Deflection* (Oxford: Oxford University Press, 2014), 23–25.

82. Frances Power Cobbe, "Criminals, Idiots, Women and Minors," *Fraser's Magazine for Town and Country* 78 (1868): 778. I thank Jennifer Pitts for drawing this article to my attention.

83. Jacques Rancière, *Disagreement: Politics and Philosophy* (Minneapolis: University of Minnesota Press, 1999). For other treatments of the audibility – or inaudibility – of claims to justice, see Connolly, *The Ethos of Pluralization*, and Iris Marion Young, *Justice and the Politics of Difference* (Princeton: Princeton University Press, 2011).

84. J. G. A. Pocock, "The History of Political Thought: A Methodological Enquiry," in *Philosophy, Politics and Society*, eds. Peter Laslett and W. G. Runciman (New York: Barnes and Noble, 2002).

85. Cobbe, "Criminals," 785, 793.

86. Ibid., 793.

87. Hannelore Schröder, "Kant's Patriarchal Order," in *Feminist Interpretations of Immanuel Kant*, ed. Robin May Schott (University Park: Pennsylvania State University Press, 1997), 275–296.

88. Cited in Zammito, *Birth of Anthropology*, 100.

89. Kleingeld, *Cosmopolitanism*, 18.

90. Judith Butler, *Excitable Speech: A Politics of the Performative* (New York: Routledge, 1997), 89.

91. Waldron, "Theoretical Foundations," 146.

92. Mill, *On Liberty*, 18: 224.

93. McCarthy, *Race*, 42.

2

Unbending Crooked Timber

> Is this state of the perfection of humanity possible, and when is it to be hoped for? Since the germs for this are actually innate in humanity, it is thus possible that they will be developed through cultivation and can achieve perfection. But when is it to be hoped for, and how should it happen, and what can one do in connection with this in order to bring such about?
>
> Kant, *Anthropology Friedländer*

In his essay "On the common saying: That may be correct in theory, but it is of no use in practice," Kant describes the principles underlying the civil condition as preserving the freedom of every individual, the equality of all before the law and the independence of each as a citizen. In them, we easily recognize the hallmarks of the Kantian concern for the autonomy of all human beings; they ensure that "each may seek his happiness in the way that seems good to him, provided he does not infringe upon that freedom of others to strive for a like end which can coexist with the freedom of others."[1] Political order enables individual self-direction; the state preserves the conditions for every person's "[f]reedom ... the only original right belonging to every man by virtue of his humanity."[2] It comes as a surprise, then, when a few pages later, he asserts that "[t]he quality requisite to this [citizenship], apart from the *natural* one (of not being a child or a woman), is only that of *being one's own master (sui iuris)*, hence having some *property*."[3] This appears inconsistent with Kant's initial principles: political rights are, in fact, subject to both natural and conventional qualifications. Given the foundation of those rights – anchored in a humanity whose dignity, as Kant famously puts it, places it beyond mere "market price"[4] – it also seems to complicate his conception of moral equality.[5] How, then, does Kant conceptualize the status of the commonwealth's "cobeneficiaries" (or, in an equally infelicitous turn of phrase, "passive citizens"), subject to laws they're unable to shape? What kinds of citizens are endowed with full civil personality, and what capacities does that presuppose? Do these civic constraints impact

Kant's account of moral personhood, or is the divorce between ethics and politics as tenable as he claims it to be?

More problematic are Kant's writings on race, biology, anthropology, history and physical geography, which at points endorse a racial hierarchy still more directly at odds with his moral theory. In a series of essays spanning the 1770s and 1780s, Kant developed a theory of racial differentiation attributing fixed cognitive ceilings to given races.[6] Given the centrality of reason for moral personhood, it's not at all clear how he envisioned such peoples' moral standing. Feminist theorists have, still further, drawn out troubling dimensions of Kant's treatment of women from a political standpoint ("*Woman* regardless of age is declared to be immature in civil matters")[7] and a moral one ("One can only come to the characterization of this sex if one uses as one's principle not what we *make* our end, but what *nature's end* was in establishing womankind").[8]

How should we make sense of these contradictions – between the formally egalitarian and universalistic moral and political doctrines for which Kant is celebrated, and these instances of exclusion and marginalization? How are we to understand Kant's responses to human diversity and difference, and their incorporation in his philosophical system? How might Kant's views of women, non-Europeans and the unpropertied impact his liberalism, and the liberalisms that we inherit from him?

These are, broadly speaking, the puzzles that I address in this chapter and the next. In so doing, I steer between two common tendencies in the scholarship. The first is to disregard, bracket or minimize Kant's post-critical examinations of human phenomenality.[9] Much of the philosophical literature treats his expansive writings on politics, history, anthropology, education and biology as either disconnected from, or irrelevant for, the critical system – at best, sidebars to his "real" philosophy, and at worst, embarrassments best relegated to the dustbin of history. The *Critiques*' overwhelming influence, John Zammito observes, has both obscured Kant's non-critical work and quashed the impetus to explore their points of connection, despite Kant's own interest in them.[10] Even careful examinations of Kant's legal and political philosophy, such as Elisabeth Ellis's *Kant's Politics* and Arthur Ripstein's *Force and Freedom*, remain focused on its formal, universalist dimensions, elaborated in the *Groundwork*, second *Critique* and *Rechtslehre*.[11] Most of the commentary thus understands Kant's views on human diversity and moral progress as separable from presumably free-standing doctrines of ethics and right.[12] A second, more critical literature delves into Kant's treatments of gender, race, culture and civilization, but tends to read them in isolation from one another, and from the theoretical frameworks contextualizing them.[13] While contributing to a growing interest in what Robert Louden describes as Kant's "impure ethics," it also neglects important distinctions within the Kantian system.

Here and in Chapter 3, I develop an account of Kant's liberalism in the sense sketched out in Chapter 1: I elaborate his vision of moral and political life, of the kinds of persons that we are (and that we ought to aim to be), and of the conditions enabling our movement toward the realization of our moral ends.[14] I argue that Kant's understanding of moral agency incorporates not only a system of transcendentally determined duties, but also an account of the irreducibly sensible beings to whom they apply. By focusing too closely on the former, as much of the literature does, we lose track of our constitutive phenomenality; by attributing too much weight to the latter, we ignore the noumenal grounds of freedom. Building on recent efforts to excavate Kant's thought on the embodied facets of ethical life, I flesh out a fuller picture of moral personhood than the one gleaned from his formal ethics alone.[15] Kant himself consistently held that "[t]he counterpart of a metaphysics of morals, the other member of the division of practical philosophy as a whole, would be moral anthropology."[16] And yet, his encompassing view of practical ethics has largely been eclipsed by the scholarly emphasis on our obligations as strictly rational, rather than human, beings.

This is the space, between Kant's moral idealism and his pragmatic anthropology, that I delve into. I consider the kinds of agents presupposed by his moral and political thought, the conditions acculturating them to their moral duties and what happens to those unable to develop such a moral orientation. Against the strictly deontological reading of Kant's ethics – that all human beings simply *are* endowed with the rational faculty anchoring their status as free and equal – I argue that Kant's fuller conceptualization of moral agency is, in fact, developmental.[17] Our moral nature is not straightforwardly or fully inborn; human beings rather form their capacities as moral agents – their moral character, in Kant's words – over time.[18] The fulfillment of moral personhood is, then, a lifelong project that turns on particular acculturative and educational processes. This close attention to the formation of moral character is what we miss by isolating Kant's treatments of ethics and politics from anthropology and history. And while all human beings share in an inalienable dignity, I contend that these accounts of moral character and moral progress qualify its universalism in important ways. These chapters, then, elaborate Kant's distinctive notions of moral character and moral formation; show that he sees them as belonging to "the complete presentation of the system"[19] of ethics, rather than as aberrations from an otherwise strictly transcendental morality; and argue that this fuller view clarifies the deficits in women, non-Europeans and the poor throwing their moral and/or political status into question.

This serves two purposes. First, I illuminate a lesser-known Kant, whose attention to the unsystematic (and, as he recognizes, unsystematizable) dimensions of moral life is often obfuscated by the misperception of his ethics as rigid, cold and unfeeling – even inhuman. Against the rationalist caricature, I draw out his sustained engagements with the social, historical, political and institutional conditions moving us toward our moral ends. From dinner parties to global law, few features of our moral edification escaped his attention. Second, by focusing on Kant's pragmatic anthropology and philosophical history, I situate his treatments of race, gender, culture, civilization and progress within the conceptual frameworks through which he comprehended human difference. In the 1790s, Kant shifted his focus from the derivation of moral laws to their principles of application, without which, he argued, ethics could not avoid being "merely speculative."[20] It is in this context – of his historical, anthropological and teleological reflections on the species' moral development – that we are best placed to understand his views of human diversity. This aims, from a methodological standpoint, to approach Kant carefully, charitably and conscientiously, registering the distinctions and divisions shaping his philosophical architectonic. "To read historical philosophers critically," Allen Wood argues, "is to read them with intellectual sympathy ... We need to respect the unity of a philosopher's thought because we can learn most from a set of doctrines by seeing how some depend on others in ways that are not obvious."[21] Despite my criticisms of Kant, I read him, as I read Mill, with this kind of intellectual sympathy, pursuing the intuition that a fair assessment of either thinker's merits, resources and shortcomings requires it. The problems underlying Kant's views of diversity, addressed in Chapter 3, are only discernible in light of such contextualization.

This chapter begins by delving into the relationship between Kant's critical and anthropological works, starting from their seemingly incompatible notions of freedom and moral agency. While his practical philosophy describes the moral obligations incumbent on all free, rational beings, his anthropology addresses "helps and hindrances" to our moral advancement. How are we to reconcile Kant's critical account of the will's transcendental freedom with his developmental account of anthropology's assisting in our collective progress toward moral ends? I propose a resolution to the problem by arguing that Kant's transcendental and anthropological arguments attend to different dimensions of a single, cohesive conception of human moral agency. Drawing on his moral psychology, I highlight Kant's distinction between the objective, formal *derivation* of moral principle and the subjective, dispositional *volition* of moral choice. Rather than contradicting one another, I suggest, transcendental and anthropological viewpoints address distinctive components of properly human (and not just rational) moral action. This lays the groundwork for my developmental reading of Kant, which focuses on the subjective dimension of moral agency and on the formation of moral character. I argue that Kant was much more attentive to principles of moral volition, and to the conditions attuning our receptivity to moral duty, than is often recognized.

Section 2.2 excavates this wide-ranging moral acculturation in Kant's writings on pedagogy, anthropology, history, politics and ethics. I reconstruct his accounts of the structures and processes cultivating our moral dispositions at the individual level (through moral psychology and pedagogy) and group level (through civilization, culture and republican government). While Kant's ethics have long faced charges of excessive formalism, his teleological reflections on human development reveal his abiding concerns with their phenomenal conditions of application, and more generally, with the inculcation of moral personhood.

Section 2.3 considers the object of these formative processes by filling out Kant's understanding of moral character. I argue that his conceptualization of human moral agency is better captured in the *Religion*'s good human being than in the *Groundwork*'s good will. The moral personality of which we are capable, as Kant understands it, is not just transcendentally fixed – a static, inborn attribute or quality – but rather something to be worked on, and worked toward. As inexorably sensible and rational creatures equally bound by phenomenal imperfection and transcendental law, our moral vocation lies not in the realization of perfect virtue, but in an "ever-continuing striving for the better."[22]

In total, then, this chapter digs into a largely neglected dimension of Kantian ethics: the enculturation of messy, embodied human beings to their duties as moral agents. Chapter 3 considers its consequences: the challenges faced by those persons incapable of developing such a progressive moral character.

2.1 TRANSCENDENTAL GROUNDING, EMPIRICAL CONTEXTS

2.1.1 Between Critique and Anthropology

Commentators have long noted the tension between Kant's better-known, critical account of human freedom and the developmental conception recurring throughout his impure ethics (most notably, in his moral anthropology).[23] This tension has deep roots, as Kant's interest in humanity's moral advancement spanned decades and was by no means cursory. While best known for the critical philosophy elaborated over the 1780s, Kant lectured extensively on history, anthropology and physical geography over the forty-odd years of his teaching career.[24] John Zammito traces "a strong connection between anthropology and ethics" as early as 1766, suggesting that many of "Kant's anthropological considerations ... lie in his early lectures on practical philosophy."[25] This teleological thread is also visible in his early published works – notably, 1764's *Observations on the Feeling of the Beautiful and Sublime* – and cuts across the different periods of his intellectual development. Even during the critical years, Kant continued to develop his philosophy of history in essays such as "Idea for a Universal History with a Cosmopolitan Aim" (1784), his reviews of Herder (1785), "Conjectural Beginning of Human History" (1786), and in the third *Critique* (1790).

This strain of his thought came to the fore in the post-critical period, when Kant increasingly turned his attention to the phenomenal dimensions of moral personhood. He appears in his later years to have become preoccupied with lived human agency, the imperfect material to which the critical account of moral duty was to apply.[26] By the 1790s, Allen Wood observes, Kant withdrew

his earlier claim [from the *Groundwork*] that a "metaphysics of morals" can concern only "the idea and the principles of a possible *pure* will and not the actions and conditions of human volition generally" . . . Kant now no longer regards a metaphysics of morals as constituted solely by a set of pure moral principles . . . It is instead the system of duties that result when the pure moral principle is applied to the empirical nature of human beings in general.[27]

In the *Metaphysics of Morals, Religion, Anthropology, Contest of Faculties* and several shorter essays, Kant elaborates a developmental conception of human agency. Where the *Critiques* delineate our moral nature and obligations, these texts attend to our capacity and propensity to realize our moral ends. Robert Louden describes this as the "second part"[28] of morality, addressing the conditions in which we learn and ameliorate the skills for autonomous self-determination.

This presents us with a paradox: while the account of freedom advanced in the *Critique of Pure Reason* turns on the intelligible will's strict independence from the sensible world, moral anthropology speaks to "the subjective conditions in human nature that hinder people or help them in *fulfilling* the laws of a metaphysics of morals."[29] An obvious tension runs between Kant's incompatibilist conception of the intelligible will's freedom and an anthropology treating empirical circumstances affecting our moral capacities. The contradiction, Patrick Frierson notes, has long been subject to criticism. In the late 1790s, Friedrich Schleiermacher charged Kant's anthropology with subverting the *Critiques'* account of freedom, and in an 1804 review of Kant's published lectures on pedagogy, Johann Friedrich Herbart similarly pointed to the irreconcilability of moral education and transcendental freedom.[30] How are we to "learn" a freedom situated outside of time, space and experience?

Compounding the problem, Kant treats moral anthropology as a constitutive part of his system of ethics, and not a mere appendage to it. As he understands it, "a metaphysics of morals cannot dispense with principles of application, and we shall often have to take as our object the particular *nature* of human beings, which is cognized only by experience, in order to *show* in it what can be inferred from universal moral principles."[31] How, then, are we to reconcile this apparent contradiction?[32]

The distance between the two perspectives shrinks when we recognize them precisely as such: as different *perspectives* attending to different dimensions of human moral agency. The problem stems from failing to distinguish the objective derivation of the moral law (a principle of appraisal) from our subjective receptivity to it (a principle of volition). When we pull them apart, we better see Kant's transcendental and anthropological perspectives as enacting a philosophical division of labor, each attending to distinctive facets – objective and subjective – of a fuller conceptualization of moral agency, rather than as in tension.[33] Rather than treating them as issuing the same kinds of claims (leading to the question: are human beings transcendentally free or not?), we need to carefully consider what these forms of argumentation aim to do and say.

Let's begin with the transcendental grounds of freedom. In the *Critique of Pure Reason*, Kant distinguishes between empirical and intelligible character, which capture different forms of causality in which human beings partake. While empirical character concerns a person's relation, as a sensible being, with other objects in the phenomenal world, intelligible character refers to the capacity to initiate acts of will independent of, and unconditioned by, it. Our empirical character, as Henry Allison puts it, "functions as the empirical cause of [an] action";[34] it pertains to our motions within the causal order of the sensible world. As an intelligible being, however, the "subject must be considered to be free from all influence of sensibility and from all determination through appearances."[35] The possibility of human freedom turns on this intelligible character: without the ability to act on purely rational, self-given motivations, we remain bound by the causal chains of the empirical world. Freedom thus depends on our capacity to exclude sensibility from self-generated action. The autonomy of the will is predicated on its determination "in accordance with laws that are independent of any empirical condition and thus belong to the *autonomy* of pure reason ... The law of this autonomy ... is the moral law."[36]

The moral law is, of course, the beating heart of Kant's practical philosophy: our duties are determined by the moral law that stands as the very condition of our freedom. What exactly, then, is the relation between autonomy and freedom? And how does Kant understand freedom at all? Without having the space here to fully delve into this notoriously difficult question, Kant differentiates transcendental and practical senses of freedom.[37] Transcendental freedom refers to the intelligible will's capacity to act spontaneously and to initiate events or states from itself – to act as an original cause, independent of prior causation.[38] As a capacity operative solely within the constraints of the noumenal realm, it can only be the subject of speculative reason. Practical freedom, conversely, describes our particular freedom as rational and finite agents – that is, as moral actors subject to the sway of the phenomenal world. As Kant understands it, practical freedom incorporates both negative and positive characteristics. Negatively, Paul Guyer notes, it entails "independence from domination by one's own inclinations and ... independence from domination by others."[39] Its positive component is autonomy: the determination of the will by reason itself.[40] As Allison captures it, "a will with the property of autonomy is one for which there are (or can be) reasons to act that are logically independent of the agent's needs as a sensuous being."[41] The will's autonomy thus depends on transcendental freedom. "Kant's metaphysical contention," Allen Wood surmises, "is that the will can be practically free only if it is transcendentally free."[42] Transcendental freedom is "a necessary [but not sufficient] condition of practical freedom ... the ability to free oneself from the domination by one's sensory impulses presupposes the ability to initiate new series of actions, independent of natural laws."[43] While practical freedom (the capacity to act independently of inclination/coercion, and in conformity with self-legislated reason) assumes the possibility of transcendental freedom (the capacity for unconditioned and spontaneous action), it is not reducible to it; autonomy requires not just any choice, but the right kinds of choices, made for the right kinds of reasons. Whatever ambiguities remain in their relationship, this much is clear: both transcendental and practical freedom appear to strictly exclude phenomenal influences.

Neither conception, then, seems to leave much space for the influence of moral anthropology, leading us back to the "paradox that Pistorius and so many others have found in Kant's attempt to reconcile causal determinism at the phenomenal level with his incompatibilist conception of freedom."[44] That paradox is, however, attenuated by differentiating two elements in moral action: (a) the objective determination of the moral law and of the duties consequent on it (what is the moral law, and what obligations does it incur?), and (b) the subjective volition in choosing to adopt the moral law as the grounds of one's action – or, in Kantian terms, in the determination of one's maxim (should I adopt the moral law as the principle determining my action?).[45] Christine Korsgaard's analysis of Kantian motivation is instructive in this regard. For Kant, all action incorporates two basic components, which Korsgaard characterizes as "incentive" and "principle."[46] An incentive is "a motivationally-loaded or evaluative representation of an object"[47] which, roughly speaking, provides the volitional impetus for any action, moral or not. And yet, we do not act directly from it, as doing so would leave us beholden to the desire stimulating the action, and so, unfree. As Korsgaard maintains,

[a]ction, according to Kant, is the determination of our own causality, so if we are to count a movement as an action, the movement must be determined by the agent herself, not merely caused by her desires. In other words, the agent must act *on* the incentive, must take it up as a reason for action, by adopting a maxim or subjective principle of acting on it.[48]

This is the key to what Allison describes as the Incorporation Thesis. For a free being, "an inclination or desire does not *of itself* constitute a reason for acting. It can become one only with reference to a rule or principle of action, which dictates that we ought to pursue the satisfaction of that inclination or desire."[49] Human beings are perpetually assailed by competing desires and motivations to action; practical freedom lies in our capacity to adopt certain principles (or maxims, to follow Kant) as the grounds for selecting the incentives on which we choose to act.[50]

Broadly speaking, the first and second *Critiques* articulate what those principles are (or rather, what that principle is). They address the first, objective dimension of moral action by delimiting the transcendental grounds of freedom (self-determined action in conformity with the moral law) and the incentive structure demanded by moral action (immediate respect for the moral law).[51] But they pay significantly less attention to its second, volitional dimension, implicit in Kant's practical philosophy. They tell us little about how as fallible moral actors we learn to recognize and internalize this incentive structure as a lifelong orientation. While the *Critiques* establish the grounds of the moral law, Kant's post-critical works consider our receptivity to it – how we learn to choose to act as morality compels us to.[52] It's a distinction worth examining in greater detail.

2.1.2 Elateres Motiva: Moral Feeling and the Subjective Grounds of Choice

The *Groundwork* and *Critiques* address the formal qualities possessed by rational beings generally, and by human beings, subject to both empirical and intelligible motivations, more specifically. While our rational nature establishes the moral law's dominion over us, our phenomenal inclinations entail the need for the categorical imperative to determine the duties descended from it.[53] Unlike angels – rational creatures unable to act otherwise than in conformity with the moral law – our particular moral nature, wayward as it is, requires steering. While the categorical imperative responds to our sensible imperfections, the moral law that it clarifies is transcendentally fixed, based on the nature of rational, end-setting beings. The moral law and our duties are, then, determined a priori, on the basis of formal attributes of what we are, as finite, rational entities.

Yet human beings are complicated by their unique capacity – in fact, by their natural predilection – to ignore the moral law. Moral action for beings of our type requires not only a consciousness of the moral law, but also, a disposition to incorporate it within one's incentive structure. Under the heading "Of the Supreme Principle of Morality" in the *Lectures on Ethics*, Kant draws an important distinction:

We first have to take up two points here: (1) The principle of appraisal of obligation, and (2) the principle of its performance or execution. Guideline and motive have here to be distinguished. The guideline is the principle of appraisal, and the motive that of carrying-out the obligation; in that they have been confused, everything in morality has been erroneous.

If the question is: What is morally good or not?, that is the principle of appraisal, whereby I judge the goodness or depravity of actions. But if the question is: What moves me to live according to this law?, that is the principle of motive. Appraisal of the action is the objective ground, but not yet the subjective ground ... The supreme principle of all moral judgment lies in the understanding; the supreme principle of the moral impulse to do this thing lies in the heart. This motive is the moral feeling. Such a principle of motive cannot be confused with the principle of judgment. The latter is the norm, and the principle of impulsion is the motive.[54]

Kant here elaborates the distinction between the objective judgment involved in determining the moral law ("What is morally good or not?") and the subjective foundation of moral choice ("What moves me to live according to this law?"). This latter is the moral feeling, the principle of ethical impulsion particular to human beings. What, then, exactly is the moral feeling and how does it fit into Kant's accounts of freedom and moral action?

In a close examination of the good will's incentive structure in the second *Critique*, Kant asserts that

we find our nature as sensible beings so constituted that the matter of the faculty of desire (objects of inclination, whether of hope or fear) first forces itself upon us, and we find our pathologically determinable self, even though it is quite unfit to give universal law through its maxims, nevertheless striving antecedently to make its claims primary and originally valid, just as if it constituted our entire self.[55]

This is a serious problem for moral action: we are naturally disposed to prioritize phenomenal inclinations over the rational compulsion to act on moral incentives. Anticipating the *Religion*'s account of humanity's radical evil, Kant describes this "propensity to make oneself as having subjective determining grounds of choice into the objective determining ground of the will"[56] as self-love in general, and as self-conceit when the will adopts these subjective incentives as law-giving. The problem is volitional: the sanctity of moral action lies in moving the will by what Kant acknowledges is the weaker motivational impulse of respect for the moral law, as against the inducements of pleasure. Given our constitutive leanings toward our inclinations, it is hard to see how we might choose the right incentives on the right grounds.

The solution, for Kant, is the moral feeling. His account of the moral feeling sketches out both the problem and its resolution:

The understanding has no *elateres animi*, albeit it has the power to move, or *motiva*; but the latter are not able to outweigh the *elateres* of sensibility. A sensibility in accordance with the motive power of the understanding would be the moral feeling.[57]

Kant argues that the confrontation between self-love/self-conceit and the authority of the moral law generates a particular breed of feelings. By limiting self-love and striking down self-conceit, the will's immediate determination by the moral law humiliates self-conceit (a negative feeling) and creates respect for the law (a positive feeling).[58] As rationally determined affects grounded in pure respect for the moral law, these moral feelings resolve the volitional quandary by generating motivational impulses to adopt the moral law over incentives of inclination. The moral feeling enables moral action by redressing the understanding's volitional deficits before the otherwise stronger compulsions of sensibility.[59] And importantly, these moral feelings – positive and negative – remain strictly intelligible, rooted in pleasures and displeasures stimulated by the moral law, and so unconnected to the phenomenal world.[60] The moral feeling, Kant asserts, "is therefore produced solely by reason. It does not serve for appraising actions and certainly not for grounding the objective moral law itself, but only as an incentive to make this law its maxim."[61]

The moral feeling is, then, "a capacity for being affected by a moral judgment. When I judge by understanding that the action is morally good, I am still very far from doing this action of which I have so judged."[62] It thus belongs to Kant's practical ethics, connecting moral judgment and moral action. The moral feeling bridges what I ought to do as a matter of moral obligation and how I come to recognize the obligation as incumbent upon me at all, developing "the will's receptivity to finding itself subject to the law as unconditional necessitation."[63]

And importantly, the moral feeling *is* susceptible to development and to sensible influences. While inborn, it is not fixed; it is a disposition that grows or stagnates according to the attention devoted to it. Despite its resistance to strictly rational argumentation or compulsion, the moral feeling can, and must, be inculcated:

Since any consciousness of obligation depends upon moral feeling to make us aware of the constraint present in the thought of duty, there can be no duty to have moral feeling or to acquire it; instead every human being (as a moral being) has it in him originally. Obligation with regard to moral feeling can be only to *cultivate* it and strengthen it.[64]

As an innate capacity to sense the pull of intelligible duties, the moral feeling can't be commanded by duty, but we remain duty-bound to nurture and foster it. We are under an imperfect obligation to develop it as a "*subjective* condition of receptiveness to the concept of duty."[65] So while we are unable to produce the moral feeling itself, we are certainly capable of producing agents more or less receptive to it. As Kant maintains, in particularly un-Kantian sounding terms, "[t]he subject must first be habituated to morality ... the *indoles erecta* must first be excited, the moral feeling first made active, so that the subject can be actuated by moral motives."[66]

Turning back to our original conundrum – the tension between Kant's transcendental and empirical accounts of freedom – we now better see the philosophical division of labor between principles of moral appraisal and moral volition. While the *Groundwork* and *Critiques* attend to the objective, transcendental determination of the moral law (the principle of appraisal), the *Anthropology, Religion*, and certain sections of the second *Critique* address our subjective receptivity to it (the principle of volition). Seen in this light, the tension is significantly mitigated: the critical philosophy establishes the grounds of our freedom as *rational* beings, and the anthropological philosophy speaks to the moral volition implicit in the freedom of which we're capable as imperfect, embodied *human* beings. I now turn to the development of this moral volition, and to the processes of habituation, enculturation and orientation upon which it depends – in short, to moral education and character formation.

2.2   MAKING MORAL AGENTS

As we have begun to see, Kant's full account of a properly human ethics is closely attentive to the subjective and volitional aspects of moral personhood, even if these have received little critical scrutiny. This neglect is in part due to the scholarship's inclination to "make Kant more rational."[67] But it is also attributable to Kant's own inconsistencies, all the more glaring against the methodical structure of his better-known works. His "impure ethics" are scattered across a broad range of subjects: history, pedagogy, biology, aesthetics, anthropology and physical geography all concern, to varying degrees, the phenomenal character of individuals and peoples and its relevance for moral action.[68] And yet, despite its resistance to systematicity – addressing, as it does, the entirely unsystematic ways that human beings take up their moral obligations – the subjective side of ethics belongs "to the complete presentation of the system."[69] While "[t]he science of the rules of how man ought to behave is practical philosophy," Kant avers,

the science of the rules of his actual behaviour is anthropology; these two sciences are closely connected, and morality cannot exist without anthropology, for one must first know of the agent whether he is also in a position to accomplish what is required from him that he should do. One can, indeed, certainly consider practical philosophy even without anthropology, or without knowledge of the agent, only then it is merely speculative.[70]

The remainder of this chapter examines the "science of the rules of his actual behaviour" and the formation of the progressive agents at the center of Kant's liberalism. I begin by examining "micro-formative" processes – moral psychology, pedagogy and character formation – cultivating a moral disposition at the individual level. I then turn to "macro-formative" influences, the larger historical, social and political conditions enabling the development of moral agency.

2.2.1   Micro-Formation

2.2.1.1   *Moral Education*
Despite his rather fragmented treatment of the subject, Kant regards education as the foundation of moral personhood, arguing that "[t]he human being can only become human through education. He is nothing except what education makes of him."[71] While all human beings share in an intuitive sense of the moral good, our capacity to recognize and internalize the moral law's authority requires enculturation and development. The task of education is thus to "bring either a mind that is still uncultivated or one that is degraded onto the track of the morally good."[72]

This is, however, no simple task. Most of Europe's educational institutions were in Kant's view entirely misdirected. "[B]ecause everything in them works against nature," he judged, "the good to which nature has given the predisposition is far from being drawn out of the human being."[73] Properly understood, education ought to center on the practical end of forming moral character rather than imparting technical skills or speculative knowledge. Kant was an ardent supporter of the *Philanthropinum*, an institution founded in 1774 by Johann Bernhard Basedow that sought to reform Prussia's educational system by treating schools as loci for moral and civic education. Kant's enthusiasm was far-reaching: he employed Basedow's *Methodenbuch für Väter und Mütter der Familien und Völker* as the textbook for his 1776–7 course on practical pedagogy, raised money for the *Philanthropinum*, and recruited students to its ranks.[74] The *Philanthropinum* aimed to cultivate students' moral capacities and develop the inborn pleasures of learning, in marked contrast with a Prussian school system that emphasized theoretical knowledge and rote repetition.[75] Kant lauded the longer horizon of Basedow's pedagogy: schools should develop pragmatic skills, but only as means of fostering students' moral efflorescence. The "principle of the art of education," Kant argues, "is this: children should be educated not only with regard to the present but rather for a better condition of the human species that might be possible in the future; that is, in a manner appropriate to the idea of humanity and its complete vocation."[76] Given its emphasis on moral growth, Kant regarded the Basedowian institute's "perfect plan of education" as "the greatest phenomenon which has appeared in this century for the improvement of the perfection of humanity."[77] Beyond the immediate benefits of an education through which the "seed of the good itself can be cultivated and sustained,"[78] Basedow's pedagogical innovations, Kant saw, contributed to the species' broader moralization. As "the genuine educational institute that is fitting to nature as well as civil purposes," the *Philanthropinum* was "an institute in which an entirely new order of human affairs commences," whose "fruits will soon spread to all countries and to the most remote descendants."[79] Moral education was, then, as indispensable for individual advancement as for humanity's moral progress.

And yet, it remains a delicate business. A misdirected education not only fails to foster a moral disposition, but also instills pathological habits impeding future moral growth; once established, one's character is unalterable.[80] Kant argues that a well-calibrated pedagogy oscillates between freedom and discipline, striking a balance between an unruly, undisciplined agent incapable of subjecting passions to the authority of reason, and a dead soul reduced to simple, unthinking obedience. "One of the biggest problems of education," he maintains, is how one can unite submission under lawful constraint with the capacity to use one's freedom. For constraint is necessary. How do I cultivate freedom under constraint? I shall accustom my pupil to tolerate a constraint of his freedom, and I shall at the same time lead him to make good use of his freedom. Without this everything is a mere mechanism, and the pupil who is released from education does not know how to use his freedom.[81]

This concern pervades Kant's treatments of education: the tenuous equilibrium between freedom and restraint, the twin pillars of moral education, is all too easily unbalanced. A child "must always feel its freedom,"[82] Kant insists, and his pedagogy cultivates the moral capacities sustaining it.

2.2.1.2 *Discipline, Culture, Moral Training*

In his *Lectures on Pedagogy*, Kant develops a three-stage educational program consisting of discipline, culture and moral training.[83] All education begins with discipline, which Kant characterizes as "negative" instruction. Given the volitional primacy of our sensible drives, an education aiming at rational self-possession starts by mitigating the influence of our inclinations. Discipline reins in the natural impulsion for unconstrained freedom and self-indulgence, and so "prevents the human being from deviating by means of his animal impulses from his destiny: humanity . . . it is the action by means of which man's tendency to savagery is taken away."[84] By restraining our instinctive attraction to heteronomous freedom, discipline lays the foundation for rational freedom – that is, for autonomy. It underpins all positive instruction by inculcating the obedience and self-control on which it depends.

   Discipline thus clears the ground for the practical education "by which the human being is to be formed so that he can live as a freely acting being."[85] This consists of basic instruction, pragmatic instruction – both falling under what Kant describes as culture/cultivation (*Kultur* or *Bildung*, depending on the context) – and moral training.[86] Broadly speaking, this positive course of instruction imparts and develops forms of reason required for practical action in different domains of human life. Each educational stage attunes the student to distinctive types of imperatives incurred by the exercise of practical reason, along with their corresponding ends and skills. Kant distinguishes "three kinds of imperative, of skill, prudence and morality . . . The imperatives of skill are problematic, those of prudence pragmatic, and those of morality ethical."[87] The three spheres of positive instruction, then, form the capacities sustaining free action; we are incapable of pursuing our ends if we lack the technical, social/prudential and moral skills that they demand. These spheres also directly correspond to the *Groundwork*'s account of the three types of imperative implicated in the exercise of practical reason – imperatives of skill, assertoric imperatives and categorical imperatives, concerning (respectively) "*rules* of skill," "*counsels* of prudence" and "*commands* (*laws*) of morality."[88]

   Basic instruction, the first stage of positive education, serves as a foundation for future improvement by stimulating the child's natural endowments, providing the "*scholastic* formation or instruction . . . to become skillful for the attainment of all of his ends."[89] It fosters the technical skills enabling the pursuit of a wide range of different objectives. These technical skills, as Kant understands them, are the basic means through which end-setting beings undertake any and all purposive activity. Their ends are thus given by the infinite variety of goals that human beings set themselves.

The second branch of positive instruction develops pragmatic/prudential skills concerning one's happiness. While Kantian ethics are commonly portrayed as strictly ascetic, Kant in fact conceives of humanity's highest good as incorporating both moral and sensible goods, and even derides overly austere moralities as "monkish."[90] Pragmatic instruction hones an understanding of the social contexts and social rules within which we seek our own goods and pleasures. In stark contrast with moral injunctions, the prudence that it fosters aims, in Kant's words, at "using other human beings for one's purposes."[91] It educates us in the graces and refinements of civilized interaction, making us "well suited for human society, popular and influential. This requires . . . manners, good behavior and a certain prudence in virtue of which one is able to use all human beings for one's own final purposes."[92] Prudential skills thus sensitize us to the social comportments enabling the satisfaction of our ultimate end as sensible beings: our own happiness.

Discipline, basic instruction and pragmatic instruction are, then, the bedrock of Kant's practical pedagogy. By instilling the self-control and elemental skills for purposive activity, they lay the foundation for education's final stage: moral training.

2.2.1.3 *Moral Training I: Habituation*

From Hegel onward, critics of Kant's formalism have derided his inattention to the affective and habituated registers of moral life.[93] This is, perhaps, a matter of looking in the wrong places, as a fuller examination reveals his sustained preoccupation with moral development. Like Plato, Kant understands moral personality as evolving through preparatory steps awakening us to the good; and like Plato, he sees its earliest stages as concerning feeling and habituation, rather than reason itself.[94] Just as Plato's guardian-to-be learns through musical training to "praise fine things, be pleased by them, receive them into his soul . . . [even] while he's still young and unable to grasp the reason,"[95] Kant contends that "for a still undeveloped human being, imitation is the first determination of his will to accept maxims that he afterwards makes for himself."[96] While imitation and habituation are incompatible with properly moral action, they are integral for cultivating moral sensibilities. Kant accounts for the necessity of moral habit in the second *Critique*'s "Doctrine of the Method of Pure Practical Reason":

At first it is only a question of making appraisal of actions by moral laws a natural occupation and, as it were, a habit accompanying all our own free actions as well as our observation of those of others, and of sharpening it by asking first whether the action objectively *conforms with the moral law*, and with which law ... thus one teaches how to distinguish different duties that come together in an action. The other point to which attention must be directed is the question whether the action was also done (subjectively) *for the sake of the moral law*.[97]

Habituation fulfills several important functions in Kant's conceptualization of moral development that are worth teasing out.

First, through repetition, we sharpen our sensitivity to our moral obligations by forming a habit of examining the moral worth of actions. As Kant puts it, "[t]he subject must first be habituated to morality; before coming primed with rewards and punishments, the *indoles erecta* must first be excited, the moral feeling first made active, so that the subject can be actuated by moral motives."[98] Habituation awakens and attunes the moral feeling that animates the moral agency of which we're capable. The deontological rigidity associated with Kantian ethics appears to leave little space for habituation, but Kant is himself far less stringent, clearly recognizing the need for moral ballasts. Morally capable and yet prone to inclination, we are constitutively bound to develop and fortify our moral predispositions. "[B]y long practice," he argues, we "will have given strength to the moral motivating grounds, and acquired, by cultivation, a habit of desire or aversion in regard to moral good or evil. By this, the moral feeling will be cultivated, and then morality will have strength and motivation."[99]

Second, habituation forms the evaluative capacities enabling us to distinguish between: (a) moral and non-moral action, (b) action performed from duty and action performed in mere conformity with the moral law, and (c) our distinctive moral obligations. While the moral worth of any particular action turns on the will's alignment, moral action more generally requires the ability to identify morally relevant information in the world. Habituation develops our consciousness of what Barbara Herman describes as the "rules of moral salience" allowing us "to perceive situations in terms of their morally significant features."[100] Without the capability to discern moral data in our lived experience – a capability necessarily cultivated in empirical contexts – we would be incapable of moral action. Habituation thus accustoms us to recognize and appraise the morally germane information surrounding us.

Finally, habituation generates a particular affective relation toward the moral law. By fostering the moral feeling we come to *like* moral action, a pleasure that remains with us even when we come to act out of respect for the moral law. What students "have learned to *enjoy*," according to G. Felicitas Munzel, "is the expansion of their rational faculty beyond natural instincts."[101] As Philip Stratton-Lake notes, while Kant denies the moral worth of action adopted *on the basis* of sensible inclinations (such as pleasure), this does not preclude our taking pleasure in carrying out moral action (from properly moral motivations).[102] Habituation enlivens us to the pleasure of moral action – initially, as a motivation, and eventually, as an accompaniment. Far from neglecting the fine grain of moral motivation, Kant recognizes that "[t]o form a habit is to establish a lasting inclination apart from any maxim, through frequently repeated gratifications of that inclination; it is a mechanism of sense rather than a principle of thought."[103] This is, more broadly, the task of moral education: using "mechanisms of sense" to draw us toward the right "principle of thought."

2.2.1.4 *Moral Training II: Propaedeutic Aids*

These mechanisms include a wide range of pedagogical tools, including moral examples, rewards and punishment, and moral catechism. As with habituation, propaedeutic aids toe the line between inculcating a moral disposition and undermining it; and as with habituation, their utility depends on their balance.

Moral examples, for instance, "should not serve as a model but only as proof that it is really possible to act in conformity with duty."[104] Emulating moral examples, Kant contends, induces laziness in the determination of our duties; they ought rather to demonstrate that moral action is *possible*. Ideally, moral examples counter the despair to which uncultivated minds are prone when facing the seemingly insurmountable rigors of moral duty. Improperly used, however, they stunt moral growth by encouraging children to measure their worth in relation to their peers, rather than "according to the concepts of his own reason,"[105] producing envy rather than moral consciousness. "A good example," Kant holds, incites comparison not "with any other human being whatsoever (as he is), but with the *idea* (of humanity), as he ought to be."[106] Moral examples are thus edifying, but ambivalent: they ward off moral despondency and cynicism, but also risk supplanting moral judgment and shaming students into moral action rather than awakening them to it.

Rewards and punishments are likewise necessary, yet potentially damaging, sources of moral instruction. While impressing habits of discipline and self-control, sticks and carrots can instill improper incentives to moral action – namely, avoiding punishments or gaining rewards. The danger is that "both engender a low habit of mind, namely *indoles abjecta*"[107] – a submissive character – if applied incorrectly. Like moral examples, then, rewards and punishments ought never to serve as the grounds of moral action, but only as spurs to moral consciousness. Their function is to indicate morally praiseworthy and contemptible actions, shoring up moral mindfulness rather than motivating any kind of action.

Finally, Kant regards moral catechism as "an indispensable preparatory step"[108] toward moral personhood, stimulating and strengthening ethical impulses and sensibilities. Through didactic questioning in the Socratic mold, the teacher – "the midwife of the pupil's thoughts" – "guides his young pupil's course of thought merely by presenting him with cases in which his predisposition for certain concepts will develop," and so "elicits from his pupil's reason, by questioning, what he wants to teach him."[109] Proper catechistic direction provokes the student's consciousness of his own moral personality and leads him to its ensuing duties. The catechistic method is, for Kant, "a *cultivation of reason* most suited to the capacity of the undeveloped (since questions about what one's duty is can be decided far more easily than speculative questions), and so is the most appropriate way to sharpen the understanding of young people in general."[110] It initiates the transition from acting in conformity with the moral law to acting from it, a predilection constructed over time and through careful direction. And as with other tools of moral education, its functions are highly circumscribed. "In this catechism," Kant holds, "the greatest care must be taken to base the command of duty not on the advantages or disadvantages that follow from observing it ... but quite purely on the moral principles ... [lest] the concept of duty itself vanishes and dissolves into mere pragmatic precepts."[111] Through watchful steering, "by this sort of practice, the pupil is drawn without noticing it to an *interest* in morality."[112]

Moral education is, then, no afterthought in Kant's ethics, and neither are the moral abilities that it develops. "[W]e animal creatures," he maintains, "are made into human beings only by education."[113] Education cultivates the dispositions that, I argue, are central to the realization of our particular moral *vocation*, as embodied and finite moral actors. Kant's post-critical attention to the subjective dimensions of ethical life in no way attenuates the moral law's unconditionality; the force of its obligation and its transcendental grounding are equally untouched by the "principle of volition" elaborated here. It rather fills out the kind of moral agency of which we are capable. "The metaphysics of morals or *metaphysica pura*," Kant reminds us, "is only the first part of morals – the second part is *philosophia moralis applicata*, moral anthropology, to which the empirical principles belong."[114] Absent this second part, Kant's ethics *do* lapse into an empty formalism, a bare shell of unconditional imperatives. They remain incomplete, grounding our obligations as rational creatures without addressing how, as phenomenal moral agents, we might take them up. Human dignity remains anchored in our nature as rational, end-setting beings endowed with capacities for freedom, autonomy and self-determination. And yet, these are capacities to be cultivated, not fixed attributes. The subjective, volitional side of morals – how we come to recognize, internalize and actualize the moral law – is, then, integral to Kant's ethics. I now turn to flesh out this second part of ethics – moral anthropology – and its function in our moral development.

2.2.2 Macro-Formation

"Although autonomy is an essential property of individual rational wills," Barbara Herman notes, "for human beings, autonomous moral agency is realized in and through a certain form of social life with others."[115] Our ethical sentiments and propensities are, for Kant, fostered not only by moral education but also through broader social, cultural and political institutions.

As Herman, Thomas McCarthy and Sankar Muthu observe, individual moral agency relies on a backdrop of social and cultural resources.[116] And yet, I would argue that only particular *kinds* of culture, social existence and political organization are, in Kant's view, conducive to moral progress. "Cultures" are not in themselves valuable, as Muthu contends, but only in light of their role in our historical advancement toward moral perfection.[117] Certain social states are more conducive to producing morally progressive agents than others, and some (see Chapter 3) appear incapable of forming them at all. "Kantian moral education is a training to autonomy," Herman asserts, and as such, "it is not just a lifelong task for individuals, but a task of culture. The right social institutions are the background of sound moral judgment."[118] To see why this is the case, I turn to these larger-scale formative processes and to the historical-teleological framework within which Kant addresses them.

2.2.2.1 History, Culture and Civilization

As is well known, Kant understands humanity as fundamentally progressive: history, writ large and from a philosophical perspective, reveals our collective progress, tracing our movement from nature to freedom.[119] Kant conceives of nature (and of humanity's place within it) in teleological terms, as a purposively organized system of ends in which all creatures develop their naturally given capacities.[120] Humanity is in the unique position of only being able to do so at a species-wide, rather than individual, level. This is a result of the kind of being that we are: rational and finite. Our capacity for reason obligates us to perfect our rational faculties, and our finitude prevents us from doing so as individuals. We are thus bound to improve ourselves collectively, over generations, moving toward an ever-greater realization of our shared capability for autonomous moral action.[121] That natural end – the perfection of our rational faculty – anchors a teleological account of historical development centering on humanity's moral realization. As we have seen, our progress in this regard turns on the formation of our moral propensities. While moral education addresses that formation at the individual level, Kant's anthropology speaks to the broader "subjective conditions in human nature that hinder people or help them in *fulfilling* the laws of a metaphysics of morals. It would deal with the development, spreading, and strengthening of moral principle."[122]

Crucial among these conditions, Kant argues, is culture. Kant describes "nature's plan, of a supreme and, to us, inscrutable wisdom: to bring about the perfection of the human being through progressive culture."[123] Culture, as he understands it, is cultivation, comprehensible in relation to our acculturation to our moral ends. In a general sense, it refers to "the procurement of skillfulness [*Geschicklichkeit*]"[124] enabling human beings to undertake purposive action – to set and pursue moral ends. As such, it touches on both individual and social development. As Louden observes, culture "is often used in a double sense by Kant: sometimes it refers to the general formation of humanity out of animality in the human race as a whole; sometimes it refers to more specific educational processes directed at particular groups as well as individuals."[125] How, then, do these two conceptions of culture – individual and collective – relate to one another?

As we have seen, culture in the narrow sense – at the individual level – denotes the course of positive instruction in Kant's moral pedagogy developing our technical and prudential skills. As Kant puts it in the third *Critique*, "[t]he production in a rational being of an aptitude for any ends in general of his own choosing (consequently of his freedom) is *culture*."[126] Our moral evolution, however, is not just individual, but also species-wide. Culture thus also concerns humanity's wider formation, our movement through stages of social progress, and in this second sense it refers to a given juncture in that collective advancement. In this context, Kant understands culture in roughly similar terms to the more familiar, contemporary sense: as a particular form of social life. And yet, it remains tethered to cultivation: culture does not refer to *any* instantiation of social life (in the sense that we would understand it: Latin culture, queer culture, café culture, etc.), but rather to the specific *form* of social life associated with a given stage of historical development. In this sense, it demarcates a point of historical-social achievement. But Kant also "makes a further distinction," Louden notes, "between general culture and 'a certain kind of [*gewisse Art von*] culture, which is called *civilization*'."[127] Culture captures our collective life as the sphere within which we cultivate the skills, aptitudes and dispositions required to set our own ends, and which depend on social intercourse. Civilized culture, then, refers to a particular *kind* of social life enabling the enlargement of equally particular skills and aptitudes.

Individual and collective iterations of culture are thus intimately related: given variants of social life develop – or fail to develop – our rational faculties. Our rational abilities and propensities are fostered not only by moral education, but also through the broader institutions of civilized social existence. We progress both *as* societies and *in* societies, their coevolution fixed by Kant's linking individual rational growth with particular phases of social improvement. Individual and collective cultivation are inexorably intertwined and mutually reinforcing: as we emerge from our "self-incurred immaturity," we forge social and political institutions increasingly dependent on the exercise of reason. These successive social stages are directly analogous with the stages of individual development structuring Kant's pedagogy. Early, or "savage," societies stand in need of discipline, just as do children; "culture" represents an intermediary point of social advancement, a preparatory stage honing the skills for moral action; and moralization comprises our collective end. Kant identifies these stages of social progress with distinctive achievements in our moral capacities:

We are *cultivated* to a high degree by art and science. We are *civilized* to the point of excess in all kinds of social courtesies and proprieties. But we are still a long way from the point where we could consider ourselves *morally* mature. For while the idea of morality is indeed present in culture, an application of this idea which only extends to the semblances of morality, as in love of honour and outward propriety, amounts merely to civilization.[128]

Kant's conceptualization of culture is, then, framed in relation to the long arc of humanity's moral perfection. And, importantly, our movement through these stages of moral development is enabled by specific social and political conditions: only advanced, civilized societies produce the habits, dispositions and propensities orienting us toward moral ends. "The human being," Kant concludes, "is destined by his reason to live in a society with human beings and in it to *cultivate* himself, to *civilize* himself, and to *moralize* himself by means of the arts and the sciences."[129]

Through our immersion in civilized social contexts, we internalize the "small" virtues that Kant associates with the duty "to use one's moral perfections in social intercourse."[130] The exercise of these social virtues "cultivate[s] a disposition of reciprocity – agreeableness, tolerance, mutual love and respect."[131] Civilized, European cultures "promote a virtuous disposition,"[132] one of the "*many* duties of virtue"[133] rounding out a properly moral character. In the *Anthropology*, Kant addresses the moral worth of fashion, good living, luxury and fine art; moderate alcohol consumption, dinner parties and reading poetry all comprise morally edifying activities. While hardly irreplaceable pillars of moral life, they reveal the particularity of Kant's conceptualization of a morally progressive culture, and of the social institutions, habits and proprieties forming moral consciousness. In a passage tellingly entitled "On Permissible Moral Illusion," he maintains that

the more civilized human beings are, the more they are actors. They adopt the illusion of affection, of respect for others, of modesty, and of unselfishness without deceiving anyone at all, because it is understood by everyone that nothing is meant sincerely by this. And it is also very good that this happens in the world. For when human beings play these roles, eventually the virtues, whose illusion they have merely affected for a considerable length of time, will gradually really be aroused and merge into the disposition.[134]

Duplicity and affectation clearly have no place in genuinely moral action, but they nonetheless foster a moral disposition, as do civilized social graces. Socially necessary attitudes such as "*affability, sociability, courtesy, hospitality* and *gentleness*," Kant tells us, "promote the feeling for virtue itself by striving to bring this illusion as near as possible to the truth."[135] These social virtues perform two vital functions: they cultivate moral feelings and develop the social habits sustaining progressive social and political institutions. Through our participation in social decencies and in the arts and sciences – in short, in civilized culture – we shed the crudity of our animal nature and develop the orientations, tendencies and character of self-governing agents.

It is, still further, *only* civilized cultures that fulfill this pivotal developmental role. As Allen Wood observes, "savage" societies foster an unmitigated desire for freedom that, without the pacifying effects of discipline and culture, manifests itself through natural drives rather than rational endowments.[136] Uncultivated forms of social life inhibit the moral faculty's formation by pandering to, rather than reigning in, our instinctual impulsions. This has long-term impacts: given that "by nature the human being has such a powerful propensity towards freedom ... when he has grown accustomed to it for a while, he will sacrifice everything for it. And is it precisely for this reason that discipline must be applied very early."[137] Savages' failure to apply this discipline generates social distortions that aren't easily remediable, if at all. "[I]n savage nations," Kant observes,

> though they may be in the service of Europeans for a long time, they can never grow accustomed to the European way of life. But with them this is not a noble propensity towards freedom, as *Rousseau* and others believe; rather it is a certain raw state in that the animal in this case has so to speak not yet developed the humanity inside itself.[138]

Without civilization's mollifying effects, our primordial drive for unconstrained independence inhibits the capacity for rational self-possession. As a result, the savage's "complete humanity is not yet developed, because they do not have the opportunity to unfold all of the attributes of humanity."[139] Bereft of European civilization's moral influence, savages treat women as property,[140] express themselves through symbol (rather than concepts),[141] and "show few traces of a character of mind which would be disposed to finer sentiments."[142] Their collective life thus fails to cultivate moral propensities, and even entrenches pathological habits proscribing their future development. Still worse, Kant considers certain non-European races – as shown in Chapter 3, Native Americans in particular – as entirely incapable of culture, cultivation and development.

   Not all forms of sociality, then, move us toward our moral ends. Civilized societies alone compel us to subject the propensity for freedom to reason's authority, transforming it from unfettered impulsion to an ennobled desire for rational self-government – which is to say, for true freedom. Uncivilized social forms fail to move us toward what Kant describes as an autocracy of the mind; they fail to bridge nature and freedom, indulging the former to the detriment of the latter. While Robert Louden observes that "moralization ... necessarily presupposes the preparatory steps of culture and civilization,"[143] Kant specifies that

> not just any culture is adequate for this ultimate purpose of nature. The culture of *skill* is indeed the foremost subjective condition for an aptitude to promote purposes generally ... Th[e] other condition could be called the culture of discipline [*Zucht (Disziplin)*]. It is negative and consists in the liberation of the will from the despotism of desires, a despotism that rivets us to certain natural things and renders us unable to do our own selecting.[144]

Only civilized societies foster the capacities required for moral action, and the cultures/cultivation sustaining them. They alone develop cultures of discipline, reducing the sway of inclination and skill, forming the technical and pragmatic talents required for purposive activity.[145] Here, in the third *Critique*, Kant incorporates the pillars of his moral pedagogy (discipline and skill) into an account of the social contexts harboring and strengthening them; we see the intersection of individual and collective processes shaping our moral development. And these are the very processes lacking in non-European social forms. Savage societies fail to arrest the influence of sensible impulsions, leaving their inhabitants too close to nature to actualize themselves as free agents. The discipline, self-mastery and sociality characteristic of European culture, Kant tells us,

mak[es] room for the development of our humanity, namely, by making ever more headway against the crudeness and vehemence of those inclinations that belong to us primarily as animals and that interfere most with our education for our higher vocation … [For we have] the fine art[s] and the sciences, which involve a universally communicable pleasure as well as elegance and refinement, and through these they make man, not indeed morally [*sittlich*] better for society, but still civilized [*gesittet*] for it; they make great headway against the tyranny of man's propensity to the senses, and so prepare him for a sovereignty in which reason alone is to dominate.[146]

This capacity for rational self-government – individual and collective – is also at the heart of the "perfect civil constitution":[147] the republic.

2.2.2.2 *Political Education*
At its base, political association is for Kant a shared condition of right harmonizing our equal entitlements to external freedom. Kant's political philosophy rests on the "Universal Principle of Right" ("Any action is *right* if it can coexist with everyone's freedom in accordance with a universal law, or if on its maxim the freedom of choice of each can coexist with everyone's freedom in accordance with a universal law"),[148] and on the "*one innate right*" derived from it: "*Freedom* (independence from being constrained by another's choice), insofar as it can coexist with the freedom of every other in accordance with a universal law, is the only original right belonging to every man by virtue of his humanity."[149] From a strictly formal perspective, a "rightful condition" is a system of enforceable duties preserving every person's freedom to the degree that it can be made conformable with everyone else's; or, in Arthur Ripstein's more elegant recapitulation, "[i]ndependence is the basic principle of right. It guarantees equal freedom, and so requires that no person be subject to the choice of another."[150] "[T]his normative starting point," Ripstein maintains, "leads Kant to reject anthropological and empirical factors in general, and benefits and burdens in particular"[151] as a basis for political association.

And yet, a second strain of argument runs through Kant's politics: political institutions also *form* their citizens, for better and for worse. While it's certainly true that "Kant argues in the *Rechtslehre* in the ideal style, drawing conclusions intended to be valid for 'every rational being as such',"[152] the formal account – as with his moral philosophy – neither captures nor exhausts his fuller view of political life. Despite famously proclaiming a republic's capacity to rule a nation of devils, Kant sees governments, laws and constitutions as doing more than erecting barriers between Hobbesian monads. Political institutions influence citizens by their laws, and to their laws. The republic is, Kant holds, "the only constitution that accords with right,"[153] but it also serves an important pedagogic function in our moral advancement. After briefly sketching Kant's principled defense of right, I will draw out this less familiar – and surprisingly Aristotelian – line of argument on virtue and law.

Kant's system of right incorporates domestic, international and cosmopolitan spheres. Each arm presupposes the others, and all belong to a full account of right.[154] At the domestic level, "the sole constitution that issues from the idea of the original contract, on which all rightful legislation of a people must be based – is a *republican* constitution."[155] That constitution enables a system of self-authored laws governing the relations of free individuals within a state by creating "a will that is *omnilateral* . . . [f] or only in accordance with this principle of the will is it possible for the free choice of each to accord with the freedom of all."[156] At the international level, "[t]he right of nations shall be based on a *federalism* of free states."[157] International law ensures rightful exchange between states, removing them from a global state of nature in which "a state, as a moral person, is considered as living in relation to another state in the condition of natural freedom and therefore in a condition of constant war."[158] Finally, at the cosmopolitan level, the "*right to visit*" secures individual entitlements to "present oneself for society"[159] to a foreign state, as a condition for free interchange with other human beings. Cosmopolitan right regulates the relation between individuals and states (in which they are not citizens), sustaining "the possible union of all nations with a view to certain universal laws for their possible commerce."[160] While political institutions are strictly instrumental – they have no inner moral value – we are nonetheless obligated to enter into a rightful condition to harmonize our freedoms and seek peace. "A civil constitution, though its realization is subjectively contingent," Kant argues, "is still objectively necessary, that is, necessary as a duty."[161]

Kant's account of politics, however, extends beyond the *Rechtslehre*, which only delineates the grounds of the rightful condition and of our duty to enter into it. This misses the implication of political life in humanity's moralization: progress toward our natural perfection – toward enlightenment – is at least in part a political movement. While the civil condition is a necessity of right, "civil society is [also] the means whereby the cultivation of the human being is produced and in which he gets closer and closer to his final destiny."[162] And yet, this formative capacity is not the property of all social and political orders, but only rather of particular forms of it:

Since only in society, and indeed in that society which has the greatest freedom, hence one in which there is a thoroughgoing antagonism of its members and yet the most precise determination and security of the boundaries of this freedom so that the latter can coexist with the freedom of others – since only in it can the highest aim of nature be attained, namely, the development of all the predispositions in humanity ... therefore ... a perfectly *just civil constitution* must be the supreme problem of nature for the human species, because only by means of its solution and execution can nature achieve its remaining ends for our species.[163]

The compulsion to enter into law-governed relations with others follows from our shared right of freedom, in conjunction with the "determinate limits" imposed by inhabiting the finite space of a *"globus terraqueus."*[164] This more particular end, however – the perfection of our moral capacities – entails a different and thicker set of political obligations. By turning from the determinative perspective of right to the reflective perspective of history, we better perceive our imperfect moral compulsion to pursue "that which nature has as its aim ... a universal *cosmopolitan condition*, as the womb in which all original predispositions of the human species will be developed."[165]

Beyond its principled necessity, then, a rightful condition – the *right* rightful condition – contributes to the inculcation of moral personality. Republican states, G. Felicitas Munzel contends, are for Kant "an indispensable vehicle of moral cultivation,"[166] fostering "moral judgment and the formation of moral character."[167] Republican government, of course, conforms to the idea of right. But it also fuels moral and political improvement by soliciting citizens' active engagement, encouraging the use of their rational capacities in tandem with others. While freedom of the pen and the exercise of public reason enable republican self-direction and self-correction, safeguarding against the sovereign's misjudgments, they also develop citizens' critical faculties and act as conduits for public self-scrutiny. In these latter functions, public reason generates progressive political dispositions: engaging in individual and collective self-examination, speaking out against injustice and participating in a shared and self-directed political life. This kind of joint public action advances the process of enlightenment through which a citizen comes to "extricate himself from the minority that has become almost nature to him."[168] "[F]*reedom of the pen*," Kant asserts, "kept within the limits of esteem and love for the constitution within which one lives by the subjects' liberal way of thinking, which the constitution itself instills in them ... is the sole palladium of the people's rights."[169] Republican institutions depend on this "liberal mindset" and also produce it, shaping particular kinds of citizens who learn to exercise their civic responsibilities; an enlightened public becomes disposed to improve itself and to cultivate its talents and abilities through the exercise of republican freedom. "[I]t is not the case that a good state constitution is to be expected from inner morality," Kant maintains, "on the contrary, the good moral education of a people is to be expected from a good state constitution."[170] This formative function also extends to other spheres of right. Kant persistently characterizes cosmopolitan federation, for instance, as "a pious wish" and "an unattainable idea". As such, he argues, it is best understood not as an achievable end, but as "a regulative principle: to pursue this diligently [is] the vocation of the human race."[171] Like the republican one, the cosmopolitan ideal anchors a progressive political disposition, an orientation toward the tasks of political life informed by the imperatives of humanity's moralization.

Kant's declamations against variously distorted political constitutions are similarly attuned to their deleterious formative impacts. Beyond his principled opposition to ecclesiastical and paternalistic political orders (their failure to respect present and future citizens' autonomy), Kant castigates them for shaping passive citizens. Overweening governments treat subjects "like minor children who cannot distinguish between what is truly useful or harmful to them, [and] are constrained to behave only passively";[172] they form an indolent citizenry unable to develop capacities for self-direction and autonomy. They "have made their domesticated animals dumb and carefully prevented these placid creatures from daring to take a single step without the walking cart in which they have confined them," inhibiting "further progress in enlightenment. This [is] a crime against human nature, whose original vocation lies precisely in such progress."[173] These are not just transgressions of right, but failures of orientation: despotic governments perpetuate the immaturity that Kant decries in "What is Enlightenment?" – the disinclination to enhance one's rational and moral faculties. While the "inner moral edifice is indeed affirmed as being the work of the individual," Munzel recognizes, political misgovernment "can present (and on Kant's view, thus far has done so) nearly insurmountable obstacles to this endeavor."[174]

Kant's defense of republicanism is most often interpreted in terms of: (1) its conformity with principles of right, and (2) the consequentialist argument, in "Toward Perpetual Peace" and *The Contest of Faculties*, concerning republics' aversion to go to war (the progenitor of the democratic peace theory).[175] Less frequently noted is this third, developmental argument: republics form good, morally progressive citizens. "[T]he final destiny of humanity will then be reached," Kant argues, "if we have a perfect civil constitution, i.e., if we find ourselves in the highest degree of cultivation, civilization, and moralization."[176] In a remarkable passage connecting his rights-based, pedagogical and teleological arguments, he asks:

On what, then, rests the achievement of the ultimate vocation of human nature? The general foundation is the civil constitution; the union of human beings into a whole, which serves to achieve the cultivation of all talents, and also for one person's giving the other the freedom for that cultivation – through this it happens that the predisposition to talents is developed; through this the human being is elevated out of his animality.[177]

Under republican constitutions, "the development of the moral predisposition to immediate respect for right is actually greatly facilitated ... thereby a great step is taken *toward* morality (though it is not yet a moral step)."[178] "[O]nly in a state overseen by a politically just constitution," Jennifer Mensch concludes, "would the crooked wood of humanity be finally made straight."[179]

2.3 FROM THE GOOD WILL TO THE GOOD HUMAN BEING

Kant's liberalism – his fuller vision of moral and political life, of human nature and of our movement toward our natural ends – is, then, closely attuned to the developmental and affective facets of human personhood. By widening beyond the critical view, Kant's extensive, decades-spanning attention to the subjective side of ethical life comes into clearer focus. In this final section, I turn to the object of the formative processes traced out above: the moral character encapsulated not in the *Groundwork*'s good will, but rather, in the *Religion*'s good human being. The good human being, I argue, is the center of Kant's conceptualization of humanity's moral vocation.

2.3.1 Virtue and Moral Character

"*Morality*," Kant tells us, "is a matter of character"[180] – and yet, what that character consists of requires some elaboration. Kant distinguishes two sense of character in the *Anthropology*:

on the one hand, it is said that a certain human being has *this* or that (physical) character; on the other hand that he simply has *a* character (a moral character), which can only be one, or nothing at all. The first is the distinguishing mark of the human being as a sensible or natural being; the second is the distinguishing mark of the human being as a rational being endowed with freedom.[181]

Strictly speaking, physical (or empirical) character has no bearing on our status as free, moral agents, as "[p]hysiological knowledge of the human being concerns the investigation of what *nature* makes of the human being."[182] This falls outside anthropology's purview, which as a pragmatic endeavor comprises "the investigation of what *he* as a free-acting being makes of himself, or can and should make of himself."[183]

Anthropology, then, addresses moral character. As Manfred Kuehn observes, moral character is intimately related to virtue, "the moral strength of a *human being's* will in fulfilling his *duty*."[184] Kuehn in fact treats character as the anthropological analogue of Kant's conception of virtue in the *Metaphysics of Morals*.[185] It is worth considering their relationship in some detail.

Virtue describes the moral actor's singular capacity to act from duty in spite of the more immediate compulsion of inclinations.[186] As such, it is a defining characteristic of human beings: as holy beings can't help but conform to the moral law and animals are beholden to their natural impulses, we alone are susceptible to both forms of impulsion, and we alone can choose between them.

Virtue is thus the uniquely human capacity to ensure "the will's conformity with every duty, based on a firm disposition."[187]

Character, in the most basic sense (as distinguished from moral character), is a capacity for principled action. It describes the proclivity to persistently act from principled rather than sensible grounds. As Kant accounts for it in the *Critique of Practical Reason*, character inheres in "a consistent practical cast of mind in accordance with unchangeable maxims."[188] At this level of generality, character can be rightly or wrongly oriented because "even before a good or evil character is formed, a character must in fact be formed ... [we] must first be accustomed to act from principles."[189] Good or moral character, then, refers to the unfailing predilection to act from the *right* principles, fixed by the moral law. As Kant understands it, "to have a character signifies that property of the will by which the subject binds himself to definite practical principles that he has prescribed to himself irrevocably by his own reason."[190]

Virtue is thus "the moral and ideal concept; 'character' refers to the empirical reality."[191] Character is a condition for acting virtuously, and so, for moral agency. If character concerns the propensity to act from principles, rather than from volatile inclinations, then virtue – exercising the strength of will to act from moral principles – requires it.

The relationship between virtue and character draws out the vital importance of moral constancy and disposition: moral acts do not, in and of themselves, make moral actors. A properly moral character lies in the *consistent* predisposition to fulfill our moral obligations, in spite of sensible inclinations and as a matter of principle. A person who regularly flouts their moral duties but occasionally refrains from doing so clearly lacks a moral character, as does one whose actions unswervingly conform to the moral law, but from phenomenal motivations.[192] To lack a moral character is to fail to grasp the necessity of principled action as a condition of moral personhood; without it, we might occasionally act on moral grounds, but otherwise fail to do so. Moral character turns on the constancy and fidelity of our intentions, on the internalization and persistent prioritization of moral motivations, rooted in a firm commitment to principled action. It "entails possession of fixed principles and a secure basis, such that we shall never live otherwise than virtuously."[193] Kant's pedagogy aims precisely at the acquisition and strengthening of these "fixed principles," recognizing that "[t]he first effort in moral education is the grounding of character."[194] And it *is* an effort: if virtue requires acting on moral principles opposed to our natural incentive structure, we are bound to develop the propensity to act from principles, to sensitize ourselves to the right ones, and to strengthen our disposition to do so over the course of a lifetime. While "[c]*haracter constitutes inner worth*," then, it is not simply fixed within us. It is, rather, the object of constant striving and improvement. "*Good character does not come from nature*," Kant recognizes, "*but must be acquired. To be sure, one has the predisposition for it, but these seeds of nature must be cultivated through understanding and reason, so that principles emerge. The acquisition of good character in the human being occurs through education."*[195]

Moral pedagogy, civilized culture, republican institutions: these are the mechanisms stimulating, developing and shoring up moral character, along with the broad-ranging enculturation that Kant elaborates in the *Tugendlehre*'s treatment of "moral endowments." These are naturally occurring tendencies that we cannot be compelled to acquire but are nonetheless bound to ameliorate, and include injunctions to seek our own perfection and others' happiness, to cultivate the moral feeling, to foster one's conscience, to love and respect others (entailing corollary duties of beneficence, gratitude and sympathy), and to develop our natural abilities. They also prohibit defiling ourselves by lust, stupefying ourselves with food and drink, being avaricious, making ourselves servile, and being arrogant, defamatory or inclined to ridicule others.[196] This panoply of necessarily imperfect duties fills out Kant's view of moral character: they show us what virtuous human beings ought to do and, generally, be like. They "lie at the basis of morality, as *subjective* conditions of receptiveness to the concept of duty,"[197] upholding our moral sensitivity and moral resolve. In short, they build up a moral character that, Kant contends, "cannot become vicious, and even if he lapses into a few vices, [he] always returns to the path of virtue, because his principles have already become firmly rooted in him."[198]

This moral character is the defining feature of the good human being. Much of the scholarship on Kant's practical philosophy centers on the *Groundwork*'s good will, the figuration of the only unqualified good imaginable. And yet, the good will isn't a human will; it is an idealization that models the good of free, rational agents. To understand Kant's fuller view of the *human* good, we turn from the good will to the good human being.

2.3.2 Moral Revolution, Moral Disposition: The Good Human Being

Kant's account of the good human being appears in *Religion within the Boundaries of Mere Reason*. Broadly speaking, *Religion* explores the relationship between the various (provisional) "historical faiths" adopted by an imperfect humanity and "the pure faith of religion [that] will rule over all"[199] – the religion of pure reason – toward which we progress. It thus falls within Kant's wide-ranging treatments of the historical-teleological conditions advancing our moral perfection. The *Groundwork*'s good will, "the will of a rational being, in which ... the highest and unconditional good alone can be found"[200] is, of course, the moral beacon that we are bound to approximate. In the *Religion*, however, Kant considers "[h]ow it is possible that a naturally evil human being should make himself into a good human being."[201] Radical evil refers to our propensity to prioritize sensible impulses over intelligible ones in contexts in which we ought to do the opposite ("evil"), despite an awareness of our moral duty ("radical evil"). It describes the misalignment of incentives endemic in our constitution: human beings, as we have seen, are naturally disposed to act on their sensible impulses, even in the face of moral obligations of which they're conscious.[202] Radical evil thus constitutes a problem to which the good will is unresponsive. While the good will delineates the ends that we ought to pursue as free, rational beings, it does not attend to how creatures of our kind come to recognize or choose them at all.

As we have also seen, moral education weakens these phenomenal inclinations and strengthens our receptivity to duty, laying the foundation for moral character. And yet, being a good human being, endowed with that moral character, does not simply consist in resisting the imperatives of a misaligned will. The good human being, Kant maintains, emerges from an internal revolution that fundamentally reorients the will's motivational structure. Without this deep-seated turn in the maxims governing our incentives, we remain incapable of bridging the chasm between moral and merely legal action:

so long as the foundation of the maxims of the human being remains impure, [moral goodness] cannot be effected through gradual *reform* but must rather be effected through a *revolution* in the disposition of the human being ... And so a "new man" can come about only through a kind of rebirth, as it were a new creation ... and a change of heart.[203]

By changing the grounds on which we base our actions, and not just our actions themselves, we undergo the motivational transformation redirecting us from evil to moral goodness. This "revolution" alters the maxims governing the will, turning us away from a predilection to act on sensible incentives and toward the ends set by the good will. This moment of moral epiphany – as Kant puts it, "the grounding of character" – "is like a kind of rebirth ... which makes the resolution and the moment when this transformation took place unforgettable to him, like the beginning of a new epoch."[204] The good human being is born of this tectonic shift, this subjective reorientation from a condition of unprincipled volatility to moral virtue.

And yet, this internal revolution is only the initial point in the good human being's metamorphosis. While the transition to moral goodness *begins* from this moment of revelation, it *consists* in the lifelong commitments to principled action, rational self-determination and moral improvement following from it. The moral awakening realigning the will's incentive structure is no mere temporary change, but rather instills an ongoing orientation toward, and dedication to, the principled pursuit of moral action. For true moral conversion, Kant argues, "a revolution is necessary in the mode of thought"; but it also demands

a gradual reformation in the mode of sense (which places obstacles in the way of the former), and [both] must therefore be possible also to the human being. That is: If by a single and unalterable decision a human being reverses the supreme ground of his maxims by which he was an evil human being (and thereby puts on a "new man"), he is to this extent, by principle and attitude of mind, a subject receptive to the good; *but he is a good human being only in incessant laboring and becoming*; i.e. he can hope – in view of the purity of the principle which he has adopted as the supreme maxim of his power of choice, and in view of the stability of this principle – to find himself upon the good (though narrow) path of constant *progress* from bad to better … the change is to be regarded only as an ever-continuing striving for the better.[205]

The good human being's transition from radical evil to moral rectitude thus incorporates two distinctive, if related, dimensions: a moral revolution, and the enduring dedication to moral amelioration following from it.

This "ever-continuing striving for the better" captures the specifically human task of reaching for, but never reaching, the good will and moral virtue. It illuminates the moral imperative not to realize virtue, but to develop the capacities enabling us to approach it. Despite our constitutive inability to achieve absolute virtue, we are nonetheless bound to treat it as an ideal "to which one must continually approximate."[206] As imperfect and phenomenal beings, then, our moral vocation is not to be perfectly virtuous, but rather to continuously strive for it. "Virtue," Kant maintains, "is always *in progress* and yet always starts *from the beginning*. – It is always in progress because, considered *objectively*, it is an ideal and unattainable, while yet constant approximation to it is a duty."[207] As a result, Paul Guyer observes, "while it makes no sense to say that *to be virtuous* is a duty, it makes sense to say that to *strive to make progress towards becoming virtuous* is a duty … the general obligation to be virtuous can be perfectly well understood as a duty to strengthen our natural disposition to be moral."[208] All human beings share an inborn, intuitive sense of the moral good, Kant tells us in "Theory and Practice," however distant it might be from the divine will of sages and angels. Our moral commission is ultimately to reduce this space by cultivating the propensity to seek virtue and the capacities enabling us to do so.

While Kant's attention to this subjective, developmental register of moral agency is most pronounced in the post-critical period, it stretches back to (at least) the second *Critique*'s account of the "moral disposition." As with the moral feeling, the moral disposition is not amenable to compulsion; nothing can "command us to *have* this disposition in dutiful actions but only to *strive* for it."[209] Kant here recognizes what he would elaborate in later years: the moral revolution does not turn us, once and for all, from self-love to moral goodness. We only *become* moral agents over time, by shoring up the moral disposition. For beings of our kind, constitutionally bound to our sensible inclinations, moral agency can only ever be a process, and not an end. Moral action, autonomy and freedom are not only abstractions fixed by the dictates of a stringent Archimedean moral law, but also goals that we need to work toward. Our moral objective, then, is to foster the moral disposition to do that work.

While the good will models the moral ideal incumbent on all rational beings, the good human being draws out a fuller, more robust conception of moral agency. The figuration of the good human being shows that while practical freedom is rooted in intelligible character – the capacity to initiate action and set unconditioned ends – *human* freedom, our kind of freedom, remains inexorably subject to the sway of phenomenality.[210] Practical reason enjoins us to pursue the ideal of holiness, but the will's complete conformity with the moral law is "a perfection of which no rational being of the sensible world is capable". Our good, then, "can only be found in an *endless progress* toward that complete conformity ... it is necessary to assume such a practical progress as the real object of our will."[211] Our moral task is not to achieve a perfection that Kant clearly sets beyond us, but rather to cultivate the inclination, disposition and capacities to always reach for it. This is the moral agency of which we are capable; it is our moral calling. The good human being's "incessant labouring and becoming," Kant holds, is "the moral vocation of our nature."[212] It is to foster the disposition orienting us toward our moral ends, and the character cementing our lifelong commitment to their pursuit.

2.4   A FULLER MORAL AGENCY

This chapter has aimed to develop a fuller, more comprehensive view of Kant's liberalism by drawing out his expansive, if under-examined, attention to the subjective dimensions of moral and political life. Shifting the focus from Kant's critical philosophy to his teleological-developmental writings on anthropology, education, politics and history sheds light on several important features of his considered views.

First, against the common perception of his excessive formalism, we better recognize Kant's sustained engagement with the affective, habituated and enculturated features of human life. Kant's complete ethics – beyond the *Critiques, Groundwork* and *Metaphysics of Morals* alone – is a moral system that lives and breathes; it has brains, heart, and even guts. Seen in its fullness, it is an ethics not for purely rational actors, but for phenomenal, limited moral creatures whose reasoning faculties – the heart of dignity and freedom – require cultivation. Properly understood, the transcendental-teleological divide is less reflective of any conceptual confusion (or outright contradiction) than of the boundaries delimiting distinctive forms and spheres of inquiry. Principles of appraisal and volition ought never to be confused, Kant recognizes, but neither should consideration for one supplant consideration for the other.

Second, and relatedly, a practical system of ethics must incorporate both sides of our moral agency; "the subjective conditions in human nature," Kant maintains, "cannot be dispensed with."[213] While isolating Kant's empirical ethics from his critical philosophy might well better preserve the latter's systematicity, it is won at the cost of misrepresentation. Kant's wide-ranging and long-lasting attention to the phenomenality of moral agency attests to the incompleteness of a strictly formal ethics. The richer, developmental account of moral personhood encapsulated in the good human being speaks to our moral vocation. It speaks to the important question of how we might bridge the gap between who we are and who we ought to be – or, how we come to realize those capacities in which our dignity inheres. These conditions of realization are neither negligible for, not incidental to, Kant's complete reckoning of our moral and political nature. They belong to it.

Finally, as we've begun to see, these conditions of realization are rather particular, and in certain ways, rather exacting. Moral personality – the orientation and character of moral actors – is no small achievement, and neither does it develop under all circumstances. We need a careful pedagogy to balance freedom and restraint, to develop a moral character and to avoid stunting the moral growth of the young. We need civilized societies to curb our barbaric predilections and inculcate moral dispositions. We need republican institutions to foster the public-mindedness and impulsion for freedom sustaining enlightenment.

How, then, should we make sense of the moral and political standing of those vast tracts of humanity that are *not* subject to this kind of acculturation? If, as Kant suggests, our moral vocation lies in an "ever-continuing striving for the better," how might we regard people(s) who, for either natural or circumstantial reasons, are incapable of moral development? Despite our shared, inalienable dignity, Kant's account of moral character certainly thickens the view of moral agency, and so appears to circumscribe the kinds of people capable of moral realization. How, ultimately, are we to understand the moral status of human beings unable to move toward the realization of their natural ends or participate in the moral life of which human beings are capable? This is the question we turn to consider in Chapter 3.

NOTES

1. Immanuel Kant, "On the Common Saying: That May Be Correct in Theory, but It Is of No Use in Practice," in *Practical Philosophy*, ed. and trans. Mary J. Gregor (New York: Cambridge University Press, 1996), 8:291. Given hereafter as TP.

2. Kant, MS, 6:237. Kant describes this "innate right" of all persons as "prior to any rightful deed" (Kant, TP, 8:293), inhering in human beings as rational – and hence, moral – agents. For careful treatments of the innate right of humanity's foundational status in Kant's political philosophy, see Ripstein, *Force and Freedom*, ch. 2, and Leslie A. Mulholland, *Kant's System of Rights* (New York: Columbia University Press, 1990), ch. 7.

3. Kant, MS, 8:296.

4. Immanuel Kant, *Groundwork of the Metaphysics of Morals*. In *Practical Philosophy*, ed. and trans. Mary J. Gregor (New York: Cambridge University Press, 1996), 4:435. Given hereafter as G.

5. While Kant sharply distinguishes political right and moral obligation – the objects, respectively, of the Doctrine of Right (*Rechtslehre*) and Doctrine of Virtue (*Tugendlehre*) – the line between them, Ronald Beiner and Susan Mendus

observe, is rather tenuous. See Ronald Beiner, "Paradoxes in Kant's Account of Citizenship," in *Responsibility in Context: Perspectives*, ed. Gorana Ognjenovic (Dordrecht: Springer, 2010); and Susan Mendus, "Kant: 'an Honest but Narrow-Minded Bourgeois'?" in *Essays on Kant's Political Philosophy*, ed. Howard Williams (Cardiff: University of Wales Press, 1992). For a strong defense of Kant's consistency in demarcating right and ethics, see Ripstein, *Force and Freedom*.

6. Immanuel Kant, "Of the Different Races of Human Beings," (given hereafter as RM), "Determination of the Concept of a Human Race" (BM hereafter), and "On the Use of Teleological Principles in Philosophy" ("Teleological Principles" hereafter). All three essays appear in *Anthropology, History, and Education*, eds. Günter Zöller and Robert B. Louden (Cambridge: Cambridge University Press, 2007). Kant's thoughts on race are further elaborated in his lectures on physical geography and anthropology, *Observations on the Feeling of the Beautiful and Sublime*, and *Anthropology from a Pragmatic Point of View*, all of which are treated in detail in Chapter 3. For the authoritative study of Kant's role in the development of eighteenth-century natural sciences and anthropology, see Zammito (2002).

7. Kant, *Anthropology*, 7:209.

8. Ibid., 7:305. See Susan Moller Okin, "Women and the Making of the Sentimental Family," *Philosophy & Public Affairs* 11, no. 1 (1982): 65–88; Jean Bethke Elshtain, *Meditations on Modern Political Thought: Masculine/Feminine Themes from Luther to Arendt* (New York: Praeger, 1986); Jean P. Rumsey, "The Development of Character in Kantian Moral Theory," *Journal of the History of Philosophy* 27, no. 2 (1989): 247–265.

9. For an insightful analysis of such bracketing techniques, see Pauline Kleingeld, "The Problematic Status of Gender-Neutral Language in the History of Philosophy: The Case of Kant," *The Philosophical Forum* 29 (1993): 134–150.

10. Zammito exposes the continuities between Kant's pre-critical works and interests – particularly, in the mid-to-late eighteenth-century German *Popularphilosophie* out of which anthropology emerged – and his critical philosophy. "[T]he future of Kant studies," he suggests, "lies with the 'informal' impulse … the reenvisioning of the entire Kantian system as precisely an anthropology" (Zammito, *Birth of Anthropology*, 349).

11. Ripstein, *Force and Freedom*; Elisabeth Ellis, *Kant's Politics: Provisional Theory for an Uncertain World* (New Haven: Yale University Press, 2005).

12. As Karl Ameriks puts it, "[f]or an orthodox Kantian, any focus on 'development' can thus appear to be either a mere secondary issue concerning contingent 'subjective,' 'psychological' or pedagogical considerations, or, even worse, a subversion of the very idea of pure philosophy" (Karl Ameriks, "The Purposive Development of Human Capacities," in *Kant's 'Idea for a Universal History with a Cosmopolitan Aim': A Critical Guide*, eds. Amélie Oksenberg Rorty and James Schmidt (Cambridge: Cambridge University Press, 2009), 47). While Kant's writings on anthropology and history have long faced charges of inconsistency with his critical philosophy, Zammito credits the "sharply antihistorical, systemic direction" (Zamitto, *Birth of Anthropology*, 258) of Peter Strawson's interpretation with the neglect of Kant's non-critical works in Anglo-American philosophy.

13. See, for instance, Emmanuel Chukwudi Eze, "The Color of Reason: The Idea of 'Race' in Kant's Anthropology," in *Anthropology and the German Enlightenment: Perspectives on Humanity*, ed. Katherine M. Faull (Cranbury: Bucknell University Press, 1995); C. W. Mills, "Kant's *Untermenschen*," in *Race and Racism in Modern Philosophy*, ed., Andrew Valls (Ithaca: Cornell University Press, 2005); Robert Bernasconi, "Kant as an Unfamiliar Source of Racism," in *Philosophers on Race: Critical Essays*, eds. Julie K. Ward and Tommy Lee Lott (Malden: Blackwell Publishers, 2002); Robert Bernasconi, "Who Invented the Concept of Race," in *Race* (Malden: Blackwell Publishers, 2001), 11–36; Pauline Kleingeld, "Kant's Second Thoughts"; and Jean P. Rumsey, "The Development of Character." I treat this literature in detail in Chapter 3.

14. While orthodox Kantians will undoubtedly resist my associating Kant's ethics and politics, given "Kant's adamantine boundary between right and ethics" (Ernest J. Weinrib, "Poverty and Property in Kant's System of Rights," *Notre Dame Law Review* 78, no. 3 (2003): 799), I argue that that boundary is in fact rather more fluid. I am, also, not alone in drawing out the connections between Kant's moral and political thought. G. Felicitas Munzel, for instance, argues that "Kant deems the republican constitution an indispensable vehicle of moral cultivation" (Munzel, *Moral Character*, 17), and Patrick Riley suggests that "politics serves primarily to make morality, or at least moral ends, more nearly possible" (Patrick Riley, *Kant's Political Philosophy* (Totowa: Rowman & Littlefield, 1983), 9). Allen D. Rosen locates the origins of Kant's theory of justice "in other parts of Kant's moral philosophy" (Allen Rosen, *Kant's Theory of Justice* (Ithaca: Cornell University Press, 1996), 3), and for Howard Williams, "Kant's political philosophy grows out of his moral theory" (Howard Williams, *Kant's Political Philosophy* (New York: St. Martin's Press, 1983), 39). On the broader question of whether Kant's moral theory underlies the *Rechtslehre*, see Paul Guyer, "Kant's Deductions of the Principles of Right," in *Kant's Metaphysics of Morals: Interpretative Essays*, ed. Mark Timmons (Oxford: Oxford University Press, 2002), 23–64; Thomas W. Pogge, "Is Kant's *Rechtslehre* a 'Comprehensive Liberalism'?" in ed. Mark Timmons (Oxford: Oxford University Press, 2002), 133–158; and Robert B. Pippin, "Mine and Thine? The Kantian State," in *The Cambridge Companion to Kant and Modern Philosophy*, ed. Paul Guyer (Cambridge: Cambridge University Press, 2006), 416–446. Whether one understands Kant's doctrine of right as underwritten by his moral theory or not, Paul Formosa observes, "in either case, morals and politics are not in conflict" (Paul Formosa, "All Politics Must Bend Its Knee before Right," *Social Theory and Practice* 34 (2008): 160).

15. While this remains a minority position, recent years have witnessed a rising interest in Kant's "impure ethics." See Louden, *Impure Ethics*; Wood, *Ethical Thought*; Frierson, *Freedom and Anthropology*; Munzel, *Moral Character*; Kain and Jacobs, *Essays on Kant's Anthropology*; Barbara Herman, *The Practice of Moral Judgment* (Cambridge: Harvard University Press, 1993); Wilson, *Kant's Pragmatic Anthropology*; Susan Meld Shell, "Kant's 'True Economy of Human Nature'," in *Essays on Kant's Anthropology*, eds. Patrick Kain and Brian Jacobs (Cambridge: Cambridge University Press, 2003), 194–229; Alix Cohen, ed. *Kant's Lectures on Anthropology: A Critical Guide* (Cambridge: Cambridge University Press, 2014); and Rorty and Schmidt, *Critical Guide*.

16. Kant, MS, 6:217.
17. This is a controversial claim open to varying interpretations, which I will clarify in this chapter and the next. For a few particularly compelling readings of the developmental features of Kant's moral philosophy, see Paul Guyer, "The Obligation to Be Virtuous: Kant's Conception of the *Tugendverpflichtung*," *Social Philosophy & Policy* 27, no. 2 (2010): 206–232; Paul Guyer, *Kant's System of Nature and Freedom: Selected Essays* (Oxford: Oxford University Press, 2005); and Anne Margaret Baxley, "Autocracy and Autonomy," *Kant-Studien* 94 (2003): 1–23.
18. Munzel's *Moral Character* is the authoritative English-language treatment of Kant's conceptualization of moral character. While my reading is deeply indebted to it, we diverge in two respects. First, Munzel argues that "Kant's mature conception of moral character is essentially a critical concept" (8), a position that she shares with Werner Stark and that, by her own admission, is a "strong stance" (8, n. 14). Where Munzel treats character as part of Kant's critical philosophy, I argue that it belongs to what Robert Louden describes as "the second part of morals" – the unsystematizable facets of human moral agency that fall outside of critical philosophy, but remain importantly connected to it. Second, Munzel does not address the implications of Kant's "thicker" conception of moral character – in particular, how it limits the universalism of his ethics. This is the subject of Chapter 3.
19. Kant, MS, 6:469.
20. Kant, VA, 27:244.
21. Wood, *Ethical Thought*, 4.
22. Immanuel Kant, *Religion within the Boundaries of Mere Reason and Other Writings*, eds. Allen W. Wood and George Di Giovanni (Cambridge: Cambridge University Press, 1998), 6:48. Given hereafter as R.
23. See, for example, Frierson, *Freedom and Anthropology*; Kain and Jacobs, *Essays on Kant's Anthropology*; Louden, *Impure Ethics*; Munzel, *Moral Character*; Wilson, *Kant's Pragmatic Anthropology*; and Wood, *Ethical Thought*.
    Kant's conceptualization of anthropology – what he took as its precise object and purview, and how he understood its relationship to other fields of study and to his practical and critical philosophies – is subject to considerable interpretive variation, for a few reasons. First, as Zammito shows, Kant was, along with Herder, a pioneer in the development of anthropology as a discipline. Its novelty, in conjunction with Kant's treatments spanning his pre-critical, critical and post-critical periods, lends itself to a certain inconsistency. Kuehn traces shifts in Kant's views from the 1770s, when he saw anthropology as central to moral philosophy, through the 1780s, when the critical turn steered him away from the empirical circumstances studied by anthropology, before finally settling in the 1790s on the view that anthropology addressed the "sociological and historical developments which are relevant to morality" (xxiii). Allen Wood raises additional complications stemming from Kant's view of anthropology as *pragmatic*, distinguishing four distinctive senses of the term: (1) as pertaining to what human beings make of themselves as free beings; (2) as a form of practically oriented knowledge, in contrast to purely "scholastic," or speculative, knowledge (Zammito traces this diremption to the important break between Wolffian *Schulphilosophie* and the rise of *Popularphilosophie* in mid–late eighteenth

century German philosophy); (3) as knowledge required for the pursuit of moral ends (knowledge of "helps and hindrances" to moral action); and (4) as prudential knowledge enabling human happiness. Finally, as Zammito and Brian Jacobs note, Kant's primary engagement with anthropology came in the context of the popular lectures that he offered at the University of Königsberg for close to three decades, which were explicitly intended to disseminate pragmatic, and not speculative, knowledge. This isn't to suggest that anthropology is strictly prudential, rather than moral; as Allen Wood points out, the 1798 *Anthropology*'s preoccupation with humanity's moral destiny clearly demonstrates anthropology's moral orientation (Wood, "Introduction," 10).

Despite these complications, it is clear that as an "investigation of what *he* as a free-acting being makes of himself, or can and should make of himself" (Kant, *Anthropology*, 7:119), Kant regarded anthropology as integral for understanding human moral nature. I follow Reinhardt Brandt in treating Kant's anthropology as primarily concerned with "the vocation of humanity" – that is, with our ultimate moralization. For all of these arguments, see Zammito, *Birth of Anthropology*; Manfred Kuehn, "Introduction," in Immanuel Kant, *Anthropology from a Pragmatic Point of View* (Cambridge: Cambridge University Press, 2006), vii–xxix; Allen W. Wood, "Kant and the Problem of Human Nature," in *Essays on Kant's Anthropology*, eds. Brian Jacobs and Patrick Kain (Cambridge: Cambridge University Press, 2003), 38–59; and Reinhardt Brandt, "The Vocation of the Human Being," in *Essays on Kant's Anthropology*, eds. Brian Jacobs and Patrick Kain (Cambridge: Cambridge University Press, 2003), 85–104.

24. Wood, "Introduction," 1–10; Kuehn, "Introduction," vii–xxix; and Zammito, *Birth of Anthropology*.
25. Zammito, *Birth of Anthropology*, 294.
26. Vincent M. Cooke traces the increasing emphasis of teleological argument in Kant's late-critical and post-critical writings, and Manfred Kuehn notes Kant's rising interest in empirical matters – specifically, relating to religious and political controversies in the early 1790s – over the same period. See Vincent M. Cooke, "Kant, Teleology, and Sexual Ethics," *International Philosophical Quarterly* 31, no. 1 (1991): 3–13; and Manfred Kuehn, *Kant: A Biography* (Cambridge: Cambridge University Press, 2001), 329–385.
27. Wood, *Ethical Thought*, 196.
28. Robert Louden, "The Second Part of Morals," in *Essays on Kant's Anthropology*, eds. Patrick Kain and Brian Jacobs (Cambridge: Cambridge University Press), 60–84.
29. Kant, MS, 6:217.
30. Frierson, *Freedom and Anthropology*, 1; Louden, *Impure Ethics*, 56.
31. Kant, MS, 6:217.
32. For an overview of commentators' efforts toward this reconciliation, see Frierson, *Freedom and Anthropology*, 68–94, and Inder S. Marwah, "*Elateres Motiva*: From the Good Will to the Good Human Being," *Kantian Review* 18, no. 3 (2013): 413–437.
33. This is not a rigid or categorical division, but rather distinguishes between the central objects of Kant's critical and anthropological writings, described by Kant himself as, respectively, principles of moral appraisal and principles of moral

volition. Neither strictly excludes or disregards matters of concern to the other as both contribute to Kant's fuller conception of moral agency. The point is elaborated in notes 51 and 52.

34. Henry Allison, *Kant's Theory of Freedom* (Cambridge: Cambridge University Press, 1990), 5.

35. Immanuel Kant, *Critique of Pure Reason* (London: Macmillan and Co., 1953), A541/B569. Given hereafter as KrV.

36. Immanuel Kant, *Critique of Practical Reason*, in *Practical Philosophy*, ed. and trans. Mary J. Gregor (New York: Cambridge University Press), 5:43. Given hereafter as KpV.

37. Kant's accounts of freedom are riddled with interpretive difficulties. For a few helpful attempts to untangle them, see Allison, *Theory of Freedom*; Lewis White Beck, "Five Concepts of Freedom in Kant," in *Philosophical Analysis and Reconstruction: A Festrschrift to Stephan Körner*, ed. Jan J. T. Srzednicki (Dordrecht: Martinus Nijhoff, 1987); Wood, *Ethical Thought*; Paul Guyer, *Kant on Freedom, Law, and Happiness* (Cambridge: Cambridge University Press, 2000); and Paul Guyer, *Kant's System of Nature and Freedom: Selected Essays* (Oxford: Oxford University Press, 2005). I here address Kant's two most common (and most widely debated) conceptualizations of freedom, but it is by no means clear that they stand alone (Beck, for example, distinguishes five "concepts" of Kantian freedom).

38. "By freedom . . . I understand the power of beginning a state *spontaneously*. Such causality will not, therefore, itself stand under another cause determining it in time, as required by the law of nature. Freedom, in this sense, is a pure transcendental idea" (Kant, KrV, A533/B561).

39. Guyer, *Nature and Freedom,* 118.

40. While Guyer and Wood diverge from Allison's interpretation of Kant's transcendental idealism, Allison understands practical freedom in much the same way as Guyer does here, "defined negatively in terms of independence of pathological necessitation (although not affection) and positively in terms of a capacity to act on the basis of reason" (Allison, *Theory of Freedom*, 55).

41. Ibid., 97. This is borne out by KrV, A533/B561, where Kant maintains that "the practical concept of freedom is based on this *transcendental* idea."

42. Wood, *Ethical Thought*, 172.

43. Guyer, *Nature and Freedom*, 121–122. While Guyer's interpretation of the relationship between transcendental and practical freedom is compelling, Allison notes deep inconsistencies in Kant's own accounts. The central difficulty lies in determining whether or not practical freedom depends on transcendental freedom, a question on which Kant contradicts himself and so fails to provide any clear resolution. See Allison, *Theory of Freedom,* 54–70, Wood, *Ethical Thought*, 171–178, and Guyer, *Nature and Freedom*, 115–126. For the purposes of this chapter, I set aside this difficult question to focus on the relationship between Kant's practical and anthropological arguments.

44. Allison, *Theory of Freedom*, 41.

45. Pauline Kleingeld similarly distinguishes between "the *creation* and the *discovery* of a moral principle" (68), but focuses on the distinction as it pertains specifically to Kant's philosophy of history. See Pauline Kleingeld, "Kant, History, and the Idea of Moral Development," *History of Philosophy Quarterly* 16, no. 1 (1999):

59–80, and Kleingeld, "Debunking Confabulation: Emotions and the Significance of Empirical Psychology for Kantian Ethics," in *Kant on Emotion and Value*, ed. A. Cohen (Basingstoke: Palgrave Macmillan, 2014), 146–165.

46. Philip Stratton-Lake similarly distinguishes between the *motive* and *maxim* of duty: while the former describes the immediate source of impulsion behind any given action, the latter provides the principles of motivation that agents adopt in structuring their incentives more generally. See Philip Stratton-Lake, "Moral Motivation in Kant," in *A Companion to Kant*, ed. Graham Bird (Malden: Blackwell Publishing, 2006), 322–334.

47. Christine Korsgaard, "Natural Motives and the Motive of Duty: Hume and Kant on Our Duties to Others," *Contemporary Readings in Law and Social Justice* 1, no. 2 (2009): 19.

48. Ibid., 20.

49. Ibid., 40.

50. Both Paul Guyer and Philip Stratton-Lake note that the ability to choose our motivations, rather than simply being subject to them, is central to Kant's account of ethical freedom. While we are able to conform to principles for any number of reasons (which Stratton-Lake describes as moral rightness), moral action depends on choosing principles of virtue from the right grounds, namely, out of respect for the moral law (which constitutes moral goodness). See Guyer, "The Obligation to be Virtuous" and Stratton-Lake, "Moral Motivation," 323.

51. Kant devotes considerable attention to moral action's incentive structure in the second *Critique* (5:71–5:89), which may appear to undermine the broad division of labour drawn out here between, as Kant puts it, principles of moral appraisal and moral volition. And yet, the second *Critique*'s account of moral motivation remains largely formal: it describes the *form* to which a morally upright incentive structure must adhere, regardless of time and place. As such, it remains closely bound to Kant's analytical account of what moral action *is*: no action is moral unless it is adopted from the right motivations. The second *Critique*'s account of moral motivation thus remains largely, though not strictly, within the sphere of "principles of appraisal": it delimits the incentives that we must adopt in order to act morally. It tells us little, however, about how imperfect human beings come to internalize those principles of moral action, or the authority of the moral law more generally. So while the second *Critique* addresses the formal attributes of moral volition (at 5:72–5:89), it largely disregards the "moral disposition" to which Kant briefly alludes at 5:83–5:85, whose cultivation is elaborated in his anthropological works. For a few helpful examinations of incentive and the good will, see Patrick Frierson, "Kant's Empirical Account of Human Action," *Philosophers' Imprint* 5, no. 7 (2005): 1–34; Andrews Reath, *Agency and Autonomy in Kant's Moral Theory: Selected Essays* (New York: Oxford University Press, 2006); and Korsgaard "Natural Motives."

52. This is, again, only roughly the case; Kant's critical writings do occasionally touch on empirical concerns. The second *Critique*'s discussions of moral education (5:152–5:163) and moral feeling (5:74–5:81), for example, address the subjective, developmental side of moral agency. Similarly, Kant's anthropological works consistently refer back to his formal accounts of right and ethics. There is, then, interchange between Kant's transcendental and anthropological perspectives, as well there should be. And yet, the rough division holds: Kant's critical and practical

works largely attend to the grounds of freedom and moral principles, while anthropology treats their conditions of realization. Anne Margaret Baxley's distinction between autonomy and autocracy, as distinctive properties of the free will, is helpful in clarifying these two dimensions of moral personhood. "Autonomy", Baxley explains, "designates the property of the will to give particular sorts of laws to itself ... Autocracy, on the other hand, describes the executive power of the will to enforce principles that have been given ... autocracy represents the strength that a rational autonomous being must strive to acquire so that she is master over her inclinations" (Baxley, "Autocracy and Autonomy," 11–12).

53. For astute reflections on the implicit phenomenality of the categorical imperative, see Nancy Sherman, "Kantian Virtue: Priggish or Passional?" in *Reclaiming the History of Ethics: Essays for John Rawls*, eds. Barbara Herman and Christine Korsgaard (Cambridge: Cambridge University Press, 1997a), 270–96.

54. Kant, VA, 27:275. While I cite the *Lectures on Ethics*' formulation here for its clarity, Kant draws the same division in the *Metaphysics of Morals*: "practical laws of reason ... take no account of these [moral] feelings ... since they have nothing to do with the *basis* of practical laws but only with the subjective *effect* in the mind when our choice is determined by them" (6:221). Kant's caution regarding the conflation of objective and subjective principles is also echoed in the *Blomberg Logic*: "All error arises when we hold subjective grounds of our judgment to be objective ones" (cited in Zammito, *Birth of Anthropology*, 276).

55. Kant, KpV, 5:74.

56. Ibid., 5:74.

57. Kant, VA, 27:1429. While Kant's views on the relation of morality and feeling shifted over time, his mature conclusion – that affects bear on moral motivation, but not on the derivation of moral principles – is traceable to the early 1770s. In the 1760s, still under Hume's sway, he "had emphasized the importance of the moral sense for *both* the first formal and the first material principles of morals" (Kuehn, *Kant*, 201), but settled on the distinction between moral feeling and moral principle in the early years of the silent decade, well before the publication of the first *Critique*.

58. Kant, KpV, 5:74. For informative treatments of the role of respect in motivating moral action, see Reath, *Agency and Autonomy*, and Sherman, "Kantian Virtue."

59. As Kant explains in a rather convoluted passage: "sensible feeling, which underlies all of our inclinations, is indeed the condition of that feeling we call respect, but the cause determining it lies in pure practical reason; and so this feeling, on account of its origin, cannot be called pathologically effected but must be called *practically effected*, and is effected as follows: the representation of the moral law deprives self-love of its influence and self-conceit of its illusion, and thereby the hindrance to pure practical reason is lessened and the representation of the superiority of its objective law to the impulses of sensibility is produced and hence, by removal of the counter-weight, the relative weightiness of the law (with regard to a will affected by impulses) in the judgment of reason" (Kant, KpV, 5:75–76).

60. For Kant's distinction between intelligible and sensible pleasures, see Frierson, "Account of Human Action," and Munzel, *Moral Character*, 128–129.

61. Kant, KpV, 5:76.

62. Kant, VA, 27:1428.

63. Kant, TP, 8:283.
64. Kant, MS, 6:400.
65. Ibid., 6:399.
66. Kant, VA, 27:287.
67. Munzel, *Moral Character*, 5.
68. Several sets of Kant's pupils' lecture notes on anthropology, pedagogy and ethics have been published since the early 2000s. These span from the 1770s to the 1790s, and have been invaluable in illuminating the genesis of Kant's long-standing interests in anthropology and human development. While they cannot be treated as authoritative articulations of Kant's views, they nevertheless substantiate arguments developed in his written work. They also serve as the connective tissue between published texts, tracing out the development of Kant's ideas. Throughout this book, I treat them with all due caution regarding the limits of their reliability. As such, I draw on them only to corroborate arguments contained in published works, and not to introduce stand-alone or original ideas.
69. Kant, MS, 6:469.
70. Kant, VA, 27:244. Despite slight variations, Kant echoes this sentiment in the 1784–5 *Anthropology Mrongovius* ("Anthropology is pragmatic, but is of service for the moral knowledge of the human being, for one must create the motives for morals from it, and without it morals would be scholastic, not at all applicable to the world, and not agreeable to the world" (25:1212)), and still earlier, in the 1781–1782 *Menschenkunde* ("All morals require knowledge of the human being ... I must know which avenues to human dispositions I can have in order to bring forth resolutions; knowledge of the human being can give us the opportunity for this" (25:858)). Kant's appraisal of pragmatic anthropology's moral value thus appears to have held consistently, even during the critical period. See Immanuel Kant, "Anthropology Mrongovius," in *Lectures on Anthropology*, eds. Allen W. Wood and Robert B. Louden (Cambridge: Cambridge University Press, 2012); and Immanuel Kant, "Menschenkunde," in *Lectures on Anthropology*, eds. Allen W. Wood and Robert B. Louden (Cambridge: Cambridge University Press, 2012).
71. Immanuel Kant, "Lectures on Pedagogy," in *Anthropology, History, and Education*, eds. Günter Zöller and Robert B. Louden (New York: Cambridge University Press, 2007), 9: 443. Given hereafter as VP. Kant's writings on education appear in the second *Critique's* "Doctrine of the Method of Pure Practical Reason," the *Metaphysics of Morals'* "Doctrine of the Methods of Ethics," and, more obliquely, in the *Anthropology*. The *Lectures on Pedagogy* (coalesced into a published volume posthumously in 1803 by D. Friedrich Theodor Rink, to whom Kant entrusted his lecture notes on the subject), *Lectures on Anthropology*, and *Lectures on Ethics* provide a much richer view of his moral pedagogy. Given their considerable elaboration over Kant's written treatments, I draw on these lectures – particularly, the *Lectures on Pedagogy* – here, with all due wariness of working from unpublished materials. These concerns are somewhat mitigated by the fact that despite minor terminological inconsistencies, Kant's assessments of the aims, procedures, divisions and value of pedagogy remain relatively stable, across both lectures and published work, over the two decades (1770s–1790s) that he treated them.
72. Kant, KpV, 5:152.

73. Immanuel Kant, "Essays Regarding the *Philanthropinum*," in *Anthropology, History, and Education*, eds. Günter Zöller and Robert B. Louden (New York: Cambridge University Press, 2007), 2:449.
74. For discussions of Kant's enthusiasm for the *Philanthropinum*, see Munzel, *Moral Character*, 266–274; Robert B. Louden, "Introduction" to *Lectures on Pedagogy*, in *History, Anthropology, Education* (Cambridge: Cambridge University Press, 2007), 434; Louden, *Impure Ethics*, 44–47; and Kuehn, *Kant*, 229.
75. Munzel, *Moral Character*, 266–274. The *Philanthropinum*'s radical and broad-ranging pedagogical mandate, Kuehn notes, was controversial, contravening the common view that education should groom Prussians to fill their stations in life, rather than stimulating their higher faculties. See Kuehn, *Kant*, 227–230.
76. Kant, VP, 9:448.
77. Immanuel Kant, "Anthropology Friedländer," in *Lectures on Anthropology*, eds. Allen W. Wood and Robert B. Louden (New York: Cambridge University Press, 2012), 25:772–773. It is worth noting that Kant's appraisal of education's moral value was not limited to his enthusiasm for Basedowian pedagogy; "concerning the well-being of the world," he maintained in the 1784–5 *Anthropology Mrongovius*, "everything depends on education" (Kant, *Mrongovius*, 25:1429).
78. Kant, "Essays," 2:451.
79. Ibid., 2:447–448.
80. Kant, *Anthropology*, 7:293.
81. Kant, VP, 9:454.
82. Ibid., 9: 464.
83. For detailed analyses of these pedagogical stages, see Munzel, *Moral Character*, ch. 5; Louden, *Impure Ethics*; Louden, "Second Part"; Wood, *Ethical Thought*; and Wood, "Human Nature." Kant's treatments of education suffer from terminological inconsistencies – the result of Rink's piecing together the *Lectures on Pedagogy* from Kant's loose lecture notes, of variations between translators and their source materials, and of changes in Kant's own presentations (he offered the course on practical pedagogy in 1776–7, 1780, 1783–4 and 1786–7). However, its substantive and structuring elements – centrally, the division between: (a) basic instruction, (b) pragmatic instruction, and (c) moral instruction – are broadly consistent. For an instructive discussion of education, morality and anthropology, see G. Felicitas Munzel, "Indispensable Education of the Being of Reason and Speech," in *Kant's Lectures on Anthropology: A Critical Guide*, ed. Alix Cohen (Cambridge: Cambridge University Press, 2014).
84. Kant, VP, 9:442.
85. Ibid., 9:455.
86. To clarify Kant's terminology: education falls into three basic stages (discipline, culture and moral training), which are here split into slightly more detailed sub-stages. Following the negative, preparatory stage (discipline), the first two forms of positive instruction listed here (basic and pragmatic instruction) fall within the second stage of education (culture). The third form of instruction (moral training) belongs to the final stage of education, and is treated in detail in subsections 2.2.2.3 "Moral Training I: Habituation" and 2.2.2.4 "Moral Training II: Propaedeutic Aids."
87. Kant, VE, 27:245.
88. Kant, G, 4:415–416.

89. Kant, VP, 9:455.
90. "Now, inasmuch as virtue and happiness together constitute possession of the highest good in a person, and happiness distributed in exact proportion to morality (as the worth of a person and his worthiness to be happy) constitutes the *highest good* of a possible world, the latter means the whole, the complete good" (Kant, KpV, 5:111). Kant's conceptualization of the highest good is subject to a vast literature; I refer to it here only to draw out his attention, in both ethics and pedagogy, to imperatives of happiness. For a few treatments of the highest good, see Stephen Engstrom, "The Concept of the Highest Good in Kant's Moral Theory," *Philosophy and Phenomenological Research* 52, no. 4 (1992): 747–780; Paul Guyer, "Beauty, Systematicity, and the Highest Good: Eckart Förster's *Kant's Final Synthesis*," *Inquiry* 46, no. 2 (2003): 195–214; Pauline Kleingeld, "What Do the Virtuous Hope For? Re-Reading Kant's Doctrine of the Highest Good," in *Proceedings of the Eighth International Kant Congress*, ed. Hoke Robinson (Memphis: Marquette University Press, 1995): 91–112.; Eoin O'Connell, "Happiness Proportioned to Virtue: Kant and the Highest Good," *Kantian Review* 17, no. 2 (2012): 257–279; and Matthew Caswell, "Kant's Conception of the Highest Good, the *Gesinnung*, and the Theory of Radical Evil," *Kant-Studien* 97, no. 2 (2006): 184–209.
91. Kant, *Anthropology*, 7:201.
92. Kant, VP, 9:450.
93. For a few recent examples, see Stocker's, Schiller's and Williams's critiques of Kant's formalism, outlined in Stratton-Lake (2006). Allen Wood nicely captures the spirit of this line of critique, which sees in Kant's ethics "a theory that accords moral worth only to actions done from duty, treats our entire emotional nature as worthless, and places moral principles ahead of human experience at every turn" (Wood, *Ethical Thought*, 3).
94. As Nancy Sherman suggests, for Kant, "cultivated emotions become an important expression of the dominion of practical reason" (Nancy Sherman, *Making a Necessity of Virtue: Aristotle and Kant on Virtue* (Cambridge: Cambridge University Press, 1997b), 135). Pauline Kleingeld similarly identifies "natural feelings that lead us to act in ways that accord with moral demands" (Kleingeld, *Kant and Cosmopolitanism*, 168, and more generally, 165–169). For more treatments of affects, passions and desires in Kant's thought, see essays by Patrick Frierson, Allen Wood and Paul Guyer in Alix Cohen, ed., *Kant's Lectures on Anthropology: A Critical Guide* (Cambridge: Cambridge University Press, 2014); Alix Cohen, "Kant on the Moral Cultivation of Feelings," in *Thinking About the Emotions: A Philosophical History*, eds. Alix Cohen and Robert Stern (Oxford: Oxford University Press, 2017); Alix Cohen, "Rational Feelings," in *Kant and the Faculty of Feeling*, eds. K. Sorensen and D. Williamson (Cambridge: Cambridge University Press, 2018), 9–24; and Alix Cohen, "Kant on Moral Feelings, Moral Desires and the Cultivation of Virtue," in *Begehren/Desire*, eds. Sally Sedgwick and Dina Emundts (Berlin: De Gruyter, 2018), 3–18. Regrettably, much of Cohen's insightful work on Kant, virtue and moral feelings was published too close to this book's publication to more fully integrate throughout.
95. Plato, *Republic*, trans. G. M. A. Grube (Indianapolis: Hackett Publishing Co., 1992), 402a.

96. Kant, MS, 6:480.
97. Kant, KpV, 5:159.
98. Kant, VE, 27:287.
99. Ibid., 27:362.
100. Herman, *The Practice of Moral Judgment*, 83.
101. Munzel, *Moral Character*, 309.
102. Stratton-Lake, "Moral Motivation."
103. Kant, MS, 6:480.
104. Ibid., 6:593.
105. Kant, VP, 9:491.
106. Kant, MS, 6:480.
107. Kant, VE, 27:287–288.
108. Munzel, *Moral Character*, 316.
109. Kant, MS, 6:478–480.
110. Ibid., 6:484.
111. Ibid., 6:483
112. Ibid., 6:484.
113. Kant, "Essays," 2:449.
114. Kant, *Moral Mrongovius II*, in Louden, *Impure Ethics*, 6.
115. Barbara Herman, "Training to Autonomy," in *Philosophers on Education: New Historical Perspectives*, ed. Amélie Rorty (London: Routledge, 1998), 1; see also Herman, "A Cosmopolitan Kingdom of Ends," in *Reclaiming the History of Ethics: Essays for John Rawls*, eds. Andrews Reath, Barbara Herman and Christine Korsgaard (Cambridge: Cambridge University Press, 1997), 187–213.
116. Herman, "Training to Autonomy"; Muthu, *Enlightenment against Empire*; and Thomas McCarthy, "Multicultural Cosmopolitanism: Remarks on the Idea of Universal History," in *Letting Be: Fred Dallmayr's Cosmopolitical Vision*, ed. Stephen Schneck (Notre Dame: University of Notre Dame Press, 2006), 188–213.
117. I elaborate on Kant's understanding of culture in section 2.2.2.1, and in Chapter 3, section 3.4.4. For a fuller critique of Muthu's reading of Kant, see Inder S. Marwah, "Bridging Nature and Freedom? Kant, Culture and Cultivation," *Social Theory and Practice* 38, no. 3 (2012): 385–406.
118. Herman, "Training to Autonomy," 269.
119. Kant's philosophy of history is elaborated in several essays spanning his critical and post-critical periods ("Idea for a Universal History with a Cosmopolitan Aim" (1784), "Conjectural Beginning of Human History" (1786), "The End of All Things" (1794)), "A Renewed Attempt to Answer the Question: 'Is the Human Race Continually Improving?'" (1798), and the *Anthropology* (1798), and, most importantly, the third *Critique* (1790). For a seminal analysis, see Yirmiyahu Yovel, *Kant and the Philosophy of History* (Princeton: Princeton University Press, 1980). For treatments in relation to Kant's impure ethics, see Wood, *Ethical Thought*, and Louden, *Impure Ethics*. For a critique of its Eurocentric features, see McCarthy, *Race*. For its incompatibility with Kant's political philosophy, see Ellis, *Provisional Theory*. For its compatibility with Kant's critical philosophy, see Kleingeld, "Idea of Moral Development" and Sharon Anderson-Gold, *Unnecessary Evil: History and Moral Progress in the Philosophy of Immanuel Kant* (Albany: State University of New York Press, 2001). My views on the relationship between Kant's philosophy of history and

his moral and political philosophy are laid out in this chapter, Chapter 3, and Chapter 6.

120. It cannot be stated strongly enough that Kant's teleology is regulative, and not objective. Kant's claims stand apart from an Aristotelian view because they concern how we ought to *regard* human nature (a perspectival/interpretive claim), and not what it *is* (an ontological/foundationalist claim). In Kant's view, we are unable to know nature's purposes in any objective sense. However, we are compelled to conceive of a purposive natural order if we're to understand humanity as progressive. As Kant himself explains in the third *Critique*, "these principles [of teleology] pertain merely to reflective judgment: they do not determine the actual [*an sich*] origin of these beings, but only say that the character of our understanding and of our reason is such that the only way we can conceive of the origin of such beings is in terms of final causes" (5:429). Teleological claims are, then, reflective postulates concerning how we can understand ourselves as a species, and not what we are. Allen Wood makes the distinction particularly clear: "the entire idea of natural purposiveness always has only regulative use in organizing our cognitions; it is misunderstood if viewed as an explanatory hypothesis of any kind, or even as an object inviting such purposes" (Wood, *Ethical Thought*, 218). For interpretations of the role of teleology in Kant's thought, see Louden, *Impure Ethics*; Wood, *Ethical Thought*; Bernasconi "Concept of Race"; McCarthy, *Race*, ch. 2; and Lea Ypi, "*Natura Daedala Rerum*? On the Justification of Historical Progress in Kant's 'Guarantee of Perpetual Peace'," *Kantian Review* 14, no. 2 (2010): 118–148.

121. As Kant puts it in "Idea": "*All natural predispositions of a creature are determined sometime to develop themselves completely and purposively ... In the human being* (as the only rational creature on earth), *those predispositions whose goal is the use of his reason were to develop completely only in the species, but not in the individual.*" Immanuel Kant, "Idea for a Universal History with a Cosmopolitan Aim," in *Anthropology, History, and Education*, eds. Günter Zöller and Robert B. Louden (New York: Cambridge University Press, 2007), 8:18–9. Cited hereafter as I.

122. Kant, MS, 6:217.

123. Kant, *Anthropology*, 7:322.

124. Louden, *Impure Ethics*, 40.

125. Ibid.

126. Immanuel Kant, *Critique of Judgment*, ed. and trans. Werner S. Pluhar (Indianapolis: Hackett Publishing Co., 1987), 5:431. Given hereafter as KU.

127. Louden, *Impure Ethics*, 40. Louden argues that Kant sees "civilization" as a distinct stage of socio-historical development, distinguishable from (and set above) "cultivation" (see Louden, *Impure Ethics*, 40–44). It's not entirely clear whether or not this is the case. While Kant unambiguously distinguishes "civilized" and "barbaric" societies, it is less clear that he treats "civilization" as qualitatively distinct from "cultivation," rather than as a variant of it.

128. Kant, I, 8:26.

129. Kant, *Anthropology*, 7:324. Kant distinguishes these social stages and assigns them a moral value at least as early as the mid-1780s. In the *Anthropology Mrongovius*, for instance, he observes that "[t]he natural predispositions aim at

the development of our talents through 1. the highest cultivation 2. civilization 3. moralization" (25:1426).

130. Kant, MS, 6:473.
131. Ibid.
132. Ibid.
133. Ibid., 6:411.
134. Kant, *Anthropology*, 7:151.
135. Kant, MS, 6:474.
136. Wood, *Ethical Thought*, 253–256.
137. Kant, VP, 9:442.
138. Ibid.
139. Kant, *Menschenkunde*, 25:857.
140. Kant, *Anthropology*, 7:304.
141. Ibid., 7:191.
142. Kant, BS, 2:254.
143. Louden, *Impure Ethics*, 41.
144. Kant, KU, 5:432.
145. For the argument that Kant values cultures of discipline and skill insofar as they support "[t]he primacy of moral development within the flourishing of the human species," see Lara Denis, "Individual and Collective Flourishing in Kant's Philosophy," *Kantian Review* 13, no. 1 (2008).
146. Kant, KU, 5:434.
147. Immanuel Kant, "Conjectural Beginning of Human History," in *Anthropology, History, and Education*, eds. Günter Zöller and Robert B. Louden (New York: Cambridge University Press, 2007), 8:117. Given hereafter as MA.
148. Kant, MS, 6:231.
149. Ibid., 6:237.
150. Ripstein, *Force and Freedom*, 16. Elisabeth Ellis similarly holds that "[t]he doctrine of right, based on the moral law, is for Kant the fundamental basis of all politics" (Ellis, *Provisional Theory*, 36).
151. Ripstein, *Force and Freedom*, 5.
152. Ibid., 35.
153. Kant, MS, 6:341.
154. "[I]f the principle of outer freedom limited by law is lacking in any one of these three possible forms of rightful condition, the framework of all the others is unavoidably undermined and must finally collapse" (Kant, MS, 6:311).
155. Immanuel Kant, "Toward Perpetual Peace," in *Practical Philosophy*, ed. and trans. Mary J. Gregor (New York: Cambridge University Press, 1996), 8:350. Given hereafter as EF.
156. Kant, MS, 6:263.
157. Kant, EF, 8:350.
158. Kant, MS, 6:343.
159. Kant, EF, 8:358.
160. Kant, MS, 6:352.
161. Ibid., 6:264.
162. Kant, *Mrongovius*, 25:1425. Kant's view of the civil condition's formative capacity can be traced back to (at least) the 1775–6 *Anthropology Friedländer*: "When such a [political] state will be attained, in which everything will be

instituted in accordance with complete rules of justice and morality, this will then be a condition under which everyone will be able to make himself more perfect" (25:690–691, square bracket in the original). While this predates Kant's formal distinction between ethics and right (which would become entrenched – albeit, inconsistently – in the division between the *Tugendlehre* and the *Rechtslehre*), his broader view of the state's pedagogic function remains well into the 1790s. At this early stage, however, Kant confesses to a lack of clarity with respect to the relation between individual and collective formation: "What then serves to be able to produce such [a state]? Here one is still uncertain whether one should start from the bottom, or from the top. Should such a [political] state first be established, so that every single individual could be made perfect, or should every single individual first thus be made perfect through education, in order that finally later, when it has passed through many members, such a state could be established? Does the perfection of every single human being depend on the perfection of the state, or does the perfection of the state depend on the perfection of every single human being?" (25:691). For an analysis of the relationship between individual and collective formation in Kant's early (1770s) anthropology lectures, see Catherine Wilson, "Kant on Civilization, Culture and Moralisation," in *Kant's Lectures on Anthropology: A Critical Guide*, ed. Alix Cohen (Cambridge: Cambridge University Press, 2014), 191–210.

163. Kant, I, 8:22.
164. Kant, MS, 6:352.
165. Kant, I, 8:28.
166. Munzel, *Moral Character*, 259.
167. Ibid., 323.
168. Immanuel Kant, "An Answer to the Question: What is Enlightenment?," in *Practical Philosophy*, ed. and trans. Mary J. Gregor (New York: Cambridge University Press, 1996), 8:36. Given hereafter as WA.
169. Kant, TP, 8:304.
170. Kant, EF, 8:367. Kant makes the point somewhat more forcefully in the *Anthropology Mrongovius*: given that "[v]irtue and vice, religion, and arts and sciences are products of the political constitution" (25:1420), "the government should think more about religion and morality in order to make human beings better" (Kant, *Mrongovius*, 25:1428).
171. Kant, *Anthropology*, 7:331.
172. Kant, EF, 8:291.
173. Kant, WA, 8:36, 8:39.
174. Munzel, *Moral Character*, 324.
175. "[U]nder a constitution in which subjects are not citizens of the state, which is therefore not republican, [deciding upon war] is the easiest thing in the world; because the head of state is not a member of the state" (Kant, EF, 8:351).
176. Kant, *Mrongovius*, 25:1428.
177. Immanuel Kant, *Anthropology Pillau*, in *Lectures on Anthropology*, eds. Allen W. Wood and Robert B. Louden (New York: Cambridge University Press 2012), 25:843.
178. Kant, EF, 8:376.
179. Jennifer Mensch, "What's Wrong with Inevitable Progress? Notes on Kant's Anthropology Today," *Cogent Arts and Humanities* 4 (2017).

180. Kant, VP, 9:487. For an exhaustive treatment of character as the lynchpin binding Kant's critical and anthropological endeavors, see Munzel, *Moral Character*. For the relationship between intelligible and empirical character, see Frierson, "Account of Human Action." For a view of character as a necessary but not sufficient condition for virtuous personhood, see Patrick Frierson, "Character and Evil," *Journal of the History of Philosophy* 44, no. 4 (2006): 623–634; and Kuehn, "Introduction," vii–xxix. For an overview of Kant's occasionally contradictory conceptualizations of character, see Brian Jacobs, "Kantian Character and the Problem of a Science of Humanity," in *Essays on Kant's Anthropology*, eds. Patrick Kain and Brian Jacobs (Cambridge: Cambridge University Press, 2003), 105–134.

181. Kant, *Anthropology*, 7:285.

182. Ibid., 7:119.

183. Ibid.

184. Kant, MS, 6:405.

185. Kuehn, "Introduction," xxvi.

186. Kant distinguishes virtue (the strength of will in acting on moral motives despite the pull of inclinations) from virtues (the social skills and behaviors cultivating moral dispositions conducive to virtue). In his words, "there is only *one* obligation of virtue, whereas there are *many* duties of virtue; for there are indeed many objects that it is also our duty to have as ends, but there is only one virtuous disposition, the subjective determining ground to fulfill one's duty" (Kant, MS, 6:411). For a close examination of the distinction, see Guyer, "The Obligation to be Virtuous."

187. Kant, MS, 6:395.

188. Kant, KpV, 5:152. Munzel traces the development of Kant's views on this "practical cast of mind" from his earliest lectures and writings in the 1750s to the anthropological turn of the 1790s, in which it figures most prominently. Kant's attention to character, she demonstrates, falls within philosophical debates on the "conduct of thought" (*Denkungsart*) in the seventeenth and eighteenth centuries, spanning from Antoine Arnauld, to Blaise Pascal, to – most importantly, for Kant – Rousseau's *Emile*. In the German context, Munzel takes Kant's, Herder's and Goethe's treatments of *Denkungsart* to "indicate a genuine issue of the age, capturing the attention of its major thinkers" (Munzel, *Moral Character*, 34). See Munzel, *Moral Character*, ch. 1.

189. Kant, *Friedländer*, 25:630–631.

190. Kant, *Anthropology*, 7:292.

191. Kuehn, "Introduction," xxvi.

192. Despite variations across Kant's treatments of moral character, its central feature – a persistent disposition to act from principles – remains fixed in written works and lectures from the mid-1770s onward. In the lectures from the early 1770s (*Anthropology Collins* (1772–1773) and *Anthropology Parow* (1772–1773)), Kant's views on character remain indistinct, inconsistent, and unformed. But as of 1775–1776 – perhaps unsurprisingly, given Kant's rising interest in moral education during the same period – he comes to describe character as "the employment of our power of choice to act according to rules and principles" (Kant, *Anthropology Friedländer*, 25:630), a formulation which recurs in 1781–1782 ("Character is that which marks a resolution in principles in the

human beings ... a settled way of thinking and not merely a feeling" (Kant, *Menschenkunde*, 25:1169)), 1784–1785 ("Character is the will of the human being in accordance with principles" (Kant, *Anthropology Mrongovius*, 25:1385)), and – somewhat more obliquely – in 1788–9 ("The character of a human being as a free being is posited in his will" (Immanuel Kant, "Anthropology Busolt," in *Lectures on Anthropology*, eds. Allen W. Wood and Robert B. Louden (New York: Cambridge University Press 2012), 25:1530)). This of course conforms to the account in the published *Anthropology* of 1798.

193. Kant, VA, 27:464.
194. Kant, VP, 9:481.
195. Kant, *Menschenkunde*, 25:1172.
196. Kant, MS, 6:400–6:468.
197. Ibid., 6:399.
198. Kant, VA, 27:464.
199. Kant, R, 6:121.
200. Kant, G, 4:401.
201. Kant, R, 6:45.
202. Kant's doctrine of radical evil is subject to considerable debate, most notably between Allen Wood and Henry Allison; see Wood, *Ethical Thought*; Henry E. Allison, "Kant on Freedom: A Reply to My Critics," *Inquiry* 36, no. 4 (1993): 443–464; Henry E. Allison, *Idealism and Freedom: Essays on Kant's Theoretical and Practical Philosophy* (Cambridge: Cambridge University Press, 1996); and Henry E. Allison, *Kant's Theory of Taste: A Reading of the Critique of Aesthetic Judgement* (Cambridge: Cambridge University Press, 2001).
203. Kant, R, 6:47.
204. Kant, *Anthropology*, 7:294. It is unclear whether Kant understands this moral epiphany as affecting intelligible or empirical character. On one hand, this "tectonic shift" certainly appears to impact the maxims governing our actions, and so, our intelligible character. On the other, Kant persistently situates the "revolution" within a temporal order, as inaugurating a moral character. Henry Allison's "epistemological" approach provides a particularly compelling resolution: the moral revolution concerns a fundamental shift in how we *think* of ourselves – as beings who choose to elevate moral maxims over maxims founded on self-love – which naturally entails an engrained commitment to moral self-improvement (what I describe as the second dimension of the good human being). It is entirely plausible to treat Kant's "moral revolution" not as *occurring* in an ontologically distinctive sphere, but rather, as *describing* the epistemological shift in our maxims giving rise to the good human being's "incessant laboring" toward moral self-cultivation.
205. Kant, R, 6:48, my italics.
206. Ibid., 6:383.
207. Ibid., 6:409.
208. Guyer, "The Obligation to be Virtuous," 224–225.
209. Kant, KpV, 5:83.
210. In this, I follow Henry Allison's argument that "the transcendental idea of freedom, which provides the content to the otherwise empty thought of an intelligible character, has a merely regulative, nonexplanatory function. What it regulates is our conception of ourselves as rational agents ... the basic idea is

simply that it is a condition of the possibility of taking oneself as a rational agent, that is, as a being for whom reason is practical, that one attribute such spontaneity to oneself" (Allison, *Theory of Freedom*, 45).

211. Kant, KpV, 5:122.
212. Ibid.
213. Kant, MS, 6:217.

3

Difference, Diversity and Exclusion

> Does the author really mean that if the happy inhabitants of Tahiti, never visited by more cultured nations, had been destined to live for thousands of centuries in their tranquil indolence, one could give a satisfying answer to the question why they exist at all, and whether it would not have been just as good to have this island populated with happy sheep and cattle as with human beings who are happy merely enjoying themselves?
>
> Kant, "Review of J. G. Herder's *Ideas for the Philosophy of the History of Humanity*"

> Without these qualities of unsociability from which the resistance arises, which are not at all amiable in themselves, qualities that each of us must necessarily encounter in his selfish pretensions, all talents would, in an arcadian pastoral life of perfect concord, contentment and mutual love, remain eternally hidden in their germs; human beings, as good-natured as the sheep they tended, would give their existence hardly any greater worth than that of their domesticated beasts; they would not fill the void in creation in regard to their end as rational nature.
>
> Kant, "Idea for a Universal History with a Cosmopolitan Aim"

No shortage of ink has been spilled over Kant's infamous denigration of the Tahitians in his review of Herder's *Ideas*, from Gayatri Spivak's contention that Kant's "raw man ... *cannot* be the subject of speech or judgment in the world of the *Critique*,"[1] to Emmanuel Chukwudi Eze's criticism of its evident race-thinking, to Robert Louden and Allen Wood's observation that "Kant's main animus is directed not at Tahitians per se but at human beings everywhere who are 'merely enjoying themselves'."[2] From either perspective, the Tahitians are taken to exemplify or explain Kant's racism or Eurocentrism – either confirming its transcendental foundations, or, conversely, demonstrating its disconnectedness from his critical philosophy.

And yet, Kant's assessment of the Tahitians also sharpens the question raised by the account of moral agency developed in Chapter 2. If Kant understands our moral vocation as an "ever-continuing striving for the better" – as forming the consistent, lifelong orientation toward moral duty encapsulated in the good human being – how are we to understand the moral status of those people(s) that fail to adopt that orientation, or that appear unable to progress toward our natural ends? While the strictly deontological reading of Kant's ethics treats our moral worth as fixed and inborn, the view I've advanced complicates it by drawing out the capacities we're bound to cultivate as moral actors. These are precisely the complications raised by the Tahitians: what is the value, Kant asks, in a life that fails to develop those rational capacities in which our dignity inheres – a life that does not advance toward moral realization? Can we "give a satisfying answer to the question why they exist at all" if they do not "fill the void in creation in regard to their end as rational nature"? If not for the fortuitous (or perhaps providential) intervention of Europeans, would the lives of Tahitians – barely more rational than the sheep which they tend – actually be beyond "market price"?

This chapter aims, broadly speaking, to assess the worth of Tahitians' lives in Kant's eyes. It aims to consider how the developmental dimensions of moral agency impact Kant's liberalism – or, more specifically, how Kant's thicker view of the kinds of agents capable of moral progress stands to constrain his ethics' universalism. My central claim is this: if a properly human moral nature is necessarily developmental – that unlike divine rational beings, we are bound to develop our moral capacities in moving toward our natural end – then we ought to take seriously the moral quandary facing the swathes of humanity that, either "naturally" or circumstantially, are unable to cultivate those capacities. If, as constitutively imperfect, phenomenal creatures, our moral task is to continually *approximate* virtue and strengthen our moral dispositions and resolve, then the inability to foster them at all constitutes a signal failure of our specifically human moral vocation. To put it plainly, Kant's liberalism faces profound challenges if certain kinds of people(s) appear unable to develop the capabilities bridging nature and freedom. Without suggesting, as some critics do, that the teleological framework surrounding Kant's treatments of race and gender directly impugns his moral theory, I argue that it only poorly registers the full moral worth of certain categories of people (if at all), and so seriously troubles his liberalism's coherence. It is in this space – between moral idealism and moral advancement – that Kant makes sense of human difference, and that we best understand its attendant problems.

Kant's account of the Tahitians (this time, from the *Anthropology Mrongovius*) also illuminates the connections between the moral and political deficits of improperly cultured agents. "[T]ight civil association," Kant tells us,

is further brought about by … unsociability; this produces more culture and refinement of taste. Without this unsociability there would never have arisen a firm civil association, but at most only the arcadian life of a shepherd … whereby the human being would never be perfected or cultivated and would not be more esteemed than any other animal species. One still finds such a life in Tahiti.[3]

Our moral and political lives are, for Kant, more entwined than tends to be recognized. Beyond harmonizing our entitlements to freedom, politics – or rather, certain forms of politics – also contributes to our moral advancement. More often than not, though, the moral and political inequities in Kant's conceptualizations of race and gender are treated as separate matters; little attention has been devoted to their interconnections.[4] Without losing sight of important distinctions between doctrines of virtue and right, I want to suggest that many of the exclusionary proclivities in Kant's moral and political philosophies share common foundations. Their supposed isolation from one another has, moreover, contributed to the view that these are mere irregularities, rather than systematic problems – failures to apply universalistic commitments consistently, and so, little more than historically contained aberrations from an otherwise cohesive, inclusive and egalitarian liberalism. I argue, conversely, that we misapprehend the limitations in Kant's political thought by setting it apart from the moral theory animating it, and from the broader account of human progress contextualizing it.

The chapter proceeds in three sections. The first explores problems of political exclusion by scrutinizing Kant's distinction between active and passive citizenship. Despite their subjection to and equality before republican law, neither women nor the un-propertied are "active" (law-giving) citizens; they are, rather, co-beneficiaries of the state. To see why exactly this is the case, I begin by sketching out Kant's accounts of republican citizenship, focusing on the citizen–co-beneficiary divide in "Theory and Practice" and the *Rechtslehre*'s active–passive formulation. The answer, I argue, lies in "deficiencies" in the exercise of the understanding, cognitive shortcomings – temporary in the case of the poor, permanent for women – detracting from republican public life. As we have seen, republican governments both shape and depend on particular kinds of citizens, oriented toward public reason, self-direction and deliberation. In this section, I show that the un-propertied fail to cultivate the forms of judgment required for responsible public action.

Section 3.2 shifts from strictly political concerns to the overlap of morality and politics by delving into Kant's treatment of women. I argue that women's political deficits are rooted in their moral nature, elaborated in Kant's anthropology. Women's character, Kant holds, is only comprehensible in light of the ends that nature sets them, and not by the ends they might set themselves. Their civil immaturity is, then, epiphenomenal: their civic incapacities are not only a political problem, but rather reflect entrenched limitations that affect their standing as moral agents. If human dignity inheres in rational, autonomous self-determination, it's not clear how we should regard the moral status of persons endowed with a permanently stunted understanding, whose capacity for purposive action is, at best, indeterminate.

Section 3.3 examines problems of moral exclusion, focusing on Kant's conceptualization of race. As we saw in Chapter 2, human moral agency is a matter of formation: our moral duty doesn't just enjoin us to undertake moral *actions* (though it does that too), but rather to develop a moral *character*, oriented toward the moral law and developed by particular pedagogical, cultural and political conditions. How, then, should we understand the moral nature of agents unable to cultivate such a character? I turn to Kant's engagements with the non-European world to consider the problem.

In total, this chapter aims to situate Kant's treatments of difference and diversity within their teleological and anthropological contexts, and to assess the challenges that they present for his liberalism. By drawing together his writings on ethics, politics, anthropology, history, biology and pedagogy, I develop a broad-ranging picture of his moral and political vision, and of the human beings at its center. Ultimately, I argue that it leaves remarkably little space for recognizing the worth of human diversity. The tensions between Kant's transcendental view of moral nature and teleological view of moral development – tensions most clearly manifest in his response to human difference – make for a particularly unsteady liberalism. These tensions are, of course, easily avoided by simply bracketing the human part of the equation. But as Kant himself saw, this would yield but an impoverished and hollow account of the moral and political lives of which we – or at least, some of us – are capable.

3.1   POLITICAL EXCLUSION

3.1.1   Citizens and Co-beneficiaries

Recent years have witnessed a growing interest in Kant's political philosophy.[5] While the grounds of his system of right are well-served, his account of citizenship – turning from abstract matters of justification to concrete conditions of realization – is somewhat less clearly spelled out.

The principles underpinning republican citizenship, Kant tells us in "Theory and Practice" (1793), preserve the freedom of every individual, the equality of all subjects and the independence of each citizen. Full citizenship, however, is qualified by both natural (not being a child or a woman) and conventional (*"being one's own master (sui iuris)*, hence having some *property"*)[6] constraints. While all subjects enjoy negative rights securing their external freedom,

it is not the case that all who are free and equal under already existing public laws are to be held equal with regard to the right to give these laws. Those who are not qualified for this right are still, as members of the commonwealth, subject to compliance with these laws and thereby enjoy protection in accordance with them, not, however as *citizens* but as *cobeneficiaries of this protection.*[7]

The division recurs in the *Rechtslehre* (1797), where Kant elaborates the qualities distinguishing "active" and "passive" citizens:

being fit to vote presupposes the independence of someone who, as one of the people, wants to be not just a part of the commonwealth but also a member of it, that is, a part of the commonwealth acting from his own choice in community with others. This quality of being independent, however, requires a distinction between *active* and *passive* citizens ... an apprentice in the service of a merchant or artisan; a domestic servant (as distinguished from a civil servant); a minor (*naturaliter vel civiliter*); all women and, in general, anyone whose preservation in existence (his being fed and protected) depends not on his management of his own business but on arrangements made by another (except the state). All these people lack civil personality and their existence is, as it were, only inherence.[8]

The active/passive distinction is notoriously unconvincing, as the egalitarianism implicit in Kant's ideal of civil independence – equal freedom from the choice of others – is clearly undermined by restricting the political rights of a particular class of citizen, and by subjecting certain citizens to the decisions of others.[9] The qualifying criteria – natural and property-based – are, still further, as arbitrary as they are theoretically unsatisfying; the prima facie conflict between the innate right to self-determination and a property requirement, Leslie Mulholland maintains, "makes Kant's treatment of the principle of civil independence suspect."[10] If Kant's political philosophy rests, as Arthur Ripstein suggests, "on the simple but compelling normative idea that, as a matter of right, each person is entitled to be his or her own master ... [in the] sense of not being subordinated to the choice of any other particular person,"[11] then passive citizens' subjection to laws they are powerless to affect appears by all rights unjustifiable.

Commentators have nonetheless sought to reconcile Kant's account of citizenship with his political philosophy's broader egalitarianism. Ripstein, for instance, suggests that Kant "concedes that qualifications for voting can be consistent with a rightful condition, but require that each person be able to change from being a passive to an active citizen, precisely because such arrangements could not be made binding on individuals."[12] While this holds true for menial laborers and male children, it does little to redress women's inborn civil immaturity. Howard Williams claims that "Kant discusses the theory of the State at two levels," distinguishing the "philosophical idea" of republicanism (in which all citizens are active) from the "idea of the State as it effects actual states."[13] The radical egalitarianism of Kant's ideal republicanism is, then, tempered by a "pragmatic conservatism" regarding existing states. And yet, Kant's distinction between baseline rights (to freedom and equality) and active citizens' political rights (to law-giving) is elaborated at the theoretical level of pure principles of right, conceding nothing to actual political conditions. Williams also fails to ask *why* certain citizens shouldn't be enfranchised, accepting as unproblematic that "[b]eing in the employ of another person, in

Kant's view, automatically confers an inferior status upon an individual. The employee has, therefore, no right to claim the same freedom as is enjoyed by the full citizen."[14] Jacob Weinrib more directly addresses women's disenfranchisement, arguing that Kant revised his account of citizenship between "Theory and Practice" and the *Rechtslehre*, and that the mature formulation abandons naturalistic and conventional restrictions. An active citizen, Weinrib holds, is subject to the state's omnilateral will and not any person's private will, a condition accessible to all. "Although the women in Kant's own society lacked independence ... there is nothing about women *as such* that render them perpetually immature,"[15] as their passive citizenship "reflects a contingent fact rather than a natural deficiency."[16] And yet, Kant's purported shift between 1793 and 1797 is difficult to square with his 1798 claim that "[w]*oman* regardless of age is declared to be immature in civil matters; her husband is her natural curator ... women cannot personally defend their rights and pursue civil affairs for themselves."[17] The differentiations in Kant's account of citizenship are, then, not easily conformable to the principle of right's egalitarian pretensions.

While poorly defended, Kant's argument is not uncommon. Dependent citizens are politically unreliable, the story goes, both because of their susceptibility to their benefactors' influence and because reliance breeds self-interest. They are far more likely to employ public means for private ends than active citizens, whose material independence eliminates bad incentives and enables public-mindedness. And yet, these arguments from persuasion and privation miss Kant's broader view of the deficits incurred by dependency, which ultimately concern the exercise of the understanding. Dependency creates a cognitive problem: women and the poor are unable to cultivate the political judgment sustaining a progressive, republican polity. I begin by examining the poorer classes' circumstantial shortcomings before considering the more entrenched naturalistic ones attributed to women.

3.1.2 Self-Mastery, Non-Mastery and Political Judgment

Much of the commentary treats Kant's property qualification in strictly material terms, as an "economic proviso"[18] that "excludes all but property holders"[19] from full citizenship on the basis of some version of the argument(s) from privation and/or persuasion. Yet property is in fact ancillary to independence/self-mastery. Full, active citizenship, Kant argues, requires "*being one's own master (sui iuris)*, hence having some property (and any art, craft, fine art or science can be counted as property) that supports him – that is, if he must acquire from others in order to live, he does so only by *alienating* what *is his* and not by giving others permission to make use of his powers."[20] Through a rather idiosyncratic taxonomy, Kant designates (in "Theory and Practice") domestic servants, shop clerks, day laborers and barbers as "mere *operarii* ... not qualified to be citizens,"[21] along with (in the *Rechtslehre*) apprentices, woodcutters, Indian blacksmiths, private tutors and tenant farmers – "mere underlings of the commonwealth."[22] These he distinguishes from tailors, wigmakers, artists and craftsmen, European carpenters, school teachers and leasehold farmers, endowed with the "property" required for civil personality.

As Kant himself concedes that it is "somewhat difficult to determine what is required in order to be able to claim the rank of a human being who is his own master,"[23] self-mastery does not appear straightforwardly indexed to wealth or fungible property, as the argument from privation would suggest. It rather concerns the life-activities through which we sustain ourselves: skills in particular arts, trades and crafts, for example, comprise relevant types of property. Kant thus conceptualizes property in relation to the faculties we employ to set our ends and meet our needs, rather than in explicitly material terms. It concerns how we go about living our lives, and not how comfortable or deprived that life might be. What's important about property is not that it alleviates our susceptibility to private interests (our own or others'), but that it reflects a capacity to set ends and maintain one's "preservation in existence"[24] through purposive, self-directed action. The relevant distinction, then, is between persons who sustain themselves by alienating what's theirs (their property) and those that do so by selling a general permission to use their capacities. Where the carpenter exercises self-mastery "in pursuing his trade, thus exchang[ing] his property with another," the servile laborer "[grants] the use of his powers ... to another."[25]

Kant's self-master retains control over the choice of his actions, and property is the endowment that enables him to do so. The non-master's lack of property, conversely, forces him to relinquish the capability for self-direction altogether by contracting out the use of his abilities, which are determined by another person.[26] Both alienate something that belongs to them, but while the active citizen exchanges his own property – be it skill-based or material – the non-master trades his power for self-chosen, purposive activity, the power to set and pursue his own ends. As a result, he fails to develop the skills, aptitudes and habits of judgment entailed by autonomous, self-directed action. As shown in Chapter 2, Kant understands the capacity to set ends of all kinds – technical, pragmatic and moral – as subject to formation. By alienating that capacity, non-masters experience deficits in the *exercise* of certain cognitions that constrain their civic capacities:

An understanding that is in itself sound (without mental deficiency) can still be accompanied by deficiencies with regard to its exercise, deficiencies that necessitate either a *postponement* until the growth to proper maturity, or even in the *representation* of one's person through that of another in regards to matters of a civil nature. The (natural or legal) incapacity of an otherwise sound human being to use his *own* understanding in civil affairs is called *immaturity*. If this is based on immaturity of age, then it is called *nonage* (being a minor); but if it rests on legal arrangements with regard to civil affairs, it can then be called *legal* or *civil* immaturity.[27]

Non-masters' shortcomings are, then, failures of practice. Their life-activity compels them to abandon the power to seek their own ends, stunting the development of skills demanded by an active civic life.

This is, ultimately, a problem of judgment. In the *Anthropology*, Kant sketches out the three divisions of the higher cognitive faculty: understanding[28] (a general ability to identify and follow rules), judgment (applying general rules to particular cases) and reason ("deriving the particular from the universal"[29]). "*Correct* understanding, *practiced* judgment, and *thorough* reason," he maintains, are required for "competence in promoting ends"[30] generally. But more narrowly, each of these cognitive powers' distinctive qualities lends itself to particular usages:

> The domestic or civil servant under express orders needs only to have understanding. The officer, to whom only the general rule is prescribed for his entrusted tasks, and who is then left alone to decide for himself what to do in cases that come up, needs judgment. The general, who has to judge all possible cases and has to think out the rules for himself, must possess reason – The talents necessary for these different dispositions are very distinct.[31]

While understanding (in the narrow sense) enables us to recognize and follow rules, judgment designates the capacity to fix a particular course of action in light of general principles. And, importantly, whereas "understanding can be enriched through instruction with many concepts and furnished with rules ... *the power of judgment* (*iudicium*) – cannot be *instructed*, but only exercised. That is why its growth is called *maturity*, and its understanding that which comes only with years."[32] This gets to the heart of non-masters' cognitive, and ensuing civil, shortcomings. The faculty of judgment only develops through the *use* of our end-setting capacities, honed and cultivated through practical experience, and this is the very power that non-masters relinquish to sustain themselves. The cognitive deficits at the root of their civil immaturity stem from their inability to determine themselves in their everyday lives; by permitting others to use their powers for their own purposes, non-masters have no opportunity for self-direction. Their life-activity employs little more than their basic understanding, and so fails to cultivate the ability to decide what to do as a matter of principle under given circumstances.

And *this* is a political problem. An active political life requires neither the understanding's rule-following nor reason's universalism, but rather judgment in determining how to realize general principles (of civil freedom, equality and right) in particular institutional contexts. It requires the capacity to evaluate the laws best suited to formalizing civic ideals in given circumstances – as Kant describes it, "the power of judgment[,] the faculty of discovering the particular in so far as it is an instance of these rules."[33] Passive citizens lack the maturity, fostered by active citizens' life-activity, on which sound political judgment depends. This ability to think in the place of others and assess "whether something is an instance of the rule or not"[34] is a minimal condition for the exercise of political rights. While he wouldn't elaborate his fuller system of right for another decade, Kant drew the connection between judgment and civic competence as early as 1784/5:

> Jurists need excellent power of judgment, for there can be fewer *casus in terminis* and more *casus discretivi*, that is, the law contains fewer cases according to the letter and more according to the spirit. Even when someone has the theory, he can still lack the *praxis*, and very often it is missing in the beginning until one has first exercised his power of judgment.[35]

For jurists as for citizens, civic fitness turns on the cultivation of measured political judgment.

This capability is the lynchpin of republican states in particular, which solicit the active engagement of their citizenries. Where despotic governments perpetuate their citizens' immaturity by "representing the danger of making use of one's *own* understanding without the guidance of another as very great, even lethal,"[36] republics foster and rest on the exercise of citizens' political judgment, informally (though public reason) and formally (through law-giving and voting). Beyond entrenching the "right to manage the state itself as *active* members of it, [and] the right to organize it or to cooperate for introducing certain laws,"[37] republics invite citizens to discuss public affairs and exercise their critical faculties.[38] The viability of republican institutions, then, turns on the exercise of sound political judgment honed through the purposive, end-setting activity that non-masters relinquish. Given this, Kant's distinction between active and passive citizens becomes clearer.[39] If the success of republican public life turns on the populace's civic aptitude, passive citizens' failures of judgment unravel the conditions for right. They also by implication threaten the advancing moralization to which, as shown in Chapter 2, republics contribute.

While these cognitive constraints certainly trouble Kant's liberalism, they clearly comprise circumstantial rather than inborn deficiencies. Under republican institutions, Kant assures, "anyone can work his way up from this passive condition to an active one."[40] Domestics, day laborers, tenant farmers and Indian blacksmiths may well raise themselves out of immaturity. Women, on the other hand, face an entirely different prospect.

3.2   POLITICAL EXCLUSION, MORAL EXCLUSION

3.2.1   What Nature Makes of Her

Why *exactly* does Kant treat women as perpetually stunted in civil affairs? Much of the commentary lands on a truth that's hard to avoid: Kant was a product of his time and shared in many of its less palatable views. While undoubtedly true, this doesn't tell us much: if prejudice serves as a sufficient explanation, there's little reason to consider precisely why Kant saw women as politically incapable. The deeper problem, I want to suggest, is only visible when we examine the theoretical framework surrounding Kant's understanding of women's nature. We need, then, to turn back to the historical-teleological perspective fleshed out in Chapter 2, through which Kant conceptualizes women's character, virtues and ends.

While Kant's views on women are most fully elaborated in the 1798 *Anthropology*, they are traceable through his lectures on anthropology in the 1770s–1780s, and still further back, to 1764, with his *Observations on the Feeling of the Beautiful and Sublime*. Their substance and teleological framing remain remarkably consistent over this thirty-year span: from his earliest reflections on the subject, Kant casts women's nature in relation to humanity's moral advancement. Women play an instrumental role in furthering civilization, he argues, by curbing the barbaric urges to which men are naturally prone and which inhibit the development of their rational faculties. Women's qualities – docility, vanity, loquacity, coquettishness – are providentially instilled to enable them to manipulate and exercise some measure of control over men, despite their weaker physical constitution. In so doing, women bring about the refinements of a morally progressive culture, distinguished by its distance from our primeval crudity. Such civilizations further moral progress by making "great headway against the tyranny of man's propensity to the senses, and so prepare him for a sovereignty in which reason alone is to dominate."[41]

But this invites us to wonder *why* women might be inclined to advance such a culture at all. Kant argues that women's particular attributes – their virtues and character – only become expressible in civilized contexts, impelling them to bring those contexts about. Feminine qualities, he observes, remain latent in savage societies, effectively depriving women of their measure of social power. In savage nations, "the woman is a domestic animal";[42] women are treated as property under a "barbaric civil constitution"[43] whose rule by force is indifferent to the feminine characteristics comprising women's tools of social control. "In the crude state of nature," Kant asserts, "one can no more recognize these features ... culture does not introduce these feminine qualities, it only allows them to develop and become recognizable."[44] Refined social conditions generate a responsiveness to forms of compulsion beyond mere force; women are thus inclined to push men toward the civilized contexts within which their qualities translate into social power. A wise and providential nature motivates women to advance the civilization in which their particular character can flourish, drawing the species to higher stages of moral development.

Like much of his writing on humanity's empirical character, Kant's account of men's and women's natures is inconsistent and morally ambiguous. While gender should by his own reckoning be morally irrelevant, Kant persistently treats women's character and virtues in ethical terms, and in relation to humanity's moralization. Still more directly, he draws substantive distinctions between women's and men's ends and cognitive capacities, which clearly bear on their moral standing. In the *Anthropology Mrongovius*, he describes "the character of the sexes" as belonging to "the moral character of the human being itself, where I consider him as a free being," rather than to "what is characteristic of the human being, where I consider the human being as a product of nature."[45] Women's character, then, and gender relations more generally, comprise a particularly murky area in the ostensibly strict division between humanity's moral and sensible features.

As a result, Kant's treatments of gender frequently lapse, as Robert Louden observes, between observational and normative claims.[46] Women's and men's character and virtues are qualitatively distinct: while men's character aims at the sublime, women's is – and ought to be – gauged by the standard of the beautiful.[47] Both sexes participate in humanity's moral development, but differently, through the gender-specific virtues comprising their proper points of reference. "Feminine virtue or lack of virtue," Kant maintains, "is very different from masculine virtue or lack of virtue, not only in kind but also as regards incentive."[48] Kant's panoply of gendered virtues is not unpredictable: women's nature is patient, sensitive and driven by a desire for domination, where men are sensible, tolerant and better suited to govern. But more significant is the *character* standing as the measure of both genders' moral perfection:

in a woman all other merits should only be united so as to emphasize the character of the beautiful, which is the proper point of reference, while by contrast among the male qualities the sublime should clearly stand out as the criterion of his kind. To this must refer all judgments of these two genders, those of praise as well as those of blame. All education and instruction must keep this before it, and likewise all effort to promote the ethical perfection of the one or the other, unless one would make unrecognizable the charming difference that nature sought to establish between the two human genders.[49]

Kant here toes the line between descriptions accounting for each sex's natural attributes and normative imperatives: men and women *ought* to develop the character and virtues advancing their distinctive ethical perfections.

In this normative guise – pertaining to the character toward which each sex should strive, and to the education forming it – Kant clearly wanders onto moral turf. As shown in Chapter 2, we develop a receptivity to our moral obligations through cultivation and learning, as the "outcome of an extensive educational process."[50] This process is, however, differentiated according to women's and men's particular natures. Educating women to masculine virtues, or vice versa, orients them toward the wrong ends, detracting from humanity's moral-historical progress. In the *Anthropology Friedländer*, Kant distinguishes nature's "two aims ... with regard to the two sexes": the propagation and preservation of the species (the end of our animal inclinations), and "[t]he greatest social union and the most perfect state of society" (the end of our rational capacities). The latter, he contends, "does not happen other than through inclination, therefore by means of women."[51] Given their distinctive nature and particular role in advancing our moral perfection, "the education of women . . . must be of a completely different kind than that of the masculine sex. With regard to morality, the instruction must be completely different."[52] Where men's education fosters a capacity for principled action, women "are incapable of these principles, [so] the whole of morality must be presented from the point of view of honor."[53]

While the *Friedländer* notes (1775–1776) predate Kant's critical turn, the *Mrongovius* (1784–1785) reiterate the same differentiation: "good character does not originate from nature, but must be acquired. The acquisition of character includes: I. education – for males it must rest on principles, for females, on honor."[54] Both effeminate, coquettish men and intellectually driven women fail to actualize their particular character, measured by the gender-appropriate standard. "Laborious learning or painful pondering," for instance, "even if a woman should greatly succeed in it, destroy the merits that are proper to her sex"[55] by detracting from the beautiful character stimulating men's moral, and not just animal, dispositions. Kant here distinguishes men's coarse sexual desires from those grounded in a "finer taste," responding to women's moral qualities. The moralization of men's desire – from sexual possession to moral inclination – depends on women cultivating a specifically *beautiful* character; its masculinization through "laborious learning" undermines men's moral impulsions toward them.[56] Kant similarly chides preening, fastidious men whose propensities for the beautiful pull away from a rational character, properly awed by the sublimity of the moral law.

Each sex thus partakes in moral life and moral advancement through its particular character and virtues. Still more problematically, gendered differentiations extend to women's and men's cognitive capacities. "The fair sex has just as much understanding as the male," Kant maintains, "but it is a *beautiful understanding*, whereas ours should be a *deep understanding*, an expression that signifies identity with the sublime."[57] The sublimity of men's character lies in its capacity for properly moral action, the principled fulfillment of the moral duties incumbent on all rational beings. The beauty in women's character, conversely, awakens the moral feeling in men, arousing the virtuous disposition attuning them to their moral obligations. Given that "[t]here is a specific difference between the corresponding properties that we attribute to the male and female sexes," Kant tells us, "completely different standards are to be assumed for the male and female understanding."[58] Where men's understanding lends itself to directly moral purposes, women's moral nature is realized by acting on and through the natural inclinations that refine and civilize men. Women "cultivate the taste of the male sex, but do not cultivate it themselves."[59] Men's understanding and "the understanding which [women] can attain according to their nature"[60] are thus substantively different.

Women's nature is, then, only comprehensible from the teleological perspective, in light of their role shepherding men from crude animality to the civilized cultures enabling their rational efflorescence. For Kant, Holly Wilson observes, "[t]he proper nature of the female sex is civilization itself."[61] Women participate in moral life indirectly, by stimulating the moral feeling rather than acting from moral principle. A woman's "philosophy is not to reason," in Kant's view, "but to sense. In the opportunity that one wants to give to women to cultivate their beautiful nature, one must always keep this relation before his eyes."[62] Women's and men's virtues, character, and understanding are measured by the beautiful and sublime benchmarks mediating our moral existence and comportments; we exercise our moral perfections by acting on the qualities appropriate to our gender.[63] For men, a sublime character is noble, rational and principled, set by and aligned toward the moral law. For women, the "moral expression of the sublime"[64] is articulated through their beautiful character, and in relation to nature's ultimate end – humanity's moralization. "The female sex," as Kant most succinctly captures it, "is for the cultivation of the male sex."[65]

3.2.2 Three Kinds of Wrong: Masculinism, Moral Ends and Teleology

Feminist scholars have drawn out several challenges that Kant's treatment of women present for his moral and political thought.[66] To begin with, his account of gender is in the simplest and most banal way entirely androcentric, pervaded by a masculinist bias that directly and indirectly relegates women to a subordinate status. He adopts and even furthers the worst tropes of his era by characterizing women as incapable of principled action, intellectually deficient, unable to govern themselves and beholden to their emotions. His assessment of women's cognitive capacities is persistently unclear and often contradictory, and appears to share Aristotle's view that "the female indeed possesses [reason], but in a form which remains inconclusive."[67] While we can't fault Aristotle for failing to jump over Rhodes, Kant lived in an age of Enlightenment which he self-consciously sought to advance. As Robin May Schott and Susan Moller Okin point out, the inequities in his treatment of women are all the more glaring in light of his otherwise steadfast, principled egalitarianism.[68] This is no merely presentist critique: Kant's conservatism, while prevalent, was by no means unchallenged in his day by figures such as Condorcet, Wieland and Hippel. Kant not only resisted his contemporaries' efforts to recognize women as political equals, but actively opposed them by entrenching their subservience in a naturalized account of gendered virtues. By the end of the eighteenth century, John Zammito observes, "women's rights had already become a matter of public debate ... Kant cannot be excused on the grounds of anachronism."[69]

That androcentrism also works its way into the underpinnings of his thought. Drawing on Carol Gilligan's critique of Kohlberg, Sally Sedgwick exposes the narrowness of Kant's atomistic view of moral personhood, observing that "female identity development essentially involves community rather than detachment."[70] Kant's account of moral action neglects the social embeddedness and affective interactivity of human agency, which Gilligan and Sedgwick associate with female identity formation. His ideal of moral autonomy thus privileges an especially masculine perspective that disregards the distinctive features of women's experiences. Jean Bethke Elshtain similarly traces that masculinism in his moral philosophy's abstract universalism, as noumenal freedom's divorce from the phenomenal world "cannot begin to get at the complexities of women's embodied experiences."[71] Women's purported subjection to emotion makes them, still further, "a suspect category within a Kantian framework";[72] Kant's mistrust of the emotions, Elshtain suggests, is indirectly transferred on to women themselves.

A second set of problems concerns women's ends. Human autonomy and intelligible freedom turn on our capacity, as rational beings, to set unconditioned ends, on our unique ability to transcend the causal chains binding all natural creatures to phenomenality through the will's self-determination. Our highest end, then, lies in the capacity to set our *own* ends. Women's highest end, however – their natural end – lies not in their own autonomous self-government, but in the mediate moral goal of drawing humanity toward its realization. "One can only come to the characterization of this sex," Kant stipulates, "if one uses as one's principle not what we *make* our end, but what *nature's end* was in establishing womankind ... These ends are: 1) the preservation of the species, 2) the cultivation of society and its refinement by womankind."[73] Where men's freedom inheres in the capacity to set ends independently of natural causality, women's ends are derived from, and fixed by, nature's own design. Kant measures women's character in relation to the *functional* goal of advancing the species' moralization, teleological history's ever-receding endpoint, rather than by their own moral capabilities. As Jean P. Rumsey notes, "Kant's primary reason for holding that women are morally immature is that their own purposes are co-opted by nature's. Unlike men ... women must serve nature's purposes."[74] "[T]he principle for characterizing woman," Kant himself states still more directly, is "a principle which does not depend on our choice but on a higher purpose for the human race."[75] Rather than partaking in the autonomous end-setting characterizing free agency, then, women appear beholden to the ends that nature sets them.

Finally – and, in my view, most problematically – women's incapacity for self-determination is inseparable from, and not incidental to, Kant's teleological framework. Humanity's moral advancement *requires* that women cultivate a character that undermines their moral capacities. Of course, Kant tries to fence teleological claims off from determinative ones by maintaining that "these principles pertain merely to reflective judgment: they do not determine the actual [*an sich*] origin of these beings."[76] But the segregation is untenable: his conceptualizations of moral agency and moral development *depend* on the cultured civilization that women bring about, such that we cannot understand ourselves as progressive beings outside of this framework. This is why his account of women's nature persistently slips from the reflective judgments to which he claims to confine them to the normative imperatives through which, more often than not, they issue. Far from merely observing their character, Kant exhorts women to develop the beautiful qualities realizing, in his words, their ethical perfection – qualities that directly detract from their capacities as autonomous, end-setting beings. To put it simply, the character that makes women good from the *teleological* perspective is precisely what makes them bad by the *transcendental* standards of moral agency. The beautiful virtues realizing the sublimity of their character are diametrically opposed to those demanded of rational, self-governing agents. Women participate in moral life through the beautiful qualities drawing men into affective and sexual partnership, softening the edges of their barbarism and so advancing human progress. Their virtues appeal to (and draw on) inclinations and emotions, rather than the faculty of reason, whose cultivation in fact deforms women's character and detracts from their naturally given ends. Humanity's moralization hinges on women's capacity to awaken moral impulses and nudge the species toward its moral end.

Commentators have responded to the teleological framework undergirding Kant's view of women in a few ways. Robert Louden, for instance, regards it as a regrettable deviation from Kant's otherwise strict moral egalitarianism, criticizing his elision of physical and moral character, his indulging in a "naïve teleologism," and his easy acceptance of his era's prejudices.[77] And yet, Louden remains inconclusive with respect to these lapses' implications for Kant's ethics, vacillating between bracketing his views on women as aberrations from his moral theory, on one hand, and suggesting that Kant perceives women "as still being in a state of *Unmundigkeit*: they do not yet have the courage to use their own reason,"[78] on the other. Neither approach is entirely convincing. As I have argued in this chapter and in Chapter 2 – following Louden's own view – Kant's teleological developmentalism belongs to a full account of human moral agency and so cannot be isolated from his ethics. And given that women's "immaturity" is anchored in their character, there's little to suggest their ever outgrowing this "state of *Unmundigkeit*."

Rather more directly, Jean P. Rumsey recognizes that "Kant's teleological arguments about the contribution of women to the civilizing and thus the moralizing of the race are basically contrary to Kantian tenets,"[79] but suggests that "this apparent inconsistency vanishes when one takes a broader perspective which includes Kant's theory of character."[80] Rumsey argues that women's "civilizing" function produces the very conditions in which they can flourish as moral agents. Kant's view of women, then, pertains to their role in this moralizing process; he does not deny women's "fundamental moral capacity," but rather explains "why she is unable to develop it properly, because of her function."[81] While he appears to disallow women's moral abilities, Kant is in fact preoccupied with the circumstances under which "women would then find it possible to develop their latent but undeniable moral capacities."[82] Rumsey thus falls back on a version of Louden's argument from maturity: the world's state of imperfection requires women to adopt a temporarily "functional" character to bring about the conditions enabling their full moral development. But not only does this treat existing women as means for the realization of future others – untenable from a moral standpoint – it also runs into Louden's problems. First, women's character is natural and permanent; nothing in Kant's accounts suggests their ever transcending its "beautiful" defects to cultivate a properly "sublime" understanding. Second, such a future end-state – the state of maturity in which women would shed their functional role and realize their moral potential – appears unattainable, a regulative, not objective, end. Unless and until we transcend our corporeal imperfections, human beings remain destined for immaturity.

Holly Wilson addresses women and teleology in the context of Kant's much-maligned thoughts on marriage. While nature bestows certain physical advantages on men, she contends, women enjoy a developmental advantage through their ability to manipulate men's impulses. Marriage thus unites the sexes in a relation of approximate reciprocity through which gendered differences balance each other out, generating an "equality of agency"[83] between them. But this treats these differences as essentially equivalent, neglecting the moral asymmetries between men's and women's characters. Women's "developmental advantages," as we have seen, in fact *detract* from their capacities as moral agents. Their virtues are neither morally benign nor equal to men's, as the character ostensibly empowering women in the context of marriage also renders them morally defective. The "equivalence of inequalities" that marriage is claimed to achieve papers over those inequalities' moral non-equivalence.

Women's civil immaturity is, then, epiphenomenal: their political shortcomings are rooted in deeper deficiencies concerning their moral standing. Their exclusion from political life isn't reducible to Kant's prejudices (though these are clearly at work as well), but rather points to a substantive moral problem stemming from their function in humanity's progress: women are agents of moralization, not moral agents. Beyond the evident moral infraction in treating them as means rather than ends, this also attributes them virtues undermining their capacities as moral agents. Theirs is to sense, Kant reminds us, and not to reason. Women's moral realization lies not in their *own* end-setting capacities but in drawing humanity toward *its* natural ends. Their nature thus sits at the uneasy juncture of Kant's transcendental account of rational agency and teleological account of human development.

And here, we might consider a final objection, limned but undeveloped above: that my view is insufficiently attentive to the *reflective* status of teleological judgments. As mere postulates of reflection, the objection goes, teleological principles enable us to interpret the world and make (conjectural) sense of human progress, but have no place in the normative construction of our moral duties. They tell us how beings of our kind might understand ourselves, but not how we ought to act.

Yet, as we've seen, Kant's assessments of women's character and virtues consistently burst the banks of reflective judgments and spill into normative ones. They extend well beyond what might reasonably be construed as postulates of reflection: women's nature, their "ethical perfection," *compels* them to cultivate the beautiful character driving humanity's moral development. This doesn't just make sense of women's naturally occurring attributes, as a strictly reflective teleology might, but rather belongs to a prescriptive, gendered account of human – and not just rational – nature. What makes us human is precisely the imperfection that women are bound to ameliorate. Strange though it is to suggest, an objective teleology might be less problematic: we might then, with Louden and Rumsey, interpret Kant as pinning women's (temporary) ethical and political nonage on humanity's current state of imperfection. But this is unwarranted on two fronts. First, it clearly is *not* Kant's view: "*Woman* regardless of age is declared to be immature in civil matters"[84] due to a permanent "incapacity" in her understanding. As John Zammito observes, for Kant, "women have no true moral personhood ... they are perpetual minors, *unmündig* by nature."[85] Second, as constitutionally phenomenal moral agents, we are by our very nature destined for perpetual immaturity. At no point will we transcend the corporeal limitations making us the kind of beings that we are. It is, then, difficult to envision a state in which women might shed their natural/functional character and gain ethical and political maturity.

And so we come to see the depth of the problem. The problem, ultimately, is that teleology belongs to a full human ethics. Kant's account of women's beautiful character is not an addendum to an independent, transcendental moral philosophy. It is, rather inextricable from his understanding of humanity's moralization. We cannot isolate the teleological from the transcendental if the teleological comprises a qualifying condition for the ethical development of our kind of being. "If we lift Kant's concept of the person out of his system," Anthony J. La Vopa asks, "what gives it philosophical cogency?"[86] This strikes me as fundamentally correct. We cannot excise Kant's view of human agency, of women, and of our morally progressive nature from an otherwise strictly rational ethics; our impurities shape our moral nature. Women aren't, then, incidentally marginalized or even intentionally denigrated by Kant's schema. They rather belong – in the worst sense of the word – to a teleological account of humanity's moralization.

Arthur Ripstein finds the essence of Kant's political philosophy in the ideal of self-mastery, that none should be subordinated to the choice of others. And yet, it's difficult to reconcile this guiding intuition with Kant's steadfast insistence that women *should* be subordinated to the choice of others, and in perpetuity. While the unpropertied retain the capacity to work themselves up to active citizenship, women's civil deficits points to a deeper problem, and to deeper questions concerning Kant's liberalism. How are we to conceptualize the moral status of agents who, despite sharing in humanity's inalienable dignity, are unable to develop the capacities in which that dignity inheres? What are the consequences of the slippage between transcendentally derived moral equality and the anthropological account of our progress – or failure to progress – toward it? How, in a word, should we understand the moral standing of persons unable to cultivate the dispositions sustaining the fulfillment of our moral vocation?

These are, ultimately, questions that emerge from the intersection of Kant's critical and anthropological philosophies, and that are most clearly drawn into focus in his treatments of race, culture and the non-European world.

3.3 MORAL EXCLUSION

Kant's principled myopia to the heteronomous features of human life – race, class, gender, culture – is central to his moral (and to a lesser degree, political) egalitarianism. The appeal of Kant's ethics and politics lies precisely in the willful neglect of those markers that might qualify their universalism: our dignity anchors inalienable rights to which all rational, end-setting beings are entitled.

A closer examination, however, yields a rather different story. Kant is less than consistent in differentiating pure principles of ethics and right from their empirical and anthropological conditions of realization. The ostensibly extraneous facts of human variability – poorer classes' failures of judgment, women's immaturity – work their way up into the formulation of those principles (in, for instance, the property qualification distinguishing active citizenship), and down into their application (in qualifying women's civil status). The difference-blind egalitarianism that we might have celebrated is, then, tethered to a certain reading of his ethical and political commitments. Kant's liberalism is far from exhausted, or even captured, by the *Rechtslehre*'s and *Tugendlehre*'s treatments of our rights and duties, as rational agents. And when we descend from the Archimedean perch, the foundations of that liberalism grow murkier. From the transcendental standpoint, we all share in an incontrovertible dignity, we all stand to participate in political life, and we all enjoy the capacity to set and pursue our own ends. And yet, that dignity inheres in a rational faculty that we are bound to cultivate (and that we can fail to cultivate); most human beings suffer from "deficits of understanding" that constrain, temporarily or permanently, their political rights; and the conditions developing our end-setting powers appear far from universal (recall the Tahitians). These limitations are perhaps most pronounced, and most problematic, in Kant's views on race.

3.3.1 Race: The Genesis of an Idea

While Kant's treatments of race are scattered across his writings on anthropology, history, natural science and physical geography, his racial theory is most clearly elaborated in three essays spanning a little over a decade: "Of the Different Races of Human Beings" (1775/1777), "Determination of the Concept of a Human Race" (1785) and "On the Use of Teleological Principles in Philosophy" (1788). These lay out the central pillars of his racial theory, but don't entirely capture his conceptualization of human difference. Kant's fuller views on race and diversity are best understood in light of their development, from a patchwork of unsubstantiated bigotries to a fully articulated and conceptually robust account of human variation in relation to natural purposiveness. In this section, I draw on several iterations of his lectures on anthropology to fill the spaces between these essays and trace the progression of the substantive, structural and methodological-epistemological facets of Kant's racial theory.[87] I then turn, in the next two sections (3.3.2 and 3.3.3), to its contents and consequences.

While Kant's thoughts on race date back to the 1750s, *Observations on the Feeling of the Beautiful and Sublime* (1764) contains the first relevant published account – relevant because, as John Zammito notes, *Observations* outlines roughly the basic structure and some of the substantive content that the lectures on anthropology would adopt over the next three decades.[88] Race falls into *Observations*' final section, treating the character of the human species (what would become the "Anthropological Characteristic" in the better developed anthropology of the 1780s–1790s). At this point, Kant divides the investigation into the character of human beings "in general," the character of the sexes and the character of the world's nations. These early views on race are, quite simply, riddled with baseless and uncritical prejudices. On Hume's authority, for example, Kant infamously declares that

Negroes of Africa have by nature no feeling that rises above the ridiculous ... while among the whites there are always those who rise up from the lowest rabble and through extraordinary gifts earn respect in the world. So essential is the difference between these two human kinds, and it seems to be just as great with regard to the capacities of mind as it is with respect to color.[89]

Kant's views are at this point more indicative than any kind of racial theory. While his substantive assessment of Africans' capacities would in later years vary unfortunately little, the conceptual apparatus through which he would come to make sense of them as a racial type is here absent. Several important elements of his mature account are missing. First, he fails to distinguish the morally irrelevant character of nations (by which he designates Europeans, principally differentiated through non-hereditary temperamental variations) from the character of races that, despite ambiguities, consistently carries moral weight. From the mid-1770s on, this distinction would shape his anthropology (and racial theory). Second, he does not clearly separate moral and physical-empirical character. While noting that the "characters of mind of the peoples are most evident in that in them which is moral" (2:245), Kant's "observations" frequently confound the moral and empirical attributes whose divorce would structure the critical project. Finally, he has as yet to develop the teleological framework enabling us to comprehend racial difference. *Observations*' treatment of racial character is, then, less a racial theory than a disjointed set of unreflective cogitations. This desultoriness held into the early 1770s: both the *Collins* and *Parow* (1772–1773) notes share in the *Observations*' lack of systematicity, and neither appears particularly concerned with race or national character.

Kant's race-thinking gains greater coherence as of the mid-1770s – not surprisingly, following the 1772–1773 split of his lecture course into physical geography and anthropology and subsequent publication, in 1775, of "Of the Different Races of Human Beings."[90] Given that this essay comprised the course announcement for his summer lectures on physical geography, race would appear to fall under its purview. And yet, its final paragraph distinguishes between the "cosmological" study of "*nature* and the *human being* ... the first instruction [being] *physical geography* ... the second one I call *anthropology*";[91] in this case, race belongs to the study of anthropology. While Kant's understanding of race begins to adopt a more systematic form – the subject of anthropology, the pragmatic examination of human nature – these kinds of ambivalences remain at this early stage. Important conceptual elements of his racial theory – specifically, his account of racial predispositions (*Anlagen*) and germs (*Keime*) – are similarly discernible in a nascent form in the 1775–1776 *Friedländer* lectures on anthropology (rather than geography; race appears to have decisively migrated from geography to anthropology by 1776). "Innate to human nature," Kant holds, "are germs which develop and can achieve the perfection for which they are determined"; even the "savage Indian or Greenlander" has

the same germs as a civilized human being, only they are not yet developed. We equally have reason to believe that there are germs for greater perfection innate to human nature, which could well be developed, and [that] humanity must achieve the degree of perfection for which it is determined, and for which it has the germs within itself.[92]

While unrefined, Kant introduces the theoretical apparatus framing race (innate "germs" whose efflorescence develops the four human races), the philosophical basis for monogenism (the shared presence of identical germs, *in potentia*, in all human beings), and the ideal of human perfection anchoring his teleological developmentalism. He also advances one of the racial theory's central claims: that racial traits are innate, unfailingly hereditary characteristics activated by climate.[93] "[T]hrough long duration, through climate and other causes," nations "in the end receiv[e] a unique ingrained constitution," a "determination of the character [that] must not be taken from contingent matters ... [but] rather ... hereditary peculiarity."[94]

Despite inconsistencies, then, Kant's views on race begin to adopt a more systematic organization by the mid-1770s. We can discern, in embryonic form: (1) his categorization of race/nation (still undistinguished at this point) under the anthropology's treatment of the character of nations, one of the 3–6 divisions (depending on the year) structuring what would become the "Anthropological Characteristic"; (2) his account of the germs and predispositions dividing humanity into four distinctive races (American/ Kalmuckian, Negro, Hindustani and White); and (3) the teleological viewpoint that would become instrumental for understanding human diversity and racial differentiation. The central structural, substantive and methodological-epistemological elements of Kant's mature racial theory thus begin to take shape at this point, and coalesce in the 1775/1777 "Of the Differences Races of Human Beings." Of these elements, the last is undoubtedly the most significant: it's at this point (and in this essay) that the teleological framework surrounding Kant's racial theory begins to take a firmer shape, which he would develop in the distinction between "natural history" and a "description of nature" in the two essays of the 1780s. "The discovery worth announcing in 1775," Jennifer Mensch observes, was "an increasing sense on Kant's part of the positive explanatory role that could be played by teleology in the search for a rationally unified order."[95] The 1777–1778 *Pillau* lectures' ruminations on "what kinds of germs lie hidden in the soul of the human being" and on the "predispositions for morality that lie in human nature"[96] – germs and predispositions whose development Kant explores in different races/ peoples, and in relation to "the vocation of human nature"[97] – further substantiate this temporalization. The mid-1770s thus mark the beginning point of Kant's considered thoughts on race, even if they remain at this point inchoate and riddled with irregularities.

In the early 1780s, as we enter into the critical period, they become sharpened in a few distinctive ways. In *Menschenkunde* (1781–1782), Kant distinguishes between the "physical" and "moral" causes leading to "[t]he variety of natural gifts among the many diverse nations [which] cannot be explained entirely by incidental causes, but must lie in the nature of the human being himself,"[98] disentangling the moral and strictly physical-empirical facets of pragmatic anthropology. This also marks a more explicit, if still inconsistent, treatment of racial character's moral features. A second shift accentuates these changes: following his regular appraisal of European nations' characters (the gallant Frenchman, the disciplined German, the lazy Spaniard, the witty Briton and so on), Kant declares that "[t]here are *Four Races on Earth*,"[99] decisively demarcating Europeans' contingent national variations from inborn racial characteristics. In the 1780s, then, he starts to pull apart national character (defined in terms of mutable, non-hereditary temperamental dispositions, carrying no moral value, and having no explanatory function in a teleological natural history) and racial character (defined in terms of immutable hereditary attributes, some endowed with a moral weight, and central to his account of humanity's moralization).[100]

By the mid-critical period, Kant firms up much of the structure and organization surrounding the racial theory, in large part responding to challenges from Herder and Forster.[101] In the *Anthropology Mrongovius* (1784–1785), he clearly separates "what is characteristic of the human being, where I consider the human being as a product of nature" (addressing natural aptitudes and temperaments) from "the moral character of the human being itself, where I consider him as a free being"[102] (treating the sexes, nations and species), reflecting the critical diremption of empirical and intelligible character. The division holds through the remainder of the 1780s and 1790s, to the 1798 publication of the *Anthropology* (and, presumably, to the end of Kant's life). In 1785, Kant also published his second essay on race, "Determination of the Concept of a Human Race," in the *Berlinische Monatsschrift*. Beyond skewering Herder's philosophical history, the essay clarifies both the conceptual core of race (the unfailing heredity of given characteristics within and across variations in a single human species) and the methodological standpoint from which to make sense of it ("natural history"). Two of the essay's features are worth noting. First, Kant develops the teleological framework contextualizing race and further distinguishes it from a mere "description of nature" (I elaborate on this in section 3.3.2. "Race, Teology and Natural History"). Second, he holds that "those four differences in color are the *only ones* among all hereditary characters that are *unfailingly* hereditary"[103] – that skin color alone differentiates the different races.

However, by 1788, in "On the Use of Teleological Principles in Philosophy," the third and final essay on race, Kant's view appears realigned with its iterations from the 1770s. Far from remaining confined to skin color, racial characteristics concern a broad range of inborn capacities. The essay responds to Georg Forster's accusation that Kant's racial theory and natural history favor philosophical conjecture over ethnological observation by, essentially, doubling down – Kant deepens and strengthens the teleological framework. Beyond defending a monogenetic account of human origins against Forster's postulation of the Negro race's distinctive filiation, the essay expands on Kant's contention that race is only comprehensible in relation to a "*system of final causes.*"[104] While much of its substance – its assessments of the different races' capacities and characteristics – remains largely congruent with his "Of the Different Races" (1775), its teleological structure is, by 1788, much more pronounced, sophisticated and significant. Kant's later treatments of race are, then, neither cursory nor a merely a backward turn. They rather entrench the concept of race in a methodical and better-refined philosophical architectonic.

This chronological overview shows that while Kant's thoughts on race are traceable to *Observations* (and, still earlier, to the 1750s' lectures on physical geography), they remain relatively unformed until the mid-1770s. More importantly, they lack any kind of systematic organization. His observations on Negroes' indolence and Amerindians' stuntedness remain, at these early junctures, unreflective speculations, little more than what he would later describe as mechanistic "descriptions of nature." In the mid-1770s, he began developing the conceptual framework surrounding his mature theory of race, whose structure, substance and standpoint were expanded and honed during the 1780s. By the mid-late 1780s, Kant integrated them into a well-developed racial theory explaining human variation in relation to natural purposiveness; both published essays and lecture notes emphasize the teleological natural history through which race was comprehensible. We now turn to consider that racial theory's contents in some detail.

3.3.2 Race, Teleology and Natural History

Alongside Voltaire, Hume, Lord Kames, Platner, Meiners, Blumenbach and Buffon, Kant was among the eighteenth century's progenitors of an early natural science seeking to develop a systematic account of humanity's phyletic origins. Robert Bernasconi understands Kant's as the first full, modern typology of the human races.[105]

Kant turned his attention to the "science of man" and human biology after 1770, when he delved into the question of biological generation in the works of Maupertuis, Bonnet, Haller and Buffon.[106] His first essay on race, as we have seen, appeared in 1775, the same year that Johann Friedrich Blumenbach published his dissertation, *On the Natural Variety of Mankind*, another seminal text in the development of eighteenth-century race discourse.[107] Both Kant and Blumenbach aimed to respond to Lord Kames's *Sketches of the History of Man*, and more particularly, to refute its polygenism.[108] Kant drew on *"Buffon's* rule, that animals which produce fertile young with one another (whatever difference in shape there may be) still belong to one and the same physical species,"[109] to propose a monogenetic account of human origins. His racial theory sought a plausible and parsimonious explanation of humanity's shared origins despite our external differences. This analytical abstemiousness opposed the "opinion which needlessly multiplies the number of causes" that "many local creations would have to [assume]";[110] while conjectural, Kant's monogenism had "at least sufficient ground to counterbalance other conjectures which find the differences in the human species so incompatible that they rather assume on that account many local creations."[111]

Kant's theory instead identifies four races of human beings, descended from a single phyletic source: "1) the race of the *whites*, 2) the *Negro race*, 3) the *Hunnish* (Mongolian or Kalmuckian) race, 4) the Hindu or *Hindustani* race."[112] This original human being contained all four germs (*Keime*), each equipped with its own particular predispositions (*Anlagen*), from which the different races evolved. These "various germs and natural predispositions," Kant contends, "had to lie ready in him to be on occasion either unfolded or restrained, so that he would become suited to his place in the world and over the course of the generations would appear to be as it were native to and made for that place."[113] As human beings spread across the globe, climatic variations activated given germs in different populations, developing over time the racial character best suited to their particular environments. This character "takes root over a long series of generations in the same climate until it becomes a persistent race which preserves itself even if such a people afterward acquires new residences in milder regions."[114] Once a germ takes root, it becomes permanent, hereditary and exclusive, extinguishing the others and fixing a population's race. While climate-based explanations were a staple of eighteenth-century race theories, Kant's is distinctive in treating racial differentiation as permanent; once set, racial character becomes impervious to further changes through transplantation. Race is, then, irreversible. No "mixing of different races according to a certain proportion could restore still the shape of the human phylum."[115]

As John Zammito observes, Kant's racial theory is centrally preoccupied with limiting the moral and metaphysical excesses pervading the nascent sciences of man.[116] It aims not only to undercut the implied superiority of Europeans' distinctive filiation, but also to clarify the agencies and mechanisms of racial differentiation. For instance, he carefully distinguishes human beings' latent racial predispositions, endowed with a generative power, from the climatic and environmental triggers activating and extinguishing them. While external stimulants *actuate* a given inborn racial character, they have no generative capacity to produce or shape it. Racial character also does not itself capture the full breadth of human variation. While race describes *"the classificatory difference of the animals of one and the same phylum in so far as this difference is unfailingly hereditary,"*[117] Kant also addresses the "varieties," "sorts," "kinds" and "strains" capturing the endless contingent forms of human difference. While the phenotypical manifoldness of human varieties is propagated through interbreeding, environmental influences and a broad range of other conditions, however, race alone is inextinguishable once set. Kant thus draws a firm line between fixed racial characteristics and superficial dissimilarities attributable to external stimulus (such as tanned skin) or mutable hereditary traits (such as hair or eye color). Reflecting this growing attention to the subject's finer details, his lectures on anthropology come to more clearly differentiate racial and national character as he systematically parses distinctive forms of human diversity.

Most importantly, Kant's analytical parsimony shapes the methodological and epistemological framework surrounding race – that is, his account of how we might understand it at all. In "Determination" and "On the Use of Teleological Principles," Kant distinguishes between teleological natural history (*Naturgeschichte*) and a mechanistic description of nature (*Naturbeschreibung*) to determine "the principles according to which natural history could be enlarged" while avoiding "harm from the carelessness of letting the boundaries of the sciences run into each other."[118] Given the *Critiques'* preoccupation with delimiting the claims and objects of distinctive forms of inquiry, Kant's rising interest in teleology and race – embryonic in 1775, better developed in 1785, and the central object of the 1788 essay – is unsurprising. "Oriented by the language of destiny and purpose," Jennifer Mensch observes, "Kant discovered that with a teleological approach he could avoid the pitfalls of subreption, even while invoking the beneficence of nature's care for her chosen species."[119] Kant argues that race falls under the auspices of a natural history rooted in reflective judgment, and not a "mere *description of nature*"[120] treating phenomena in terms of mechanistic causality. Where descriptions of nature *observe* the world, natural history seeks to *explicate* it in relation to a (necessarily) conjectural natural purposiveness. As part of a *"system of final causes,"* Kant holds, our place in the natural world "only leaves the teleological but not the physical-mechanical mode of explanation."[121] Natural history's reflective standpoint casts the phenomenal world in relation to our moral ends, to which a merely mechanistic or observational perspective is blind. "[T]here can be no thought," therefore, "of sparing us *teleological* grounds of explanation in order to replace them with physical ones, in the case of organized beings as regards the preservation of their kind."[122] As Robert J. Richards observes, Kant insists that "in comprehending the organization and operation of creatures, an investigator had to assume a teleological causality – since no application of merely mechanistic laws could make biological processes intellectually tractable."[123]

Racial differentiation is, then, only intelligible in relation to the larger purposive organization of the natural world and to our place within it. The teleological mode of inquiry provides the principles guiding an investigation into humanity's function in a system of natural ends. While "necessary with respect to natural history," then, the concept of race "does not figure in a system of the description of nature"[124] with which it is incompatible. From a descriptive standpoint, racial divergences are merely phenotypic dissimilarities indistinguishable from those of variety or strain; it neither discriminates between human distinctions nor has any explanatory capacity to account for them. From the perspective of natural history, however, race becomes comprehensible as the mechanism enabling a human species of shared phyletic origins to populate the globe in accordance with nature's intentions. It explains the purpose of human differentiation in relation to our natural ends. By providing the four germs sustaining environmental adaptation, nature equips us with the tools to spread across and moralize the entire world: "the evolving seeds were distinct but originally implanted in one and the same line of descent *purposively suited for the first general populating of the earth* through their offspring."[125] For Kant, the concept of race provides the only viable way to conceive of human origins, human differentiation and human development in relation to the natural world's purposive organization and ultimate end – our rational perfection.

3.3.3   The Substance of Race

How, then, does Kant understand the *substance* of race? Does racial character concern merely physical attributes (what nature makes of us), or does it also entail morally relevant qualities (what we make of ourselves, as free beings)?

Read in the most charitable light – as morally benign – Kant's racial theory is understood as either: (a) sufficiently disconnected from his moral philosophy as to isolate his ethics from his race thinking, as Bernard Boxill and Thomas Hill suggest, or (b) defending humanity's unity against Kames's and Forster's polygenisms.[126] Robert Louden, for instance, takes Kant's insistence on our common phyletic ancestry – that we were all potentially white, yellow, black or red – as indicating the four races' fundamental equality.[127] Both incarnations of the view are best supported by "Determination," where Kant insists that "not a single [attribute] can be found within a class of human beings characterized merely by skin color that is necessarily hereditary – but that this latter character, insignificant as it may appear, is universally and *unfailingly* hereditary."[128] While other phenotypic traits might recur in given races and even be passed on through generations, skin color's invariable heredity sets it apart as the sole marker of race. This is, of course, also congruent with Kant's broader commitment to shelving heteronomous features of human life as morally inconsequential.

The ambiguities, inconsistencies and outright contradictions pervading the racial theory, however, render the morally benign view hard to sustain.[129] To begin with, Kant oscillates between advancing and resisting a racial hierarchy based on proximity to the original human form. In certain cases – as above, in "Determination," for instance – the four seeds' primeval coexistence suggests that it is "impossible to guess the shape of the first human phylum (as far as the constitution of the skin is concerned); even the character of the whites is only the development of one of the original predispositions that together with the others were to be found in that phylum."[130] As products of environmental adaptation, the four races here appear as equal deviations of, rather than degenerations from, the species' phyletic source – distinctive but equivalent paths of human evolution, rather than degradations from an originary stock. And yet, in "Of the Different Races," Kant maintains that

the region of the earth from the 31st to the 52nd degree of latitude in the ancient world (which also with respect to its population appears to deserve the name of the ancient world) is rightly taken for that region of the earth in which the most fortunate mixture of the influences of the colder and hotter regions are found ... and where also the human being must have diverged the least from his original formation, given that he is equally well prepared for all transplantings from there. Now here we do indeed find inhabitants that are white, however they are *brunette*, which shape we thus want to assume to be the one closest to that of the phyletic species.[131]

This grounds a natural hierarchy structured by each race's distance from the "original" human being:

Phyletic Species Whites of brunette color.
First race High blondes (Northern Europeans) from humid cold.
Second race Copper-reds (Americans) from dry cold.
Third race Blacks (Senegambia) from humid heat.
Fourth race Olive-yellows (Indians) from dry heat.[132]

This phyletic ranking clearly carries an evaluative weight: the white European is, here, least deviated from the original human form (itself white) and so most adaptable. Kant's further cogitations on Amerindians' stuntedness, Negroes' "lazy, soft and trifling"[133] nature, and the white race's superior "talent" and "perfection" make it particularly difficult to sustain the equi-primordial view.

Of course, one might dismiss "Of the Different Races" as an artifact of Kant's early, pre-critical conceptualization of race, predating his disentangling of intelligible and empirical character. But while the essays from the 1780s shed the explicit hierarchy, his substantive assessment of the races persists. The American race, he contends in 1788's "Teleological Principles," "which is too weak for hard labor, too indifferent for industry and incapable of any culture – although there is enough of it as example and encouragement nearby – ranks still far below even the Negro, who stands on the lowest of all the other steps that we have named as differences of the races."[134] Kant's later treatments also expand and deepen the range of inborn racial characteristics well beyond skin color to include traits that clearly impact agentive capacities. "Should one not conclude," he muses, reflecting on the passivity of non-European races,

that, in addition to the *faculty* to work, there is also an immediate drive to activity (especially to the sustained activity that one calls industry), which is independent of all enticement and which is especially interwoven with certain natural predispositions; and that Indians as well as Negroes do not bring any more of this impetus into other climates and pass it on to their offspring than was needed for their preservation in their old motherland and had been received from nature; and that *this inner predisposition extinguishes just as little as the externally visible one.*[135]

In its final and best-developed incarnation, then, Kant's account of race entails a broad range of attributes: "inner predispositions," "the faculty to work," "industry," "drive to activity" – all "interwoven with certain natural predispositions" – are racially determined and equally subject to activation or extinction as are variations in skin color.[136] These are, moreover, forms of character that Kant had ascribed to non-European races for over two and a half decades. In *Observations* Kant treats the Negro as indolent, as bereft of talent (his measure of naturally occurring cognitive capacity), as unaccomplished in any art or science and as far removed from the white race "with regard to the capacities of mind as it is with respect to color."[137] The Negro "seed" clearly carries more baggage than mere skin color, cementing a racial character that inhibits the full development of rational faculties. This is hardly surprising, given Kant's teleological framework: if racial adaptations enable us to populate vastly different environments, there's no reason why they should remain restricted to pigmentation. Across his essays and lectures on race, "Determination" in fact stands alone in *not* treating race as shaping "inner dispositions," often in morally salient ways. While the conceptual architecture surrounding Kant's racial theory sharpened over the 1780s, his evaluations of the different races' capacities underwent no substantive change. They instead became entrenched in a teleological history tracking humanity's movement from nature to freedom. "The critical turn and his mature ethics did not displace Kant's concerns," Mark Larrimore observes, "[t]hey reframed them and, as they did, 'race' became a term claiming at once scientific, providential and pragmatic significance."[138]

Still further, white Europeans continue to enjoy an elevated status well into the critical period. "The white race," Kant maintains in the 1781–1782 *Menschenkunde*, "contains all incentives and talents in itself"[139] – all the more troubling given that "by *talent* (natural gift) we understand that excellence of the cognitive faculty which depends not on instruction but on the subject's natural predisposition."[140] Talent most explicitly bridges natural endowments and rational capacities. It's also among the most persistent markers of race, leading Emmanuel Chukwudi Eze to argue that Kant's attribution of talent anchors a naturally fixed moral ordering of the races.[141] While Eze overstates the case, talent *is* distributed along racial lines and appears to ascribe cognitive ceilings to given peoples: the Negro has none, the Hindustani's is "meager," and the American – incapable of culture and "well below" the Negro – lacks it entirely. This is further borne out by Kant's contention, in *Anthropology Pillau* (1778), that "Americans have such relations in their nature that they now should become no more perfect," and that Negroes are "no longer susceptible of any further civilizing."[142] Still more directly, and in a published essay, he stipulates that "Americans and Negroes are each a race, sunk beneath the remaining members of the human species in their mental predispositions"[143] – and this in 1785, well into the critical period.

Kant's estimation of Native Americans' capacities perhaps best illustrates the moral limitations implicit in his envisioning of the non-European world. Native Americans are an "incipient" and "incompletely adapted race,"[144] whose adaptation was "interrupted halfway through [its development] ... establishing the persistent state of this cohort of human beings."[145] Sufferers of genealogical, climatic and migratory misfortunes, "their natural disposition did not achieve a *perfect* suitability for any climate," Kant avers, relegating them to "the lowest of all the other steps that we have named as differences of the races."[146] Native Americans are marked by a permanent stuntedness, a "half extinguished life power"[147] rendering them as indisposed to exert themselves as they are incapable of developing themselves. These inborn failures of drive, reason and culture clearly throw into question their capacity to participate in humanity's moral advancement. And again, Kant's view has deep roots. "We find nations that do not appear to have progressed in the perfection of human nature, but have come to a standstill," he proclaims a decade earlier, in 1777–1778,

while others, as in Europe, are always progressing. If the Europeans had not discovered America, the Americans would have remained in their condition. And we believe even now that they will attain to no perfection, for it appears that they will all be exterminated, not through acts of murder, for that would be gruesome! but rather that they will die out.[148]

Passages such as this certainly support Robert Bernasconi's contention that non-Europeans are, in Kant's philosophy of history, destined either to become suitably civilized or fade into extinction.[149] But more broadly, they illustrate how racial character conditions both our progress toward "the perfection of human nature" – our end, within the structure of a purposive natural order – and our moral status as rational, end-setting beings. Certain races appear incapable of developing the subjective capacities on which moral advancement depends, and in which moral dignity inheres. Kant could hardly put it more bluntly: "Americans have such relations in their nature that they now should become no more perfect."[150] "If a people in no way improves itself over centuries," he suggests further, "then one may assume that there already exists in it a certain natural predisposition which it is not capable of exceeding."[151] As with the Tahitians, the moral worth of Americans, a people whose "natural predisposition" renders it unable to approach moralization, remains an open and vexing question. Unlike the Tahitians, Americans' inborn limitations appear, in a profoundly sinister way, self-extinguishing.

Of course, the relationship between Kant's racial theory and his moral and political thought is widely contested.[152] In different ways, Robert Louden, Thomas McCarthy, Thomas E. Hill and Bernard Boxill treat Kant's race-thinking as separable from his practical philosophy. While Kant's prejudices infect his impure ethics, the greater weight and sophistication of his moral egalitarianism ought to carry the day. "Kant's theory," Louden assures, "is fortunately stronger than his prejudices."[153] But this doesn't get around the depth of their imbrication: a fuller view of Kant's "theory" – his ethics and politics – shows its boundedness to the anthropological-teleological contexts to which his prejudices would be banished. As Larrimore reminds, "Kant's theory of race shows the importance of reading together elements of his oeuvre that tend to be studied in isolation: practical philosophy, philosophy of history, anthropology, physical geography."[154] Kant's interest in race was, still further, far from negligible, rooted in the 1750s–1760s, systematized in the 1770s, and entrenched in the 1780s.

Eze and Charles Mills, conversely, see Kant's racial theory as directly undermining his moral universalism. Non-Europeans fail to qualify as full persons at all; they are, rather, *Untermenschen*, sub-persons outside the sphere of moral consideration.[155] This isn't quite the case either. As a matter of regulative, reflective judgment, Kant's racial theory is of a different order than the normative, determinative judgments comprising his ethics and politics. Each makes importantly different kinds of claims – the former, conjectures orienting our understanding of the human condition, and the latter, imperatives derived from our nature as rational beings. As such, they are not amenable to flat-out contradiction. This doesn't suggest that they're unrelated. As I have argued throughout, Kant's critical and teleological projects persistently spill into one another, and Mills is not wrong to treat Kant's racial theory as leaving non-Europeans "*below the threshold* for normatively equal treatment."[156] But that theory must nonetheless be accounted for within the regulative framework to which Kant consigned it. Suggesting that Kant "makes whiteness a prerequisite for full personhood"[157] or that "[t]he inferiority of the Negro, as proposed by Hume, is now in Kant successfully grounded in transcendental philosophy"[158] conflates different orders of judgment. Also, despite the force of their criticisms, neither Mills nor Eze clearly distinguishes between lecture notes and published texts, pre-critical, critical and post-critical writings, or the division of anthropology and physical geography.[159]

In a particularly nuanced and influential reading, Pauline Kleingeld argues that Kant abandoned his racial theory at some point after 1792 (the racial hierarchy still figures in the 1792 *Dohna* physical geography lecture notes) due to its incompatibility with his cosmopolitanism.[160] Kleingeld takes the brevity of the published *Anthropology*'s "Character of the Races" (a single page), his condemnation of chattel slavery in "Toward Perpetual Peace," and his anti-imperialism as evidence of a late-life desertion of race-thinking.[161] The case is, however, in certain respects questionable. Kant's anti-imperialism turns on a doctrine of right that simply disregards race, rather than revaluating its character. Unless we assume that prior to 1792, Kant would have taken racial inferiority as a warrant for imperial conquest (nothing in his racial theory, even at its worst, suggests as much), we have no reason to treat his opposition to colonial adventurism as altering his view of race.[162] Race-thinking and anti-imperialism are not necessarily at odds, and certainly don't preclude one another.[163] As for the concision of the published *Anthropology*'s treatment of race, Larrimore points out that by the 1790s, Kant's racial theory was so well established as to need no further elaboration. The essays on race were republished, either in full or separately, in 1793, 1795, 1797/8 and 1799, and were the object of scholarly engagement by Herder, Blumenbach and Girtanner throughout the 1790s.[164] While the published *Anthropology*'s account of race is indeed reduced to one page, it also refers the reader to Girtanner's work on the subject – which explicitly supported Kant's own racial theory. Finally, the inconsistency between Kant's racial theory and his cosmopolitanism pales in comparison to its disjuncture with his moral egalitarianism – and yet, he appears to have had little difficulty reconciling them throughout the 1780s.[165]

Still further, as Kleingeld herself observes, Kant accepted the institution of slavery with little reservation throughout the 1780s (and earlier), and only changed his views in the early 1790s – the result, she argues, of his "second thoughts" on race. But beyond race-thinking's easy compatibility with a tepid abolitionism, Inés Valdez has persuasively demonstrated that Kant's opposition to slavery and colonialism concerned its damaging effects on European peace, rather than on non-Europeans.[166] Colonial conflict between European states (chiefly France and Britain), Kant saw, threatened peaceable inter-European relations. His opposition to slavery, late coming as it was, appears motivated less by a change of heart regarding the rights of non-Europeans than by a practical concern with European stability. The evidence of his opposition to chattel slavery is, also, tenuous. While Kant condemns slavery in the drafts of the essay on perpetual peace, he fails to do so in the published text, despite growing European resistance to the slave trade that would have rendered the position palatable to his audience. The passages in the *Metaphysics of Morals* from which Kleingeld extrapolates his views on slavery (6:283, 6:270, 6:231) also do not address slavery itself, but rather work through various prohibitions on treating human beings as things. The case supporting Kant's abolitionism (and subsequent reformed view of race, so the logic goes) is, then, built on writings that he opted *not* to publish, and on slavery's incompatibility with the injunction against treating persons as things – a claim of non-contradiction. But as we've seen, Kant clearly contradicts himself on various fronts, particularly where pure principles of right meet impure conditions of application. There is, then, little to indicate that Kant's views on race changed substantively in the 1790s, even if he warmed to abolitionism.

Kant's racial theory and racial thinking do have moral gravity. Race affects the development (or non-development) of our rational faculties and of the subjective dispositions orienting us toward our moral ends. While it does not impugn his practical philosophy as directly as Eze and Mills contend, race shapes Kant's vision of the progress comprising our moral vocation. "Even if racism is not seen in the core principles (such as the Categorical Imperative)," Kleingeld notes, "racist prejudice can (and in Kant's case does) influence how the most basic moral and political principles are applied in the elaboration of the full theory."[167] It's precisely this influence – the sway of Kant's conceptualization of race over the elaboration of his moral and political theories – that I have aimed to illuminate here. It's worth considering a few of the features and implications of the view I've sketched out.

To begin with, the account presented here captures Kant's mature theory of race, elaborated over his late pre-critical, critical and post-critical periods. The challenges that it presents for his practical philosophy do not, then, proceed from his early and more inflammatory – and unsystematic – race-thinking, such as we find in *Observations* and the lectures on geography. I have instead focused on the racial theory developed between 1775 and 1788 whose substantive, structural and epistemological commitments remain, despite variations, consistent. My account also weighs the distinctions (and relations) between published essays and lecture notes on anthropology to show the genesis of Kant's thoughts on race, and particularly, their steady entrenchment in a teleological framework that "for the first time promised a truly scientific natural history of man."[168] The racial theory that I have drawn out, and the problems associated with it, thus belong to Kant's mature critical and post-critical thought. Mark Larrimore suggests that "race became an a priori concept"[169] through its integration in the teleology propounded in the third *Critique*. While this puts the case somewhat strongly, its teleological grounding undoubtedly pushes Kant's notion of race into the critical project's exploration of what we, as human beings, might hope for.

Kant's mature racial theory also reaches well beyond the merely physical character demarcated by skin color. It concerns a wide range of morally salient "inner dispositions" impacting different races' rational and cognitive faculties, and so, their capabilities as free agents. Of his many treatments of the subject, published and unpublished, one essay alone – "Determination" – keeps race within the strict bounds of physical character and avoids racial rankings and hierarchies. In this, it is an outlier. While the conceptual architecture surrounding race shifted considerably across the decades, Kant's substantive assessments of race-based capacities and incapacities are remarkably stable. Many of the most problematic elements in 1788's "Teleological Principles" are traceable to at least 1777 (in the case of Amerindians) and 1764 (in the case of Negroes). It is, then, difficult to sustain the view that Kant's racial theory became incompatible with his critical or post-critical thought, and still more that race can be cleanly extirpated from his moral philosophy. How given races' developmental paralysis, their unfitness for cultivation, their becoming "no more perfect" and their talent-based cognitive limitations might be reconciled with a moral standing predicated on precisely those rational faculties is hard to see.

Finally, Kant's racial theory entrenches non-Europeans' moral deficits in a teleological framework transmuting race from an inconsequential afterthought to an integral facet of humanity's moralization. Cast in the light of natural history, race is solely intelligible in relation to our moral perfection. Kant's early observations on race are little more than superficial conjectures, easily dismissed as philosophically trivial. Their progressive integration over the late 1770s and 1780s into his theorization of moral evolution, however, elevates its conceptual significance. Race comes to account for how beings of our kind – moral, but imperfect – fit within the purposive organization of the natural world. To speculate on non-Europeans' inborn laziness, developmental torpor or cognitive shortages is of little theoretical import; to anchor them in a teleological schema explaining human variation as part of the species' advancement problematizes their moral character. As the mechanism enabling the earth's moralization, race – and the character it carries – is only comprehensible relative to the fulfilment of nature's highest end, creating at least two problems.

First, and most straightforwardly, non-Europeans' racially fixed cognitive and developmental shortcomings undermine their moral status. If, as I have argued, our particular moral task lies in an ever-continuing striving for moral improvement – in strengthening our powers and resolve in approximating, but never achieving, virtue – non-Europeans' incapacities in this exact regard proscribe their participation in humanity's moral vocation. Kant's evaluation of the American race best captures the concern: if "[t]he American people acquires no culture"[170] and "should become no more perfect,"[171] it is unclear why they should not simply "die out."[172] As with the Tahitians, Americans' congenital failures of formation challenge their basic moral stature: without "fill[ing] the void in creation in regard to their end as rational nature,"[173] their worth is difficult to discern. Racial attributes enable the *species* to bridge the gap between nature and freedom, but also prevent a great many people, and peoples, from doing so.

Second, as with gender, Kant treats racial difference in strictly functionalist terms. As with women, he understands non-Europeans in relation to humanity's moralization and nature's ends, rather than as ends in themselves. As with women, non-Europeans are not autonomous, self-determining, purposive actors, but conditions of realization – conduits – for nature's purposiveness. As with women's beautiful virtues, racial attributes comprise adaptive traits anchored in a system of natural ends, rather than their own. Still worse – and again, as with women – that racial character limits the rational, end-setting faculty that is the object of our moral worth. As with women, race stumbles from the observational standpoint describing humanity's empirical character to the teleological standpoint accounting for moral character.[174] Like gender, race is rooted in an evaluative and morally salient developmental framework (how else should we understand the "human perfection" against which Kant measures different races?). At bottom, then, Kant's natural history *instrumentalizes* racial difference.[175] As with women, non-Europeans' moral worth is measured not by the dignity of end-setting beings, but in terms of their functional role in humanity's moral advancement. Like women, non-Europeans are transitory figures, paving the way for a perfection denied to them by their very racially fixed deficits.

3.4 THE KIND OF MORAL AGENTS WE CAN BE

Where, then, does this leave the Tahitians with whom we began? Tahitians and Americans, Hottentots and Hindustanis, Arabs and Africans: all fall into the uncomfortable juncture between who we are – imperfect, finite, embodied – and the rational, autonomous, self-governing moral actors we're bound to approximate. Of course, they are not alone: we all inhabit the space between nature and freedom, between the perfect will of angels and the phenomenal world's mechanistic determinism. This is the kind of moral being we are, and it delimits our moral work: we are destined to endlessly seek rational perfection and develop the capacities, dispositions and faculties orienting us to it.

And yet, Kant's sustained attention to that space, to the anthropological conditions shaping our moral and political nature, has largely been eclipsed by the singular focus on his critical and formal accounts of ethics and right. The ensuing picture is not only incomplete, but also unfaithful to Kant's view of the task at hand. As Mark Larrimore observes, Kant

did not think you could responsibly do practical philosophy without physical geography and pragmatic anthropology, and wasn't trying to. We misread his ethics if we do not also read his accounts of human diversity and their implications for respecting the humanity in everyone, treating none as a means only. We misunderstand his philosophy of history and politics if we forget the potentially fatal imprint of the earth and its regions on human populations.[176]

Kant's liberalism is not isolated, or isolatable, from the conception of human nature at its center, neither does it treat moral subjects as separable from the conditions characterizing their humanity (and not just their rationality). Thomas McCarthy similarly recognizes Kant's impure ethics not as "a merely convenient but unnecessary addition to pure ethics; it is, as Derrida might say, a necessary supplement, if morality is to have any purchase at all on human life."[177] This is the intuition that I have aimed to flesh out. Kant's full ethics addresses moral principles derived from our rational nature, along with a careful consideration of how, as sensible beings, we develop a subjective receptivity to them. Moral agency is not simply fixed within us, then, but rather consists by Kant's own reckoning in an endless progress toward moral betterment. My effort here is to take this standpoint seriously and work through its implications.

Because this is where we best see the challenges facing women, Tahitians, Amerindians and so many others. Women and non-Europeans do not develop toward the human perfection that is our natural end; they do not participate in our moral vocation, as human beings. So long as we remain bound to sensibility, we remain between nature and freedom, and so long as we remain between nature and freedom, our moral imperative lies in pushing ever closer to the latter. Women's beautiful character, Amerindians' stuntedness, Negroes' lack of talent: all limit the capacity to cultivate the orientations, skills and dispositions enabling us to do just that. Todd Hedrick suggests that "Kant must think that all peoples have *some* predisposition for the development of culture,"[178] but it's not clear that this is the case, given, for instance, Native Americans' inbuilt limitations in this exact regard. Women and non-Europeans, then, do not share in the rational and ethical advancement constituting our moral nature. While we all remain between nature and freedom, their immobility signals a failure of our distinctively human moral vocation.

Still worse, Kant's account of *how* we move from nature to freedom makes it impossible to envision things otherwise. Race and gender are comprehensible only relative to humanity's moralization, as instruments of progress. Their moral nature and moral intelligibility remain strictly tied to, and mediated by, the natural world's purposive organization, and not their own capacities for autonomy and self-determination. Kant's liberalism – his moral and political vision – contains no conceptual resources to understand human difference in non-instrumental terms, as anything other than conduits for a future state from which they are, by all appearances, excluded.[179] By stepping back from pure principles of right and virtue, we better perceive diversity's place within that liberalism, and what precious little space it leaves to recognize the worth of human heterogeneity. Teleological histories are convergent histories, and like all convergent histories, Kant's unavoidably treats differences as deficits. Non-European lives and practices aren't valuable, they're simply further behind, mired in the "raw state" of an undeveloped humanity.

Whether or not Kant's accounts of race and diversity directly contradict his moral philosophy, we ought to be wary of an ethics whose developmentalism constrains its universalism. While reflective judgment and normative principles make very different kinds of claims, Kant's moral theory remains incomplete and speculative – non-practical – without the teleology bridging a strictly rationalist ethics and a properly human one. As Hedrick suggests, "even if we agree with Kant that judgments regarding the *character* of individuals and judgments about the *moral worth* of persons are analytically distinct modes, it would surely be naïve to believe that, at the level of impure historical reality, the two modes have nothing to do with one another."[180] To rise above mere formalism, Kant's ethics have to address *how* we move from nature to freedom, even if that raises discomfiting questions concerning *who* is able to do so at all. Ultimately, an ethics whose conditions of realization exclude vast swathes of the human beings for whom they're intended is one that should invite skepticism.

It isn't hard to retreat behind the many walls that Kant erects – between transcendental moral dignity and the mess of embodied heteronomy, between morality and politics, between normative and reflective judgments, between nature and freedom. It's equally easy to isolate Kant's treatments of pure right and ethics from his slipperier anthropology, and to minimize the latter as "unfortunate but largely disposable elements of his political cosmopolitanism and moral teleology."[181] But we can't do so without willfully disregarding the many junctures bridging them, for better and for worse, and the fuller liberalism they evince. Whether Kant understands women and non-Europeans as full members of a possible kingdom of ends, as autonomous or as endowed with moral dignity (or at least, with an equal moral dignity) remains an open question. From the strictly critical standpoint, it seems inconceivable that he wouldn't. But Kant's account of our moral nature exceeds mere formalism: the substance of our moral worth lies in the capacity to *set* our ends, to *be* autonomous, and to *develop* the rational capacities in which dignity inheres. This is not a weakness, but a strength of his ethics: against common misperceptions, Kant's practical philosophy is profoundly attuned to the cultivation of reason and lifelong moral development. Women's and non-Europeans' deficiencies in precisely these aspects of our moral lives must, then, strike us as all the more troubling.

What remains of Kant's moral universalism and political egalitarianism when women and the unpropertied are disenfranchised, the former in perpetuity; when non-Europeans are cognitively stunted, culturally stillborn and unable to partake in our collective moral ends; when women and non-Europeans are agents of moralization, rather than moral agents; when their ends are set by nature and not by themselves; when neither appears capable of developing dispositions to morality; and when their worth is measured in instrumental terms, relative to a moral progress from which they're excluded? If we extricate the human being from Kant's ethics, these problems dissolve. But if, along with Kant, we consider how human beings realize their moral nature, it becomes abundantly clear just how few of us in fact fall under those egalitarian pretensions.

A great deal of liberalism's appeal lies in just this egalitarianism – not only in a formal sense, but in the deep moral parity grounding liberal commitments to civil equality. This is what we like about liberalism, if we like it at all: the recognition of all persons' substantive equality and moral worth, and the promise of political institutions preserving them. It's the promise that Kant's liberalism holds out: a difference-blind egalitarianism predicated on our shared capacities for individual and political self-determination, self-government and autonomy. This is, from the contemporary perspective, perhaps what we most value in liberalism. It articulates a vision of associational life predicated on vastly different people's equal moral worth and political entitlements. But it isn't Kant's liberalism. At its core, Kant's liberalism is closed to the forms of human difference that, arguably, make the most pressing claims on its universalism. Despite its conceits, it remains constitutionally blind to the dignity of different races, cultures and genders – to the dignity in human difference itself. And yet, Kant's liberalism does not encompass liberalism altogether. It is only one liberalism among others.

NOTES

1. Gayatri Chakravorty Spivak, *A Critique of Post-Colonial Reason: Toward a History of the Vanishing Present* (Cambridge: Harvard University Press, 1999), 26.
2. Louden and Wood, "Introduction," 9.
3. Kant, *Mrongovius*, 25:1422.

4. For a notable exception, see Eduardo Mendieta, "Geography is to History as Woman is to Man: Kant on Sex, Race, and Geography," in *Reading Kant's Geography*, eds. Stuart Elden and Eduardo Mendieta (SUNY Press, 2011): 345–368.

5. For lucid treatments of Kant's system of right, see Ripstein, *Force and Freedom*; Mulholland, *Kant's System of Rights*; Rosen, *Kant's Theory of Justice*; Williams, *Kant's Political Philosophy*; Ellis, *Provisional Theory*. For his views on revolution, see Lewis W. Beck, "Kant and the Right of Revolution," *Journal of the History of Ideas* 32, no. 3 (1971): 411–422; Christine Korsgaard, "Taking the Law into Our Own Hands: Kant on the Right to Revolution," in *The Constitution of Agency: Essays on Practical Reason and Moral Psychology* (Oxford: Oxford University Press, 2008); David Cummiskey, "Justice and Revolution in Kant's Political Philosophy," in *Rethinking Kant Volume I*, ed. Pablo Muchnik (Newcastle: Cambridge Scholars Publishing, 2008), 217–240; and Katrin Flikschuh, "Reason, Right and Revolution: Kant and Locke," *Philosophy and Public Affairs* 36, no. 4 (2008): 375–404. For cosmopolitanism and global right, see Habermas, "Perpetual Peace"; Otfried Höffe, *Kant's Cosmopolitan Theory of Law and Peace* (Cambridge: Cambridge University Press, 2006); Benhabib, *Another Cosmopolitanism*; Bohman and Lutz-Bachmann, *Perpetual Peace*; Pauline Kleingeld, "Kantian Patriotism," *Philosophy of Public Affairs* 29, no. 4 (2000); Pauline Kleingeld, "Kant's Cosmopolitan Law: World Citizenship for a Global Order," *Kantian Review* 2 (1998): 72–90; and Kleingeld, *Kant and Cosmopolitanism*.

6. Kant, TP, 8:296.

7. Ibid., 8:294.

8. Kant, MS, 6:314.

9. For a few incisive criticisms of active/passive citizenship, see Beiner, "Paradoxes"; Mendus, "Narrow-Minded Bourgeois?"; and Mulholland, *System of Rights*.

10. Mulholland, *System of Rights*, 322. Wolfgang Kersting criticizes the property qualification still more strongly, arguing that it "transforms the rational state, which makes all humans into citizens, into a state of property owners, which degrades those without property into second-class political beings" (Wolfgang Kersting, "Politics, Freedom and Order: Kant's Political Philosophy," in *The Cambridge Companion to Kant* (Cambridge: Cambridge University Press, 1992), 357). The criticism is echoed by John Kenneth Baynes's observation that "the condition of independence excludes all but property-holders from taking part" (John Kenneth Baynes, "Kant on Property Rights and the Social Contract," *The Monist* 72 (1989): 445). Elisabeth Ellis is critical of "Kant's rather dated theory of citizenship," but lauds "the intuition behind Kant's distinction" – namely, that the exercise of public reason should be free of private interests (Ellis, *Provisional Theory*, 197). While Jacob Weinrib differentiates the citizen–cobeneficiary distinction in "Theory and Practice" from the *Rechtleshre*'s active–passive formulation, his view is in the minority; virtually all other commentators treat them as substantively similar. I engage Weinrib's argument in section 3.1.1.

11. Ripstein, *Force and Freedom*, 4. One might reply that passive citizenship subjects co-beneficiaries to the will of a particular *class* of people, and not the arbitrary whims of other individuals, but the will in question, even if group-based, remains particular, rather than omnilateral (as the law ideally ought to be).

12. Ripsten, *Force and Freedom*, fn. 54, 213.

13. Williams, *Kant's Political Philosophy*, 178–179. Elisabeth Ellis similarly attributes the active/passive distinction to the provisionality and imperfection of existing political states, noting Kant's "awareness of the difficult problem of the gap between contractarian demands on citizen capacity and the reality of widespread citizen incapacity" (553). See Elisabeth Ellis, "Citizenship and Property Rights: A New Look at Social Contract Theory," *The Journal of Politics* 68, no. 3 (2006): 544–555.

14. Williams, *Kant's Political Philosophy*, 180.

15. Jacob Weinrib, "Kant on Citizenship and Universal Independence," *Australian Journal of Legal Philosophy* 33 (2008): 14.

16. Ibid., 10.

17. Kant, *Anthropology*, 7:209. Weinrib treats Kant's view of women's civil immaturity (in 1797) as reflecting the "contingent fact" that "[w]omen were dependent on others for their existence and preservation in 18th century Prussia." Kant's proclamations on women's civil immaturity, the argument goes, are best interpreted as declarative fact (about Prussian society and its existing legal arrangements) rather than normative judgment. Yet, the *Anthropology*'s 1798 account of women's civil immaturity rests on the "deficiencies with regard to [the understanding's] exercise, deficiencies that necessitate ... the *representation* of one's person through that of another in regard to matters of a civil nature" (Ibid., 7:209). The problem concerns women's *understanding*, not their contingent state of dependence. These were, also, long-held convictions. In the *Anthropology Mrongovius*, 14 years prior to the published *Anthropology*, Kant draws the same connections between women's immaturity and their understanding: "Immaturity is the inability to use one's own understanding without guidance from another ... in civil life everything is artificial, hence we become mature later. There is an immaturity of sex, namely, of woman ... The immaturity of the second sex is in public affairs" (Kant, *Mrongovius*, 25:1298–1299). Reaching still further back, this conforms to views on women's civil rights and rational capacities that Kant held consistently since 1764's *Observations*. There is, then, little to suggest that his assessment of women's status and capabilities underwent a dramatic change in the mid-1790s. The contention that he substantively revised his conception of citizenship between 1793 and 1797 is further undermined by the *Rechtslehre*'s appeal to the same three criteria ("lawful freedom," "civil equality" and "civil independence") as appear in "Theory and Practice." His accounts of self-mastery and independence are also nearly identical in both texts.

18. Mulholland, *System of Rights*, 323.

19. Baynes, "Property Rights," 445. For additional material/economic readings of the property qualification, see Kersting, "Politics, Freedom"; and Joseph Grcic, "Kant on Revolution and Economic Inequality," *Kant-Studien* 77 (1986): 447–457.

20. Kant, TP, 8:290.

21. Ibid., 8:295.

22. Kant, MS, 6:315.

23. Kant, TP, 8:296.

24. Ibid.

25. Kant, TP, 8:295.

26. Contractual subservience of this kind is limited by the duty of rightful honor (to "not make yourself a mere means for others" (Kant, MS, 6:237)) and so does not violate right. The problem concerns the cultivation of judgment.

27. Kant, *Anthropology*, 7:208–209.

28. Kant distinguishes between "understanding" in the broad sense ("the faculty of *thinking*" (Kant, *Anthropology*, 7:197)) and its narrower variant ("when it is subordinated to understanding in a general sense as one member of a division with two other members" (7:197)). The broad sense of understanding, which Kant also calls "the *higher* cognitive faculty," thus consists of a tripartite division (*"understanding, the power of judgment,* and *reason"* (7:197)) which contains the narrower sense.

29. Kant, *Anthropology*, 7:199. It may seem curious to focus on the *Anthropology*'s account of cognition, rather than the critical one. However, the *Anthropology*'s "Anthropological comparison of the three higher cognitive faculties with one another" and the larger division within which it appears ("On the cognitive faculty, in so far as it based on understanding") most directly treat the questions raised here, pertaining to cognition's relation to civil maturity.

30. Ibid., 7:198.

31. Ibid.

32. Ibid., 7:199.

33. Ibid.

34. Ibid.

35. Kant, *Mrongovius*, 25:1297.

36. Kant, *Anthropology*, 7:209.

37. Ibid.

38. Munzel similarly observes that the republican state "positively facilitates the cultivation of human capacities of judgment by both providing the freedom for and calling upon its citizens actively to exercise their capacity of thought" (Munzel, *Moral Character*, 323) and that Kant's defense of philosophers' civic value turns on "their being citizens who are exemplary instances of the 'free exercise of judgment'" (326).

39. As Pauline Kleingeld notes, "[t]he description of the active citizen as a free and equal, co-legislating member of the state implies that a republic can exist only when its citizens support and are involved in its core institutions" (Kleingeld, *Kant and Cosmopolitanism*, 30).

40. Kant, MS, 6:315.

41. Kant, KU, 5:434.

42. Kant, *Anthropology*, 7:304.

43. Ibid.

44. Ibid., 7:303. Kant's conviction that women's character only develops in civilized states is traceable to (at least) 1775–6, *Anthropology Friedländer*: "[a]ll the woman's art to get the man, her charms, her amenities, have no effect at all in the unrefined state … the art of the feminine sex is only visible in [the state of] refinement" (25:699). His views of "savage" societies are likewise consistent, as he contends that "among all savages the woman is to be regarded as a domesticated animal" (Kant, *Friedländer*, 25:700), and that "the feminine sex must be studied in the refined state where the predisposition of the germs of its nature has been able to

develop" (Ibid., 25:700). These arguments also recur in the 1781-2 *Menschenkunde* (25:1189) and 1784-5 *Mrongovius* (25:1393).

45. Kant, *Mrongovius*, 25:1368.
46. Louden, *Impure Ethics*, 82.
47. Kant's thoughts on the beautiful and the sublime concern his aesthetic theory and are extensive. I restrict myself here to his appeals to beauty and sublimity only as these relate to gender. For feminist scholarship illuminating the relationship between Kant's aesthetic and moral theories, as regards their impacts on his views of women, see Okin, "Sentimental Family," and Cornelia Klinger, "The Concepts of the Sublime and the Beautiful in Kant and Lyotard," in *Feminist Interpretations of Immanuel Kant*, ed. Robin May Schott (University Park: Pennsylvania State University Press, 1997), 191–211.
48. Kant, *Anthropology*, 7:308.
49. Kant, BS, 2:228. While one might object to treating *Observations*, predating the critical turn by fifteen years, as representing Kant's mature understanding of women, there is little evidence to suggest that his later assessments changed in any substantive way. Reinhard Brandt, Steven Lestition and John Zammito in fact share in the view that "Kant's conception and his delivery of the anthropology course was entirely unaffected by the 'critical revolution' of the 1780s" (Zammito, *Birth of Anthropology*, 301). Zammito also notes that the "Anthropological Characteristic," in which Kant addresses women's nature, "followed very closely the agenda and often the very examples and language of his *Observations*" (301). The central elements of Kant's account in *Observations* are consistent with the *Anthropology*, published more than three decades later. In both texts, Kant: (a) differentiates men's and women's character and virtues; (b) frames women's nature in relation to humanity's moralization; (c) regards civilization as a precondition for the development of women's character; (d) distinguishes between the standards, methods and goals anchoring men's and women's educations; and (e) treats women's ends as set by nature, rather than themselves. Given that "the crucial source of material (and structure) for the balance of the anthropology course was Kant's own *Observations*" (Zammito, *Birth of Anthropology*, 295), it does not appear that the critical revolution affected his evaluation of women, even if later years witnessed an attenuation of some of its more outlandish judgments.
50. Louden, *Impure Ethics*, 38.
51. Kant, *Friedländer*, 25:701.
52. Ibid., 25:722.
53. Ibid.
54. Kant, *Mrongovius*, 25:1392.
55. Kant, BS, 2:229.
56. Sarah Kofman argues that, as objects of non-animalistic desire, the moral qualities in women's beautiful character enable a form of attraction respecting both sexes' humanity. See Sarah Kofman, "The Economy of Respect: Kant and Respect for Women," *Social Research* 49, no. 2 (1982): 383–404.
57. Kant, BS, 2:229. For two compelling arguments drawing on this passage to show the impacts of women's cognitive defects on their moral agency, see Jean P. Rumsey, "Re-Visions of Agency in Kant's Moral Theory," in *Feminist Interpretations of Immanuel Kant*, ed. Robin May Schott (University Park:

Pennsylvania State University Press, 1997), 125–144; and Klinger, "Kant and Lyotard."

58. Kant, *Mrongovius*, 25:1394.
59. Ibid. Susan Meld Shell similarly observes that women's role "lies, above all, in bringing about civil order and refinement 'through inclination' rather than compulsion" (Shell, "True Economy of Human Nature," 211).
60. Kant, *Friedländer*, 25:543.
61. Wilson, *Kant's Pragmatic Anthropology*, 290.
62. Kant, BS, 2:230.
63. "The virtue of a woman is a *beautiful virtue*. That of the male sex should be a *noble virtue*." Kant, BS, 2:232.
64. Ibid., 2:236.
65. Kant, *Mrongovius*, 25:1394.
66. For two enduring critiques of Kant's treatment of women as second-class subjects, politically and morally, see Jean Bethke Elshtain, "Woman as a Suspect Category," in *Meditations on Modern Political Thought: Masculine/Feminine Themes from Luther to Arendt* (University Park: Pennsylvania State University Press, 1992); and Okin, "Sentimental Family."
67. Aristotle, *Politics of Aristotle*, in *The Politics and the Constitution of Athens*, ed. Stephen Everson (Cambridge: Cambridge University Press, 1996), 1260a7.
68. See Robin May Schott, "Feminism and Kant: Antipathy or Sympathy?" in *Autonomy and Community: Readings in Contemporary Kantian Social Philosophy*, eds. Jane Kneller and Sidney Axinn (New York: State University of New York Press, 1998), 87–100; and Okin, "Sentimental Family." Manfred Kuehn, conversely, treats Kant as reproducing the tropes of his day, concluding that "not much more could be expected" of him (Kuehn, *Kant*, 118).
69. Zammito, *Birth of Anthropology*, 126.
70. Sally Sedgwick, "Can Kant's Ethics Survive Feminist Critique?" in *Feminist Interpretations of Immanuel Kant*, ed. Robin May Schott (University Park: Pennsylvania State University Press, 1997), 94; see, also, Rumsey, "Re-Visions," 133. For a lucid analysis of androcentrism in Kant's language, see Kleingeld, "The Problematic Status of Gender-Neutral Language.
71. Elshtain, *Masculine/Feminine Themes*, 26.
72. Ibid.
73. Kant, *Anthropology*, 7:305–306. As with much of his conceptualization of women's nature, Kant's view here was deeply rooted, appearing in the *Friedlander* lecture notes and the *Menschenkunde*: "The end of nature in the most perfect unity of connection between two so very different sexes was: 1) to maintain the species, and then also: 2) to promote the social condition in the human sexes" (25:1189).
74. Rumsey, "Development of Character," 260.
75. Kant, *Anthropology*, 7:305.
76. Kant, KU, 5:429.
77. Louden, *Impure Ethics*, 82–87.
78. Ibid., 87.
79. Rumsey, "Development of Character," 262.
80. Ibid., 251.
81. Ibid.

82. Ibid., 262.
83. Holly Wilson, "Kant's Evolutionary Theory of Marriage," in *Autonomy and Community: Readings in Contemporary Kantian Social Philosophy*, eds. Jane Kneller and Sidney Axinn (New York: State University of New York Press, 1998), 291.
84. Kant, *Anthropology*, 7:208–209.
85. Zammito, *Birth of Anthropology*, 128.
86. Anthony J. La Vopa, "Thinking About Marriage: Kant's Liberalism and the Peculiar Morality of Conjugal Union," *The Journal of Modern History* 77 (2005): 33–34.
87. Mark Larrimore chronicles important shifts in Kant's views of race without tracing them, as I do here, through the lectures on anthropology. While my account is very much aligned with (and indebted to) his, I do not focus on Kant's account of temperament (which he does), given the distinction that Kant's mature anthropology draws between morally inconsequential differences of temperament and morally salient differences of race. I demonstrate that Kant's early (1770s) anthropology fails to distinguish between racial and national character, but the division becomes entrenched as of the mid-1780s and remains central from that point onward. Todd Hedrick similarly draws an equivalence between national and racial character to which Kant's later treatments do not conform. See Mark Larrimore, "Antinomies," and Todd Hedrick, "Race, Difference, and Anthropology in Kant's Cosmopolitanism," *Journal of the History of Philosophy* 46 (2008): 245–268.
88. Zammito, *Birth of Anthropology*, 301; see also Larrimore, "Antinomies of Race," 347. Jennifer Mensch notes that *Observations* "brought together the various strands that Kant was then pulling together as he began to think about the proper scope of anthropology: a field that could include an account of character, taste, and morality alongside consideration of native differences between sexes, nations, and the races" (Jennifer Mensch, "From Crooked Wood to Moral Agency: On Anthropology and Ethics in Kant," *Estudos Kantianos* 2, no. 1 (2014): 190). Those interests would, Zammito remarks, remain remarkably consistent across pre-critical, critical and post-critical periods (John Zammito, "What a Young Man Needs for his Venture into the World: The Function and Evolution of the 'Characteristics'," in *Kant's Lectures on Anthropology: A Critical Guide*, ed. Alix Cohen (Cambridge: Cambridge University Press, 2016), 230–248).
   Kant's lectures on physical geography, however, comprise his earliest reflections on race, preceding the *Observations* by at least half a decade. While their exact dating is uncertain, the relevant sections (9:311–9:320, "Concerning Human Beings," in the "Second Part" of the lectures) are prior to 1759. I largely set aside Kant's treatments of race in these lectures, for a few reasons. First, they predate Kant's critical turn by over two decades, and his more systematic account of anthropology by around fifteen years. Virtually all of the conceptual, epistemological and disciplinary divisions structuring Kant's mature thinking – between intelligible and noumenal realms, empirical and moral character, reflective and determinative judgment, anthropology and physical geography – are, at this point, absent. The reflections on race that remain are superficial bigotries with little bearing on the ethical theory he had yet to develop. Second, Eric Watkins points out that Kant's notes were hurriedly assembled and printed by

Friedrich Theodor Rink following Jakob Wilhelm and Gottfried Vollmer's unauthorized 1801 publication of his physical geography lectures. Already in the twilight of his life and in frail mental and physical health, Kant entrusted a rough manuscript to Rink, whose own failing health impacted his editorial capacities and who supplemented it with student notes. The resulting text, Watkins concludes, "is neither a document that Kant himself wrote nor a reliable indicator of what Kant said in his class ... there is no straightforward and unequivocal sense in which it can be taken to represent his actual views" (Eric Watkins, "Introduction to *Lectures on Physical Geography,*" in *Natural Science* (Cambridge: Cambridge University Press, 2012), 436. See, also, Bernasconi, "Third Thoughts," 297). This doesn't suggest that Kant's considered views on race depart radically from what appears in these lectures, but given these qualifications, I draw on them only to temporalize the development of his racial theory.

89. Kant, BS, 2:253.
90. The essay was subsequently revised and reprinted in a collection of essays in 1777. For a careful chronicling of the development of Kant's lectures on anthropology from his courses on physical geography and metaphysics, see Mensch, "Crooked Wood."
91. Kant, RM, 2:443.
92. Kant, *Friedländer*, 25:694.
93. For a careful treatment of the integration of epigenetic and preformationist arguments in Kant's germ-based account of racial generation, see Phillip R. Sloan, "Performing the Categories: Eighteenth-Century Generation Theory and the Biological Roots of Kant's *A Priori,*" *Journal of the History of Philosophy* 40, no. 2 (2002): 229–253.
94. Kant, *Friedländer*, 25:655.
95. Jennifer Mensch, *Kant's Organicism: Epigenesis and the Development of Critical Philosophy* (Chicago: University of Chicago Press, 2013), 106.
96. Kant, *Pillau*, 25:838.
97. Ibid., 25:839.
98. Kant, *Menschenkunde*, 25:1181.
99. Ibid., 25:1187.
100. Alix Cohen draws temperament – along with race, gender and nationality – under the broad umbrella of what nature makes of humanity, rather than what humanity makes of itself. Temperament and nationality, however, carry no moral value, while race and gender do. See Alix Cohen, "Kant on Epigenesis, Monogenesis and Human Nature: The Biological Premises of Anthropology," *Studies in History and Philosophy of Biological and Biomedical Sciences*, 37 (2006): 686–690.
101. For a detailed historical account of Kant's disputes with Herder and Forster, and of their impacts on the development of his racial theory in the 1780s, see Phillip R. Sloan, "Kant on the History of Nature: The Ambiguous Heritage of the Critical Philosophy for Natural History," *Studies in History and Philosophy of Biological and Biomedical Sciences* 27 (2006): 627–648, and Jennifer Mensch, "Kant and the Skull Collectors: German Anthropology from Blumenbach to Kant," in *Kant and his German Contemporaries. Volume 1, Logic, Mind, Epistemology, Science and Ethics*, eds. C. W. Dyck and F. Wunderlich (Cambridge: Cambridge University Press, 2018), 192–210.
102. Kant, *Mrongovius*, 25:1368.

103. Kant, BM, 8:98.
104. Kant, "Teleological Principles," 8:179.
105. Bernasconi, "Concept of Race"; see also Mark Larrimore, "Antinomies of Race," 341, and Charles Mills, "Kant and Race, *Redux*," *Graduate Faculty Philosophy Journal* 35, nos. 1–2 (2014): 131–132. Kant's precise role in the generation of the period's racial science is subject to some debate. While Jon M. Mikkelsen treats Kant's work in the natural sciences as pivotal for late eighteenth-century race discourse, John Zammito emphasizes the influence of such figures as Blumenbach, Buffon and Wolff. See Jon M. Mikkelsen ed. and trans., *Kant and the Concept of Race: Late Eighteenth-Century Writings* (Albany: State University of New York Press, 2013), and John Zammito's review of this same, at http://ndpr .nd.edu/news/45502-kant-and-the-concept-of-race-late-eighteenth-century-writings/. For careful reconstructions of the intellectual contexts surrounding Kant's racial theory, focusing on the life sciences and theories of generation in particular, see Jennifer Mensch, "Crooked Wood," and *Kant's Organicism*. For a narrower parsing of the scope, divisions and aims of the period's racial theories, see Mensch, "Skull Collectors."
106. Zammito, *Birth of Anthropology*, 302. Kant's racial theory is enmeshed in eighteenth-century debates surrounding evolution, generation, preformation and epigenesis in embryology and natural descent. As these do not directly inform my argument, I largely set them aside here. A substantial literature treats those debates' impacts on Kant's epistemology; see, for instance, Mark Fisher, "Metaphysics and Physiology in Kant's Attitudes towards Theories of Preformation," in *Kant's Theory of Biology*, eds. Eric Watkins and Ina Goy (Boston: De Gruyter, 2014), 25–42; Robert J. Richards, "Kant and Blumenbach on the *Bildungstrieb*: A Historical Misunderstanding," *Studies in History and Philosophy of Science Part C* 31, no. 1 (2000): 11–32; and Philippe Huneman, ed., *Understanding Purpose: Kant and the Philosophy of Biology* (Rochester: University of Rochester Press, 2007).
107. It is not clear whether Kant read Blumenbach in the 1770s, as his first reference to Blumenbach's work appears in 1788's "Teleological Principles." Blumenbach, however, lists Kant in the second edition of his *De generis humani varietate native* (1781).
108. Larrimore, "Antinomies of Race," 346; Zammito, *Birth of Anthropology*, 304. For an account of Kant's racial theory as primarily concerned with monogenesis (and epigenesis), see Cohen, "Biological Premises."
109. Kant, RM, 2:429.
110. Ibid., 2:430.
111. Ibid., 2:440.
112. Ibid., 2:432.
113. Ibid., 2:435. For a detailed treatment of Kant's usage of *Keime* and *Anlagen* in the context of mid-century debates between preformationist and epigenetic accounts of generation, see Sloan, "Performing the Categories."
114. Kant, RM, 2:437.
115. Kant, BM, 8:105.
116. Zammito, *Birth of Anthropology*, 302.
117. Kant, BM, 8:100.

118. Kant, "Teleological Principles," 8:162. For the epistemological implications of Kant's distinction between natural description and natural history, see Phillip R. Sloan, "Buffon, German Biology, and the Historical Interpretation of Biological Species," *The British Journal for the History of Science* 12, no. 2 (1979): 109–153, and Mensch, *Kant's Organicism*, ch. 5. For shifts in Kant's views on the distinction stemming from his disputes over human generation with Forster and Herder in the mid-1780s, see Sloan, "Ambiguous Heritage."
119. Mensch, *Kant's Organicism*, 106.
120. Kant, "Teleological Principles," 8:161.
121. Ibid., 8:179.
122. Ibid., 8:169.
123. Richards, "*Bildungstrieb*," 27.
124. Kant, "Teleological Principles," 8:163.
125. Ibid., 8:169.
126. Thomas E. Hill Jr. and Bernard Boxill, "Kant and Race," in *Race and Racism*, ed. Bernard Boxill (Oxford: Oxford University Press, 2001), 145–166. Mark Larrimore points out that Kant's monogenism in no way implies its greater egalitarianism; many of the era's monogenetic racial theories treated non-Europeans as degenerations from a superior – invariably white – phyletic origin. Forster in fact directly challenged monogenists to show that their view resulted in any more humane treatment of African slaves.
127. Louden, *Impure Ethics*, 104.
128. Kant, BM, 8:96
129. I restrict myself here to the deeper moral incoherences in Kant's racial theory, largely setting aside the inconsistencies pervading his racial taxonomy and rankings. For a detailed account of these irregularities, see Mark Larrimore, "Sublime Waste: Kant on the Destiny of the 'Races'," *Canadian Journal of Philosophy* 25 (1999): 99–125.
130. Kant, BM, 8:106.
131. Kant, RM, 2:441.
132. Ibid.
133. Ibid., 2:438.
134. Kant, "Teleological Principles," 8:176.
135. Ibid., 8:174. My italics.
136. "Human character," Sloan observes, "both as physiognomy, and also as a moral property, is closely related to the inborn *Keime*. Some individuals possess these inborn principles for moral development, whereas others lack them" ("Performing the Categories," 240).
137. Kant, BS, 2:253.
138. Larrimore, "Antinomies of Race," 342.
139. Kant, *Menschenkunde*, 25:1188.
140. Kant, *Anthropology*, 7:220.
141. Eze, "Color of Reason."
142. Kant, *Pillau*, 25:843.
143. Immanuel Kant, "Review of J. G. Herder's *Idea for the Philosophy of the History of Humanity. Parts 1 and 2*," in *Anthropology, History, and Education*, eds. Günter Zöller and Robert B Louden (Cambridge: Cambridge University Press 2007), 8:62.

144. Kant, RM, 2:438.
145. Kant, "Teleological Principles," 8:176.
146. Ibid.
147. Kant, RM, 2:438.
148. Kant, *Pillau*, 25:840.
149. For the "Europeanization" argument, see Louden, *Impure Ethics*; for the "extinction" argument, see Bernasconi, "Unfamiliar Source of Racism," 159–160. For a similar view – that Kant "conceived of the (non-white) races as an unsalvageable waste, a mistake, meaningless in the grand teleological scheme of things," see Larrimore, "Sublime Waste," 118.
150. Kant, *Pillau*, 25:843.
151. Kant, *Menschenkunde*, 25:1181.
152. In what follows, I sketch out a few approaches to this relationship. More broadly, one can differentiate two basic camps: those that see Kant's race-thinking as impacting his wider moral and political theory, and those that believe, roughly, that they can be set apart. For the former, see Bernasconi, "Third Thoughts," "Concept of Race" and "Unfamiliar Source of Racism"; Mills, "Kant's *Untermenschen*" and "Kant and Race, *Redux*"; Eze, "Color of Reason"; Larrimore, "Antinomies" and "Sublime Waste"; Hedrick, "Race, Difference"; Inés Valdez, "It's not About Race: Good Wars, Bad Wars, and the Origins of Kant's Anti-Colonialism," American Political Science Review 111, no. 4 (2017): 819–834; and my argument here. For the latter, see Kleingeld, "Second Thoughts on Race" and her "Kant's Second Thoughts on Colonialism," in Flikschuh and Ypi, *Kant and Colonialism*; Muthu, *Enlightenment*; Hill and Boxill, "Kant and Race"; Louden, *Impure Ethics*; McCarthy, *Race, Empire*; Wood, *Ethical Thought*; and Ian Storey, "Empire and Natural Order in Kant's 'Second Thoughts' on Race," *History of Political Thought* 36, no. 4 (2015): 670–699.
153. Louden, *Impure Ethics*, 105.
154. Larrimore, "Antinomies of Race," 342.
155. Mills, "Kant's *Untermenschen*"; Eze, "Color of Reason."
156. Mills, "Kant and Race," 138.
157. Mills, "Kant's *Untermenschen*," 169.
158. Eze, "Color of Reason," 105.
159. The tendency to draw a rough equivalency between different kinds of texts is not uncommon. Lea Ypi, for instance, suggests that Kant changed his view of non-Europeans' political status between "Conjectural Beginning of Human History" (1786) and the 1797 *Rechtslehre*. But these are distinctive forms of writing with disjunctive aims and claims. The former is – as the title suggests – conjectural, and largely a polemic against Herder, satirizing Book 10 of his *Ideen zur Philosophie der Geschichte der Menschheit*; the latter is a systematic account of the rightful condition preserving our external freedom. To treat their claims as continuous – such that a shift between them implies a change of mind – is unwarranted. See Lea Ypi, "Commerce and Colonialism in Kant's Philosophy of History," in Katrin Flikschuh and Lea Ypi, *Kant and Colonialism: Historical and Critical Perspectives* (Oxford University Press, 2014), 119.
160. Kleingeld, "Second Thoughts on Race." For an expansion of the argument, suggesting that Kant's anti-colonialism also emerges from a mid-1790s change of heart, see Kleingeld's "Second Thoughts on Colonialism." While agreeing

that Kant underwent a "change of attitude" concerning colonialism, Jennifer Mensch argues that he nonetheless "remained committed to his scientific account of the physiological grounds for racial difference" (Mensch, "Crooked Wood," 199). "[W]hile Kant dropped the language of racial hierarchy in the 1790s," then, "he by no means retracted his scientific essays offering a physiological anthropology of racial difference" (Mensch, "Inevitable Progress," 8).

161. Kant does appear to have changed his views on a race-relevant subject in the 1790s, even if it isn't the change that Kleingeld proposes. Phillip Sloan argues that Kant altered his account of generation (along with the account of *Keime* it sustained) as of 1790, in the wake of Blumenbach's all-out attack on leading preformationist theories (including his own, from the late 1770s). Kant did not, however, change the substance of the racial theory tethered to it, but rather modified and adapted his account of generation – which already charted a "middle course" between strong preformationist and epigenetic theories – to nudge it closer to the epigenetic position. While Kant minimizes references to *Keime* in the 1790s (without abandoning it altogether; it appears in the *Religion, Anthropology*, and lectures on physical geography and pedagogy), there is no indication that he substantively altered his account of race as a consequence. "[I]n the *moral* realm, at least," Sloan holds, "Kant did not give up his reliance on some kind of preformed *Keime* that lie within the human stock, even in the face of the arguments he seems to have generally accepted in 1790 in favor of Blumenbach's *Keime*-free epigenetic theory" (Sloan, "Performing the Categories," 251). Still further, the change was not prompted by the egalitarian implications of his cosmopolitanism (as Kleingeld suggests), but by the need to adapt a theory of biological generation that had become unsustainable.

162. Kleingeld and Ypi pursue just this line of argument, taking Kant's early denigrations of non-Europeans, along with his failure to criticize slavery, as evidence that he supported colonialism (prior to 1792). This is unwarranted. Beyond the speculativeness of treating non-criticism as an endorsement of political domination, the evidence demonstrating Kant's ostensible (early) support for colonialism is drawn from his writings on race, history, geography and anthropology, while the post-1792, anti-colonial Kant is culled from his writings on right. These are, again, different forms of writing with distinctive vantage points issuing in claims that are unassimilable. Kant's reflective judgments on non-Europeans' deficits do not bear on questions of right: they situate Europeans at the apex of civilization, but provide no consequent warrant to impose that civilization on others. Charles Mills similarly conflates reflective and determinative judgments in suggesting that Kant's racial theory treats "races of blacks and Native Americans [as] natural slaves who may be colonized and enslaved" ("Kant and Race," 146). This is, again, unwarranted: racial hierarchy does not countenance such a violation of rights. See Kleingeld, "Kant's Second Thoughts on Colonialism," Lea Ypi, "Commerce and Colonialism," and Charles Mills, "Kant and Race."

163. Robert Bernasconi makes a similar observation concerning Kant's views on slavery: "[i]t would be perfectly possible to be against slavery and still maintain a racial hierarchy and indeed in his *Lectures on Physical Geography* in 1792 Kant did so" (Bernasconi, "Third Thoughts," 304).

164. Larrimore, "Antinomies of Race," 358.
165. Robert Bernasconi is rightly wary of the interpretive temptation to "have a reading of Kant that imposes consistency on him from outside when it seems that there is none," a tendency that he sees in both critics (Mills) and defenders (Kleingeld). See Bernasconi, "Third Thoughts," 293.
166. Valdez, "Good Wars". Bernasconi echoes the point; see "Third Thoughts," 302.
167. Kleingeld, "Second Thoughts on Race," 585–586.
168. Larrimore, "Antinomies," 343.
169. Ibid., 362.
170. Kant, *Menschenkunde*, 25:1187.
171. Kant, *Pillau*, 25:843.
172. Ibid., 25:840.
173. Kant, I, 8:21.
174. Kant's "assumption that the non-white race have inferior agential capacities," Kleingeld observes, "plays a crucial role in his teleological account of race, in explaining why the stability of racial features is purposive" (Kleingeld, *Kant and Cosmopolitanism*, 105).
175. For another treatment of the problem of instrumentalization entailed by Kant's philosophy, see Hedrick, "Race, Difference." I elaborate on this further in Chapter 5, section 5.5.
176. Larrimore, "Kant's Antinomies," 362; see, also, Kleingeld, *Kant and Cosmopolitanism*.
177. McCarthy, *Race, Empire*, 47.
178. Hedrick, "Race, Difference," 263.
179. Bernasconi similarly suggests that Kant doubted the capacity of "whole race[s] to be raised to the level that would allow them to participate fully in the ultimate end nature had set for the human species" (Bernasconi, "Third Thoughts," 312).
180. Hedrick, "Race, Difference," 267.
181. Ibid., 265.

4

Democratic Character and the Affective Grounds
of Politics

> If I am asked, what system of political philosophy I substituted for that which, as
> a philosophy, I had abandoned, I answer, no system: only a conviction that the
> true system was something much more complex and many-sided than I had
> previously had any idea of, and that its office was to supply, not a set of model
> institutions, but principles from which the institutions suitable to any given
> circumstances might be deduced.
>
> J. S. Mill, *Autobiography*

Kant's views on human diversity require some excavation. Having never set foot
beyond the city of his birth, and widely perceived as eschewing such
phenomenal dreck, the sage of Königsberg seems an unlikely candidate for
reflections on humanity's heterogeneity. Mill's, on the other hand, appear
somewhat closer to the surface, and all the more so in recent years, as the
imperial entanglements of his social, political and moral thought have come
under scrutiny. His failure to recognize the moral worth or political capacities
of non-Europeans seem less incongruous than Kant's for both philosophical and
biographical reasons. Conceptually, Mill is understood to have conjoined the
Scottish Enlightenment's conjectural history with a utilitarian calculus to
develop an index of civilization warranting pedagogical imperialism.
By adapting and moralizing the four-stages theory of socio-historical
development, he purportedly treats all societies as moving through fixed
stages of progress. Only through a well-calibrated imperial tutelage, then,
could the uncivilized be raised up to a society of laws. His 35-year tenure at
the East India Company also suggests that he saw non-Europeans as morally,
intellectually, culturally and politically backward, as does James Mill's well-
documented influence over him. J. S. Mill's liberalism has thus come to
exemplify the tradition's impulses toward the domination and
marginalization of non-liberals (and more pointedly, of non-Europeans),

perhaps among the clearest illustrations of what Uday Singh Mehta describes as liberal strategies of exclusion.[1]

And yet, Mill's views are as poorly served by a quick reading as Kant's. While criticisms of Mill's liberal imperialism are well-warranted and illuminating, they also misrepresent his fuller liberalism and its accounts of racial, cultural, social and political diversity. Here and in Chapter 5, I argue that Mill's liberalism can only be portrayed as closed to human difference, as reflecting the tradition's implicit exclusionism, or as blind to the worth of non-European social forms by setting aside his expansive writings on national character, human development and political life. I also argue that the critical perspective misconstrues the philosophy of history and sociological conception of progress framing his understanding of human plurality. Many of the presumptions upholding the critical view – that Mill reproduced his father's prejudices, that he saw social evolution as fixed and universal, that he regarded non-Europeans as frozen in time, that he drew a Manichean divide between civilized and uncivilized societies, and more – are, in fact, mistaken. My central aim is to elaborate Mill's treatments of human diversity and difference within the conceptual architecture surrounding them. Understood properly, they are not continuous with Kant's, nor with a great many other liberals'. Far from sharing in the "continental chauvinism and implicit and explicit racism ... inherent to the Western canon,"[2] Kant's and Mill's liberalisms are not of a kind. Their responses to human diversity diverge substantively, generating accordingly different political ideals and programs.

To make the case, these chapters proceed much as the last two did with Kant. I take a wide view of Mill's liberalism, gleaned from his writings on ethics, politics, history, sociology and ethology (his ill-fated foray into a science of character formation), to contextualize his notion of human diversity.[3] This pursues the intuition guiding my reading of Kant. If we're to understand how human difference fits within Mill's liberalism, we need to expand beyond *On Liberty, Considerations on Representative Government*, and the few essays (most often "Civilization" and "A Few Words on Non-Intervention") containing his most parochial assessments of non-Europeans. Without neglecting or minimizing its impacts on his political philosophy, we also need to expand beyond Mill's imperialism to capture his fuller vision of human pluralism. While empire and chauvinisms clearly shape his thinking, Mill's liberalism is not reducible to an apologetics for empire, nor is his view of human diversity reducible to his chauvinisms. His international engagements far exceeded his commitments as an imperialist: from the American Civil War and abolitionism, to international law and treaty obligations, to Britain's conflict with Russia over the 1856 Treaty of Paris, Mill threw himself into a wide array of transcontinental causes now obscured by the long shadow of his imperialism.[4] By widening the lens, I ultimately aim to better capture his considered views of social, cultural and racial diversity, along with the historical and social sciences framing them.

Reading Mill this way, comprehensively, exposes a certain elusiveness in his thinking. Despite its ambiguities, the nerve center of Kant's moral and political philosophy – autonomy and rational self-determination – is clear. Mill has no such equivalent. He is, of course, widely recognized as a founding father of liberalism, but its precise contours are less easily discerned. George Kateb and Nadia Urbinati, for instance, treat dignity as the cornerstone of his ethics and politics, which sits uncomfortably with the utilitarianism that John Gibbins, Don Habibi and Uday Mehta take as Mill's governing principle.[5] For Isaiah Berlin, utilitarianism vanishes almost entirely from his mature thought, the vestigial trace of James Mill's and Bentham's waning influence; with C. L. Ten and Jeremy Waldron, Berlin finds in Mill a thoroughly anti-foundationalist, pluralist liberalism.[6] That liberalism is itself not without its critics: Maurice Cowling and Alistair McIntyre take its (ostensibly) withering individualism as emblematic of the tradition's atomism.[7] Mill is also accused of not being liberal enough. Charles Larmore, Dana Villa and John Rawls criticize his (again, purported) utilitarian perfectionism for infracting political liberalism's neutrality (Bruce Baum more reasonably locates him somewhere in the middle, as a "liberal socialist").[8] Against strictly liberal readings – for or against – Martha Nussbaum, John Gray, Nadia Urbinati and Nicholas Capaldi draw out Mill's latent Aristotelianism, while Peter Berkowitz, Wendy Donner and Bernard Semmel treat him as an outright virtue ethicist.[9] Depending on who you ask, Mill is an unabashed democrat in the Athenian mold,[10] a hesitant democrat,[11] no democrat at all,[12] a civic republican,[13] an imperialist despot,[14] an ethical perfectionist,[15] a fallibilist,[16] a "Romantic deontologist,"[17] a multiculturalist,[18] a libertarian,[19] a liberal,[20] a moral authoritarian in liberal clothing,[21] a socialist,[22] a conservative,[23] the "Saint of Rationalism,"[24] a Benthamite reformer[25] – and the list goes on. Perhaps most confounding is that none of these is particularly wrong – elements of each sit elbow to elbow in his thought. Beyond the catch-all liberalism draped around his shoulders, then, Mill is not reducible to any single ideological mantle.[26]

This elusiveness is attributable to a few sources. First, Mill was an inordinately prolific writer who touched on every subject that we might expect to capture the attention of Victorian England's preeminent public intellectual (and many that we might not). The *Collected Works'* 33 tomes bear witness to his sustained engagements with politics, history, sociology, political economy, moral psychology, ethics, human development, international law, religion, philosophy, national character and much more. Second, Mill underwent profound personal and philosophical transformations over the course of his life. Raised an impeccable utilitarian, he was a burgeoning leader of the Philosophical Radicals in the 1820s before his deep and years-long depression pushed him toward St.-Simonism, Romanticism and conservatism in the 1830s, all influences that he would spend a lifetime integrating. Mill's views changed over time, and quite dramatically. Third, he was neither doctrinaire nor terribly precise with the distinctions structuring his moral and political philosophies, leaving in his wake a long trail of tensions (between, for instance, his utilitarianism and his defense of liberty or his elitism and his democratic theory). As Nicholas Capaldi observes, Mill's overarching concern with his ideas' social and political implications led him to prize practical orientation over analytical rigor, for better or worse; he treated as apparent "[t]he error ... of those who would deduce the line of conduct proper to particular cases from supposed universal practical maxims," arguing that "rules of conduct [should] only be considered as provisional."[27] Mill also occupied different posts during his life – East India Company functionary, editor of the *London Review* (and subsequently, of the *London and Westminster Review*), Member of Parliament and, through it all, "public moralist"[28] – each of which impacted his thought. Finally, and perhaps most importantly, Mill's indefinability is a corollary of his longstanding conviction, most eloquently articulated in *On Liberty*, that the truth on any given matter is invariably spread across ideological lines. He took seriously the view that dissent and heterodoxy couldn't help but reveal a fuller understanding of any particular subject, cause or idea. More than almost any other moral and political thinker – and certainly more than any as canonized as he's been – Mill remains most firmly committed to synthesizing seemingly irreconcilable perspectives and most persistently unconstrained, on principle, by ideological rigidity.

The resulting ambivalences have generated both a wider range of interpretations and a broader scope for reasonable disagreement than we get from many other political theorists. Mill's philosophical ecumenism, however, is neither lazy nor dilettantish. It is, rather, grounded in a sociologically and historically informed skepticism toward the utility of universal maxims generally, and all the more so in relation to the social and political theory at the center of his concerns. Given this, it's no surprise that the tensions in his views are not reducible to his intellectual shifts: his mature political philosophy holds together Romanticism and utilitarian rationalism, democratic tendencies and elitist retrenchments, experiments in living and a taxonomy of pleasures, and other contradictions, or seeming contradictions. We need only recall that *On Liberty* and *Utilitarianism*, whose accounts of the relationship between ethics and politics are at best difficult to reconcile, were published just two years apart to see the unusually wide berth for disagreement that Mill provides. One suspects that he wouldn't have wanted it any other way.

While Mill covers a lot of ground, I focus on his liberalism's principal blind spot: the uncivilized people(s) that he regarded as incapable of democratic self-government, as benefiting from despotism and as unfit for the liberties enjoyed by their intellectual and political superiors.[29] I address the Mill drawn out by critics of liberal imperialism, whose thought is qualified by a Eurocentric developmentalism relegating non-Western peoples to, as Dipesh Chakrabarty characterizes it, a permanent state of "not yet."[30] As a result, I devote less attention to his treatment of women and the working classes, of whose rights he was a tireless champion. While I touch on them throughout (particularly in my account of democratic affects), I center on the non-Europeans falling outside his liberalism's ambit, and on the conceptualizations of historical progress, civilization and human development framing their moral and political standing.

I begin by elaborating Mill's account of the aims and ends of government generally, and more particularly, of representative government – the "ideally best form of government"[31] for advanced, civilized peoples (but, we will see, not for all of them). This clarifies Mill's measure of the worth of governing institutions and his account of their enabling conditions to show what makes for a desirable politics at all. It also delves into his account of democratic fitness, which critics take as demarcating civilized, democratically capable societies from uncivilized ones based on citizens' cognitive abilities. From this perspective, democratic competence turns on a fixed cognitive threshold distinguishing distinctively different kinds of societies, defined by their capacity or incapacity for fruitful self-government.

Section 4.2 challenges this view. Rather than treating the division as a strictly cognitive-rational one – as a matter of civilizational-intellectual achievement – I argue that Mill is in fact concerned with the development of democratic *character*.[32] Mill, I suggest, understood democracy as a uniquely character-dependent form of government whose success, measured by the standard of utility, hinged on the development of particular habits, orientations and affects. More than others, democratic institutions rest on public-mindedness, civic trust and political engagement, and on the "schools of public spirit" cultivating them. Mill was accordingly wary of the affective deficits threatening a democratic polity, to which the uncivilized and a range of civilized people(s) – particularly, the civilized poor – are subject. Given this, I argue that Mill's account of democratic competence turns less on a strict assessment of rational capability (though he weighs this as well) than on citizens' acculturation to the *habitus* of democratic life. It reflects Mill's concern with democracy's affective conditions – conditions that he saw as lacking in some of the most advanced, civilized societies of his day – more than a facile division between advanced and retrograde peoples.

The chapter's final section elaborates on the associationist moral psychology underpinning this affective register of political life. Mill's moral psychology was rooted in, but ultimately departed from, his father's work on the subject (he read James Mill's *Analysis of the Phenomena of the Human Mind* as it was being written, in the summers from 1822 to 1829, and re-published it with his own expansive notes in 1869). The younger Mill's associationism bridges his politics and utilitarianism by showing how citizens learn to want the higher pleasures of social virtue. It thus keeps utilitarianism from lapsing into a self-serving hedonism by accounting for the socialized dispositions and habits sustaining a progressive, liberal polity. This does not, however, entail the moral perfectionism that critics have attributed to Mill. It is, rather, a "procedural perfectionism"[33] preserving the conditions for ongoing individual and collective self-development (rather than self-perfection, as Kant would have it). Mill's political ideal does not advance any particular end-goal or thick utilitarian ethics, but is thoroughly fallibilistic and intentionally undefined. It rests on the presumption that our good – the "permanent interests of man as a progressive being"[34] – lies in our inexhaustible capacity for development.

As will become evident, the "affective" standpoint developed here helps us to understand Mill's view of the uncivilized without depicting it any more favorably than the "cognitivist" perspective on which I expand. If anything, Mill comes out looking worse than he did coming in, as I in no way defend his reprehensible opinions of the uncivilized, much less the imperialism that they supported. My defense of Mill, like my critique of Kant, is qualified, not root and branch: it aims to understand his views of diversity and difference within their textual and conceptual contexts. I thus neither disregard nor diminish the impacts of Mill's prejudices on his liberalism, but rather – as with Kant – situate them within the architectonic through which he made sense of cultural, national and racial diversity. There is much to criticize in Mill's treatment of non-Europeans; he fares no better here than in the critical literature. But the fuller picture to which it contributes will, I hope, bear out my contention that Mill's liberalism is singularly receptive to the claims of culture and difference, even if he is not.

4.1   GOVERNMENT

4.1.1   The Art of Life and the Social Science

Mill's championing of liberty and self-government have long served as the flashpoint for interpreting, and misinterpreting, his political philosophy. At one end of the spectrum, John Hospers and Charles Murray read Mill as a libertarian (or as a fount for their own libertarianisms) whose defense of liberty guts the state of all but the most night-watchman-like of powers, overstating "Mill's unequivocal advocacy of liberty and his wish to expand it almost without limit."[35] At the other, John Rawls, William Galston and Charles Larmore treat him as an ethical perfectionist all too willing to countenance an overweening state to achieve utilitarian goals.[36] How, then, does Mill actually understand the aims, ends and conditions of government, and the nature of political life more generally?

In *Considerations on Representative Government*, his best-developed account of the purposes of political organization, Mill stipulates that "the influence of government on the well-being of society can be considered or estimated in reference to nothing less than the whole of the interests of humanity."[37] Utility "in the largest sense, grounded on the permanent interests of man as a progressive being"[38] comprises the measure of all government, representative or not. And yet his conceptualization of utility and its connection to politics as a "first principle" remain unclear without the guiding light of the *System of Logic*'s "Art of Life."[39]

In the *Logic*'s final chapter, "Of the Logic of Practice, or Art; Including Morality and Policy," Mill addresses two constituent elements of practical action: the end-guiding norms of "art" and the truth-generating domain of "science." These he places in relation to moral, prudential and aesthetic spheres, and to the meta-principle of utility anchoring them. Art speaks in the "imperative mood"[40] and supplies "the original major premise, which asserts that the attainment of [a] given end is desirable"[41] – the normative goal steering practical action. "The Method, therefore, of Ethics, can be no other than that of Art."[42] "Science," Mill goes on to explain, "then lends to Art the proposition (obtained by a series of inductions or of deductions) that the performance of certain actions will attain the end,"[43] taking up the principles and laws enabling that goal's pursuit and delimiting its conditions of possibility. In total,

The relation in which rules of art stand to doctrines of science may be thus characterized. The art proposes to itself an end to be attained, defines the end, and hands it over to the science. The science receives it, considers it as a phenomenon or effect to be studied, and having investigated its causes and conditions, sends it back to art with a theorem of the combinations of circumstances by which it could be produced. Art then examines these combinations of circumstances, and according as any of them are or are not in human power, pronounces the end attainable or not.[44]

At first glance, Mill's distinction appears to countenance a relatively straightforward division of labor between the ethical direction of art ("that which enunciates the object aimed at, and affirms it to be a desirable object")[45] and the "[p]ropositions of science [that] assert a matter of fact."[46] In this case, ethical principles provide the normative direction steering "the Social Science" (sociology, ethology and political science). The "traditional" criticism of Mill's political philosophy, as John Gray describes it – that the science of politics follows from the art of morality, rendering it subservient to a perfectionist ethics – turns on precisely such a reading.

However, it misrepresents Mill's argument. The division of art and science is not neatly overlaid onto ethics and politics, but rather clarifies the relationship between action-directing norms and their conditions of possibility across multiple spheres of practical life, not just the moral. Art pertains less to any particular ethical principles governing political life than to the contextually variable ends orienting practical action in different domains of human experience, in tandem with the relevant "theorems of science."[47] From these premises, Mill deduces "a body of doctrine, which is properly the Art of Life, in its three departments, Morality, Prudence or Policy, and Aesthetics; the Right, the Expedient, and the Beautiful or Noble, in human conduct and works."[48] Morality is, then, one of three divisions of the Art of Life (themselves divided into more "particular art[s]," including the art of government), and not a *higher* principle guiding or constraining politics. Morality, policy and aesthetics comprise the equi-primary spheres to which "all other arts are subordinate; since its principles are those which must determine whether the special aim of any particular art is worthy and desirable."[49]

Art, then, does not refer to morality per se, but to the variable ends anchoring practical action in different realms. And while the coherence of all forms of inquiry rests on some such "Doctrine of Ends," "a writer on Morals and Politics requires those principles at every step," given that they "undertake to say not merely what is, but what ought to be."[50] Mill's conviction that a clearly enunciated "ultimate standard"[51] should steer social advancement animated his critique of Comte, whose mechanistic philosophy of history obviated the need, or even the possibility, for any kind of concerted guidance. Even the best exposition of the laws of social progress, as Mill considered Comte's to be, remained as futile as it was rudderless without a normative thread to lead it. Comte's failure was to proceed "on the conviction, that if he [could] produce a theory of society as it is, and as it tends to become, there [was] nothing more to be done,"[52] a scientistic determinism that Mill found equally objectionable in Bentham and in the Philosophical Radicals.

This practical bent also informs the *Logic*'s critique of moral intuitionism. Without a clear-sighted "first principle of Teleology," moral and political theory inevitably lapses into the groundless supposition that "a moral sense, or instinct, inherent in our constitution, informs us ... what principles of conduct we are bound to observe."[53] To avoid this kind of baseless subjectivism, Mill argues, practical action requires "some standard by which to determine the goodness or badness, absolute and comparative, of ends, or of objects of desire," a non-speculative "ultimate principle of Morality, as for that of Prudence, Policy, or Taste."[54] That "general principle," he declares (in a self-avowedly under-justified way), "to which all rules of practices ought to conform, and the test by which they should be tried, is that of conduciveness to the happiness of mankind, or rather, of all sentient beings; in other words, that the promotion of happiness is the ultimate principle of Teleology."[55] Utility is, then, the governing meta-principle orienting morality, policy, and aesthetics; it figures, as John Gray puts it, "not as a moral principle from which may be derived in any very direct way judgments about the rightness of actions, but as an axiological principle specifying that happiness alone has intrinsic goodness."[56] While Mill understands the task of politics as advancing that ideal of happiness, this is less an ethical stricture specifying any particular conception of the good than what Alan Ryan describes as "the imperative major premise of the whole Art."[57] The standard of utility is "a general principle of valuation"[58] split into subsidiary divisions and norms delimited by the narrower spheres of practical action to which they apply.

Mill's account is thus structured lexically: utility is the governing principle postulating the inherent worth of happiness; the arts of morality, prudence and aesthetics comprise the broad fields of practical life, whose norms (the right, the expedient, and the beautiful/noble) orient the more particular subfields of human activity (ethics, government, public policy, fine art, etc.); and the sciences associated with them delimit the relevant conditions, laws and truths within which their ends might be pursued. His approach to the design of political institutions is accordingly under-defined and circumstantially flexible, set against the tendency (here attributed to French speculators) of deriving "what is called the general principle of the government"[59] from "large and sweeping practical maxims."[60] The principle of utility is no moral code yielding specific political arrangements, but rather an overarching touchstone orienting all domains of practical life, including the political *and* the moral. Far from subsuming practical and political action under an all-encompassing morality, his tripartite division explicitly eschews the intuitionists' ethical over-extension. Even if their principles were proven true, Mill argues, they "would provide only for that portion of the field of conduct which is properly called moral. For the remainder of the practice of life some general principle, or standard, must still be sought."[61] This criticism of moral sprawl extended to all political thinkers holding "the untenable position that morality has authority over large areas of practical life,"[62] including Comte (to whom he referred as a "morality-intoxicated man")[63] and Bentham. Politics and morality are, for Mill, distinctive arenas of practical life, each governed by its own ends and subject to its own sciences. The social science, then, explores the "combinations of circumstances" enabling differently situated societies to pursue their collective ends.

4.1.2 Aims, Ends and Conditions of Government

While utility orients the social sciences generally, *Considerations* specifies subsidiary principles relating to politics and statecraft. Two things are worth noting about its account. First, it reflects the *Logic*'s art–science divide and indeterminate view of governments, which, "being only a means," Mill asserts, "must depend on their adaptation to the end."[64] As a result, "the proper functions of a government are not a fixed thing, but different in different states of society."[65] Second, Mill's steadfast resistance to ideological stringency surfaces from the book's first pages, which set out his conviction that "a better doctrine must be possible" than either conservatives' or liberals', and "not a mere compromise, by splitting the difference between the two, but something wider than either, which, in virtue of its superior comprehensiveness, might be adopted by either."[66] These characteristic features – politics as art and science, the contingency of institutional forms, ideological hybridity – structure Mill's mature view of politics.

Considerations starts from the premise that political orthodoxies, liberal and conservative, are irredeemably deficient.[67] Despite his liberal sympathies, Mill took umbrage at their overly scientistic reformism, which treated government as "a problem, to be worked like any other question of business."[68] Steeped in the rigidly rationalist "philosophy of the 18th century"[69] that he decried in

Benthamite radicalism, liberals saw "the form of government which combines the greatest amount of good with the least of evil"[70] as determined a priori, and the mechanics of implementation ("persuad[ing] others that it is the best")[71] as little more than a technicality to be worked out further down the road. Mill had rejected this kind of crude utilitarianism more than two decades earlier in the essays on Bentham and Coleridge, "the culmination of [his] attempt to free philosophic radicalism from what he called 'sectarian Benthamism'."[72] In the 1830s, under the sway of German and English Romanticism, he developed the abiding conviction that political institutions should be fitted to the nature, mores and character of the vastly different peoples over whom they presided. Treating political systems as context-sensitive rather than rationally predetermined, Mill held, "may be regarded as the main point of superiority in the political theories of the present above those of the last age"[73] and is central to *Considerations'* account of government.

He was, however, equally set against the conservative conception of political institutions as natural outgrowths of a people's inborn character, an organicism that resisted concerted direction by suggesting that "forms of government are not a matter of choice," and that a citizenry's "will has had no part in the matter."[74] The glint of conservatism in Mill's political thought, Nicholas Capaldi observes, "was never a defense of the status quo"[75] as his attraction to its holism diminished neither his commitment to reform, nor his faith in individual and collective self-development. He also criticized the conservative "partition of the exigencies of society between the two heads of Order and Progress (in the phraseology of French thinkers) [or] Permanence and Progression, in the words of Coleridge,"[76] treating the dichotomy as "unscientific and incorrect."[77] This was, however, a view that he only came to over time, as the order-progress split figured in his own political thinking for decades. In the 1831 essay series "The Spirit of the Age," he distinguishes "natural" and "artificial"/"transitional" states of society, quite directly borrowing from the St. Simonians' cycle of "organic" and "critical" historical periods.[78] In the *Logic*, the distinction shifts from philosophical history to social science, adopting Comte's social statics and social dynamics to examine "the conditions of stability in the social union" and its "laws of progress."[79]

Considerations' settled view, then, emerged from three decades of contemplating social order and progress from liberal, conservative, rationalist, Romantic and sociological vantage points. That settled view, understood properly, suggests that principles of progress and permanence do not in fact conflict. "The fundamental antithesis which these words express do not lie in the things themselves," Mill avers, "so much as in the types of human character which answer to them."[80] A given population's "social exigencies" are best determined not by such abstractions as order and progress (which in any case presuppose one another, he points out), but from a careful assessment of "the qualities of the human beings composing the society over which the government is exercised."[81] Conservatives and liberals alike misconstrue national character: while the former treat a people's habits, *moeurs* and culture as fixed, the latter sees them as inconsequential. Against both, Mill understands it as a government's central object and limiting condition: the best governments shape themselves to their people's character and further their active, moral and intellectual capabilities. The first criterion of good government is "the degree in which it tends to increase the sum of good qualities in the governed, collectively and individually"[82] (call this the "pedagogic criterion"). The second lies in the capacity of the state's institutional arrangements – the administration of justice, electoral forms, the judicial system and so on – to best harness and employ its citizens' existing abilities (call this, following Mill, the "machinery criterion"). Taken together, the "twofold division of the merit which any set of political institutions can possess ... consists partly of the degree in which they promote the general advancement of the community ... and partly of the degree of perfection with which they organize the moral, intellectual and active worth already existing."[83] True to Millian form, pedagogic and machinery criteria are entwined and mutually reinforcing, rather than opposed; the state's institutions, for instance – its machinery – ought equally to develop a population's capabilities and manage its existing resources.

These two measures of good government – "how far they tend to foster in the members of the community the various desirable qualities, moral and intellectual" and "the quality of the machinery itself; that is, the degree in which it is adapted to take advantage of the amount of good qualities which may at any time exist"[84] – certainly depart from liberal neutralism, and still more from the crude libertarianism sometimes attributed to Mill. Mill was no simple champion of liberty or representative institutions: to treat any particular form or principle of government as uniformly desirable was to misunderstand the nature and tasks of government altogether. As early as 1829, he criticized Comte's contention that governments should direct "all the forces of society to some one end," countering that "[g]overnment exists for all purposes whatever that are for man's good; and the highest & most important of these purposes is the improvement of man himself as a moral and intelligent being."[85] Governments shouldn't necessarily maximize liberty, or pursue any other fixed principle divined in a speculative vacuum, but should instead be crafted to a people's character and oriented to their self-development.

The design of government is, then, for Mill an evaluative and context-dependent art drawing on practical and prudential judgment, and not Bentham's legislative science. This vantage point registers not only the ends of government, but also its enabling conditions. For any government to function, Mill holds,

The people for whom the form of government is intended must be willing to accept it; or at least not so unwilling, as to oppose an insurmountable obstacle to its establishment. They must be willing and able to do what is necessary to keep it standing. And they must be willing and able to do what it requires of them to enable it to fulfil [*sic*] its purposes ...

They must be capable of fulfilling the conditions of action, and the conditions of self-restraint, which are necessary either for keeping the established polity in existence, or for enabling it to achieve [its] ends.[86]

Against political idealism's abstraction and universalism, Mill's three conditions draw out the intimate connection between national character and political institutions. As the lawmaker's art lies in forging a political system aligned with "the opinions, tastes, and habits of the people," he maintains, "it would be a great mistake in any legislator not to shape his measure so as to take advantage of such pre-existing habits and feelings."[87] Mill's assessment of a government's worth turns on its alignment with citizens' customs and predilections – what Nadia Urbinati describes as "the cultural criterion for judging government [which] set the tone for Mill's political thought as a whole."[88] Governments both foster and depend on the bonds of solidarity securing citizens' acquiescence, bonds cultivated not just politically, but through the broader affective networks of particular civil societies.

These three conditions and the social unity they secure are hard-won achievements. Mill is acutely conscious that "the very first element of the social union, obedience to a government of some sort, has not been found so easy a thing to establish in the world,"[89] and can't be commanded by political powers alone. It rather turns on the sociological and educational supports forming a population willing and able to satisfy the requirements of government. Political societies aren't just aggregates of interchangeable laws, rights and institutions, but rather sit at the intersection of culture, history and politics. Their stability is upheld by "a system of *education*, beginning with infancy and continued through life"; "the feeling of allegiance, or loyalty"; and "a strong and active principle of cohesion among the members of the same community or state."[90] Nationally particular social webs – military training, religious teaching, political ideologies, common ancestry – shore up civic attachments, tying citizens to one another and to their institutions, and generating a willingness to shoulder the burdens of cooperation. They nurture the nationalist sentiments that "enable society to weather ... storms, and pass through turbulent times without any permanent weakening of the securities for peaceable existence."[91] In short, they form a people capable of fulfilling the conditions for government.

Mill's attention to the aims, ends and conditions of government bespeaks a subtler view of politics than the catch-all liberalism he's often made to ventriloquize. If governments are to shape themselves to a people's character and foster its capacities, if they're to command and maintain social solidarity, and if they're to balance order and progress, they're bound to account for that people's cultural, sociological and historical circumstances. They're bound to lean on the pedagogical and institutional networks sustaining unique and idiosyncratic forms of collective life. Government, Mill saw, is neither neutral, minimal nor a bare guard for liberty. It is, rather, embedded in the affective, dispositional and habituated fabric of social and political life.

4.2 AFFECT, CHARACTER AND DEMOCRACY

Given Mill's close attention to the contingency of political forms generally, his account of its ideal – democratic, representative government – is, unsurprisingly, a qualified and contextually sensitive one. This ideal, he avers, "must be constructed of the form of government most eligible in itself, that is, which, if the necessary conditions existed for giving effect to its beneficial tendencies, would, more than all others, favour and promote not some one improvement, but all forms and degrees of it."[92] This "ideally best form of government is that in which the sovereignty, or supreme controlling power in the last resort, is vested in the entire aggregate of the community; every citizen not only having a voice in the exercise of that ultimate sovereignty, but being, at least occasionally, called on to take an actual part in the government."[93]

This tentativeness and sensitivity to context, critics rightly observe, also underpin Mill's conviction that the uncivilized are incapable of self-government. While advanced, civilized societies should govern themselves through representative institutions, the uncivilized benefit from the despotic rule of their moral and intellectual superiors. And yet, Mill's account of *why*, exactly, differently situated peoples are best suited to different institutions is somewhat less clear. For much of the literature, his conception of democratic fitness turns on a fixed cognitive threshold distinguishing rational, self-directing societies from intellectually backward ones. As Uday Mehta and others understand it, it's a philosophical distinction setting categorically different types of peoples apart on the basis of their intellectual capacities (or lack thereof), and it frames Mill's wider understanding of the non-western world. I call this the cognitivist view.

In this section, I expand on the strictly cognitivist reading to draw out Mill's attention to the *affective* register of democratic public life – to the emotive, habituated and dispositional bonds connecting citizens to their social and political institutions. His account of democratic capacity, I suggest, concerns the development of a democratic character, rather than any fixed civilizational-intellectual measure. For Mill, democracy is a character-dependent good: more than other forms of government, it relies on citizens' public-mindedness, civic trust and public engagement, and not just on their rational capacities. To be sure, he weighs those as well. But his distinction between self-governing and democratically unfit populations is neither as clear, stark nor categorical as the critical view suggests (I elaborate on this argument in Chapter 5).

Much of the commentary on Mill's democratic theory (rather than on his imperialism) focuses on *Considerations'* more controversial institutional reforms, such as plural voting and Hare's representational scheme – on the machinery balancing civic participation and competence, and countering the pathologies of class-based factionalism.[94] Its pedagogical dimensions have received less scrutiny, despite their centrality to Mill's vision of democratic goods.[95] It is to these pedagogical, affective, character-building facets of his democratic thought that we turn our attention.

4.2.1 Democratic Fitness: The Cognitivist View

The cognitivist view treats Mill's notion of democratic fitness as distinguishing civilized and uncivilized societies on the basis of their citizens' rational capacities.[96] This is anchored in a stage-based theory of historical progress portraying societies as moving through fixed stages of development reflecting their cognitive evolution. The resulting conception of socio-historical advancement, Mehta contends, "derives centrally from premises about reason as the appropriate yardstick for judging individual and collective lives."[97] Mill is thus understood to countenance a "stark binary of the backwards and the progressive, with nothing in between"[98] these two distinctive modes of social existence. For Bhikhu Parekh, it's a "Manichean divide": while Europeans value "individuality, rationality and other liberal principles," non-Europeans remain entrapped in "traditions, custom and religion."[99] From the cognitivist standpoint, then, a capacity for reason cleanly demarcates civilized and uncivilized societies as, respectively, democratically fit and unfit.

There is much in Mill's treatments of the uncivilized to sustain the view, beginning, most prominently, with *On Liberty*'s declaration that self-government applies only "to human beings in the maturity of their faculties ... [and] has no application to any state of things anterior to the time when mankind have become capable of being improved by free and equal discussion."[100] Given their insensitivity to rational deliberation, "[d]espotism is a legitimate mode of government in dealing with barbarians."[101] The sentiment is hardly isolated. In "A Few Words on Non-Intervention" (1859), Mill warns that "[t]o suppose that the same international customs, and the same rules of international morality, can obtain between one civilized nation and another, and between civilized nations and barbarians, is a grave error" as "barbarians will not reciprocate. They cannot be depended on for observing any rules. Their minds are not capable of so great an effort, nor their will sufficiently under the influence of distant motives."[102] The assessment was, also, long-held: "wanting in intelligence," Mill proclaimed nearly 25 years earlier, the "savage cannot bear to sacrifice, for any purpose, the satisfaction of his individual will."[103] These and similar passages support the contention that Mill espoused a "cognitive-development model"[104] positing "a direct correspondence between a society's stage of historical development and the mental capacities of its members."[105] "[S]ocietal development" was, then, for Mill "a matter of the improvement of individuals' cognitive capacities."[106] The view is taken to apply to "non-European peoples" generally, who "were not deemed to have the necessary *qualified* reason to enjoy equal rights of liberty."[107]

The cognitivist argument thus focuses almost entirely on the rational deficits of the uncivilized as democrats-in-waiting. To be civilized is precisely to have developed the intellectual capacity for fruitful self-direction. Barbarians, non-Europeans, the uncivilized (or under-civilized): all fall on the wrong side of a cognitive fence attributing democratic competence to the civilized alone. But is this so clearly the case?

4.2.2 Affective Failures I: Passivity and Passion

Two related problems, pertaining to the conditions and aims of government examined above, bedevil the uncivilized. First, while they might accept representative government, they're incapable of fulfilling its conditions of action and self-restraint. Second, representative institutions not only fail to improve the uncivilized, but actually exacerbate their pathological character, detracting from government's ultimate end. What remains unclear is why exactly they're harmed by democratic institutions that Mill otherwise regards as invaluable schools of public spirit.

The answer surfaces in *Considerations*. While *On Liberty* most famously expresses Mill's view of the uncivilized as democratically unfit, *Considerations* clarifies its substance:

A people may prefer a free government, but if, from indolence, or carelessness, or cowardice, or want of public spirit, they are unequal to the exertions necessary for preserving it; if they will not fight for it when it is directly attacked; if they can be deluded by the artifices used to cheat them out of it; if by momentary, or temporary panic, or a fit of enthusiasm for an individual, they can be induced to lay their liberties at the feet even of a great man, or trust him with powers which enable him to subvert their institutions; in all these cases they are more or less unfit for liberty ... a people may be unwilling or unable to fulfil the duties which a particular government requires of them.[108]

As Mill characterizes it, the problem with the uncivilized lies in their passivity, variously manifested as indolence, carelessness, a lack of public spirit, cowardice and so on – an affective deficit. This broad-ranging inactiveness results from a lack of habituation to the demands of sociality and law. "[A] people in a state of savage independence, in which every one lives for himself"[109] is unaccustomed to the burdens of political association, and so falls short of Mill's second condition of government: citizens will not do what it takes to sustain the polity. Unbowed by social institutions, their natural egoism discourages any greater social exertion than is required by a bare obeisance to the law. A citizenry that cares little about institutions of law, that fails to stop crimes when they see them performed, that is unmotivated to learn about political representatives, and that is generally indifferent to public life cannot, he argues, maintain a democratic state.[110] The problem is an engrained civic apathy, a lack of affective connection binding citizens to one another and to their institutions. Mill's concern is not so much with their rational incapacities (though they fall short here as well), but more fundamentally, that they haven't learned to *care* about public life at all. It lies in the "deplorable states of feeling, in any people who have emerged from savage life."[111]

This presents a particular challenge for democracies, which are uniquely dependent on public-mindedness absent in a citizenry unaccustomed to seeing itself in its politics. "[R]epresentative institutions are of little value," Mill reflects, "when the generality of electors are not sufficiently interested in their own government to give their vote."[112] Without any particular desire to see those institutions preserved, an apathetic citizenry all too easily slides from democracy into despotism; for Mill, Graham Finlay observes, democratic fitness turns on a people's willingness to fight for their enfranchisement and rights.[113] Without public spirit, without internalizing a commitment to laws, without the sense that a citizen "feel[s] himself one of the public, and whatever is for their benefit to be for his benefit,"[114] democracies cannot achieve their ends. Democratic societies take work – active, public engagement motivated by feelings of kinship connecting citizens and their public establishments. The passive character of the uncivilized, conversely, "is favoured by the government of one or a few."[115] "Inactivity, unaspiringness, absence of desire, are a more fatal hindrance to improvement than any misdirection of energy," the very character traits "which retain in a savage or semi-savage state the great majority of the human race."[116] Public indifference is, in fact, the single greatest impediment to representative government, "it being easier, in most cases, to change the direction of an active feeling, than to create one in a state previously passive."[117] Mill's argument thus turns on a sociological account of democracy's affective foundations, rather than on a strict philosophical division yielding, as Mehta sees it, a "civilizational classification that determines whether or not savages can, for example, be members of independent societies."[118]

Compounding these defects, the uncivilized are, paradoxically, also incapable of curbing their passions. Both too passive to shoulder the responsibilities of democratic citizenship and too impassioned to govern themselves, they're doubly damned, caring too much for their own interests and not enough for the public good. A rude people is "unable to practice the forbearance [civilized society] demands: their passions may be too violent, or their personal pride too exacting, to forego private conflict, and leave to the laws the avenging of their real or supposed wrongs."[119] This unregulated fervor is politically problematic in two senses. As citizens, the uncivilized fail to elevate law over their impulses, and as political actors, they are incapable of rational deliberation. But rather than curbing these pathologies, representative institutions worsen them:

How can a representative assembly work for good if its members can be bought, or if their excitability and temperament, uncorrected by public discipline or private self-control, makes them incapable of calm deliberation, and they resort to manual violence on the floor of the House, or shoot at one another with rifles? How, again, can government, or any joint concern, be carried on in a tolerable manner by people so envious that, if one among them seems likely to succeed in anything, those who ought to cooperate with him form a tacit combination to make him fail?[120]

Incapable of dispassionate debate, violent, intemperate, envious and vindictive: these are less the natural character traits of the uncivilized than those developed by exposure to democratic procedures. This isn't just a matter of affective failure, but of institutional mismatch: the unmitigated compulsions of ego are exacerbated by representative institutions giving them vent. Under democracy, then, the uncivilized fail to fulfill both conditions and ends of government: far from ameliorating their active, moral and intellectual qualities, democratic processes deepen their anti-social impulses.

4.2.3 Affective Failures II: Self-Interest, Moral and Institutional

These affective shortcomings are, of course, problematic in themselves. But still worse, they also entrench the self-interest characteristic of the uncivilized condition. More than any other defect, self-interest stunts the associative and affective bonds cementing democratic citizenship, and for "the savage . . . social [sentiments] cannot even temporarily prevail over his selfish feelings, nor his impulses bend to his calculations."[121]

Self-interest generates both moral and practical problems. In his discussion of justice in *Utilitarianism*, Mill describes the moral faculty as depending on the socialization of certain natural impulses. Justice, he argues, stems from an inborn desire to avenge wrongs (the "natural" core of the moral sentiment), extended (through learning and socialization) by sympathetic association to those surrounding us.[122] Lacking the stable, long-term associative networks generated by civilized society ("thinly scattered over a vast tract of country"[123] as they are), the uncivilized do not forge the bonds of sympathetic extension socializing, and so moralizing, otherwise self-centered instincts for punition and advantage. Unable to alienate their immediate interests, recognize the gains of cooperation, or pursue a broader social good, the uncivilized fail to develop the public spirit undergirding representative government. "When the general disposition of the people is such that each individual regards those only of his interests which are selfish and does not dwell on, or concern himself for, his share of the general interest," Mill tells us, "in such a state of things good government is impossible."[124]

In a democratic context, this moral deficit entails at least two practical-institutional challenges. First, self-interested citizens fail to check their governments' excesses. Democracy demands the solicitousness and engagement not only of political delegates, but of a citizenry entrusted to select their representatives on the right grounds and limit their powers when need be. This means that "[i]f the agents, or those who choose the agents, or those to whom the agents are responsible, or the lookers-on whose opinion ought to influence and check all these, are mere masses of ignorance, stupidity and baleful prejudice, every operation of government will go wrong."[125] A self-governing demos, in other words, requires a self-governing ethos extending beyond governing castes to encompass the social body. As Nadia Urbinati observes, Mill's democratic theory balances legislators' "skilled" competence against ordinary citizens' "deliberative" competence, which is all too easily corrupted by self-interest.

Second, misformed – or, rather, unformed – citizens elect representatives for private rather than public reasons. Citizens who "do not bestow their suffrages on public grounds, but sell them for money, or vote at the beck of some one who has control over them, or whom for private reasons they desire to propitiate"[126] ultimately erode civic life. Under the sway of self-interest, without "the degree of interest in the general affairs of the State necessary to the formation of a public opinion,"[127] democratic institutions become conduits for social oppression. The very mechanisms intended to improve a people's moral and intellectual faculties lead to parochialism, factionalism and the tyranny of the majority when citizens use "the right of suffrage ... to serve their private interest, or the interest of their locality."[128] "[I]n this state of public feeling" – the state that Mill attributes to variously uncultivated populations – citizens invariably treat their electoral powers "solely as a means of seeking their fortune."[129] This kind of partiality also animates the class-based voting that many of *Considerations'* institutional reforms seek to mitigate.[130]

While Mill most directly identifies pathologies of self-interest with the uncivilized, they also recur in his criticisms of advanced, democratic states. Class-based rule, electing panderers, intellectually unsophisticated representatives, treating political office as a means of enrichment, antipathy toward the unconventional: these are not particularly uncivilized shortcomings, but rather pervade improperly formed democracies of all kinds. They are, all, failures of democratic character.

4.2.4   Schools of Public Spirit and Democratic Character

As the cognitivist view observes, Mill treats democratic government as conditional on a population's "speculative faculties." This is, however, not a sufficient condition. As we have begun to see, Mill is acutely conscious of the broader social institutions forming the habits, dispositions and character translating representative government into a social good. And yet, despite its centrality to his democratic thinking, his attentiveness to the pedagogic criterion is often overlooked. In his lucid examination of Mill's democratic theory, for instance, Dennis Thompson suggests that he "did not seriously consider the problem of how to activate an inactive citizenry ... [and] really offers only institutional opportunities for citizens who wish to participate, not means of stimulating a desire to participate."[131] Jonathan Riley similarly treats *Considerations'* central preoccupation as balancing class-based variations in civic competence, rather than inculcating public-mindedness in the working class.[132]

Mill's writings on democracy are, however, persistently attuned to the sentiments upholding public life, and to the institutions forming them. His early (1830s) reflections on democracy show his skepticism toward strictly rationalist measures for suffrage, suggesting that "between an average Birmingham gun-maker, an average London shopkeeper, and an average country gentleman, we suspect the differences of intelligence are more apparent than real."[133] Tocqueville (among others) drew him to see that public life wasn't just upheld by reason, but by the imbrication of the intellectual, dispositional and habituated facets of democratic citizenship. "It is a fundamental principle in his political philosophy, as it has long been in ours," Mill asserts in his 1835 review of *Democracy in America*, "that only by the habit of superintending their local interests can that diffusion of intelligence and mental activity, as applied to their joint concerns, take place among the mass of a people."[134] This habit does not spring from political participation alone. Social bodies such as "[p]olitical Unions, Anti-Slavery Societies, and the like; to say nothing of the less advanced, but already powerful organization of the working classes"[135] develop democratic inclinations for public engagement and self-direction. Such smaller-scale, locally driven "associations are not the machinery of democratic combination, but the occasional weapons which that spirit forges as it needs them."[136]

This concern with public spirit became entrenched in Mill's mature political thought, which addresses a broad range of social and political mechanisms cultivating democratic dispositions. Through "the instruction obtained from newspapers and political tracts,"[137] for example, citizens learn to recognize themselves as engaged in a joint social enterprise, rather than as mere subjects of political authority. For Mill, newspapers are "[t]he real Political Unions of England which tell every person what all other persons are feeling, and in what manner they are ready to act: it is by these that the people learn, it may truly be said, their own wishes, and through these that they declare them."[138] By forging mutuality and common interest, such social glues strengthen citizens' investment in a shared public life, with shared public aspirations. They belong to what Mill describes as humanity's education writ large: beyond their immediate aims and goods, institutions such as jury trials, public service, accessible education, and "industrial and philanthropic enterprises by voluntary associations"[139] comprise invaluable schools of public spirit, drawing us past our parochial interests. Service to juries and parish offices are modern equivalents of the Athenian dicastery and ecclesia, developing public-mindedness, while newspapers and railroads serve as Britain's agora.[140] These and other such social institutions are "parts of national education," being, in truth, the peculiar training of a citizen, the practical part of the political education of a free people, taking them out of the narrow circle of personal and family selfishness, and accustoming them to the comprehension of joint interests, the management of joint concerns – habituating them to act from public or semi-public motives, and guide their conduct by aims which unite instead of isolating them from one another. Without these habits and powers, a free constitution can neither be worked nor preserved.[141]

This common space, at the intersection of public, private and civil society organizations, educates us to our responsibilities beyond the mere strictures of law, generating the democratic solidarity and generosity connecting citizens to one another and to their institutions. "[L]ectures and discussion, the collective deliberations on questions of common interest, the trade unions, the political agitation," Mill asserts, "all serve to awaken public spirit, to diffuse a variety of ideas among the mass."[142] What Mill sees here is that democracies are not just governments, but regimes. They work through the lattice of public and semi-public institutions and organizations through which every citizen "learns to feel for and with his fellow-citizens, and becomes consciously a member of a great community."[143]

Of all such institutions, Mill regards democratic political action itself as the fount of public spirit. Local democracy, he maintains, is "the school as well as the safety-valve of democracy in the state,"[144] as citizens "cultivat[e] habits of collective action"[145] by engaging in smaller-scale, municipal politics. Democracies do, of course, enable self-determination through rational deliberation. But more profoundly, they harbor the *dispositions* at the center of a properly public life. Political participation enculturates the predilection to look beyond our immediate desires and seek more remote public goods. By contributing to local government, we become habituated to incorporating co-citizens' goods in our political choices, we are awakened to the interests of distant others, we foster social sentiments, and we extend our sympathetic identification to an ever-widening circle of compatriots.[146] Drawing together his central insight and concerns, Mill describes

the moral part of the instruction afforded by the participation of the private citizen, if even rarely, in public functions. He is called upon, while so engaged, to weigh interests not his own; to be guided, in case of conflicting claims, by another rule than his private partialities; to apply at every turn, principles and maxims which have for their reason of existence the common good ... He is made to feel himself one of the public ... Where this school of public spirit does not exist, scarcely any sense is entertained that private persons, in no eminent social situation, owe any duties to society ... There is no unselfish sentiment of identification with the public ... The man never thinks of any collective interest, of any objects to be pursued jointly with others, but only in competition with them ... Thus even private morality suffers, while public is actually extinct.[147]

Without these social ballasts, social sentiments, social sympathies and social habits – without, in short, the public spirit expanding our sphere of interests – representative governments cease to function. This is all the more true in capitalist-industrial societies (as most democracies are), as "the spirit of a commercial people will be, we are persuaded, essentially mean and slavish, wherever public spirit is not cultivated by an extensive participation of the people in the business of government."[148] Given their implicit privatism, market-based democracies need to "[b]alance these tendencies by contrary ones" by giving citizens "something to do for the public, whether as a vestryman, a juryman, or an elector" so that their "ideas and feelings are taken out of this narrow circle."[149]

While the institutional reforms in *Considerations* and "Thoughts on Parliamentary Reform" (1859) address Mill's concerns with political incompetence and class-based voting, they also speak to this affective, democratic spirit. His advocacy for the open ballot, for instance, reflects his conviction that "there will never be honest or self-restraining government unless each individual participant feels himself a trustee for all his fellow citizens and for posterity."[150] As an institutional concern, the private ballot is subject to private influences, irresponsible choices or simple neglect. But equally problematically, it fails to develop the sense of communal responsibility for the polity's well-being. Mill was skeptical that "the social feelings connected with [voting], and the sense of social duty in performing it, can be expected to be as powerful when the act is done in secret."[151] As citizens, we are constantly assailed by public and private interests; the publicity of the open ballot moves us to weigh those interests properly, as democratic life demands. Even if problems of class- and interest-based voting vanished, Mill argues, the open ballot would remain invaluable for developing the inclination to raise public over private goods.[152] These and other institutional reforms enhance what Nadia Urbinati characterizes as the "cultural and political climate of public interaction and trust"[153] that, for Mill, democracy cultivates. The greater security of private property afforded by democratic states "fosters all those feelings of kindness and fellowship towards others, and in the general wellbeing of the community"; even a progressive system of taxation "tends in an eminent degree to educate the moral sentiment of the community."[154]

Ultimately, democratic life and representative government turn less on rational sufficiency than on being disposed the right way. Democracies require citizens with a distinctively public orientation, whose identification with the common good runs deeper than show, and who value social cooperation above self-interest. By participating in shared public institutions, we not only learn to care about others, but become the kinds of persons that *want* to care about others. "The food of feeling is action," Mill tells us: "[l]et a person have nothing to do for his country, and he will not care for it."[155] For Kant, a good republic enables a race of devils to coexist; for Mill, democracy is a character-dependent good. Bad citizens can't be good democrats – but not only the uncivilized make bad democrats.

4.2.5   The Civilized Poor and the Poorly Civilized

The more we tug at the edges of the cognitivist view, the less clear it becomes, and the affective perspective complicates it in two more ways. First, the deficits associated with the uncivilized are not theirs alone, as Mill expresses identical concerns regarding the (civilized) working classes' capacities for fruitful self-government. Second, Mill saw some of the world's most advanced, civilized societies as lacking the public habits for representative government, and so, as unfit for democracy. Both points suggest that civilization, reason and democratic fitness are not as neatly overlaid as the cognitivist argument suggests.

Let's begin with the civilized poor. As with the uncivilized, the working classes' defects stem from contingent social, historical and sociological circumstances. The uncivilized progress through advances in military, economic, cultural and industrial organization, the various "operations [by which] mankind learn the value of combination,"[156] alienate their self-interest, and develop a social orientation. The working class, Mill argues, requires the same shift. Under modern conditions, "[t]he poor have come out of leading-strings, and cannot any longer be governed or treated like children," but must rather cultivate "the virtues of independence" and "be made rational beings."[157] This "rationalization" is not, however, strictly cognitive, but also entails a refusal to submit to the "mere authority and *prestige* of superiors," along with ensuing desires for self-government and to see their interests reflected in law – all dispositional shifts.[158] Their advancement thus consists not only in an "increase of intelligence, of education, and of the love of independence," but also, in "a corresponding growth of the good sense which manifests itself in provident habits of conduct."[159] Along with an improved capacity to perceive long-term and collective interests, the poorer classes develop an increasing their social consciousness and propensity for collective action. More than a capacity for rational deliberation, they learn to *feel* themselves invested in a shared civic life through the socialization imparted by schools of public spirit.

And yet – again, as with the uncivilized – "the too early attainment of political franchises by the least educated classes might retard, instead of promoting, their improvement."[160] Despite Mill's indefatigable advocacy for working-class suffrage, *Considerations* remains better known for its institutional constraints on enfranchisement. In light of variations across the population's educational levels, "the benefits of completely universal suffrage cannot be obtained without bringing with them, as it appears to me, a chance of more than equivalent evils."[161] This tension – between the value and dangers of inclusive democratic participation – perhaps best captures the schism between Mill's egalitarianism and elitism. The middle chapters of *Considerations* explore the institutional mechanisms navigating this divide, including a plural voting scheme endowing the better educated with greater civic power, Hare's single-transferable vote, and conditional restrictions on sections of the population. As Dale Miller observes, these respond to Mill's concerns with working-class educational deficits (and with class-based voting) by limiting the franchise of the uneducated, tax defrauders and welfare recipients.[162]

These constraints, however, don't just mitigate the lower classes' irrationalism, but inculcate a socially minded disposition while limiting the damages that Mill associated with full enfranchisement. His advocacy for plural voting "contributes to and encourages the education of citizens, in the broad sense of 'education' well captured by the German *Bildung*"[163] by stimulating their active, intellectual and moral faculties. For Mill, Miller argues, a weighted voting scheme promoting the value of education would "improve the 'tone' of 'public feeling,' even if plural voting were to have no 'direct political consequences'."[164] Wendy Donner similarly notes that beyond containing the potentially detrimental influence of uneducated voters, such institutional mechanisms cultivate the working class's sense of civic responsibility.[165] Without this social orientation, Mill sees full voting rights as harming both the polity and poorer citizens themselves. A democratic citizen "is bound to give [his vote] according to his best and most conscientious opinion of the public good," and to think of it – or to use it – otherwise "is to pervert, not to elevate his mind ... it awakens and nourishes in him the disposition to use a public function for his own interest, pleasure or caprice."[166] As with the uncivilized, then, an unregulated franchise not only detracts from the public good, but also distorts the poorer classes' public-mindedness. It comprises an institutional mismatch that, without checks and balances, exacerbates antisocial tendencies rather than stimulating public ones. Along with the schools of public spirit sketched here, Mill's institutional reforms aim to instill a democratic ethos in the working class and develop "the habit of seeing public matters from the perspective of the general interest."[167]

Mill does of course differentiate democratically fit and unfit peoples – but their diremption is, we can now see, less categorical than it appears from the cognitivist standpoint. Far from strictly dividing civilized and uncivilized societies, Mill understands the civilized poor and the uncivilized as sharing in the same democratic deficits, leading to the same pathological outcomes, in spite of their evidently different circumstances. In both cases, unrestricted enfranchisement inhibits public-mindedness, entrenches self-interest and deepens factionalism and class-based division. And in both cases, citizens' failures are not just intellectual, but rather concern deficits of public feeling, habit and disposition.

These democratic shortcomings also extend still more broadly. The affective view explains why Mill treated some entirely progressive, civilized societies as democratically unfit. Despite their social maturity, Mill argues, certain peoples lack the institutions and schools of public spirit enabling representative governments to fulfill their ends. As Georgios Varouxakis observes, "Mill spoke of countries which he considered to be at the same level or stage of civilization as exhibiting differences in their states of

society"[168] impacting their democratic capacity. For all of their civilizational
sophistication, Mill saw the French, for instance, as unfit for representative
government because of their "superficial love of freedom, in the face of
a practical habit of slavery."[169] Citing Tocqueville, he muses that "the
question whether or not the French are to be a free people, depends ... upon
the possibility of creating a spirit and a habit of local self-government,"[170]
a possibility about which he harbored serious doubts, given defects in the
French national character:

> though a republic, for France, was the most natural and congenial of all the forms of free
> government, it had two great hindrances to contend with. One was, the political
> indifference of the majority – the result of want of education, and of the absence of
> habits of discussion and participation in public business. The other was the dread
> inspired by the remembrance of 1793 and 1794 ... These two causes prevented the
> French nation in general from demanding or wishing for a republican government; and
> as long as those causes continue, they will render its existence, even now when it is
> established, more or less precarious.[171]

France's central problem, then, is that

> [w]hile the equalization of conditions was thus rapidly reaching its extreme limits, no
> corresponding progress of public spirit was taking place in the people at large.
> No institutions capable of fostering an interest in the details of public affairs were created
> by the Revolution ... A political act, to be done only once in a few years, and for which
> nothing in the daily habits of the citizen has prepared him, leaves his intellect and moral
> dispositions very much as it found them ... everything was done for the people, and
> nothing by the people.[172]

This is what the cognitivist view misses: not all civilized societies cultivate the
public spirit sustaining self-government. Even the most advanced societies need
to develop the "habits of discussion and participation in public business"
enabling self-government to serve as a social good. Mill evidently doesn't see
the French as rationally deficient; the problem is, rather, a lack of enculturation
to free government, a problem that clearly cuts across civilized and uncivilized
contexts. No matter how civilized a state might be, a "democratic constitution,
not supported by democratic institutions in detail, but confined to the central
government, not only is not political freedom, but often creates a spirit precisely
the reverse."[173] Civilization, it seems, is no guarantee of a people's fitness for
political self-determination.

4.3   MORAL PSYCHOLOGY AND POLITICAL VIRTUE

Mill's account of democracy's goods and of the kinds of people(s) capable of
benefiting from it is, then, less straightforward than it initially appears. His
liberalism wanders well beyond the rationalism, neutralism and atomism often
associated with the tradition, and by extension, with his own political thinking.
It's certainly a thicker liberalism than has come to be the norm – very much to its

credit, in my view – and the more we delve into it, the further it drifts from the emaciated individualism so often (and so erroneously) tethered to Mill, and to liberalism itself. Mill devoted a great deal of attention to who we are, and to how we think, feel, learn and develop, all matters treated by the utilitarian moral psychology underlying his liberalism, and more narrowly, the affective register of politics central to it.[174]

4.3.1   Utility, Virtue and Morality

As with Kant's good human being, Mill's utilitarianism fleshes out his fuller conception of moral agency and its social moorings. Moral actors balance tranquility and excitements; they "cultivate a fellow-feeling with the collective interests of mankind"; they foster interests in "the objects of nature, the achievements of art, the imaginations of poetry, the incidents of history, the ways of mankind, past and present, and their prospects in the future"; they maintain "genuine private affections, and a sincere interest in the public good"; and they pursue "good physical and moral education, and proper control of noxious influences."[175] A virtuous person also avoids comportments subject to moral (but not legal) censure, such as "[c]ruelty of disposition; malice and ill-nature; that most anti-social and odious of all passions, envy; dissimulation and insincerity, irascibility on insufficient cause, and resentment disproportioned to the provocation; the love of domineering over others; [and] the desire to engross more than one's share of advantages," all "moral vices [that] constitute a bad and odious moral character."[176] Like Kant's imperfect duties and social virtues, Mill's prescriptions and proscriptions are neither exhaustive nor strictly binding, but rather illustrate the social comportments and moral orientations of progressive, publicly disposed citizens.

Utilitarianism expands on the social character demanded by utility, and on the mechanisms fostering it:

As between his own happiness and that of others, utilitarianism requires him to be as strictly impartial as a disinterested and benevolent spectator ... As the means of making the nearest approach to this ideal, utility would enjoin, first, that laws and social arrangements should place the happiness, or (as speaking practically it may be called) the interest, of every individual, as nearly as possible in harmony with the interest of the whole; and secondly, that education and opinion, which have so vast a power over human character, should so use that power as to establish in the mind of every individual an indissoluble association between his own happiness and the good of the whole; especially between his own happiness and the practice of such modes of conduct, negative and positive, as regard for the universal happiness prescribes; so that not only he may be unable to conceive the possibility of happiness to himself, consistently with conduct opposed to the general good, but also that a direct impulse to promote the general good may be in every individual one of the habitual motives of action, and the sentiments connected therewith may fill a large and prominent place in every human being's sentient existence.[177]

This remarkable passage exposes the imbrications of Mill's political, social, psychological and moral thinking. And yet, their interconnectedness does not imply their collapse. Mill remains faithful to the *System of Logic*'s axiological structure: politics and morality remain distinct, but both anchored in the meta-principle of utility. As such – and as *Considerations*' pedagogic criterion makes clear – government, law, education and morality all contribute to forming citizens oriented toward utility, in a broad sense. This does not, however, entail moral monism or a singular vision of human ends, the very fault he decried in Comte's system (the presumption that "all human life should point but to one object, and be cultivated into a system of means to a single end").[178] Rather than countenancing any particular conception of the good life, Mill's utilitarianism aims to inculcate social behaviors conducive to individual and collective self-development. "If we wish men to practice virtue," he reasons, "it is worthwhile trying to make them love virtue and feel it an object in itself ... It is worth training them to feel, not only actual wrong or actual meanness, but the absence of noble aims and endeavours, as not merely blameable but also degrading."[179] The cultivation and internationalization of such socially virtuous habits and feelings is the object of Mill's moral psychology.

4.3.2 Better to be Socrates Dissatisfied: Associationism and Complex Pleasures

Mill's associationist psychology is elaborated in chapter 4 ("Of the Laws of Mind") of the *System of Logic*'s sixth book, addressing the laws of ethology. Starting from the premise that "[a]ll states of mind are immediately caused either by other states of mind, or by states of body,"[180] Mill's psychology is resolutely empiricist, and equally resolute in its opposition to two forms of fatalistic determinism denying or substantially curtailing the ambit of individual freedom.

The first is the physiological determinism of Comte's social science, which attributes all mental phenomena to originating physical states. While Mill and Comte shared in the ambition to establish a social science as firmly grounded as the natural sciences, Comte, in Mill's words, "rejects totally, as an invalid process, psychological observation properly so called," treating the "the science of Psychology ... with contempt" and reducing the "study of mental phenomena ... [to] a branch of physiology."[181] Comte aimed to "extricate[e] the mental study of man from the metaphysical stage, and elevat[e] it to the positive"[182] by anchoring it in observable physical/physiological processes, thereby drawing mental phenomena under the umbrella of phrenology, the nascent "science" to which he was unabashedly committed and which Mill roundly rejected. Mill indulged Comte's phrenological interests to a point, reading Franz Joseph Gall's treatment of the subject on Comte's recommendation in 1842, but came away wholly unconvinced by its methods and conclusions.[183] "This great mistake" was for Mill "not a mere hiatus in M. Comte's system, but the parent of serious errors in his attempt to create a Social Science."[184] Comte's overly ambitious scientism reduced human agency and intellectual capacity to brute facts of nature, immune to rectification or redress; no educative or environmental formation could alter a human character fixed by the vagaries of natural endowment. As Nicholas Capaldi observes, "[t]he fundamental disagreement in methodology between Comte and Mill centers on individual autonomy,"[185] which Comte's biological determinism effectively eradicates. This divergence also shaped their respective views on social and political reform: where Comte envisioned social advancement as steered by an enlightened "scientific-industrial-managerial elite,"[186] Mill saw it as contingent on individual autonomy, self-government and mass education. While Mill's associationist psychology *is* deterministic – its aim, as he states in the *System of Logic*, is to reconcile liberty and necessity – it is not fatalistic, and so resists absolutist scientific determination.

If Comte's social science denies the existence of purely psychological phenomena, James Mill's Owenite associationism treats it as an iron cage. Comte understood mental capacities as biologically fixed, and consequently, as impervious to environmental conditioning. The elder Mill, conversely, saw character as entirely formed by external forces, a *tabula rasa* shaped from the outside – again reducing human freedom to the space carved out by predetermined influences. This view animated J. S. Mill's infamously strict education: convinced that psychological makeup was molded wholly from without, James Mill endeavored to form his son into a perfect utilitarian. Though the younger Mill followed in a long line of British associationists, from Locke, Hume and Hartley down to his father, he departed from this last by positing our capacity for self-formation. Without denying that character conditioned choices, desires and preferences, J. S. Mill saw the self as *among* the influences shaping it, rather than as simply (and passively) subject to it.[187] "To the Owenite," as Alan Ryan puts it, "one's character appeared as a straightjacket constraining one's actions; to Mill it was a suit, to be altered and reshaped should it not fit what we wanted to look like."[188] Mill thus rejected Owenite moral psychology and Comte's social science on the same grounds: their common determinism denied human capacities for freedom, self-cultivation and self-development.[189]

For Mill, psychology properly understood concerns "the uniformities of succession, the laws, whether ultimate or derivative, according to which one mental state succeeds another."[190] His exposition of these laws rests on a few basic principles. First, any state of consciousness produced by either mental or physical stimulus can be reproduced by the mind alone. Human beings can recreate ideas, or "secondary mental states," in the absence of their initial causes. Second, these

secondary mental states are excited by our impressions, or by other ideas, according to certain laws which are called Laws of Association. Of these laws the first is, that similar ideas tend to excite one another. The second is, that when two impressions have been frequently experienced (or even thought of) either simultaneously or in immediate succession, then whenever one of these impressions, or the idea of it, recurs, it tends to excite the idea of the other. The third law is, that greater intensity in either or both of the impressions, is equivalent, in rendering them excitable by one another, to a greater frequency of conjunction.[191]

Simple pleasures or pains, originating from rudimentary sensory or mental experiences, become linked through three associative relations: similarity, frequency/conjunction, and intensity. Most basically, our cognitions are shaped by the simultaneous association of sensations forming our conceptions of objects (such that the concurrence of a given color, shape, odor, flavor and so on are associated to form the idea of an orange, to follow Mill's example), or by the successive association of sensations forming our conceptions of events. Through these associations, we draw simpler mental phenomena into more complex compounds. These composites bear resemblances to other such comparable mental states, developing still more complex associations with them. These in turn might recall pleasures/pains emanating from different sources, drawing together initially separate experiences or states of consciousness; and so on and so forth. Our associations are, then, a product of *what* and *how* we learn: states of mind that share similarities, that are often experienced together (or in repeated succession), or that mark us deeply become cemented over time in our habits, predilections and preferences. The same associative relations govern higher-order cognitions: "[a] desire, an emotion, an idea of the higher order of abstraction, even our judgments and volitions when they have become habitual, are called up by association, according to precisely the same laws as our simpler ideas."[192] These associative channels accustom us to regarding actions, objects and experiences as desirable or unpleasant, developing the complex pleasures and pains, and affections and aversions, of a human life. Like James Mill and Bentham, then, Mill believes that "that complex laws of thought and feeling not only may, but must, be generated from these simple laws,"[193] rather than from moral intuition.

And yet, his moral psychology departs from theirs in important respects – most significantly, in its rejection of the selfish hedonism driving their utilitarianisms. For James Mill, "every human being is determined by his pains and pleasures ... his happiness corresponds with the degree in which pleasures are great, and his pains are small."[194] Given the ubiquity of pleasures and pains, differences between them being a matter of degree rather than type, Mill sees human beings as moved by "self-regarding desires for material pleasures."[195] Along with David Ricardo and Bentham, he treats rational self-interest – understood as a drive for pleasure-maximization, yielded by satisfying basic material desires – as a fixed law of human nature, and so, as the basis of his system of government. Against this, the younger Mill distinguishes distinctive kinds of pleasure, recognizing its qualitative features rather than treating differences between pleasures in strictly quantitative terms, and accounting for the motivational force of social and moral sentiments.[196]

This divergence stems from a particular feature of his associationism. For J. S. Mill, while complex mental phenomena turn on relatively simple laws of association, they aren't a mere accumulation of simpler ones; they are, rather, a "blending together of several simpler ones. They better understood "to *result from*, or *be generated by*, the simple ideas, not to consist of them."[197] Higher-order cognitions, such as complex ideas and pleasures, spring from more rudimentary cognitions, but are not their aggregates. They comprise entirely independent mental states unmoored from their originating phenomena, distinct mental entities not reducible to the sum of their constituent components. Mill describes their precipitation not in additive terms, but as "mental chemistry: in which it is proper to say that the simple ideas generate, rather than that they compose, the complex ones."[198]

This is where Mill's utilitarianism deviates from Bentham's: where Bentham's felicific calculus assesses quantities of pleasure/pain (an accretive process), Mill's higher-order pleasures are of a different kind than more elementary ones (the result of a "chemical" process). For Bentham and James Mill, all ideas are constituted by genetically simpler ones, such that complex mental states are "the additive sum of real parts"[199] that careful analysis could just as easily disentangle. For J. S. Mill, higher-order mental phenomena are "states of consciousness with a wholly new intrinsic or qualitative character."[200] He thus conceptualizes the singularity of higher pleasures in strictly empiricist terms, without lapsing into an ungrounded intuitionism treating moral sentiments as innate. As higher-order mental entities, moral sentiments are generated through laws of association, but their "chemical" composition accounts for their distinctive pleasures and motivational force, even over a greater quantity of simpler hedonistic ones. Bentham's calculus treats pleasure and pain as the only psychological entities, elementary and interchangeable quanta whose only distinguishing characteristics are intensity and duration. Mill, conversely, recognizes the relational qualities of pleasure – that we are prone to different sorts of pleasures attached to distinctive experiences, associative channels and relations not reducible to their constituent parts. By incorporating quantitative and qualitative modes of evaluation, Mill's utilitarianism distinguishes between pleasures whose goods are not necessarily commensurable.

This generates the lexical separation of higher and lower pleasures: if higher and lower pleasures are qualitatively distinct, no quantity of the latter can outweigh the good of the former.[201] "Some *kinds* of pleasure," Mill holds, "are more desirable and more valuable than others"[202] (or, rather more bluntly, and famously, "[i]t is better to be a human being dissatisfied than a pig satisfied; better to be Socrates dissatisfied than a fool satisfied").[203] The distinction between higher and lower pleasures trades in, and often elides, descriptive and normative claims. On one hand, Mill is convinced that "those who are equally acquainted with, and equally capable of appreciating and enjoying, both, do give a most marked preference to the manner of existence which employs their higher faculties."[204] On the other, the principle of utility clearly *enjoins* us to seek higher pleasures – the social virtues, sentiments and habits associating one's own happiness with others'. The higher pleasures are not inborn, and if happiness is to serve as a measure of the social good (rather than lapsing into Bentham's egoistic hedonism), we are bound to cultivate a character that prefers them over the lower pleasures. We are bound, in other words, to develop what Wendy Donner describes as the standpoint of the "competent agent"[205] – properly formed, socially oriented and self-developing – if Mill's qualitative hedonism is to ground a social ethics.

4.3.3 Habituation, Purposes and Confirmed Character

As we have seen, the frequency, proximity and intensity of associative connections cement otherwise singular states of mind into complex preferences and aversions. Habituation thus plays a crucial role in cultivating the social character central to Mill's liberalism, utilitarianism and democratic theory. More than just strengthening given patterns of behavior through repetition, though, habituation introduces changes in the organization of our wills, pleasures and desires:

> As we proceed in the formation of habits, and become accustomed to will a particular act or a particular course of conduct because it is pleasurable, we at last continue to will it without any reference to its being pleasurable. Although, from some change in us or in our circumstances, we have ceased to find any pleasure in the action, or perhaps to anticipate any pleasure as the consequence of it, we still continue to desire the action, and consequently to do it.[206]

This accounts for both good and bad habits: actions initially grounded in preferences/aversions become engrained in the habitual movements of our everyday lives, to the point where pleasures/displeasures themselves cease to exert any particular motivational force. Habits consist of the inertia of our pleasures and pains, explaining why we act in certain ways without any direct reference to them. For better and for worse, habit expands the scope of our motivations beyond the unmediated influence of pleasure/pain, accounting for incentives to action untethered from direct compulsion. Mill here "augment[s] the older [utilitarians'] psychological machinery,"[207] Elijah Millgram observes, by treating habit as among our motivating forces.

We are thus driven not only by basic or even more complex pleasures and pains, but also by engrained habits that Mill describes as *purposes*, "habit[s] of willing" that are "among the causes of our volitions, and of the actions which flow from them."[208] Habituated purposes generate the stability of virtuous character, comprising more dependable grounds for socially minded action than the volatile impulsions of pleasure and pain. While these "habits of willing" develop from pleasures initially sought in and for themselves, they become fixed in our constitution over time. A properly moral character is, then, anchored in purposes and motivated by habit rather than desire. "It is only when our purposes have become independent of the feelings of pain or pleasure from which they originally took their rise," Mill avers, "that we are said to have confirmed character ... the will, once so fashioned, may be steady and constant, when the passive susceptibilities of pleasure and pain are greatly weakened, or materially changed."[209]

This account of moral character – connecting will, desire and habit – explains how we come to internalize the higher pleasures of social virtue. For Mill, virtue consists in transposing incentives to moral action from the province of desire to the dominion of habit. The acquisition of moral character isn't just a change of attitude, but rather transforms the structure of our volitions. While inclinations for justice and equality originate from pleasure-based desires for the results of social virtue (I enjoy being lauded when I act justly), a moral character lies in their habituated internalization, such that they become inseparable from one's conception of the good (to be unjust would strike against who I am). The very possibility of moral character turns on this confirmed "will to be virtuous," on the incorporation of social virtues into habits of conduct providing "unerring constancy of action."[210] To have such a character is to act virtuously as a matter of course, without the immediate incentives of pleasure and pain. And if habits are the bedrock of a socially virtuous character, transforming beneficent inclinations into confirmed purposes, "the will to do right ought to be cultivated into this habitual independence."[211] It remains for us to see how these habituated purposes and moral sentiments ultimately sustain utilitarianism's coherence as a social ideal.

4.3.4 Moral Sentiment and the Coherence of Utility

Mill's conception of moral sentiment lies between naturalism and conventionalism, incorporating both internal impulses and their socialization. While moral sentiments stem from natural inclinations, their moral worth is only realized through their subjection to social ends. "[T]he moral feelings are not innate, but acquired," as Mill understands them, but "are not for that reason the less natural ... the moral faculty, if not a part of our nature, is a natural outgrowth from it ... susceptible of being brought by cultivation to a high degree of development."[212]

That moral faculty lies in "the social feelings of mankind; the desire to be in unity with our fellow-creatures."[213] While inborn, the social impulse develops by acculturation, the advance of civilization being little more than the evolution of this tendency toward communality and cooperation. Mill's measures of progress – rising national wealth, increasingly widespread education, heightening levels of literacy, the betterment of the working classes – are all pegged to it, tracing reductions in the economic, cultural and intellectual inequalities inhibiting its realization.²¹⁴ Social and political improvements bolster this "powerful natural sentiment"²¹⁵ by "giv[ing] to each individual a stronger personal interest in practically consulting the welfare of others ... [and] lead[ing] him to identify his *feelings* more and more with their good."²¹⁶ Yet, its inherency is no guarantee of its realization, as misdirected institutions are as capable of distorting or extinguishing it as progressive ones foster it. Far from assuring the efflorescence of our inborn sociality, the historical record is littered with the memory of failed, regressive or stagnant societies.

The social inclination is anchored in sympathy. Mill argues that human beings are naturally subject to both selfish and sympathetic impulses, and the task of right-minded institutions is to "stimulat[e] the propensity to sympathy which, although weaker than self-love, is still natural and hence available for reform."²¹⁷ This propensity to sympathy is the natural core of social-mindedness and the ground of moral sentiment. Morality consists in the learned habit of elevating sympathetic impulsions over selfish ones, as sympathetic bonds moralize our natural proclivities for self-preservation and self-preference by extending them more broadly. We see this, for instance, in Mill's account of justice. Justice arises from "two sentiments, both in the highest degree natural, and which either are or resemble instincts; the impulse of self-defence, and the feeling of sympathy."²¹⁸ Rooted in the natural desire to retaliate against those who have harmed us, the instinct for vengeance is not, in itself, moral. Justice rather consists in widening, through sympathetic identification, those preserved by the retributive inclination to encompass all members of a given social body – in wanting to redress not only wrongs against oneself, but those inflicted on a larger whole. The morality in justice thus lies in its sympathetic socialization, rather than in its natural core (the drive for punition). Sympathy enables the disinterested care for distant others, the genuine concern for an abstract, collective entity that is the natural end of our inborn sociality.²¹⁹ Our capacity for sympathetic extension thus makes possible the higher-order, more complex forms of care presumed by morality. "[T]he power of sympathizing," Mill avers, "enables [man] to attach himself to the collective idea of his tribe, his country, or mankind."²²⁰ It's a power that remains, however, contingent on socialization: our natural compulsions are only moralized through their "exclusive subordination ... to the social sympathies, so as to wait on and obey their call."²²¹

And so we return to Mill's account of moral habit and engrained purposes. Progressive social and political institutions form a sympathetic habit, pushing the identification between one's own good and the social good from the domain of pleasure to that of purposes. While "the *foundation* of the moral feeling is the adoption of the pleasures and pains of others as our own,"²²² a properly moral character incorporates this sympathetic affinity into one's confirmed purposes of will. Mill's schools of public spirit – democratic participation, newspapers, unions, public service, popular education – don't just teach us to *like* socially virtuous action, leaving it to the vagaries of pleasure. They inculcate a *habit* of sympathetic association and public-mindedness, such that citizens' interests become inseparable from the social interest. This is why Mill so firmly maintains that a "people among whom there is no habit of spontaneous action for a collective interest have their faculties only half developed":[223] these socialized purposes are the foundation of democratic public life. A citizenry in which sympathetic inclinations to social virtue and justice remain subject to pleasure is unfit for self-rule, which requires the "unerring constancy of action ... acquired [by] the support of habit."[224] Sympathetic purposes are, then, the lifeblood of a stable, democratic polity.

This moral psychology also preserves the coherence of Mill's utilitarianism.[225] As is widely known, Mill's account of utility suffers from considerable argumentative deficits, chief among them the "fallacy of composition." Given that "happiness is desirable, and the only thing desirable, as an end," and that "each person's happiness is a good to that person," Mill reasons, "the general happiness [is], therefore, a good to the aggregate of all persons."[226] The problem is evident: the desirability of one's own happiness in no way implies a desire for the aggregate happiness which utility enjoins us to pursue. Mill elides the slippage between the justification of the happiness principle (a descriptive claim: happiness is desirable to me) and its generalization (a normative claim: given that we all desire happiness, we ought to seek the happiness of all). The descriptive claim alone has no moral content, and the normative one lacks motivational grounds; without its socialization, the happiness principle lapses into selfish hedonism or simple incoherence. Mill was aware of the problem. As he explains in an 1868 letter to Henry Jones,

> when I said that the general happiness is a good to the aggregate of all persons I did not mean that every human being's happiness is a good to every other human being; though I think, in a good state of society & education it would be so. I merely meant in this particular sentence to argue that since A's happiness is a good, B's a good, C's a good, &c., the sum of all these goods must be a good.[227]

Of course, this still doesn't bridge descriptive and normative claims, as the connection between individual and collective goods remains unexplained.

Mill's associationist moral psychology responds to the problem. Through habituation we learn not only to desire others' happiness, but to internalize it as a constituent element of our own. Social virtues, he argues, start out as means to our own goods – as dispositions and behaviors advancing our selfish ends. Politeness, sociability, cooperation, care for others: these are the sometimes onerous burdens securing the social harmony from which we all privately profit, and so, we submit to them. Over time and through repeated association with their advantages, however, we come to value these virtues as goods in themselves. They become fixed in our habits and purposes, shaping our conceptualizations of self and of the good – and so, of our happiness. Properly socialized citizens come to weigh the good of others and integrate the public interest into their own, such that virtue comes to be "desired and cherished, not as a means to happiness, but as a part of their happiness."[228] "What was once desired as an instrument for the attainment of happiness" comes, after some time, "to be desired for its own sake ... There was no original desire of it, or motive to it, save its conduciveness to pleasure, and especially to protection from pain. But through the association thus formed, it may be felt a good in itself."[229] Through their exercise, the social virtues become incorporated into our desires and pleasures. We come to regard ourselves as just, socially conscientious persons, such that being unjust, even if were to confer private advantages, would detract from our happiness.

In other words, the social virtues generate higher pleasures, complex mental states qualitatively distinct from their original, simpler components. Elementary pleasures – the immediate interests initially motivating other-regarding behavior – generate, but do not compose, the higher pleasures of virtuous action. These transfigure our experience of happiness: brute self-gratification loses its traction as we internalize the higher pleasures of social virtue. Through progressive socialization, our more distant, complex and abstract pleasures supersede their constituent elements and become integrated into our habits, and ultimately, into our sense of contentment. Justice comes to exert greater motivational force than material interests, and contributes more to our overall happiness; it becomes what we want, a constituent part of who we are. This is an important feature of human nature, Mill reflects, as "[l]ife would be a poor thing, very ill provided with sources of happiness, if there were not this provision of nature, by which things originally indifferent ... [to] the satisfaction of our primitive desires, become in themselves sources of pleasure more valuable than the primitive pleasures."[230] The higher-order pleasures of social virtue attest to the uniquely human capacity to develop complex moral interests and transform ourselves in doing so. Under the right institutional conditions, this social virtue becomes "a good in itself, without looking to any end beyond it ... a thing desirable in itself."[231]

Mill clearly had no compunctions melding ethics and politics, nor treating social and civil spheres as arenas for virtue, formation and self-improvement. This has, unsurprisingly, invited charges of aristocratic elitism, Aristotelianism, non-neutralism and more of the like. But Mill's social virtue and higher pleasures are neither aristocratic nor Aristotelian: they entail no thick teleology regarding human purposes, and no singular or monistic conception of the good (their dismissal of simpler pleasures is, I concede, totally snobbish). "Mill's conception of the good life," as John Gray captures it, "is a procedural perfectionism rather than a full theory of the good life."[232] His account of the higher pleasures explains their distinctiveness and motivational force; it is empiricist, rooted in laws of association rather than moral intuitionism; and most importantly, it is unrepentantly political. It is explicitly concerned with the viability of democratic public life (narrowly) and with individual and collective self-development (broadly). For Mill, the virtues have no particular metaphysical or fixed moral worth, but rather sustain the conditions for social and political progress – for the progressive interests of mankind that I turn to in Chapter 5.

4.4 A FULLER LIBERALISM

Of the many interpretive challenges that Mill presents to his reader, the sheer breadth of his scholarship is a considerable one. Few facets of the human condition remain unaddressed over the 33 volumes in the *Collected Works*, and his interests, concerns and ambitions aren't easily gathered under any particular cohesive view.

And yet, Mill was, in his way, a systematic thinker (but no system-builder) firmly convinced that the best social practices would inevitably cut across political, moral and ideological lines, whose containment he therefore steadfastly resisted. While his thought remains marked by a great many tensions, the wider lens that I've adopted here shows the connectedness of what can appear as its disparate, unrelated or even contradictory elements. When we flesh out Mill's liberalism beyond its narrower caricatures – libertarian call to arms, blind championing of liberty, thick ethical perfectionism – we see how poorly they capture his political theory's nuance and depth. Though we have good reason to doubt or reject some of his conclusions, Mill thought carefully and searchingly on the aims, ends and purposes of government, on the conditions enabling democracies to fulfill them, and on the linkages between citizens and institutions. The end result bears little resemblance to what we get out of *On Liberty* alone. This fuller picture – drawing together Mill's treatments of politics, ethics, social science and moral psychology – clarifies what liberal persons and states look like to him, for better and for worse.

It also exposes the depth of his attention to the affective register of politics, and more particularly, of democratic public life. Mill's account of democratic capacity far exceeds an appeal to rational competency: self-government, he shows, turns on the formation of a democratic character generated by social, historical and civil institutions and conditions. Stephen K. White and William Connolly have in recent years argued for the cultivation of a democratic bearing, civic generosity and critical receptiveness to resist the degradation of American civil discourse.[233] Mill saw the very same a century and half ago, at the birth of a world increasingly subject to popular government: democracies work through ethos more than logos, and democratic habits, feelings and dispositions have deeper roots than deliberative capacities. Far from drawing a categorical, binary distinction between the civilized and uncivilized, then, Mill's account of democratic fitness reflects his consciousness of the public-mindedness translating representative institutions into social goods. Human beings, he observes, are "susceptible, by a sufficient use of the external sanctions and of the force of early impressions, of being cultivated in almost any direction."[234] His "schools of public spirit" foster just this liberal, democratic character – habituated to sympathy, disposed to collective action and acculturated to the higher pleasures of social virtue. It's a character lacking not only in the uncivilized, as we have seen, but also in entirely civilized states and populations. The divide attributed to Mill's account of representative government is, then, less Manichean and more fluid than the cognitivist view allows for.

The misinterpretation reflects a deeper one – or, rather, several of them. Critics of Mill's liberal imperialism miscast his conceptualization of civilization and barbarism, along with the treatments of social progress, historical development and human diversity surrounding it. Critics rightly look to Mill's philosophy of history to map out the relationship between civilized and uncivilized peoples, as his developmentalism unquestionably shapes his understanding of cultural variation. But they fail to capture his fuller sociological view of human development and its implications for his liberalism, and for his valuation of difference. By situating Mill's views of non-Europeans within the broader architecture of his thought, Chapter 5 sets out a clearer view of his liberalism's encounter with human diversity.

NOTES

1. Uday S. Mehta, "Liberal Strategies of Exclusion," *Politics and Society* 18, no. 4 (1990): 427–454. On the liberal tradition's exclusionary appeals to "anthropological universals," see Étienne Balibar, "Difference, Otherness, Exclusion," *Parallax* 11, no. 1 (2005): 19–34.
2. Bowden, "Ebb and Flow," 93.
3. For the importance of reading Mill comprehensively, see Robert Devigne, *Reforming Liberalism: J. S. Mill's Use of Ancient, Religious, Liberal, and Romantic Moralities* (New Haven: Yale University Press, 2006); Wendy Donner, *The Liberal Self: John Stuart Mill's Moral and Political Philosophy* (New York: Cornell University Press, 1991); and Wendy Donner, "John Stuart Mill and Virtue Ethics," in *John Stuart Mill: Thought and Influence – The Saint of Rationalism*, eds. Georgios Varouxakis and Paul Kelly (London: Routledge, 2010), 84–98. For defenses of Mill as a systematic thinker, see Alan Ryan, *John Stuart Mill* (London: Routledge & Kegan Paul, 1974); Nicholas Capaldi, *John Stuart Mill: A Biography* (Cambridge: Cambridge University Press), ch. 6; and John Skorupski, *John Stuart Mill* (London: Routledge, 1991), who describes his "philosophical stance [a]s numbingly comprehensive, lucid and systematic" (xi). For the view that no system can be attributed to him, see Bernard Semmel, *John Stuart Mill and the Pursuit of Virtue* (New Haven: Yale University Press), ix.
4. Georgios Varouxakis offers the most comprehensive survey of these international engagements; see his *Liberty Abroad: J. S. Mill on International Relations* (Cambridge: Cambridge University Press, 2013).
5. George Kateb, "A Reading of *On Liberty*," in *On Liberty*, eds. David Bromwich and George Kateb (New Haven: Yale University Press, 2003), 28–66; Nadia Urbinati, *Mill on Democracy: From the Athenian Polis to Representative Government* (Chicago: Chicago University Press, 2002); John Gibbons, "J. S. Mill, Liberalism, and Progress," in *Victorian Liberalism: Nineteenth-Century Political*

Thought and Practice, ed. Richard Bellamy (London: Routledge, 1989), 91–109; Don Habibi, "The Moral Dimension of J. S. Mill's Colonialism," *Journal of Social Philosophy* 30, no. 1 (1999); Mehta, *Liberalism and Empire*.

6. Berlin, "Ends of Life"; Jeremy Waldron, "Mill and Multiculturalism," in *Mill's On Liberty: A Critical Guide*, ed. C. L. Ten (Cambridge: Cambridge University Press, 2008), 165–184; C. L. Ten, "Mill's Defense of Liberty," in *J. S. Mill's On Liberty in Focus*, eds. John Gray and G. W. Smith (London: Routledge, 2015), 212–238.

7. Maurice Cowling, *Mill and Liberalism* (Cambridge: Cambridge University Press, 1990); Alasdair C. MacIntyre, *After Virtue: A Study in Moral Theory* (Notre Dame: University of Notre Dame Press, 2007).

8. Rawls, *Political Liberalism*; Larmore, "Political Liberalism"; Villa "Maturity and Paternalism"; Bruce Baum, "J. S. Mill and Liberal Socialism," in *J. S. Mill's Political Thought: A Bicentennial Reassessment*, eds. Nadia Urbinati and Alex Zakaras (Cambridge: Cambridge University Press, 2007), 98–123.

9. Martha Nussbaum, "Mill on Happiness: The Enduring Value of a Complex Critique," in *Utilitarianism and Empire*, eds. Bart Schultz and Georgios Varouxakis (Lanham: Lexington Books, 2005); John Gray, "Mill's Conception of Happiness and the Theory of Individuality," in *J. S. Mill's On Liberty in Focus*, eds. John Gray and G. W. Smith (London: Routledge, 2015); John Gray, *Mill on Liberty: A Defence* (London: Routledge, 1996); Nadia Urbinati, "The Many Heads of the Hydra: J. S. Mill on Despotism," in *J. S. Mill's Political Thought: A Bicentennial Reassessment*, eds. Nadia Urbinati and Alex Zakaras (Cambridge: Cambridge University Press, 2007); Nadia Urbinati, "An Alternative Modernity: Mill on Capitalism and the Quality of Life," in *John Stuart Mill and the Art of Life*, eds. Ben Eggleston, Dale E. Miller, David Weinstein (Oxford: Oxford University Press, 2011), 236–265; Capaldi, *John Stuart Mill*; Peter Berkowitz, "Mill: Liberty, Virtue, and the Discipline of Individuality," in *Mill and the Moral Character of Liberalism*, ed. Eldon J. Eisenach (University Park: Pennsylvania State University Press, 1998), 13–48; Wendy Donner, "John Stuart Mill on Education and Democracy," in *J. S. Mill's Political Thought: A Bicentennial Re-Assessment*, eds. Nadia Urbinati and Alex Zakaras (Cambridge: Cambridge University Press, 2007), 250–274; Donner, *Liberal Self*; Donner, "Mill and Virtue Ethics"; Semmel, *Pursuit of Virtue*.

10. Jonathan Riley, "Mill's Neo-Athenian Model of Liberal Democracy," in *J. S. Mill's Political Thought: A Bicentennial Reassessment*, eds. Nadia Urbinati and Alex Zakaras (Cambridge: Cambridge University Press, 2007); Urbinati, *Athenian Polis*.

11. Dennis F. Thompson, *John Stuart Mill and Representative Government* (Princeton: Princeton University Press, 1976).

12. J. H. Burns, "J. S. Mill and Democracy, 1829–61," *Political Studies* 5, no. 2 (1957): 158–175; Graeme Duncan, *Marx and Mill: Two Views of Social Conflict and Social Harmony* (Cambridge: Cambridge University Press, 1973).

13. Urbinati, *Athenian Polis*; Stewart Justman, *The Hidden Text of Mill's Library* (Lanham: Rowman and Littlefield, 1990); E. F. Biagini, "Neo-Roman Liberalism: 'Republican' Values and British Liberalism, ca. 1860–1875," *History of European Ideas* 29, no. 1 (2003): 55–72; Dale Miller, "John Stuart Mill's Civic Liberalism," *History of Political Thought* 21, no. 1 (2000): 88–113.

14. See Chapter 5.

15. Larmore, "Political Liberalism"; Villa, "Maturity and Paternalism"; Semmel, *Pursuit of Virtue.*

16. Berlin, "Mill and Ends of Life."

17. Capaldi, *John Stuart Mill.* For a compelling reading of Mill's Romanticism, see Lynn Zastoupil, *John Stuart Mill and India* (Stanford: Stanford University Press, 1994).

18. Waldron, "Mill and Multiculturalism"; Richard White, "Liberalism and Multiculturalism: The Case of Mill," *Journal of Value Inquiry* 37, no. 2 (2003): 205–216.

19. John Hospers, *Libertarianism: A Political Philosophy for Tomorrow* (Los Angeles: Nash Publishing, 1971); Charles Murray, *What it Means to be a Libertarian* (New York: Broadway Books, 1997).

20. This is, of course, the ubiquitous reading of Mill.

21. Joseph Hamburger, *John Stuart Mill on Liberty and Control* (Princeton: Princeton University Press, 1999).

22. Friedrich A. von Hayek, *The Counter-Revolution of Science: Studies on the Abuse of Reason* (Indianapolis: Liberty Press, 1979); Friedrich A. von Hayek, "Liberalism," in *New Studies in Philosophy, Politics, Economics, and the History of Ideas* (Chicago: University of Chicago Press, 1978), 119–151; Bruce Baum, *Rereading Power and Freedom in J. S. Mill* (Toronto: University of Toronto Press, 2000); Ludwig von Mises, *Liberalism in the Classical Tradition,* trans. Ralph Raico (New York: Foundation for Economic Education, 1985); Harold Laski, *The Rise of Liberalism: The Philosophy of a Business Civilization* (New York: Harper and Brothers, 1936). Baum, it's important to note, situates Mill between socialism and liberalism.

23. On the influence of conservatism in Mill's thought, see Capaldi, *John Stuart Mill.*

24. Quoted in John Morley, *The Life of William Ewart Gladstone* (London: Macmillan, 1903), 544.

25. Mehta, *Liberalism and Empire.*

26. For the difficulty of attributing any fixed ideological stance to Mill, see Paul Kelly and Georgios Varouxakis, "John Stuart Mill's Thought and Legacy: A Timely Reappraisal," in *John Stuart Mill: Thought and Influence – The Saint of Rationalism,* eds. Georgios Varouxakis and Paul Kelly (London: Routledge, 2010), 15.

27. John Stuart Mill, *A System of Logic Ratiocinative and Inductive: Being a Connected View of the Principles of Evidence and the Methods of Scientific Investigation,* in *The Collected Works of John Stuart Mill, Volume VIII – A System of Logic Part II,* ed. J. M. Robson (Toronto: University of Toronto Press, 1974), 8:946.

28. Stefan Collini, *Public Moralists: Political Thought and Intellectual Life in Britain* (Oxford: Clarendon Press, 1993); Bruce L. Kinzer, Ann P. Robson and John M. Robson, *A Moralist in and out of Parliament: John Stuart Mill at Westminster, 1865–1868* (Toronto: University of Toronto Press, 1992).

29. Mill employs a number of (equally deprecating) terms to describe the uncivilized: savages, barbarians, rude peoples, peoples in their nonage and so on. He occasionally (and rather casually) distinguishes savages and barbarians, but the distinction does not affect my argument. I therefore use the term "uncivilized" throughout this book to designate peoples characterized by Mill as savage, rude, barbarian or otherwise backward.

30. Chakrabarty, *Provincializing Europe*, 8.
31. Mill, *Considerations*, 19:404. I follow the convention of citing from the University of Toronto Press's authoritative *Collected Works*, with the minor alteration of including book/essay titles (rather than citing by volume:page alone) for the benefit of non-specialists.
32. For an expansive treatment of character in Mill's philosophy, see Janice Carlisle, *John Stuart Mill and the Writing of Character* (Athens: University of Georgia Press, 1991). For an overview of character in Victorian thought, see Stefan Collini, "The Idea of 'Character' in Victorian Political Thought," *Transactions of the Royal Historical Society* 35 (1985): 29–50.
33. Gray, "Conception of Happiness," 208.
34. Mill, *On Liberty*, 18:225.
35. Hamburger, *Liberty and Control*, xi. For libertarian readings (or appropriations) of Mill, see Hospers, *Libertarianism*; Murray, *To be a Libertarian*; and Nicholas Capaldi, "The Libertarian Philosophy of John Stuart Mill," *Reason Papers* 9 (1983): 3–19. Hamburger illuminates the tendency in much of the received wisdom on Mill (including work by Gertrude Himmelfarb, Isaiah Berlin, George Kateb, Jeremy Waldron and C. L. Ten, among others) to treat his defense of liberty in generally libertarian terms, disregarding or minimizing important limits on the liberty principle. For refutations of the libertarian view, see Alan Ryan, "John Stuart Mill's Art of Living," in *J. S. Mill's On Liberty in Focus*, eds. John Gray and G. W. Smith (London: Routledge, 2015); and Hamburger, *Liberty and Control*. For a particularly sensitive reading of Mill as advocating "liberty from subjection" (10), see Urbinati, *Athenian Polis*.
36. Charles Larmore, *The Morals of Modernity* (Cambridge: Cambridge University Press, 1996), 128; Larmore, "Political Liberalism"; Rawls, *Political Liberalism*, 199–200; and William A. Galston, *Liberal Pluralism: The Implications of Value Pluralism for Political Theory and Practice* (Cambridge: Cambridge University Press), 21–23.
37. Mill, *Considerations*, 19:384.
38. Mill, *On Liberty*, 18:225.
39. Mill first formally addresses the "Art of Life" in the *System of Logic*'s 3rd edition, published in 1851 (it was first published in 1843), in the final chapter of Book 6 ("On the Logic of the Moral Sciences"). And yet, the substance of his view has deep roots. The division between arts and sciences dates back to "On the Definition of Political Economy; and on the Method of Investigation Proper to it," an essay written in 1831 and published in the *London and Westminster Review* in 1836 in which Mill posits that "[s]cience is a collection of *truths*; art, a body of *rules*, or directions for conduct ... Science takes cognizance of a *phenomenon*, and endeavours to discover its *law*; art proposes to itself an *end*, and looks out for *means* to effect it" (Mill, 4:312). This is precisely the view elaborated in the *System*. Mill's distinction between moral and physical sciences, his analysis of the methods suited (and unsuited) to conducting them, and his skepticism regarding fixed laws of social progress – all developed in the *System* – also appear in nascent form in this essay. For detailed examinations of the "Art of Life," see Ben Eggleston, Dale Miller and David Weinstein, eds., *John Stuart Mill and the Art of Life* (Oxford: Oxford University Press, 2011); Gray, *A Defence*; Donner, "Virtue Ethics"; Donner, *Liberal Self*; Stephen G. Engelmann, "Mill, Bentham, and the

Art and Science of Government," *Revue d'études Benthamiennes* 4 (2008); and
Ryan, *John Stuart Mill*, ch. 11.
40. Mill, *System of Logic*, 8:943
41. Ibid., 8:944.
42. Ibid., 8:943.
43. Ibid., 8:944–945.
44. Ibid., 8:944.
45. Ibid., 8:949.
46. Ibid.
47. Ibid., 8:947. Mill here enunciates the relationship of art and science, and their
grounding in practical action, with particular lucidity: "Art, in general, consists of
the truths of Science, arranged in the most convenient order for practice, instead of
the order which is the most convenient for thought."
48. Mill, *System of Logic*, 8:947.
49. Ibid., 8:949. Where exactly the political sphere falls, within this tripartite division,
remains somewhat nebulous given its apparent relevance for both morality and
policy/prudence. Alan Ryan argues that "morality" encompasses all interpersonal
goods, including ethics and politics; thus understood, it remains sufficiently
general a category to defuse the charge that Mill's politics are subject to any kind
of ethical perfectionism. As an "art," Ryan notes further, morality – and the
domains of politics and ethics contained within it – explicitly concerns practical
action and the norms guiding it, rather than any kind of thick, Aristotelian truth
claims. For the first argument, see Ryan, "Art of Living"; for the second, see Ryan,
John Stuart Mill, xix.
50. Mill, *System of Logic*, 8:950.
51. Ibid., 8:951.
52. Ibid., 8:950, n.51.
53. Ibid., 8:951.
54. Ibid.
55. Ibid.
56. Gray, *Defence*, 11.
57. Ryan, *John Stuart Mill*, 192.
58. Gray, *Defence*, 11.
59. Mill, *System of Logic*, 8:947.
60. Ibid., 8:946.
61. Mill, *System of Logic*, 8:947.
62. Donner, "Mill and Virtue Ethics," 878–879.
63. Mill, *Utilitarianism*, 10:336.
64. Mill, *Considerations*, 19:383.
65. Ibid.
66. Ibid., 19:373.
67. Mill's lifelong dissatisfaction with political orthodoxies is apparent as early as
1831, in a letter to John Sterling: "I cannot help regretting that the men who are
best capable of struggling against these narrow views & mischievous heresies
should chain themselves, full of life & vigour as they are, to the inanimate
corpses of dead political & religious systems, never more to be revived" (John
Stuart Mill, "Mill to John Sterling, Oct. 20–22, 1831," in *The Collected Works of
John Stuart Mill, Volume XII – The Earlier Letters 1812–1848 Part I*, ed. Francis

E. Mineka (Toronto: University of Toronto Press; London: Routledge & Kegan Paul, 1963), 12: 84). This frustration resurfaces in the essays on Bentham and Coleridge in the late 1830s/early 1840s and, of course, in *Considerations*.

68. Mill, *Considerations*, 19:374.

69. Mill, *Autobiography*, 1:161.

70. Mill, *Considerations*, 19:374.

71. Ibid.

72. Fred Rosen, "Method of Reform: J. S. Mill's encounter with Bentham and Coleridge," in *J. S. Mill's Political Thought: A Bicentennial* Reassessment, eds. Nadia Urbinati and Alex Zakaras (Cambridge: Cambridge University Press, 2007), 126.

73. Mill, *Considerations*, 19:393.

74. Ibid., 19:374–375.

75. Capaldi, *John Stuart Mill*, 79.

76. Mill, *Considerations*, 19:384. For Coleridge's accounts of permanence and progression, see Samuel Taylor Coleridge, "On the Constitution of Church and State," in *The Collected Works of Samuel Taylor Coleridge, Volume 10: On the Constitution of Church and State*, ed. John Colmer (Princeton: Princeton University Press, 2015).

77. Mill, *Considerations*, 19:384.

78. John Stuart Mill, "The Spirit of the Age, III," in *The Collected Works of John Stuart Mill, Volume XXII – Newspaper Writings Part I*, eds. John M. Robson and Ann P. Robson (Toronto: University of Toronto Press; London: Routledge & Kegan Paul, 1986), 22:252. For Mill's characterization of his own era as an "age of transition," see Mill, "Mill to Sterling," 12:77. For his debts to St. Simon, see Edward Alexander, *Matthew Arnold and John Stuart Mill* (London: Routledge, 2012), ch. 2; and Semmel, *Pursuit of Virtue*, ch. 2.

79. Mill, *System of Logic*, 8:917–918. For the intersection of St. Simonian, Coleridgian and Comtian influences in Mill's thought, see Capaldi, *John Stuart Mill*, 77–82, 169 and 295.

80. Mill, *Considerations*, 19:388.

81. Ibid., 19:389.

82. Ibid., 19:390.

83. Ibid., 19:392. Nadia Urbinati argues that "Mill uses two criteria to judge government: the *common interest* and the *common culture*" (*Athenian Polis*, 56), departing somewhat from the pedagogic and machinery criteria sketched out here (although they overlap). This results from her focus, shared by most commentators on Mill's democratic theory, on the "machinery" occupying much of *Considerations'* middle chapters, which responds to the pathologies of class-based voting ("[a]ccording to the common interest criterion, good government results when the governing class pursues the general interest of the community," *Athenian Polis*, 56). The machinery criterion that I elaborate widens beyond Mill's worries with balancing class interests (important though these are) to capture his concerns with the cultivation of democratic public-mindedness.

84. Mill, *Considerations*, 19:390–391.

85. John Stuart Mill, "Mill to Gustave D'Eichtal, Oct. 8, 1929," in *The Collected Works of John Stuart Mill, Volume XII – The Earlier Letters 1812–1848 Part I*, ed.

Francis E. Mineka (Toronto: University of Toronto Press; London: Routledge & Kegan Paul, 1963), 12:36.

86. Mill, *Considerations*, 19:379. Frederick Rosen treats Mill's three conditions as tacking between liberal reformism and conservative preservationism, while Dennis Thompson sees them as remnants of his late-lingering Comtianism. See Rosen "Method of Reform," 140; and Thompson, *Representative Government*, 141–147.

87. Mill, *Considerations*, 19:379. For Mill's sensitivity to national character, see Georgios Varouxakis, *Mill on Nationality* (London: Routledge, 2002), chs. 1 and 4.

88. Urbinati, *Athenian Polis*, 56.

89. John Stuart Mill, "Coleridge," in *The Collected Works of John Stuart Mill, Volume X – Essays on Ethics, Religion and Society (Utilitarianism)*, ed. John M. Robson (Toronto: University of Toronto Press, 1969), 10:132.

90. Mill, "Coleridge," 10:133–135. For Mill's account of public institutions' role in generating social cohesion and stability, see Berkowitz, "Liberty, Virtue, and Discipline"; Andrew Valls, "Self-Development and the Liberal State: The Cases of John Stuart Mill and Wilhelm von Humboldt," *The Review of Politics* 61, no. 2 (1999), 251–274; Wendy Donner and Richard A. Fullerton, *Mill* (Malden: Wiley-Blackwell, 2009); Donner, *Liberal Self*; and Varouxakis, *Mill on Nationality*.

91. Mill, "Coleridge," 10:134.

92. Mill, *Considerations*, 19:398.

93. Ibid., 19:403–404.

94. For illuminating treatments of Mill's democratic institutionalism, see Thompson, *Representative Government*; Urbinati, *Athenian Polis*; Jonathan Riley, "Neo-Athenian Model"; and Janine Carlisle, "Mr. John Stuart Mill, M.P., and the Character of the Working Classes," in *Mill and the Moral Character of Liberalism*, ed. Eldon Eisenach (University Park: Pennsylvania State University Press, 1998), 143–168.

   Given its ambiguities and elitist elements, Mill's democratic theory is subject to wide interpretation and equally wide criticisms. For critiques of its elitism, see Judith Shklar, *The Faces of Injustice* (New Haven: Yale University Press, 1990), and Duncan (who also suggests that Mill himself "was not a democrat of whom it could be said that he genuinely wanted democracy," 259), Duncan, *Marx and Mill*. For critiques of its inconsistencies, see Richard J. Arneson, "Democracy and Liberty in Mill's Theory of Government," *Journal of the History of Philosophy* 20, no. 1 (1982): 43–64; and Leslie Stephen, *The English Utilitarians* (London: Duckworth and Co., 1900). For a view questioning whether Mill's democratic theory is democratic at all, see Burns, "J. S. Mill and Democracy," 174–175. For the difficulties in determining Mill's relationship to democracy, see Capaldi, *John Stuart Mill*, 300–301. Despite these charges, Thompson insists – rightly, in my view – that Mill's ideal remains "fundamentally democratic" (*Representative Democracy*, 93).

95. Thompson and Urbinati briefly touch on Mill's attention to democratic pedagogy; see Thompson, *Representative Democracy*, ch. 1, and Urbinati, *Athenian Polis*, ch. 4.

96. I account for (and respond to) the critique of Mill's liberal imperialism in Chapter 5. I focus here only on the rationalism that it imputes to Mill's democratic theory.

97. Mehta, *Liberalism and Empire*, 82.
98. Ibid., 104.
99. Parekh, "Decolonizing Liberalism," 93–94. Edward Alexander concurs: "assimilat[ing] the process of history to the process of reason … Mill showed that his conception of history was … essentially Manichean" (Alexander, *Arnold and Mill*, 35).
100. Mill, *On Liberty*, 18:224.
101. Ibid.
102. John Stuart Mill, "A Few Words on Non-Intervention," in *The Collected Works of John Stuart Mill, Volume XXI – Essays on Equality, Law, and Education (Subjection of Women)*, ed. John M. Robson (Toronto: Toronto University Press; London: Routledge & Kegan Paul, 1984), 21:118.
103. John Stuart Mill, "Civilization," in *The Collected Works of John Stuart Mill, Volume XVIII – Essays on Politics and Society Part I (On Liberty)*, ed. John M. Robson (Toronto: Toronto University Press; London: Routledge & Kegan Paul, 1977), 18:122.
104. Pitts, "Empire, Progress and the 'Savage Mind'," 22.
105. Pitts, *Empire*, 127.
106. Ibid.,142. There are, unsurprisingly, variations within the cognitivist camp. Stricter proponents treat the civilized–uncivilized split as "inherently bipolar" (Parekh, "Decolonizing Liberalism," 92), such that "[w]hat represents or speaks for the savage is the location of the civilization of which he is deemed to be a part, and this in Mill's case turns on a simple binary scale of civilized or backward" (Mehta, *Liberalism and Empire*, 101). For Mehta and Parekh, self-government turns on a fixed cognitive threshold demarcating entirely different sorts of societies. Other commentators treat the distinction less starkly, recognizing the wider range of sociological measures in Mill's conceptualizations of civilization and barbarism, but nonetheless focus on its cognitive facets. For a few sensitive treatments, see Pitts, *Empire*, and "Empire, Progress"; Michael Levin, *J. S. Mill on Civilization and Barbarism* (London: Routledge, 2004), 19–20, 48; Beate Jahn, "Barbarian Thoughts: Imperialism in the Philosophy of John Stuart Mill," *Review of International Studies*, 31 (2005): 611; and Alex Zakaras, "John Stuart Mill, Individuality, and Participatory Democracy," in *J. S. Mill's Political Thought: A Bicentennial Reassessment*, eds. Nadia Urbinati and Alex Zakaras (Cambridge: Cambridge University Press, 2007), 200–220.
107. Jahn, "Barbarian Thoughts," 611.
108. Mill, *Considerations*, 19:377.
109. Ibid., 19:394.
110. Ibid., 19:377–378.
111. Ibid., 19:377.
112. Ibid., 19:378.
113. Graham Finlay, "John Stuart Mill and Edmund Burke on Empire," in *Postcolonialism and Political Theory*, ed. Nalini Persram (Lanham: Lexington Books, 2007), 63. See, also, Miller, "Mill's Civic Liberalism," 99, for democracy's dependence on active character.
114. Mill, *Considerations*, 19:412.
115. Ibid., 19:410.
116. Ibid.

117. Ibid., 19:414.

118. Mehta, *Liberalism and Empire*, 100.

119. Mill, *Considerations*, 19:377.

120. Ibid., 19:389–390.

121. Mill, "Civilization," 18:122. See also John Stuart Mill, *Principles of Political Economy*, in *The Collected Works of John Stuart Mill, Volume III – Principles of Political Economy Part II*, ed. John M. Robson (Toronto: Toronto University Press; London: Routledge & Kegan Paul, 1965), 3:708.

122. Mill, *Utilitarianism*, 10:240. I elaborate on Mill's account of moral sentiment in section 4.3.4.

123. Mill, "Civilization," 18:120.

124. Mill, *Considerations*, 19:390.

125. Ibid.

126. Ibid., 19:378.

127. Ibid., 19:414.

128. Ibid.

129. Ibid.

130. For Mill's concerns regarding class-based voting, see Urbinati, *Athenian Polis*; C. L. Ten, "Democracy, Socialism, and the Working Classes," in *The Cambridge Companion to* Mill, ed. John Skorupski (Cambridge: Cambridge University Press, 1998), 372–395; Riley, "Neo-Athenian Model"; Thompson, *Representative Government*; Carlisle, "Working Classes"; Joseph J. Miller, "J. S. Mill on Plural Voting, Competence and Participation," *History of Political Thought* 24, no. 4 (2003): 647–667; and Dale E. Miller, "The Place of Plural Voting in Mill's Conception of Representative Government," *The Review of Politics* 77, no. 3 (2015): 399–425.

131. Thompson, *Representative Government*, 51.

132. Riley, "Neo-Athenian Model." Nadia Urbinati addresses Mill's attention to cultivating a "Socratic ethos," but focuses on institutions honing citizens' deliberative and argumentative competence (such as debating societies), rather than on those developing their democratic affects (such as newspapers, unions, local governments, parish offices, etc.), which I treat here. See Urbinati, *Athenian Polis*, ch. 4. For the republicanism suffusing Mill's liberalism, see Miller, "Mill's Civic Liberalism"; Urbinati, *Athenian Polis*; Villa, "Maturity and Paternalism"; Biagini, "Neo-Roman Liberalism,"; Justman, *Hidden Text*; and Semmel, *Pursuit of Virtue*.

133. John Stuart Mill, "Rationale of Representation," in *The Collected Works of John Stuart Mill, Volume XVIII – Essays on Politics and Society Part I (On Liberty)*, ed. John M. Robson (Toronto: University of Toronto Press; London: Routledge & Kegan Paul, 1977), 18:31.

134. John Stuart Mill, "De Tocqueville on Democracy in America [1]," in *The Collected Works of John Stuart Mill, Volume XVIII – Essays on Politics and Society Part I (On Liberty)*, ed. John M. Robson (Toronto: University of Toronto Press; London: Routledge & Kegan Paul, 1977), 18:60.

135. John Stuart Mill, "De Tocqueville on Democracy in America [2]," in *The Collected Works of John Stuart Mill, Volume XVIII – Essays on Politics and Society Part I (On Liberty)*, ed. John M. Robson (Toronto: University of Toronto Press; London: Routledge & Kegan Paul, 1977), 18:165.

136. Ibid.
137. Mill, *Principles of Political Economy*, 3:763.
138. Mill, "De Tocqueville [2]," 18:165.
139. Mill, *On Liberty*, 18:305.
140. Mill, *Considerations*, 19:401; Mill, "De Tocqueville [2]," 18:165. Urbinati describes these "intermediary network[s] of communication" as mechanisms enabling "representative democracy [to] reproduce the distinctive features of Athenian democracy" (*Athenian Polis*, 73).
141. Mill, *On Liberty*, 18:305.
142. Mill, *Principles of Political Economy*, 3:763.
143. Mill, *Considerations*, 19:469. For an insightful treatment of Mill's consciousness of democracy's dependence on formal (schools, universities) and informal (newspapers, unions, democratic participation) learning institutions, see Donner, "Mill on Democracy and Education."
144. Mill, "De Tocqueville [1]," 18:63. Mill also observes the educative value of local government in "Municipal Institutions, *The Examiner*, 11 Aug, 1833," in *The Collected Works of John Stuart Mill, Volume XIII – Newspaper Writings Part II*, ed. Ann P. Robson and John M. Robson (Toronto: University of Toronto Press; London: Routledge & Kegan Paul, 1986), 23:585–590.
145. Mill, *Principles of Political Economy*, 3:942.
146. "[W]hat really constitutes education is the formation of habits ... it is only by practicing popular government on a limited scale, that the people will ever learn how to exercise it on a larger" (Mill, "De Tocqueville [2]," 18:63). I treat Mill's account of democratic habituation in section 4.3.3.
147. Mill, *Considerations*, 19:412.
148. Mill, "De Tocqueville [2]," 18:169. I treat the pathologies of commercial societies in detail in chapter 5.
149. Mill, "De Tocqueville [2]," 18:169.
150. John Stuart Mill, "Mill to George Cornewall Lewis, March 20, 1859," in *The Collected Works of John Stuart Mill, Volume XV – The Later Letters 1849–1873 Part II*, eds. France E. Mineka and Dwight N. Lindley (Toronto: University of Toronto Press; London: Routledge & Kegan Paul, 1972), 15:608. For lucid analyses of Mill's views on the public ballot, see Urbinati, *Athenian Polis*, 104–122, and Semmel, *Pursuit of Virtue*, ch. 4 (in particular, 99–101).
151. John Stuart Mill, "Romilly's Public Responsibility and the Ballot, *Reader*, Apr. 29, 1865," in *The Collected Works of John Stuart Mill, Volume XXV – Newspaper Writings Part IV*, eds. Ann P. Robson and John M. Robson (Toronto: University of Toronto Press; London: Routledge & Kegan Paul, 1986), 25:1214. I am indebted to Urbinati's *Athenian Polis* for this reference.
152. John Stuart Mill, "Thoughts on Parliamentary Reform," in *The Collected Works of John Stuart Mill, Volume XIX – Essays on Politics and Society Part II*, ed. John M. Robson (Toronto: University of Toronto Press; London: Routledge & Kegan Paul, 1977), 19:335–356.
153. Urbinati, *Athenian Polis*, 119.
154. Mill, *Considerations*, 19:386–387.
155. Ibid., 19:401.
156. Mill, "Civilization," 18:124.
157. Mill, *Principles of Political Economy*, 3:763.

158. Ibid., 763–764. Nicholas Capaldi treats Mill's advocacy for the poor here as belonging to his wide-ranging commitment to advancing the autonomy of all human beings, focusing on the working class in *Principles of Political Economy*, on women in *Subjection*, and on humanity at large in *On Liberty*. This sets Mill apart from paternalistic conservatives such as Carlyle, whose response to the working class leaned toward charity and philanthropy rather than encouraging their self-development. See Capaldi, *John Stuart Mill*, 203–204.

159. Mill, *Principles of Political Economy*, 3:765.

160. Ibid., 3:764.

161. Mill, *Considerations*, 19:287.

162. Miller, "Plural Voting," 400. Mill's thoughts on plural voting initially appear in his 1859 "Thoughts on Parliamentary Reform" and are further elaborated in *Considerations*.

163. Miller, "Plural Voting," 413.

164. Ibid., 414.

165. Donner, "Mill on Education and Democracy"; Donner and Fullerton, *Mill*. For a similar argument, linking plural voting to the inculcation of civic virtue, see Peter Berkowitz, "Liberty, Virtue, and Discipline."

166. Mill, *Considerations*, 19:299.

167. Urbinati, *Athenian Polis*, 107.

168. Varouxakis, *Mill on Nationality*, 65.

169. Mill, "De Tocqueville [2]," 18:168.

170. Ibid.

171. John Stuart Mill, "Vindication of the French Revolution of February 1848–1849," in *The Collected Works of John Stuart Mill, Volume XX – Essays on French History and Historians*, ed. John M. Robson (Toronto: University of Toronto Press; London: Routledge & Kegan Paul, 1985), 20:332. For more on democratic deficits in the French national character, see Mill, *Considerations*, 19:408.

172. Mill, "De Tocqueville [2]," 18:167–168.

173. Mill, *Principles of Political Economy*, 3:944.

174. My engagement with Mill's moral psychology is limited to its relevance for his social and political thought. I therefore (mostly) set aside voluminous debates in the philosophical literature surrounding his utilitarianism's coherence, tenability and deficits.

175. Mill, *Utilitarianism*, 10:216–217.

176. Mill, *On Liberty*, 18:278–279.

177. Mill, *Utilitarianism*, 10:218.

178. John Stuart Mill, "Auguste Comte and Positivism," in *The Collected Works of John Stuart Mill, Volume X – Essays on Ethics, Religion and Society (Utilitarianism)*, ed. John M. Robson (Toronto: University of Toronto Press; London: Routledge & Kegan Paul, 1969), 10:337.

179. John Stuart Mill, "Inaugural Address Delivered to the University of St. Andrews 1867," in *The Collected Works of John Stuart Mill, Volume XXI – Essays on Equality, Law, and Education*, ed. John M. Robson (Toronto: University of Toronto; London: Routledge & Kegan Paul, 1984), 21:254.

180. Mill, *System of Logic*, 8:849.

181. Mill, *Auguste Comte*, 10:296.

182. Ibid., 10:297.

183. Semmel, *Pursuit of Virtue*, 63–64; Capaldi, *John Stuart Mill*, 171.
184. Mill, *Auguste Comte*, 10:298.
185. Capaldi, *John Stuart Mill*, 174.
186. Ibid., 167.
187. This animates Mill's well-known valuation of active character. I treat it, and the departure from his father's moral psychology which it entails, in Chapter 5.
188. Ryan, *John Stuart Mill*, 106.
189. For Mill's resistance to Comte's and to the Philosophical Radicals' shared scientistic determinism, see Capaldi, *John Stuart Mill*, 164, 175. In a letter to Gustave D'Eichtal from October 8, 1829, Mill charged that Comte and the "French philosophers" – Saint-Simonians – "deduce politics like mathematics from a set of axioms & definitions, forgetting that in mathematics there is no danger of partial views … but in politics & the social science, this is so far from being the case, that error seldom arises from our assuming premisses which are not true, but generally from our overlooking other truths which limit, & modify the effect of the former" (Mill, "Mill to Gustave D'Eichtal," 12:36).
190. Mill, *System of Logic*, 8:852.
191. Ibid.
192. Ibid., 8:856.
193. Ibid., 8:853.
194. James Mill, "An Essay on Government," in *Utilitarian Logic and Politics: James Mill's "Essay on Government," Macaulay's Critique, and the Ensuing Debate*, eds. Jack Lively and J. C. Rees (Oxford: Clarendon Press, 1978), 55–56.
195. Fred Wilson, "Psychology and the Moral Sciences," in *The Cambridge Companion to Mill*, ed. John Skorupski (Cambridge: Cambridge University Press, 1998), 208.
196. For Mill's rejection of the egoism underpinning James Mill's and Bentham's utilitarianisms, see Semmel, *Pursuit of Virtue*, 87–89; Ryan, *John Stuart Mill*, 144; Wilson, "Psychology," 203–222; Donner, *Liberal Self*, 8–36; Thompson, *Representative Government*, 13–27; and Skorupski, *John Stuart Mill*, 295–307.
197. Mill, *System of Logic*, 8:854.
198. Ibid.
199. Ibid.
200. Skorupski, *John Stuart Mill*, 263. Fred Wilson similarly characterizes the higher pleasures as "qualitatively distinct from, and in that sense irreducible to, the more physical pleasures which they have as their associative antecedents" (Wilson, "Psychology," 218).
201. For a detailed account of lexical ordering in Mill's higher and lower pleasures, see Elijah Millgram, "Liberty, the Higher Pleasures, and Mill's Missing Science of Ethnic Jokes," *Social Philosophy and Policy*, 26, no. 1 (2009): 326–353.
202. Mill, *Utilitarianism*, 10:211.
203. Ibid., 10:212.
204. Ibid., 10:211. For an argument situating Mill's conception of happiness between Bentham's felicific calculus and Aristotle's conception of a well-lived life, see Martha Nussbaum, "Mill on Happiness."
205. Donner, *Liberal Self*. Mill's account of the competent agent suffers from a well-documented circularity: she whose evaluation determines whether higher pleasures are superior to lower ones is judged "competent" precisely due to her

preferring the higher pleasures. Mill's shift between descriptive and normative judgments is also problematic: while the test determining the higher pleasures is descriptive (experienced persons prefer it), their valuation is normative (it reflects Mill's opinion). For a clear account of both problems, see John Robson, *The Improvement of Mankind: the Social and Political Thought of John Stuart Mill* (Toronto: University of Toronto Press, 1968), 156–159. For incisive examinations of the "competent agent," see Donner, *Liberal Self*; Donner, "Democracy and Education"; Donner and Fullerton, *Mill*; Ryan, *John Stuart Mill*; Gray, "Mill's Conception of Happiness"; and Dale E. Miller, *John Stuart Mill: Moral, Social and Political Thought* (Cambridge: Polity Press, 2010).

206. Mill, *System of Logic*, 8:842.
207. Elijah Millgram, "Mill's Incubus," in *John Stuart Mill and the Art of Life*, eds. Ben Eggleston, Dale E. Miller and David Weinstein (Oxford: Oxford University Press, 2011), 174. See also Donner, *Liberal Self*, 21–22.
208. Mill, *System of Logic*, 8:842.
209. Ibid., 8:842–843.
210. Mill, *Utilitarianism*, 10:239. Mill's fuller account here is illuminating: "How can the will to be virtuous, where it does not exist in sufficient force, be implanted or awakened? Only by making the person *desire* virtue – by making him think of it in a pleasurable light, or of its absence in a painful one. It is by associating the doing right with pleasure, or the doing wrong with pain ... that it is possible to call forth that will to be virtuous, which, when confirmed, acts without any thought of either pleasure or pain. Will is the child of desire, and passes out of the dominion of its parent only to come under that of habit. That which is the result of habit affords no presumption of being intrinsically good; and there would be no reason for wishing that the purpose of virtue should become independent of pleasure and pain, were it not that the influence of the pleasurable and painful associations which prompt to virtue is not sufficiently to be depended on for unerring constancy of action until it has acquired the support of habit ... the will to do right ought to be cultivated into this habitual independence."
211. Mill, *Utilitarianism*, 10:239
212. Ibid., 10:230.
213. Ibid., 10:231.
214. "[A] phænomenon universal in all societies, and constantly assuming a wider extension as they advance in their progress, is the co-operation of mankind one with another ... Its moral effects, in connecting them by their interests, and as a more remote consequence, by their sympathies, are equally salutary" (Mill, *Auguste Comte*, 10:312).
215. Mill, *Utilitarianism*, 10:231.
216. Ibid.
217. Robson, *Improvement of Mankind*, 134.
218. Mill, *Utilitarianism*, 10:248.
219. As Mill states in the notes to his father's *Analysis of the Phenomena of the Human Mind*, "the mere idea of a pain or pleasure, by whomsoever felt, is intrinsically painful or pleasurable, and when raised in the mind with intensity is capable of becoming a stimulus to action, independent, not merely of expected consequences to ourselves, but of any reference whatever to Self; so that care for others is, in an admissible sense, as much an ultimate fact of our nature, as care for ourselves;

though one which greatly needs strengthening by the concurrent force of the manifold associations insisted on" (John Stuart Mill, "James Mill's *Analysis of the Phenomena of the Human Mind,*" in *The Collected Works of John Stuart Mill, Volume XXXI – Miscellaneous Writings,* ed. John M. Robson (Toronto: University of Toronto Press; London: Routledge & Kegan Paul, 1989), 31:232).

220. Mill, *Utilitarianism,* 10:248.
221. Ibid.
222. Mill, *Analysis,* 31:232.
223. Mill, *Principles of Political Economy,* 3:942.
224. Mill, *Utilitarianism,* 10:239.
225. This isn't to suggest that Mill's utilitarianism is, or can be made, perfectly coherent, nor is it a strong defense of it; an expansive philosophical literature points to its considerable inconsistencies. My more circumscribed aim is to show that Mill's associationism vindicates the social orientation of his utilitarianism and keeps it from lapsing into simple hedonism. For a few critiques of Mill's utilitarianism, see John M. Robson, *The Improvement of Mankind,* 155–159; Robert Scott Stewart, "Art for Argument's Sake: Saving John Stuart Mill from the Fallacy of Composition," *The Journal of Value Inquiry* 27, nos. 3/4 (1993): 443–453; Skorupski, *John Stuart Mill,* ch. 9; Ryan, *John Stuart Mill,* chs. 11–12; and Wendy Donner, "Mill's Utilitarianism," in *The Cambridge Companion to Mill,* ed. John Skorupski (Cambridge: Cambridge University Press, 1998), 255–292.
226. Mill, *Utilitarianism,* 10:234.
227. John Stuart Mill, "Mill to Henry Jones, June 13, 1868" in *The Collected Works of John Stuart Mill, Volume XVI – The Later Letters 1849–1873 Part III,* eds. Francis E. Mineka and Dwight N. Lindley (Toronto: University of Toronto Press; London: Routledge & Kegan Paul), 16:1414.
228. Mill, *Utilitarianism,* 10:236.
229. Ibid.
230. Ibid.
231. Ibid., 10:235.
232. Gray, "Mill's Conception of Happiness," 208.
233. Connolly, *Neuropolitics, Ethos of Pluralization,* and *Capitalism and Christianity;* White, *Ethos* and *Democratic Bearing.*
234. Mill, *Utilitarianism,* 10:230.

5

Complicating Barbarism and Civilization

> But was there ever any domination which did not appear natural to those who possessed it?
>
> J. S. Mill, *The Subjection of Women*

Mill's democratic theory is something of a window on to his liberalism more broadly: despite their apparent simplicity, each incorporates a sophisticated moral psychology, a deeply social ethics and a progressive, reformist and open-ended politics. And yet, its center of gravity has a clear geographical bent, tilting toward the civilized, European societies at the heart of his social and political concerns. Despite their shared pathologies, Mill evidently drew substantive distinctions between civilized and uncivilized states of society, not least concerning their basic political standing. That the working class should submit to the despotic authority that he advocated for the uncivilized was, of course, unthinkable.

I now turn to the peoples at the edges of his vision. This chapter examines Mill's philosophy of history and "the Social Science"[1] framing his conceptualizations of civilization, barbarism and human development to consider the place of the uncivilized in his account of humanity's progress, and more broadly, in his liberalism. Mill's treatment of the uncivilized is undoubtedly his liberalism's central blind spot, all the more egregious (and glaring) against that liberalism's ready incorporation of women and the working class, and has for very good reason thrown into question the viability, coherence and relevance of his political philosophy. His imperial entanglements – personal, philosophical and political – have cast doubt on the very foundations of his liberalism.

Without minimizing those entanglements, I argue that critics of Mill's liberal imperialism misinterpret his considered views of the non-European world, the developmentalism framing them, and by consequence, his liberalism's response to human diversity. The case I build expands on several arguments introduced in Chapter 4: Mill did not draw a categorical distinction between civilized and uncivilized peoples, his account of social progress is poorly captured by the stage-based theory attributed to him, and he did not treat European history in universalist terms. The presumptions I resist here (along with other related ones) attest to the sway that Mill's imperialism has come to exert over readings of his liberalism, political theory and conception of pluralism. Mill's relation to empire, I contend, is a poor proxy for his views on racial and cultural variation more generally; the imperial lens distorts his understanding of social difference and its incorporation in his moral and political philosophy. This is, again, neither a denial nor a defense of Mill's chauvinisms, and it does not suggest that these aren't implicated in his pedagogical imperialism. The idea is – as with Kant – to contextualize Mill's response to diversity within the structure of his thought to better understand the problems it incurs for his liberalism.

I begin, in section 5.1, by reviewing the account of civilization and human development imputed to Mill by recent critics, which has become something of an orthodoxy. Jennifer Pitts, Uday Singh Mehta, Bhikhu Parekh and Thomas McCarthy (among others) argue that Mill's liberalism countenances a hierarchal conception of progress justifying Europeans' right to "civilize" non-Europeans. He is understood to have, like his father, conjoined the Scottish Enlightenment's four-stages theory of social development and Benthamite utilitarianism to form a civilizational ladder justifying imperial despotism. Insensate to cultural differences, Mill ostensibly ranked societies along a fixed index of progress distinguishing self-governing from retrograde populations. His is, then, an exemplary liberal imperialism.

Sections 5.2–5.4 challenge this view by demonstrating the far greater subtlety of Mill's accounts of historical evolution, social progress and civilization. Critics attribute what I describe as an *aggregative* conception of development to him, treating societies as comprising internally correlated economic, political, industrial, cultural and cognitive elements moving through historical stages as cohesive wholes. A closer examination fails to bear this out. Mill was in fact keenly attuned to the vast differences between peoples, to the contingencies and unevenness of historical progress and to the pathological features of civilized societies. As John Robson observes, far from treating civilized and uncivilized peoples as uniformly advanced or retrograde – or, still more simply, as uniformly good or bad – Mill saw all societies as complex and idiosyncratic entities whose goods required careful evaluation and institutional steering.[2]

I launch the argument in section 5.2 by examining the biographical and intellectual contexts surrounding Mill's early political philosophy – specifically, the influence of James Mill and Jeremy Bentham. I dispute the contention that Mill reproduced, or even further entrenched, his father's conceptual commitments by tracing their divergences following the younger Mill's emergence from his mental crisis in the early 1830s. Mill's turn to

Romanticism forged his profound appreciation for the depth and worth of culture, pushing him to see cultural differences as fixed in the human condition and as shaping the political institutions best suited to any given people. It also led him to reject his father's scientistic conception of government and attuned him to the affective grounds of politics and to the obduracy of humanity's cultural variation.

In section 5.3, I sketch out the complex view of civilization emerging from this Romantic shift. As we saw in Chapter 4, the cognitivist literature reads Mill as demarcating civilized and uncivilized people(s) as particular types, "one perfect and without blemish, the other irredeemably evil."[3] His account is in fact considerably more nuanced. Mill distinguishes two concepts of civilization, differentiating its beneficial attributes from its western manifestations (of which he is deeply critical); he treats civilized and uncivilized societies as fluid and interpenetrating; he explicitly criticizes the biological determinism framing the era's common views of non-Europeans; and he envisions social development – Europeans' as well as non-Europeans' – as variable and contingent. His notion of civilization is, then, better apprehended as a matter of tentative sociological observation than strict philosophical distinction.

Section 5.4 elaborates on the sociological foundations of Mill's notion of progress. I propose a disaggregative reading of Mill's developmentalism, arguing that his philosophy of history is mischaracterized as monological, deterministic and universalist.[4] Properly understood, it registers the complexity of social advancement and the influence that cultural life – or, for Mill, national character – holds over it. Rather than treating history as convergent – as a fixed process of modernization, westernization or rationalization – Mill sees it as subject to mutable "empirical laws" swayed by sociological and historical circumstances. Progress is, then, indeterminate, mutable and indelibly shaped by a people's character. This informs his approach to government: rather than grounding political institutions on abstract, universalistic principles, Mill takes the social sciences – sociology, political science and ethology – as tools enabling differently situated societies to pursue their particular ends. Mill's sociological developmentalism thus envisages social evolution as implicitly pluralistic and culturally inflected.

Section 5.5 concludes by, in light of this fuller view, completing the contrast between Kant's and Mill's developmentalisms, and between the responses to human diversity that each frames. Despite his own parochialism, I argue that Mill's developmentalism is neither inherently disposed to social domination, nor closed to the value of human heterogeneity. In marked contrast to the singularity of Kant's historicism, Mill's philosophy of history treats progress in non-convergent, non-deterministic and culturally differentiated terms. The theoretical architecture surrounding his liberalism's incorporation of human difference is, then, more capacious and open to the claims of culture than is Kant's, even if Mill's own assessments of the uncivilized remain mired in his chauvinisms.[5] This sets the stage for Chapter 6, which considers the relationship between liberalism and pluralism – conceptual, historical and contemporary – raised by my reconstructions of Kant's and Mill's views.

5.1 AN EXEMPLARY LIBERAL IMPERIALIST: THE CASE AGAINST J. S. MILL

A varied and critical literature has in recent years developed around Mill's imperial embroilments, and by extension, around his thoughts on race, civilization and progress. Commentary ranges from outright denunciations of his racism, to treating him as a crude teleologist in the Enlightenment mold, to reading in him a peculiar sensitivity to cultural variation, despite his Eurocentrism.[6] Critics argue that Mill's liberalism is inextricable from its colonial backdrop. Beyond his long employment at the East India Company, his political philosophy is moored in a hierarchal conception of socio-historical development securing what Edward Said describes as Europeans' "positional superiority"[7] over the non-European world. The problem isn't just biographical, then, but also conceptual. While numerous commentators share in an approximation of these views, I focus on those advanced by Jennifer Pitts and Uday Singh Mehta, as their most sophisticated and well-developed expositions.

For Pitts and Mehta, Mill's personal and philosophical linkages to empire merge, his 35 years as a high-ranking colonial administrator shaping the basic contours of his political theory. Mill's celebrated thoughts on liberty, individuality, representative government and experiments in living don't arise in a vacuum; they are all, rather, qualified by a civilizational index distinguishing advanced and backward societies. This theoretical vantage point has various roots, and James Mill's ideas are chief among them. Given his well-documented influence over his son, and given the impact that his *History of British India* had on both J. S. Mill and the East India Company's colonial administration, Pitts and Mehta both turn to James Mill's views on India. These are infamously reprehensible: paternalistic, unrepentantly hubristic, and replete with judgments concerning the subcontinent's state of barbarousness. That James Mill never set foot in the subcontinent was no impediment to his assessment of its civilizational state; "[w]ith characteristic force and arrogance," Bruce Mazlish observes, he "felt that his lack of firsthand acquaintance with India guaranteed a certain impartiality."[8] James Mill clearly regarded British colonialism as the white man's burden, a superior civilization's moral imperative to draw a people in its infancy toward a higher state of social order. He merged "a standard of utility from Bentham and an idea of progressive social development from Scottish thinkers such as Smith and Ferguson" to create "an index of progress in which utility is the sole standard against which any nation can be measured."[9] In stark contrast to the Scots' more complex historicisms, however, Mill's reductive rendition ascribed a wide range of defects to the uncivilized – most problematically, concerning their mental/cognitive capacities.[10] By misappropriating elements of conjectural history and utilitarianism, he concocted a monological account of progress structured by gradations of cognitive achievement justifying the colonization of less advanced peoples. This depicted societies as discrete wholes moving through predetermined stages of advancement, each occupying a readily identifiable position on a fixed scale of civilizations. Beyond sanctifying the domination of "subject races," Mill's framework also erased the particularity of distinctive societies by "assimilat[ing] all 'rude' peoples into a single category of moral and political inferiority."[11]

For Pitts and Mehta, the sins of the father are inherited by the son. Pitts argues that J. S. Mill's conceptualizations of progress and civilization largely replicate, and even in certain respects extend, James Mill's assumptions, commitments and prejudices. "The younger Mill also retreated from the relatively subtle account of historical development elaborated by the Scots, in favor of a rough dichotomy between savage and civilized," she maintains, "and he too combined this historical argument with utilitarian ones to justify despotic, but civilizing, imperial rule."[12] Mehta concurs: "Mill plainly is assuming some version of the objective scale of civilization similar to that crafted by his father."[13] Both understand the younger Mill to adopt his father's theoretical apparatus – the conjunction of conjectural history and utilitarianism framing the distance between civilized and uncivilized peoples – root and branch. Despite acknowledging the greater sophistication of J. S. Mill's version, Pitts sees no substantive difference between them, proposing that he "supported a view of social progress that in many of its details restated and affirmed the much less complex ideas of his father."[14] James and John Mill's philosophical foundations are, then, congruent, if not identical.

They also countenance the same practical end of vindicating imperial domination. For Pitts, J. S. Mill's stage-based developmentalism presumes that "all diversity in social practices and institutions could be ranged along a scale of progress, and that the challenge for political thinkers and actors was to draw backward societies towards the state of the most advanced society."[15] Mehta arrives at the same conclusion: the Mills' shared historicism draws non-Europeans into a universalistic, Benthamite legislative framework. The civilizational hierarchy doesn't just lurk in the shadows of Mill's political thought, but rather directly informs his practical task as a colonial administrator. If "a firm line of civilizational progress, or the 'scale of nations', could be inductively established," Mehta suggests, "then the Benthamite legislator-scientist would not have to humor customs or engage with local conditions. A clear scale of civilizational development would tell the legislator precisely what was below and what was above for any civilization under consideration."[16] This civilizational scale is buttressed by the conviction, also attributed to both Mills, "that societal development is a matter of the improvement of individuals' cognitive capacity."[17] The cognitive claim further justifies colonialism: if under-developed populations suffer from intellectual deficits, then only under the most fortuitous circumstances – under the unlikely stewardship of an Akbar or a Charlemagne – or under colonial authority could they hope to climb the civilizational ladder.

J. S. Mill's "rigid hierarchy of progress"[18] is, importantly, monolithic and unified. Critics understand his conception of social development as *aggregative*, treating societies as interlinked political, economic, cultural, industrial and cognitive phenomena advancing through stages of social evolution as cohesive wholes.[19] Societies progress as unified entities, bundled totalities of interconnected sociological elements moving in lockstep through fixed stages of advancement. The view of civilization and barbarism as categorically distinct turns on just this standpoint: civilization refers to a given *type* of social organization distinguishable from an equally particular "savage" form of society. The aggregative argument thus generates the sharp dichotomy between civilized and uncivilized peoples and justifies the differentiated political rights and moral standards to which they're subject. For the critics, Mill's developmentalism treats "all realms of human endeavor as tending to progress simultaneously."[20]

It's a lens that's necessarily blind to the worth of non-European societies. "What represents or speaks for the savage," Mehta holds, "is the location of the civilization of which he is deemed to be a part, and this in Mill's case turns on a simple binary scale of civilized or backward."[21] Mill neglects cultural particularity in at least two ways: first, by reducing all societies to their position in a civilizational ranking, and second, by treating them in strictly dualistic terms, as either civilized or uncivilized. The civilizational scale in fact intentionally avoids cultural specificity: a properly calibrated legislative science *should* ignore thin cultural variations in designing institutions, basing the correct set of laws on a society's state of development. Mill thus "erased details of particular societies in favor of a single and narrow set of criteria placed along a scale of progress."[22] In his schema, Thomas Metcalf contends, "[c]ontemporary European, especially British, culture alone represented civilization. No other culture had any intrinsic validity."[23]

Dipesh Chakrabarty's distinction between two modes of historical thought, History 1 (H1) and History 2 (H2), helps to capture the harms in the developmentalism attributed to Mill. H1 is "the universal and necessary history posited by the logic of capital [in which] inhere the Enlightenment universals"[24] associated with historicism generally, and with Mill's more specifically. H1s are the totalizing histories characteristic of "Marxist or liberal views of the world," which take their "object of investigation to be internally unified, and [see] it as something developing over time."[25] By framing historical progress as singular and globe-encompassing, H1s incorporate non-Western social forms into a historical-temporal continuum that invariably positions them as lagging behind European civilization. The unifying impulse drives H1s to treat social and cultural differences as idiosyncratic and ultimately vestigial remainders that modernity would wipe away.

History 2, conversely, is a mode of historical thought "charged with the function of constantly interrupting the totalizing thrusts of History 1,"[26] capturing the recalcitrance of people(s) and events contesting H1's singular logic. They're the histories that disrupt H1's internal unity, the irreducible elements of heterogeneity and uncertainty that, despite H1's drive to "subjugate or destroy the multiple possibilities that belong to History 2,"[27] always remain at its margins. Where H1 seeks to assimilate history's elements within a fixed logical-chronological framework – a fixed global history – H2s trace "ways of being human ... in manners that do not lend themselves to the reproduction of [that] logic."[28] H2s are, then, the subaltern modernities subverting the explanatory sweep of modernity's self-understanding. They carve out the space "for the politics of human belonging and diversity"[29] and for a pluralistic understanding of social development set against western historicism. "To provincialize Europe in historical thought," then, is "to hold in a state of permanent tension a dialogue between [these] two contradictory points of view."[30] An appropriately provincialized mode of historical reflection opens itself to the H2s that can't be reduced to H1's narrative. Only by recovering these divergent histories can we register the internal worth of social and cultural differences, rather than subsuming them under the story of western progress.

Mill's liberalism, critics argue, is decidedly closed to the plurality of H2s. As "a process of translation of diverse life-worlds and conceptual horizons about being human into the categories of Enlightenment thought,"[31] his developmentalism is taken to exemplify H1's totalizing proclivities. As a universalistic theorization of humanity's rationalization, it harbors all of historicism's worst tendencies – most importantly, its obdurate closure the value of human heterogeneity. As Mehta sees it, Mill's account of civilization and human development upholds a "stark binary of the backward and the progressive, with nothing in between," pointing to "the impoverishment of the hermeneutic space that Mill imagines in the encounter with the unfamiliar."[32] Mill's imperialism is epiphenomenal, parasitic on a broader historicism denigrating any culture below a given civilizational threshold. Lacking "a set of conditions whose normative and experiential credence can be justified without reference to a future or a necessary past and prescribed path of development," the uncivilized remain "confined in the waiting room of history while some other agency has the key to that room."[33] Uncivilized peoples are non-agents, objects of historical or colonial transformation, interchangeable and consequently valueless. The converse of this was, naturally, to portray civilized, European social forms as unequivocal goods. In total, then, Mill develops "a Manichean theory of two worlds, one is an area of light, the other that of darkness, one is perfect and without blemish, the other irredeemably evil, and each governed by radically different principles and norms."[34]

5.2 INHERITING THE SINS OF THE FATHER? JAMES AND JOHN STUART MILL

The critical charge leans heavily on James Mill's influence over his son's education and career, often tracing the younger Mill's ideas on civilization and development directly to his father's conceits. Given this influence, Thomas McCarthy suggests, it appears clear that J. S. Mill "imported this idea of progressive colonial domination."[35] There is a lot to support the contention. Mill's autobiography painstakingly details his father's command over his intellectual development – both directly, through his education and the work they undertook jointly (the younger Mill read the proof sheets for the *History of British India* at the age of 11 and contributed to James Mill's *Elements of Political Economy* and *Analysis of the Phenomena of the Human Mind*), and indirectly, through "the effect my father produced on my character."[36] More broadly, he notes, "it was my father's opinions which gave the distinguishing character to the Benthamic or utilitarian propagandism of that time ... One was through me, the only mind directly formed by his instructions."[37] J. S. Mill's intellectual life clearly bears his father's impress.

James Mill was also responsible for his employment as a colonial administrator, drafting him into the East India Company as a junior clerk the day after his 17th birthday, in 1823. This was J. S. Mill's only true profession. He climbed the ranks rapidly, becoming Fourth Assistant to the Examiner within five years and rising to First Assistant by 1836, the position he occupied until he was named Examiner in 1856. Over the course of his career, Mill drafted 1522 political dispatches "concerned with the Company's non-secret relations with independent and protected princely states throughout the Indian Sub-continent,"[38] and many more in the Company's other departments. He was, then, well positioned to implement his father's reformist political agenda in India. His earlier dispatches reflect James Mill's ideas relatively faithfully, often reproducing his parochial assessments of Indian custom and his commitment to "Europeanizing" Indian education. It's also worth noting that the East India Company was something of a domestic affair: beyond father and son, two of Mill's brothers worked for the Company, one hired on the strength of John Stuart's recommendation. Imperialism ran in the family.

There are, then, compelling reasons to treat J. S. Mill as adopting James Mill's civilizational hierarchy, his science of legislation, his faith in European culture's superiority, his belief in universal history and his interest in rationalizing the subcontinent, as the critics do. The trouble, however, is that J. S. Mill shared in none of these convictions. He explicitly rejected or moved past them, and directly renounced his father's view of government, his moral psychology and much more. To clear up the picture, we begin with James Mill's thoughts on reason, civilization, government and India.

5.2.1   India as Tabula Rasa: James Mill's Enlightenment Rationalism

James Mill was "in many ways a typical product of the Scottish Enlightenment. He held strong opinions regarding the possibilities of social progress and the power of education."[39] From the Scots, he inherited a thoroughgoing rationalism, an engrained skepticism toward unwarranted authority and a penchant for conjectural history. He believed deeply in reason's emancipatory power and regarded education's mandate as dispelling the myths, traditions and hierarchies keeping much of the world enthralled to paternalistic mandarins. His steadfast resistance to aristocratic privilege was also the touchstone for the Philosophical Radicals for whom he served as an intellectual beacon in the 1820s and 1830s.

Mill's scientistic rationalism molded his political thought completely. Civil institutions were, for him, a means to the end of securing the happiness of the greatest number and nothing more. From this vantage point, any alternative conception of government could only result from a diagnostic failure – "that the ends and means have not been analyzed"[40] with sufficient clarity. "[T]o lay a foundation for the science of Government" free from the vagaries of speculation and custom, he argued, "the whole science of human nature must be explored."[41] Neatly summarized, this latter proposes that "the lot of every human being is determined by his pains and pleasures; and that his happiness corresponds with the degree in which his pleasures are great, and his pains are small."[42] It is, therefore, "the inherent principle of human nature to seek the gratification of his will,"[43] the egoist core of his utilitarianism. Mill saw these scientifically grounded and universally applicable postulates as the basis for political institutions that could supplant the "irrational, inefficient, and often oppressive tangle of the existing order."[44]

This rationalism combined with Mill's historicism to shape his *History of British India* and his administration of the subcontinent. "For James Mill," Lynn Zastoupil observes, "improvement meant bringing to India the advanced ideas of the Enlightenment."[45] His dedication to pedagogical colonialism stemmed from his faith in education's liberating capacities, along with his assessment of India's low stage of development. Mill saw India as dominated by custom and despotic authority; elite-governed social institutions and widespread attachment to regressive religious and cultural practices had stunted Indian minds, which European learning alone could rehabilitate. His rationalism, historicism, utilitarianism and colonialism intersect in his declaration that

In looking at the pursuits of any nation, with a view to draw from them indications of the state of civilization, no mark is so important, as the nature of the End to which they are directed. Exactly in proportion as Utility is the object of every pursuit, may we regard a nation as civilized. Exactly in proportion as its ingenuity is wasted on contemptible or mischievous objects . . . the nation may safely be denominated barbarous . . . To ascertain the true state of the Hindus in the scale of civilization, is not only an object of curiosity in the history of human nature; but to the people of Great Britain, charged as they are with the government of that great portion of the human species, it is an object of the highest practical importance.[46]

Mill's moral psychology informed the educational policy undertaking this highest of practical tasks. As shown in Chapter 4, his Owenite associationism treated a person's mind and character as formed fully by external forces. This was "transformed in his *History* to the notion that India too was a blank slate waiting to be shaped according to utilitarian principles," a conviction that, for Zastoupil, "obviously informed Mill's later administrative work" as "British administrators schooled in the science of politics were to create a system where Indians . . . would have their minds shaped by a new environment in which rational, self-interested character traits would be encouraged to become dominant."[47] Mill's intellectual conceits, historicist presumptions, pedagogical ambitions and political vision combined to form the Eurocentric liberalism so neatly squared with imperial domination.

His ideas were not uncontroversial; Mill figured prominently in the Anglicist-Orientalist debate on colonial policy in India. As a leading proponent of the Anglicist camp, he understood the function of education as eradicating Indian beliefs and inculcating "the clear logic of advanced ideas"[48] through scientific, European pedagogy. Eric Stokes argues that by situating India in the scale of civilizations, Mill's *History* aimed "to dispel what he considered the silly sentimental admiration of Oriental despotism which had marked earlier thinkers of the Enlightenment . . . In India there was 'a hideous state of society,' much inferior in acquirements to Europe even in its darkest feudal age."[49] Without abandoning the project of enlightening India, the Orientalists sought to integrate modern, European ideas with Indian traditions. Orientalist colonial officials such as Thomas Munro, Mountstuart Elphinstone and H. H. Wilson held out "great hopes for using [traditional Arabic and Sanskrit Indian schools] to engraft Western ideas onto traditional Indian learning,"[50] which Mill vehemently opposed. Anglicists regarded the Orientalist valuation of Indian custom as encouraging the very forces inhibiting Indians' development, and so, as undermining the progressive ideals that ought to animate colonial policy. The Orientalists, conversely, saw Indian culture as fertile ground for seeding British notions of law. This was more than a strictly pragmatic concern for educating a recalcitrant populace. The Orientalists – driven in part by William Jones, a philologist, judge and administrator who spent much of his life studying Indian languages and practices – also shared in a Burkean concern for the preservation of cultures.[51] The debate would have important repercussions for the subcontinent's government, and Mill's views carried considerable weight. Given his heavy hand in shaping India's economic, judicial, administrative and educational policy – particularly between 1827 and 1835 under the sympathetic governor-generalship of Lord William Bentinck – his Anglicist convictions had lasting political and institutional effects.

The Anglicist-Orientalist controversy thus not only concerned colonial pedagogy, but also reflected deeper divides over political stability, the value of culture, and the spread of enlightenment. How, then, did J. S. Mill approach these issues? Did he uncritically reproduce his father's views, as the critics suggest?

5.2.2   From Bentham to Coleridge: J. S. Mill's Romantic Turn

J. S. Mill's early writings on politics undoubtedly parrot Bentham's and James Mill's interests, concerns and presumptions – at times, quite directly. Letters to the *Morning Chronicle* from 1823 criticize "the present confused and heterogeneous mass of statutes and cases"[52] and advance an array of Benthamite rationalizations of the legal system. Other letters and articles lay out the battle lines that would define the Philosophical Radicals' agenda by distinguishing "the Reformers and the Anti-Reformers of this country ... the former are friends to a popular government, and the latter to an aristocracy."[53] Mill compares lawyers to Reformation priests clinging to ecclesiastical arcana to safeguard their privileges, charging that "in proportion as the law is complicated, the influence of the only class who can interpret it must increase."[54] From prison reform to Malthusian population regulation, few of Mill's ideas from the early to mid-1820s stray from Bentham and James Mill. His dispatches at the East India Company from this period also faithfully reproduce his father's views and political program.[55]

The prolonged mental crisis into which Mill fell in 1826, however, profoundly impacted his intellectual development. As is well known, Mill's great depression stemmed in no small part from the rigidly utilitarian upbringing to which his father subjected him (which Isaiah Berlin captures well as an "appalling success").[56] His "mental anguish," as he documents in the *Autobiography*, resulted from his overly analytical formation and, particularly, from its total neglect of his affective development. His education's single-minded focus on the perfection of his rational faculties was a great detriment to his emotional and aesthetic growth, failing "to create these feelings in sufficient strength to resist the dissolving influence of analysis."[57] James Mill's ambition to craft his son into a faultless utilitarian led him, unsurprisingly, to pay little attention to his sentimental life, which ultimately caught up with and unraveled the younger Mill.[58] While his early years were fulfilled by his father's imperatives – "to be a reformer of the world ... [m]y conception of my own happiness was entirely identified with this object"[59] – he recalls that the time came when I awakened from this as from a dream ... it occurred to me to put the question directly to myself, "Suppose that all your objects in life were realized; that all the changes in institutions and opinions which you are looking forward to, could be completely effected at this very instant: would this be a great joy and happiness to you?" And an irrepressible self-consciousness distinctly answered, "No!" At this my heart sank within me: the whole foundation on which my life was constructed fell down.[60]

The desolation into which he lapsed was acute and long-lasting.

Mill eventually emerged from his crisis by immersing himself into the world of Romantic poetry, finding the counter to his stringently analytical education in the works of Wordsworth and Coleridge. From them, he cultivated a lifelong sensitivity to the affective dimensions of human experience, leading him to reconsider the foundations of his father's moral and political philosophy. Mill recounts a profound transformation, as of 1828–1829 – the very moment "when the Coleridgians ... made their appearance in the Society"[61] – in his understanding of human nature and of the grounds of politics:

I found the fabric of my old and taught opinions giving way in many fresh places ... The conflicts which I had so often had to sustain in defending the theory of government laid down in Bentham's and my father's writings, and the acquaintance I had obtained with other schools of political thinking, made me aware of many things which that doctrine, professing to be a theory of government in general, ought to have made room for, and did not ... I could not help feeling ... that my father's premises were really too narrow, and included but a small number of the general truths, on which, in politics, the important consequences depend ... This made me think that there was really something more fundamentally erroneous in my father's conception of philosophical method, as applicable to politics, than I had hitherto supposed there was.[62]

This philosophical "transition," as Mill describes it, ultimately led to a "new position in respect to my old political creed" attributed to "[t]he influences of European, that is to say, Continental, thought ... They came from various quarters: from the writings of Coleridge ... from the Coleridgians with whom I was in personal intercourse; from what I had read of Goethe."[63]

During this transformational period, Mill dabbled with a range of philosophies that expanded his intellectual horizons well beyond Bentham's and his father's utilitarian liberalism. He became acutely conscious of their dogmatic rationalism's deficits and absorbed the Romantic backlash against it. This was the beginning point of his enduring intellectual ecumenicalism: his interest in reconciling eighteenth-century rationalism and nineteenth-century Romanticism was sparked in the early 1830s and molded his philosophical ambitions from that point onward. The Romantic influence was far-reaching, shaping not only his substantive views, but also his philosophical approach. His "lifelong obsession with overcoming dualisms and harmonizing antagonistic modes of thought," Nicholas Capaldi suggests, was itself "an instantiation of the methodology of Romanticism."[64] The late 1820s and early 1830s thus "marks the transition from Mill the radical proselytizer of Benthamism to

Mill the Romantic synthesizer,"[65] his emergence from the doctrinal strictures under which he was formed.

Romanticism came to Mill via two streams of thought totally antithetical to his early utilitarianism: conservatism (through Thomas Carlyle, John Sterling, Samuel Taylor Coleridge and others) and utopian socialism (through the Saint-Simonians, particularly Gustave d'Eichthal and Auguste Comte). Both personally and philosophically, Mill's commitments shifted during this period. He distanced himself from the Philosophical Radicals he'd led and became acquainted with Sterling and Frederick Maurice – the Coleridgians who appeared before the Debating Society to present "totally different grounds from Benthamism and vehemently opposed to it."[66] "The modifications which were taking place in my old opinions," Mill recollects, "naturally gave me some points of contact with them; and both Maurice and Sterling were of considerable use to my development."[67] He resigned from the London Debating Society – the Radicals' intellectual hub – in 1829 and cultivated an intimate friendship with Sterling, with whom he shared a deep appreciation of Byron and Wordsworth, leading lights of English Romanticism. "Wordsworth seems always to know the pros and cons of every question," Mill opines in an 1831 letter to Sterling; "all my differences with him, or with any other philosophic Tory, would be differences of matter-of-fact or detail, while my differences with the radicals & utilitarians are differences of principle."[68] He also met and befriended Thomas Carlyle in 1831, following the publication of "The Spirit of the Age," which Carlyle regarded highly. While they would conflict in later years, in the early 1830s Carlyle fueled Mill's disenchantment with the Radicals, shaped his early skepticism toward democracy and bolstered his Romantic leanings.

Coleridge, however, most profoundly affected Mill's intellectual evolution at this juncture. "Few persons have exercised more influence over my thoughts and character than Coleridge has," he reflects in an 1834 letter to J. P. Nichol. "I consider him the most systematic thinker of our time, without excepting even Bentham . . . On the whole, there is more food for thought – and the best kind of thought – in Coleridge than in all other contemporary writers."[69] Through him, Mill came to perceive the shortcomings of the Radicals' individualist atomism: human beings, Coleridge showed, were implicitly cultural, embedded in historically formed contexts lending meaning to their lives and stability to their institutions. While essays from the late 1830s and early 1840s (such as "Bentham" and "Coleridge") most directly reflect Coleridge's influence, Mill's sensitivity to the cultural foundations of politics clearly remains in his mature philosophy, as is evident throughout *Considerations*. From the Romantics – and from Coleridge in particular – he developed the abiding conviction that "we could not understand ourselves apart from culture and history."[70]

Mill's brief dalliance with the Saint-Simonians further reinforced his responsiveness to the political import of social, cultural and historical variation. Mill met Gustave d'Eichthal in 1828, who tried to recruit him to the Saint-Simonian cause. While he never entirely embraced it, Saint-Simonism nonetheless introduced a historicist sensibility into his political thought. The Saint-Simonians attuned him to the metamorphoses that all societies experienced over time, and to the need to adapt political institutions to them – a marked departure from James Mill's ahistorical "sciences" of government and human nature. Their historicism also imparted a certain fallibilism to J. S. Mill's political thinking by showing the contingency and transience of any era's social, moral and intellectual climate. Political systems suited to a given people at a given point would invariably fall into obsolescence, a fate which none could hope to avoid, no matter their effectiveness. This historical consciousness surfaces early in Mill's political writings – notably in "The Spirit of the Age" (1831), which most directly borrows from the Saint-Simonian lexicon (adapting, for instance, their conceptualizations of "organic" and "critical" historical periods). While he turned away from Saint-Simonism, Mill's philosophy of history only became more engrained in his political thinking. It pervades his essays from the 1830s and 1840s (most obviously, but not only, in his treatments of French historians – 1844's "Michelet's History of France" and 1845's "Guizot's Essays and Lectures on History"); it shapes his theorization of the social sciences (*System of Logic*, 1843) and political economy (*Principles of Political Economy*, 1848); it animates *On Liberty*'s fallibilism (1859); and it structures *Considerations*' account of government (1861).

These Romantic influences – Continental and British – led to significant divergences from Bentham and James Mill, and to fundamental revisions in his own political theory. "From the romantics," Zastoupil notes, "Mill learned to appreciate the mind as an organic whole in which emotions played an important part alongside the rational faculties."[71] Equipped with this fuller view, he came to recognize the poverty of moral and political philosophies that disregarded the vital role of *sentiment* in human action. The Romantic poets profoundly influenced his understanding of human nature, and more narrowly, of the affective ties underpinning political stability. Both figure prominently in his critique of "the thinkers of the eighteenth century,"[72] most clearly spelled out in the 1838 essay on Bentham.[73] "Knowing so little of human feelings," Mill charges, Bentham "knew still less of the influences by which those feelings are formed ... [No one] set out with a more limited conception either of the agencies by which human conduct *is*, or of those by which it *should* be, influenced."[74] The deficits in Bentham's moral and political theories are related: his overly rationalistic moral psychology yields a political philosophy unconcerned with – or still worse, unconscious of – the sentimental grounds of social cohesion. "Morality," Mill tells us, "consists of two parts. One of these is self-education; the training, by the human being himself, of his affections and will. That department is a blank in Bentham's system."[75] By neglecting these "affections and will," Bentham remains blind to political life's cultural valences:

Taking, as we have seen, next to no account of national character and the causes which form and maintain it, he was precluded from considering, except to a very limited extent, the laws of a country as an instrument of national culture: one of their most important aspects, and in which they must of course vary according to the degree and kind of culture already attained ... Very different institutions are needed to train to the perfection of their nature, or to constitute into a united nation and social polity, an essentially *subjective* people like the Germans, and an essentially *objective* people like those of Northern and Central Italy.[76]

From the mid-1830s on, Mill consistently treats national character as a central determinant of any given society's political institutions. Differences of national character – what we would call cultural differences – were not immaturities destined to fade through historical rationalization, but constitutive features of social and political existence. Cultural bonds comprised the civic ballasts and glues binding citizens to one another and to their institutions, the affective foundations of political life.

Mill grew equally critical of his father's moral psychology and political theory, tracing, as with Bentham, the shortcomings in his conception of government to the "science" of human nature on which it rested. In a scathing indictment of his *Essay on Government*, Thomas Macaulay accused James Mill of treating only "one-half of human nature, and to reason on the motives which impel men to oppress and despoil others, as if they were the only motives by which men could possibly be influenced."[77] The contention resonated with J. S. Mill, pushing him to question the central tenets of his father's political thought. The problem with its hedonistic grounding, he came to recognize, was that it left no space for incentives to action other than self-interest. James Mill's "geometrical" approach to government, along with the "interest-philosophy of the Bentham school" to which it belonged, treated social phenomena as "result[ing] always from only one force, one single property of human nature"[78] – egoistic selfishness. It had no capacity to account for altruistic or virtue-based motivations. J. S. Mill's qualitative utilitarianism redressed this exact deficit by advancing a moral psychology receptive to the impetus of moral ideals.

Still more personally, James Mill's associationism left only the narrowest space for individual self-determination, given the constraints of a pre-fabricated character set from the outside. With his rigidly utilitarian upbringing, J. S. Mill felt those constraints particularly acutely. The fatalism in this kind of self-understanding – that one was made by another, and limited accordingly – spurred his depression. The "doctrine of what is called Philosophical Necessity," Mill recalls,

weighed like an incubus on my existence. I felt as if I was the helpless slave of antecedent circumstances; as if the character of all persons had been formed for them by agencies beyond their control, and was wholly out of their power. I often said to myself what a relief it would be if I could disbelieve the doctrine of the formation of character by circumstances.[79]

Ultimately, this is exactly what did: he "pondered painfully on the subject, till gradually [seeing] light through it."[80] That light was a moral psychology that counted the individual's capacity for self-development as among the influences shaping one's character. The Owenite fatalist who believes that "his character is formed *for* him, and not *by* him," Mill realized, commits "a grand error". While "[h]is character is formed by his circumstances ... his own desire to mould it in a particular way, is one of those circumstances, and by no means one of the least influential."[81] From a personal standpoint, Mill's departure from his father's associationism preserved his faith in the doctrine of free will; from a political one, it led him to reconceive both the grounds and tasks of government.

There are, then, few presumptions in Bentham's and James Mill's moral and political philosophies that the younger Mill left unchallenged, if not overturned. While James Mill saw the spread of reason as advancing social and political uniformity, J. S. Mill treated variations in collective life as intractable, criticizing the view that Europe's development charted a common trajectory through which all societies would pass. He excoriated Enlightenment philosophers for "mistaking the state of things with which they had always been familiar, for the universal and natural condition of mankind,"[82] along with his utilitarian contemporaries, who "mistake their own idiosyncrasies for laws of our common being, and the accidents of their position, for a part of the destiny of our race."[83] Both labored under the false and uncritical conceit that European norms, practices and political organization were ahistorical, papering over their particularistic and contingent genesis. By contrast, Mill drew on the "Germano-Coleridgian" doctrine to argue that "[e]very form of polity, every condition of society, whatever else it had done, had formed its type of national character. What the type was, and how it had been made what it was, were questions which the metaphysician might overlook."[84] Rejecting their abstraction and parochialism, Mill theorized a politics that incorporated "the various elements of human culture and the causes influencing the formation of national character."[85] Romanticism forged a central insight of Mill's mature political thought: cultures comprise irreplaceable founts of sedimented custom and tradition that go to the core of human societies, indelibly affecting their character and institutions. It turned him away from his father's faith in humanity's historical rationalization and sparked a much more nuanced understanding of social development as variable and culturally differentiated.[86]

This departure is equally manifest in Mill's colonial work, as his critique of Benthamite utilitarianism directly contradicted James Mill's Anglicist pretentions concerning India. The contrasts that would emerge between them are stark. As Lynn Zastoupil notes, for the elder Mill, "a scientific approach to the history of that distant land would dispel many myths and prejudices, at the same time confirming the known facts of individual behavior and social development";[87] J. S. Mill, conversely, saw differences of national character pushing advancement in idiosyncratic ways, rather than in conformity with any predictive law. Against his father's faith that a properly calibrated education could raise any people's moral and intellectual standing, J. S. Mill argued that "very different institutions" would train distinctive societies "to the perfection of their nature." While the younger Mill sought to build political institutions around a people's traditions, customs and mores, James Mill thought it misguided to "rule [India] according to indigenous principles or practices, since these were obviously imperfect."[88] Where James Mill regarded Indian social life as devoid of progressive, rational content, J. S. Mill treated culturally particular affective ties as a valuable source of social cohesion.[89] Fred Wilson notes J. S. Mill's increasing willingness, during and following his depression, "to work within the limits set by existing institutions and customs ... and even to respect those institutions," recognizing that "[p]eople with those habits were not so readily to be transformed as a more mechanical view of human nature would imply."[90] In the Indian context, he came to share in the Orientalists' "sympathetic and positive use of Indigenous Indian social structures, groups and customs ... [and] to move away from his father's more narrow and more mechanical Benthamism."[91]

It is unsurprising, then, that while Mill's early writings on India echo his father's opinions, his later dispatches – particularly, those he wrote toward the end of James Mill's life – diverge from the Anglicist position. In 1836, with James Mill's failing health keeping him at a distance from East India House, J. S. Mill drafted an education dispatch that reflected and supported the Orientalist view.[92] He borrowed extensively from H. H. Wilson, arguing that "the lettered classes are still held by the people of India in high estimation, and their degradation and extinction cannot be received with indifference by their countrymen."[93] Mill encouraged the colonial administration to endow and support an educated Indian elite "whose primary responsibility would be the cultivation of learning," in order to revitalize traditional Indian learning centers, "as Wilson and Coleridge had recommended [that this] was the solution to the problem of Indian education."[94] Decades later, Mill would reflect on the impact that his consciousness of India's cultural bases exerted over his colonial policies. "Wherever there are really native states, with a nationality, & historical traditions & feelings, which is emphatically the case (for example) with the Rajpoot states," he writes, "there I would on no account take advantage of any failure of heirs to put an end to them."[95] The careful attention that he devoted to English, Irish, Indian, American and French societies bears out his Romantic bent and his sensitivity to the affective facets of politics – all in direct contrast to his father. In an 1836 letter to Edward Lytton Bulwer, Mill acknowledges that while James Mill's passing "has deprived the world of the man of great philosophical genius ... that same event has made it far easier to do that, in the hope of which alone I allowed myself to become connected with the [Westminster] review – namely, to soften the harder & sterner features of its radicalism and utilitarianism."[96]

James Mill's imprint on his son is indisputable. And yet, "[d]espite the solemn bald head, the black clothes, the grave expression, the measured phrases, the total lack of humor," Isaiah Berlin contends, "Mill's life is an unceasing revolt against his father's outlook and ideals, the greater for being subterranean and unacknowledged."[97] While Berlin puts it rather strongly, he's entirely right. Mill either disavowed, renovated or advanced well beyond his father's emaciated moral psychology, his strident, Enlightenment-derived rationalism, his ahistorical and culturally myopic view of government, his colonial policies in India, and – we will see – his account of human development. On character, history, progress, politics and culture, then, J. S. Mill grew far from his father. He neither adopted nor refined James Mill's theoretical assumptions and conceptual framework; they were, rather, a jumping-off point. The synthesis of his early radicalism and later Romanticism yielded a much more nuanced and pluralistic vision of human ends, social organization, civilization and progress.

5.3 COMPLICATING CIVILIZATION

Mill's division between civilized and uncivilized peoples is, of course, deeply problematic, and many of his writings advance some version of the categorical distinction raised by critics. But Mill's considered thoughts on civilization are neither exhausted nor even clearly represented by it, as a concept that he employs in different ways than are captured by the critical view.

5.3.1 Two Views of Civilization

Mill's clearest treatment of civilization appears, not surprisingly, in his 1836 essay "Civilization." Its opening sentence distinguishes two senses of the term: it "sometimes stands for human improvement in general, and sometimes for certain kinds of improvement in particular."[98] The former describes "a country [as] more civilized if we think it more improved; more eminent in the best characteristics of Man and Society; farther advanced in the road to perfection; happier, nobler, wiser," while the latter refers to "that kind of improvement only, which distinguishes a wealthy and powerful nation from savages or barbarians."[99] Mill thus differentiates two distinct (if related) usages of the concept precisely to distinguish civilization's broadly beneficial tendencies from its narrower manifestations – the historically contingent and culturally particular *form* of civilization embodied in European states. Far from conflating all types of civilization with its European instantiation, the essay aims rather to evaluate whether or not the latter "is on the whole a good or an evil."[100]

Mill demarcates civilized and barbarian peoples through a series of grossly infelicitous comparisons: civilization "in the restricted sense ... is the direct converse or contrary of rudeness or barbarism."[101] This characterization has drawn widespread condemnation, and for very good reason. The uncivilized are described as "wandering or thinly scattered over a vast tract of country," having "no commerce, no manufactures, no agriculture," "little or no law, or administration of justice," and as incapable of "systematic employment of the collective strength of society."[102] They are unable to engage in social cooperation – in Mill's view, the sine qua non of civilization – as the "savage cannot bear to sacrifice, for any purpose, the satisfaction of his individual will. His social cannot even temporarily prevail over his selfish feelings, nor his impulses bend to his calculations."[103] Given that "[t]heir minds are not capable of so great an effort, nor their will sufficiently under the influence of distant motives,"[104] the uncivilized are equally unfit to form bonds based on reciprocity. This short-sightedness also undermines stable inter-state associations, so the "rules of international morality"[105] upholding the principle of non-interference between civilized nations do not apply between civilized and uncivilized peoples.

Mill thus attributes the successes of civilized societies to their superior capacity for reasoned calculation, discipline, cooperation and self-sacrifice. The uncivilized, conversely, lack the foresight to recognize more remote public goods. This contrastive portrayal of civilization and barbarism is, obviously, deeply and irredeemably prejudiced. But Mill's views are in important ways tempered, and more complex than this alone suggests.

5.3.2 Biological Determinism v. Contingent History

Mill's account of civilization explicitly rejects biological determinism, ascribing the shortcomings of the uncivilized to their (contingent) social and political circumstances. He strenuously opposed the phrenology and biological essentialism espoused by many of his contemporaries, most famously in his declamation against Carlyle's "Occasional Discourse on the Negro Question."[106] Carlyle's ignorance of "laws of the formation of character," Mill charges, leads him to "the vulgar error of imputing every difference which he finds among human beings to an original difference of nature."[107] In the *Logic*, he further chastises biological determinists for failing to connect "those mental differences to the outward causes by which they are for the most part produced, and on the removal of which they would cease to exist."[108] Against this, he treated all civilizational advancement as resulting from an "extraordinary combination of advantages,"[109] and as in no way limited to white races. "The original Egyptians are inferred, from the evidence of their sculptures, to have been a negro race," he maintains; "it was from negroes, therefore, that the Greeks learnt their first lessons in civilization."[110] He also saw Jewish societies (which he characterized as "Asiatic") as implicitly progressive due to the productive antagonism between their religious and political authorities, and vigorously petitioned in favor of the Union in the American Civil War on the strength of his conviction in abolitionism's moral rectitude.[111] In each case, civilization and social development are shaped by circumstance rather than racial character.

Mill's wholesale rejection of natural determinism also emerges in his criticisms of women's social subordination, where he repudiated prevalent presumptions concerning their character. "What is now called the nature of women is an eminently artificial thing," he recognizes, "the result of forced repression in some directions, unnatural stimulation in others."[112] Education and environment were the determinants of any person's or people's mental composition, and women's apparent deficits reflected centuries of systemic disadvantage, not inborn traits. While physiological conditions might affect particular individuals' intellectual capacities, they had no bearing on groups – racial, ethnic, gendered or other – and Mill castigated dogmatists treating cognitive abilities as "ultimate facts, incapable of being explained or altered,"[113] rather than as provisional and remediable through education. He also registered the parallels between gender- and race-based discriminations, arguing that "[w]hat, in unenlightened societies, colour, race, religion ... are to some men, sex is to all women; a peremptory exclusion from almost all honourable occupations."[114]

Mill understands Europe's advanced state of civilization, then, as resulting not from any intellectual or moral superiority, but from entirely fortuitous sociological and institutional conditions. Europeans' improvement isn't due to "any superior excellence in them, which, when it exists, exists as the effect not as the cause; but [to] their remarkable diversity of character and culture ... Europe is, in my judgment, wholly indebted to this plurality of paths for its progressive and many-sided development."[115] As Mill sees it, European civilization was, historically, preserved by the balance of power between its constituent nations, none of which was sufficiently powerful to assimilate the others. The conjunction of their diversity and proximity forced Europeans to cede their immediate self-interest and seek the long-term benefits of social combination. Their capacity for cooperation thus reflects no inherent intellectual advantage, as critics suggest is Mill's view, but rather results from "a contest of rival powers for dominion of society" that under different conditions might "have stagnated, like the great stationary despotisms of the East."[116] This systemic antagonism, along with the moral influence of the Catholic clergy – which despite its many faults, Mill argues, stabilized European Christendom through the medieval era – drove Europe forward.

5.3.3   Ambivalent Civilization

Does Mill treat civilization as an unqualified good – an area of light, perfect and without blemish, as Parekh suggests? Civilization "in the narrow sense"[117] – referring to the general advancement of social progress, oddly enough – is, for Mill, unambiguously beneficial. This is characterized by a few broad trends: power shifting from individuals to masses, greater control over the natural world, rising educational levels, growing equality and increasing security of persons and property. In this qualified sense, civilization describes social improvements in humanity's lot overall. And yet, Mill is keenly aware of these tendencies' problematic features in their modern manifestations, his enthusiasm tempered by a caution regarding their pathological potential. While unreservedly endorsing civilization's general progression, he remains deeply critical of its particular embodiments in European and American societies. Far from acclaiming "the vices or the miseries of civilization,"[118] Mill asserts that while "civilization is a good … we think there is other good, much even of the highest good, which civilization in this sense does not provide for, and some of which it has a tendency (though that tendency may be counteracted) to impede."[119]

Mill's appreciation for western civilization is more ambivalent than unqualified, registering its deep-seated and enduring defects. For all of the goods bestowed by industrial, economic and institutional advances, the progress of Europeans civilization also entails

the relaxation of individual energy and courage; the loss of proud and self-relying independence; the slavery of so large a portion of mankind to artificial wants; their effeminate shrinking from even the shadow of pain; the dull unexciting monotony of their lives, and the passionless insipidity, and absence of any marked individuality, in their characters … the demoralizing effects of the great inequalities in wealth and rank; and the sufferings of the great mass of the people of civilized countries, whose wants are scarcely better provided for than those of the savage, while they are bound by a thousand fetters in lieu of the freedom and excitement which are his compensations.[120]

Far from treating civilization as an unalloyed good, Mill sees European civilizations as beset by systemic psychological, social, economic and political failures. Despite their advances, modern mass democracies corrode individuality, liberty and originality, the drivers of progress. Mill's circumspection is neither cursory nor isolated, as he consistently admonishes modern Britons for their "moral effeminacy" and civilized peoples generally for their intellectual poverty. And neither are these shortcomings incidental: the social tyranny he decries in *On Liberty* is endemic in democracy and requires concerted institutional rectification.

These problems, still further, aren't just political, but reach into every facet of modern, civilized life. The "unbalanced influence of the commercial spirit"[121] suffusing market-based societies is, Mill judges, "the most serious danger to the future prospects of mankind."[122] In Britain, he observed a widening gap between the higher classes' material advantages and moral virtues, leading to a socially pernicious condition in which wealthy elites exercised power without knowledge of, or regard for, the public interest.[123] Civilization also leads to intellectual degradation, as individuals have their minds "bowed to the yoke ... they like in crowds; they exercise choice only among things commonly done ... their human capacities are withered and starved."[124] Their social world is overrun by a crushing pressure to conformity, along with an unbridled industrialism supplanting all other values. Citizens' working lives only deepen their social alienation, as the "increasing specialization of all employments" leaves their minds and concerns "fatally narrowed," and their "feelings towards the great ends of humanity ... miserably stunted."[125] Civilized societies ultimately drift too far from the self-dependence of the barbarian condition, losing themselves in civilization's artifice, comforts and conveniences.

Civilization is, then, for Mill no panacea, but rather requires constant vigilance and restraint; it is Janus-faced, its benefits tethered to modern society's ills. This ambivalence emerges most clearly in his examination of American public life.

5.3.4 Pathologies of Civilization: Democracy in America

Following Tocqueville, Mill sees American democracy as embodying the modern world's rising spirit of equality, and like Tocqueville, he sees it as indefinite, mutable and requiring direction. "Like other great powers of nature," the democratic "tendency, though it cannot be counteracted, may be guided to the good."[126] For Mill, America's "collective despotism"[127] exemplifies its social and political risks, its radically democratic character enabling the domination of a single, unchallenged power – the public opinion of an overwhelmingly influential middle class. Over several essays, he details the mutually reinforcing relation of American culture and political systems, both shaped by its constitutionally enshrined egalitarianism. "American institutions," he reflects, "have imprinted strongly on the American mind that any one man (with a white skin) is as good as any other ... a false creed ... connected with some of the more unfavourable points in American character."[128] Founded on a rejection of elites, American democracy's unflinching egalitarianism elevates mass opinion to a position of unquestionable authority. As a result, "in no other country does there exist less independence of thought," as "when the opinion of the majority is made up, hardly any one, it is affirmed, dares to be of any other opinion."[129]

This levelling inclination generates both political-institutional and social-moral problems. From the political standpoint, America's "deference [to] numbers"[130] produces not only the conformism that Mill denounces in *On Liberty*, but a system of government that encourages pandering. Democracies work best when citizens treat their elected officials as representatives, empowered to exercise their political judgment free from their constituents' coercion, rather than as delegates, who simply voice the majority's will. Political representatives should, as Nadia Urbinati puts it, "*interpret* the public interest from the point of view of those in disadvantaged positions"[131] rather than act as "mouthpieces for the voters."[132] In the British context, this required recognizing and sympathizing with class-specific interests – hence, Mill's dogged advocacy for class-based representation, particularly for the lower classes, in democratic processes. "Every class knows some things not so well known to other people," he intoned in an 1866 speech before Parliament, "and every class has interests more or less special to itself, and for which no protection is so effectual as its own."[133]

The function of representatives isn't to articulate a class's *desires*, however, but its *interests* – that is, to interpret and realize the public good from a class-based vantage point without succumbing to privatistic class-based preferences. Herein lies the central distinction between representatives and delegates: the former serve the common interest from a class-conscious perspective, while the latter reproduce a given class's partialities (or the voting public's partialities more generally). Where a representative is "the person best qualified, morally and intellectually, to form a sound judgment of his own on political questions,"[134] delegates misuse representative institutions by encouraging politicians to "canvass" the electorate – precisely the problem in America. The radical egalitarianism of American democracy emboldens political actors to seek favor in the widest possible constituency, reproducing the electorate's whims rather than challenging them with original ideas. As Mill puts it, "the Demos, being in America the one source of power, all the selfish ambition of the country gravitates towards it."[135] This is among the gravest dangers facing democracies generally, and America in particular. "If democracy should disappoint any of the expectations of its more enlightened partisans," he opines, "it will be from the substitution of delegation for representation ... All the chances unfavourable to democracy lie here."[136] As with China or any other "stagnant" society, unchecked power – even that of a democratic majority – inevitably loses the dissent sustaining social progress.

This points to the social/moral problem: the American tendency to elect panderers stems from their inclination to value private interests over public goods. As a "republic peopled with a provincial middle class," the American spirit of industry elevates those virtues "which conduce to getting rich," entrenches "a general indifference to those kinds of knowledge and mental culture which cannot immediately be converted into pounds, shillings, and pence," and pushes citizens to "plunge into money-getting, at the earliest possible age."[137] Mill's abiding concerns with unbounded commercialism are most vividly illustrated in American public life. Lacking the social institutions to generate public-mindedness, American democracy devolves into a culturally emaciated and market-driven assemblage bound by little more than a shared zeal for private enterprise. The American's private money-getting occupation ... brings but few of his faculties into action, while its exclusive pursuit tends to fasten his attention and interest exclusively upon himself, and upon his family as an appendage of himself; making him indifferent to the public, to the more generous objects and the nobler interests, and, in his inordinate regard for his personal comforts, selfish and cowardly ... Whatever might be the case in some other constitutions of society, the spirit of a commercial people will be, we are persuaded, essentially mean and slavish, wherever public spirit is not cultivated by an extensive participation of the people in the business of government in detail.[138]

Bereft of the stabilizing counter-balances steering it toward social ends, American democracy typifies the pathologies to which entirely civilized states are prone.

While Mill's concerns are particularly sharply drawn in his assessments of American society, they were hardly unique to it. From his earlier, more skeptical treatments of democracy to his mature writings on representative government, he worries consistently about the damages of unmoored free marketeering. As early as 1829, Mill attributes "the very worst point in our national character, the disposition to sacrifice every thing to accumulation, & that exclusive and engrossing selfishness which accompanies it" to "the commercial spirit [which] is almost sure to bring with it, wherever it prevails, a certain amount of evil."[139] Despite his considerable intellectual shifts in the ensuing 30-odd years, Mill's apprehensions regarding commercialism's narrowing effects on public life remained constant. What changed was his response. In the early 1830s, during his conservative rebellion against Benthamite Radicalism, Mill found the counter to industrial society's civic anomie in the stewardship of an intellectual aristocracy. Both of his philosophical beacons from the period pushed him toward it: the Saint-Simonians envisioned social progress as steered by a scientific-technocratic elite, and Coleridge advocated the guidance of a morally enlightened clerisy. "I highly approve and commend one of the leading principles of [the Saint-Simonians'] system," Mill extols in an 1829 letter to d'Eichthal, "the necessity of a *Pouvoir Spirituel* ... in which the body of the people, i.e. the uninstructed, shall entertain the same feelings of deference & submission to the authority of the instructed, in morals and politics."[140] This was a short-lived solution, as Mill rapidly came to reject vanguardist elitism as "nothing less than a spiritual despotism."[141] From the 1840s onward, he responded to civilization's susceptibility to privatism through institutional means – the "schools of public spirit" examined in Chapter 4 and political reforms elaborated in *Considerations*.

These are precisely the ballasts lacking in American public life, yielding a democracy that amounts to Rousseau's will of all, rather than the general will – a collection of private wills, rather than a joint trust. Democracy, like civilization, undoubtedly brings about certain goods – but they're conditional goods that don't clearly fall on either side of a Manichean divide. They're sociological goods, linked to particular sociological circumstances.

5.3.5   Civilization: The Sociological View

Mill's reservations about American democracy point to his conceptualization of civilization as a multifaceted sociological condition, rather than as marking out any particular type of people. Far from treating civilization and barbarism as static or unified entities, he sees them as complex, variable and interpenetrating states of society.[142] Elements of civilization lie in barbarous peoples, just as civilized peoples retain barbarous propensities. The inclination to exercise power over others characteristic of under-developed cultures, for instance, "in many of the conditions even of civilized humanity, is far more largely exemplified."[143] Antisocial tendencies extend well into the civilized state, which without the right social, political and educational supports devolves into "a wretched competition for the selfish prizes and the petty vanities of office," developing "not the desire of freedom, but an unmeasured appetite for place and power."[144] Uncivilized traits aren't just transcended as societies achieve some measure of advancement, but rather insinuate themselves into civilization's social and political fabric, for better and for worse. For better, the modern, individual "spirit of liberty" stems from the "barbaric element" drawing Europeans away from their traditional subjection to the state – "the self-will of the savage, moderated and limited by the demands of civilized life,"[145] as Mill understands it. For worse, unchecked, European civilizations were likely to produce "a darker despotism, one more opposed to improvement"[146] than China's, Mill's perennial example of unbalanced power. Even the development of our intellectual faculties evinces the entanglements of civilization and barbarism: for all of the era's scientific advances, "men still pray for rain, or for success in war, or to avert a shipwreck or a pestilence . . . vestiges of the primitive mode of thought [that] linger in the more intricate departments of sciences which have attained a high degree of positive development."[147] Civilization and barbarism are, then, less categorically distinctive social states than unfixed and permeable ones.

From this sociological vantage point, Mill sees all societies – civilized and uncivilized alike – as developing in their own distinctive ways, on the basis of their surrounding circumstances. Social advancement follows no fixed trajectory, as a broad range of sociological phenomena – "the division of employments," military operations, "the operations of commerce and manufactures," national character – all comprise "operations [by which] mankind learn the value of combination."[148] Europe's history, still further, is as pocked and stilted as any other: Mill notes the "decline of [Spain and Portugal] in national greatness, and even in material civilization, while almost all of the other nations of Europe were uninterruptedly advancing," the result of "the Holy Inquisition, and the system of mental slavery of which it is the symbol."[149] Societies don't progress uniformly through fixed stages of development, but rather pitch and lurch forward (or in the case of Spain and Portugal, backward) according to their particular historical contingencies.

Mill's Europe is a history of mongrelization and happenstance rather than uninterrupted rationalization, as the fortuitous mixture of "Roman, Christian and Barbarian ingredients"[150] generated the conditions for its improvement. While he regards Guizot's analysis of European history as among the most accomplished theorizations of historical laws, he explicitly opposes its over-generalization. "If there be such laws," he argues, and

if the series of states through which human nature and society are destined to pass, have been determined more or less precisely by the original constitution of mankind, and by the circumstances of the planet on which we live; the order of their succession cannot be discovered by modern or by European experience alone: it must be ascertained by a conjunct analysis, so far as possible, of the whole of history, and the whole of human nature.[151]

Non-Europeans are not nascent Europeans, and Europe's evolution is no template for the rest of the world; Mill steadfastly resists extrapolating universalistic historical laws from the continent's particular genesis. This doesn't, however, suggest that he saw history as devoid of principles altogether.

5.4 MILL'S SOCIOLOGY OF HUMAN DEVELOPMENT

5.4.1 Ethology and Empirical Laws of Progress

Mill's philosophy of history conditions his understanding of human diversity and difference – it's the conceptual apparatus integrating pluralism into his moral and political philosophy. And like his account of civilization, it's subject to some misunderstanding. Without a clear view of Mill's developmentalism, and of the sociological, political and ethological sciences that it shaped, we're likely to misconstrue diversity's place in his liberalism.

Mill, early on (as of the late 1820s), came to see history as central to any coherent account of social and political life. "[H]istorical studies" and "the philosophy of the matter," he maintains, are "the foundation of sociological speculation . . . From this time any political thinker who fancies himself able to dispense with a connected view of the great facts of history, as a chain of causes and effects, must be regarded as below the level of the age."[152] While Mill's historical consciousness was sparked by the Saint-Simonians, he quickly recognized their deficits. The laws of social succession that he theorized sought to redress their overly mechanistic accounts, on one hand, and the British-rationalist tendency to ahistoricism on the other. During the 1840s, over successive editions of the *Logic* (and in other writings), Mill formulated his notion of historical causality. He also sharpened his critique of Britain's "unscientific" historians, who "studied for the facts, not for the explanation of facts,"[153] declaiming against "[t]he vulgar mistake of supposing that the course of history has no tendencies of its own."[154]

Much more fruitful were the philosophical histories developed by French historians such as Guizot, Michelet and, most importantly, Comte. But despite his admiration for Comte's philosophy of history, which he regarded as the most sophisticated of its kind, Mill criticized his confounding laws of *determination* and *causation*, conflating "two kinds of uniformities of succession, the one unconditional, the other conditional."[155] This confusion lay at the root of Comte's positivist science, which conceived of societies as cohesive bodies moving inexorably from theological, to metaphysical, to positive stages of development. In so doing, it portrayed social advancement as the unfolding of a singular, progressive impulse, neglecting the great variability of distinctive sociological phenomena for which "Mr. Comte's system makes no room."[156] Mill's sociological developmentalism thus charts a course between Benthamites, who "theorize on politics without any historical basis at all,"[157] and Saint-Simonians, who treat laws of social succession as inexorable, rather than as empirically conditioned.[158]

Properly understood, Mill asserts in the *System of Logic*, "[t]he fundamental problem ... of the social science, is to find the laws according to which any state of society produces the state which succeeds it and takes its place."[159] The *Logic*'s sixth book is a broad-ranging examination of the causal laws governing human behavior at the individual level (through psychology) and collectively (through sociology). These comprise Mill's thoughts on ethology, the study of character-formation that he regarded as the human sciences' lynchpin but failed to develop into any coherent system. Despite that failure, ethology remains central to his social and political philosophy.[160]

Mill understands human action as subject to causal laws without being determined by them, differentiating between "empirical" and "universal" laws. While universal laws are fixed, unchanging and scientifically derived, an empirical law

is an uniformity, whether of succession or of coexistence, which holds true in all instances within our limits of observation, but is not of a nature to afford any assurance that it would hold beyond those limits ... In other words, an empirical law is a generalization ... its truth is not absolute, but dependent on some more general conditions ... it can only be relied on in so far as there is ground of assurance that those conditions are realized.[161]

Sociological laws are empirical laws, derived from broad tendencies observed over time and under particular conditions. Ethological laws, governing both individual and collective character-formation, are also empirical: they concern generalizations operative in our conduct, rather than fixed principles enabling us to predict actions. While our behavior conforms to these empirical laws of succession, the innumerable conditions impacting it prevents us from determining what human beings will actually do at any given point. Human activity and the societies produced by it do, then, follow universal causal laws. But these are few, general, and most importantly, subject to the influence of circumstances – they're what Frederic Wilson describes as "gappy" laws.[162] Ethology is, and can only ever be, an empirical science accounting for tendencies swayed by our particular conditions.

Mill draws a clear connection between the application of empirical laws at individual and collective levels. If "[a]ll phenomena of society are phenomena of human nature," he contends, and "if, therefore, the phenomena of human thought, feeling, and action, are subject to fixed laws, the phenomena of society cannot but conform to fixed laws."[163] However, given their gappiness, "[t]here is, indeed, no hope that these laws, though our knowledge of them were as certain and as complete as it is in astronomy, would enable us to predict the history of society."[164] The complexity of circumstances affecting both individuals and societies prevents us from foreseeing any course of historical development. Mill approaches history and its principles of succession from a sociological rather than a philosophical perspective, and as a social scientist, he is keenly attuned to the range of factors shaping any given state of society. This sociological bent is at the root of his critique of the Saint-Simonians' universalistic and deterministic historicism. While acknowledging the usefulness of "the French school" of "philosophizing in the social science," he saw it as

chargeable with a fundamental misconception ... The misconception consists in supposing that the order of succession which we may be able to trace among the different states of society and civilization which history presents to us, even if that order were more rigidly uniform than it has yet been proved to be, could ever amount to a law of nature. It can only be an empirical law. The succession of states of the human mind and of human society cannot have an independent law of its own; it must depend on the psychological and ethological laws which govern the action of circumstances on men and of men on circumstances.[165]

While Mill's skepticism toward fixed accounts of historical progress is most fully elaborated in the 1840s, it shaped his political vision from the late 1820s onward, as he came to see the invariable plurality of societies, of their developmental paths, and of the institutions suited to them. Social advancement was neither predetermined, nor monocultural, nor reducible to European modernization. This was, in fact, his central disagreement with the French historians. "I should differ from the St Simonists chiefly in this respect," Mill writes to d'Eichthal in 1829:

they seem to think that the mind of man, by a sort of fatality or necessity, grows & unfolds its different faculties always in one particular order, like the body ... whereas I am satisfied, that better consideration would shew, that different nations, indeed different minds, may & do advance to improvement by different roads; that nations, & men, nearly in an equally advanced stage of civilization, may yet be very different in character.[166]

Far from assimilating all human difference into a convergent history, Mill rather believes that "[e]very age contains countries, every country contains men, who are in every possible state of civilization."[167] This "enlarged view of the history of mankind" recognizes that institutions unsuitable for a given people or era may "have not only been highly useful but absolutely indispensable"[168] for another. Herein lies Comte's central error. For all of the merits of his philosophical history, "in appreciating the influence which circumstances exercise . . . in producing diversities of character, collective or individual, he is sadly at fault."[169]

Mill thus clearly rejects the view that historical development follows an independent law of nature, or any kind of fixed trajectory at all. Consecutive states of mind and society are rather born of the interaction between human beings and the environments forming their character. Against deterministic historicisms, his account of progress adopts "the inverse deductive method"[170] examining the succession of social states through the interaction of generalized, empirical laws and ever-changing social phenomena. This avoids the twin errors of basing social science on unwarranted extrapolations from particular experiences ("the chemical method" that Mill attributes to Macaulay and thoroughgoing empiricists) or on unbending, abstract ideals (the apriorism of his father's and Bentham's "geometrical method"). Ethology, sociology and the study of politics treat the laws governing this interaction by assessing societies' materials and conditions.

Mill's pluralistic conceptualization of development also shapes his understanding of the social sciences' aims and utility. Political science, sociology and ethology are ultimately practical disciplines, the tools steering differently situated societies toward their respective ends. It's *because* societies evolve in unpredictable and idiosyncratic ways that Mill so values these sciences: they enable legislators to shape progressive social elements in conformity with distinctive national characters. Far from espousing a mechanistic view of progress, he treats it as essentially erratic, shaped by the vicissitudes of culture and history. Given this, the task of the social sciences is "to surround any given society with the greatest possible number of circumstances of which the tendencies are beneficial."[171] They are, for Mill, empirical instruments gauging a society's attributes – national character, history, state of civilization – in order to encourage its particular course of advancement. They also reflect the methodological commitments shaping Mill's approach to politics more generally. "The deductive science of society will not lay down a theorem, asserting in an [*sic*] universal manner the effect of any cause," he maintains, "but will rather teach us how to frame the proper theorem for the circumstances of any given case."[172] The variability of conditions affecting every society requires an according subtlety in developing its social and political institutions; the social sciences assess these conditions and how best to arrange them to further its progressive elements.

5.4.2 Disaggregating Historical Development

Mill's sociological view of development is, then, poorly captured by the aggregative account attributed to him; he does not portray societies as uniform entities moving through pre-given stages of advancement. While recognizing that "there exist Uniformities of Coexistence between the states of the various social phenomena,"[173] these comprise generalized tendencies rather than implicitly interlinked characteristics, and Mill persistently registers their differential and often disconnected evolution. Industrial and commercial growth, for example, don't necessarily entail more democratic states or heightened intelligence. As we saw in his treatments of American and French public life, democracies can lack the civil institutions sustaining good government, and mature civilizations can fall short of democratic competence. Societies don't progress as unified, cohesive entities, and ameliorations in certain spheres of collective life are no measure of social improvement overall. This is why Mill distinguishes between modernizations in particular areas of social existence (industry, commerce, economy, military, etc.) and social betterment more generally, arguing that "Progress and Progressiveness are not here to be understood as synonymous with improvement and tendency to improve."[174] This distinction – between advances in specific domains of social activity and broader social improvement – is reflected in his trepidations regarding Britain's and America's unbridled commercialism. A rationalized market, economy or industry, for Mill, is no indication of social progress.

Still more directly, Mill criticizes Tocqueville's failure to disentangle discrete sociological forces in his analysis of American character, focusing precisely on the shortcomings of its aggregationism:

M. de Tocqueville, then, has, at least apparently, confounded the effects of Democracy with the effects of Civilization. He has bound up in one abstract idea the whole of the tendencies of modern commercial society, and given them one name – Democracy; thereby letting it be supposed that he ascribes to equality of conditions, several of the effects naturally arising from the mere progress of national prosperity.[175]

Tocqueville is not alone in subsuming distinctive social phenomena under "one abstract idea": "most French philosophers," Mill complains, "insist upon only seeing *one* thing when there are many, or seeing a thing only on one side, only in one point of view when there are many others equally essential to a just estimate of it."[176] The worst culprit is Comte, whose account of civilization's advance flattens it out entirely. Comte's historical science sweeps all facets of social life under an encompassing force blind to the variances shaping human development. It's worth considering Mill's appraisal in its fullness:

There is according to M. Comte only one law of the development of human civilisation [*sic*]. You who have been in England can say whether this is true. Is it not clear that these two nations, England & France, are examples of the advance of civilisation by two different roads, & that neither of them has, nor probably ever will, pass through the state which the other is in? It is the lower animals which have only one law, that of their instinct. The order of the developement [*sic*] of man's faculties, is as various as the situations in which he is placed. It is melancholy to observe how a man like M. Comte has had all his views of history warped & distorted by the necessity of proving that civilisation has but one law, & that a law of progressive advancement; how it blinds him to all the merits of the Greeks & Romans (& the demerits of the middle ages) because there was improvement in some things at such periods, he thinks there must have been so in all: why not allow that while mankind advanced in some things, they went back in others?[177]

Comte, Guizot, Tocqueville: each indulges the same vice. Each aggregates sociological phenomena in unwarranted and over-determined ways, envisioning societies as singular entities subject to an equally singular law of progress.

And yet, it's precisely the error that critics impute to Mill himself. By treating societies as monolithic bodies marching through a determinate historical trajectory, he is accused of neglecting the particularity and value of different cultures. In Mill's "Manichean theory of two worlds,"[178] Parekh holds, civilized societies are progressive, while the uncivilized remain mired in a stationary state. But Mill's antipathy toward the "stationary state" is misinterpreted precisely by *attributing* an aggregationism to him depicting societies as *either* entirely progressive *or* entirely stationary, rather than as containing elements of both. Mehta, for instance, claims that for Mill "anything that is not aspiring to improvement or in the process of being improved must on account of that be designated as retrograde," leaving us with "the stark binary of the backward and the progressive, with nothing inbetween."[179] But the stark binary isn't Mill's, it's Mehta's. It's the *characterization* that does the work by obfuscating his detailed attention to a great diversity of social phenomena. It simply isn't Mill's view, and still further, it's a view he directly criticized. He lambasted the Saint-Simonians precisely for contending that "we must be always either standing still, or advancing, or retrograding," arguing instead that "changes may take place in a man or a nation, which are neither steps forward nor backward, but steps to one side."[180] The critical claim depends on a series of related assumptions that fail to be born out: that Mill's developmentalism is a strictly philosophical conceit derived from an Enlightenment-era universalism; that he saw Europe as charting a course through which all societies would pass; that he understood historical advancement in singular and convergent terms; and that he conceived of societies as aggregated totalities. To remain stationary, under these presumptions, would indeed be to fall behind. But Mill's sociological developmentalism neither shares in them, nor in the conclusions to which they lead. While he at points lapses into such blunt shorthand, designating certain "failed" civilizations as stagnant, his wide-ranging analyses of various states of society evince a much more nuanced view.

His writings on socialism, for example, argue for the benefits of a stationary state under conditions of advanced industrial production. Unfettered economic and industrial expansion, Mill argues, contributes to progress only at a "very early stage of human improvement"[181] – which is to say, in societies marked by poverty and under-development. Advanced societies, conversely, should institute a redistributive economic system raising the entire population's standard of living, rather than pursue continued economic growth. "This condition of society," he asserts, "is not only perfectly compatible with the stationary state, but, it would seem, more naturally allied with that state than with any other."[182] Industrial, commercial and economic progress are not unqualified goods, but are rather tethered to social imperatives. The social, moral and educative benefits accompanying a redistribution of wealth and a reorganization of labor *depend* on a stationary state of industry. The stationary state is, then, entirely compatible with an advanced society's proper measure of improvement: the moral and mental elevation of the working class. Mill in fact criticizes conceptions of progress that "regard the stationary state of capital and wealth with the unaffected aversion so generally manifested towards it by political economists of the old school," treating it as, "on the whole, a very considerable improvement on our present condition."[183] Still more clearly – and more clearly contrary to the aggregative view – he recognizes that "a stationary condition of capital and population implies no stationary state of human improvement."[184] The stigmatization of the "stationary state" thus turns on casting Mill's account in reductionist terms – as a pejorative denigrating retrograde, non-western societies – that fail to capture its complexities. The critical argument replaces Mill's actual view (that a stationary state of certain sociological phenomena is compatible with social advancement, more broadly, in certain states of society) with a cruder, aggregationist one (that all non-western societies are stagnant).

For Mehta, the categorical bifurcation in Mill's developmentalism also renders non-European social forms "inscrutable," and so justifies his "refusing to engage in the particulars of India."[185] He sees Mill as, like many of the era's imperialists, differentiating rational, civilized social forms from unintelligible, savage ones "resistant to 'all logical inquiry'."[186] While this undoubtedly captures James Mill's view, J. S. Mill's writings and colonial policy on the subcontinent are anything but blind to the distinctions of Indian society and politics. In an 1866 letter reflecting on his colonial work, he recounts distinguishing "really native states, with a nationality, & historical traditions & feelings" from

all the Mahomedan (Rampore excepted which descends from Fyzoola Khan the Rohilla chief) & most of the Mahratta kingdoms [who] are not of home growth, but created by conquest not a century ago [and whose] ruling class are almost as much foreigners to the mass of the people as we ourselves are. The Scindia & Holkar families in Central India are foreign dynasties, & of low caste too, Mahrattas who have usurped provinces from their native dynasties of Jats, Goojars, Boondelas & c. The home of the Mahrattas is in the South, & there is no really native Mahratta kingdom now standing except Kolapore. In these modern states created by conquest I would make the continuance of the dynasty by adoption not a right nor a general rule, but a reward to be earned by good government & as such I would grant it freely.[187]

India was hardly shrouded in "opacity, mystery, and unfathomable inscrutability,"[188] as Mehta suggests, hidden in the darker shadows of a binary divide. For better or worse, Mill registered the particularities of Indian society, culture, history and religion, and devised his colonial policies in light of them.

Civilized or uncivilized, Mill paid attention to the details. His sociological developmentalism is no speculative abstraction, but rather registers social, national and historical context; it is filtered through culture and grounded in social science, rather than philosophical conjecture. None of this, of course, minimizes or justifies the Eurocentrist chauvinism shaping his colonial endeavors and his parochial assessments of a great many non-Europeans. It rather clarifies the philosophical scaffolding surrounding his response to human difference and cultural pluralism, and shaping their incorporation into his liberalism. Mill's writings on non-western peoples are littered with evidence of his limitations. But these capture neither his fuller reckoning with human diversity, nor the theoretical tools through which he undertook it. Two of his central intellectual influences – Romanticism and sociology – pushed toward the same political horizon: Romanticism attuned him to the depth, inexorability and worth of cultural variation, and his sociological developmentalism integrated it. Diversity was, for Mill, embedded in the human condition.

Critics of Mill's liberal imperialism rightly draw out his moral and political philosophy's colonial entanglements, but also disregard important features of its conceptual context. The problem isn't that Mill isn't an imperialist or Eurocentrist, which he evidently is. The problem lies in miscasting the theoretical structures shaping his response to human diversity and cultural plurality, and in taking his imperialism to reflect his closure to those forms of heterogeneity more generally. Like Kant, Mill makes sense of difference through his developmentalism. Their developmentalisms, however, pull in very different directions.

5.5 LIBERALISMS, DEVELOPMENTALISMS AND DIVERSITY

Kant and Mill, we can now see, present us with two distinctive visions of historical progress, each shaping their respective understandings of human plurality. How, then, are we to evaluate them? How should we interpret their conceptualizations of diversity, difference, and the non-European world?

The Eurocentrism and racial prejudices pervading both thinkers' views of non-Europeans are well documented. What's less clear is how each encounters diversity: how their accounts of human development situate social, cultural, gender-based and racial difference, and integrate them into their moral and political theory. By focusing on their frameworks and not just their parochialisms, I want to clarify what might concern us as contemporary readers once we've exposed their own more evident limitations. I want to consider the place of diversity and difference in the structure of their ideas and the conceptual apparatus incorporating them. If our concern lies with the harms that might endure in their political thinking – and in liberalism more generally – what's of interest is less Kant's and Mill's own prejudices than the way that they fit within the broader architecture of their liberalisms. Can they make sense of – and find value in – human diversity and difference on their own terms, or do they understand them as irrationalities, evidence of historical immaturity? To return to Chakrabarty, how open are Kant's and Mill's H1s to the influence of H2s?

Kant conceives of humanity's historical progress as universalistic, stage-based, and convergent. Setting aside his racial chauvinisms, it incurs at least two substantial problems. First, his account of race – the lens through which he places diversity in relation to progress – is tied to a historicism that can only interpret differences as aberrations, more primitive forms of life destined to become Europeanized or fade away with the advent of humanity's rationalization.[189] It has no conceptual space to treat them otherwise. Non-Europeans are for Kant merely in "a certain raw state"[190] and have no future other than to ultimately adopt European social and political institutions – if, that is, they're to have a future at all (recall the Amerindians). Kant's historicism has no capacity to perceive the worth of human difference and diversity in themselves, as non-European cultural forms are only legible in relation to an all-encompassing Europe behind which they lag. Convergent histories are singular histories: progress and modernization describe precisely the process of shedding social and political immaturities. As Thomas McCarthy observes, "[t]he tendencies toward monoculturalism that surface in Kant's account of progress, the insignificant role he envisions for *reciprocal* intercultural learning, is prefigured in his fundamentally monological conceptions of reason and rationality."[191] Kant's conception of human development is unable to register any value in peoples, customs or cultures outside of universal history's explanatory framework.

Second, his philosophy of history can't make sense of racial or cultural difference in non-instrumental terms. From the perspective of a purposive natural history, racial differentiation is comprehensible only in relation to humanity's moral realization, as a mechanism enabling the globe's population and rationalization.[192] The value of non-European races is thus derived from, and contingent on, their role in the species' destiny. A purposive nature creates divergences from the original "*Phyletic Species*: Whites of brunette colour"[193] for one reason, and one reason alone: racial diversity is a condition for humanity's moral fulfilment. When Kant ponders why, left to their own devices, the Tahitians should exist at all, we should take him seriously; from within the parameters of his historicism, he's right to suggest that one simply can't give a satisfying answer. For Kant, non-European races are instruments.

They have no worth in themselves, and it's hard to see how they might share in humanity's inalienable dignity. Their "nature" can be grasped solely from a teleological rather than a transcendental perspective, in terms of their function in humanity's moralization rather than as ends in themselves. From the vantage point of Kant's philosophy of history, non-Europeans are not end-setting beings beyond market price, but vehicles for humanity's improvement.

In Chakrabarty's terms, Kant's H1 exhibits precisely those totalizing impulses suppressing human heterogeneity. It leaves no room for an H2, for the histories that might record or register the worth of cultural plurality or that might incorporate divergent standpoints. It leaves no room for any kind of view from the margins, which it obdurately excludes. Cultural, gendered and racial character are pulled into Kant's historicism, their intelligibility derived from their place in a unified account of modernization and progress. Among its many sins, Chakrabarty notes that historicism treats European history as the objective measure of historical time relative to which all other histories are situated. In Kant's case, this is plainly true. All substantive forms of human difference are made apprehensible, and derive what worth they may have, in relation to the standard set by Europe and to the European narration of history. Kant's developmentalism is, then, incapable of treating diversity on its own terms. It is constitutively closed to H2s, to plurality and to the integral dignity of non-European life, individually and collectively.

What about Mill? As with Kant, Mill's racial prejudices are as evident as they are problematic. But does he, as critics charge, understand non-Europeans as frozen in time, further back on Europe's civilizational track? Is Mill's H1 open to provincialization, to the influence of H2s?

Mill emphatically rejected the determinism, parochialism and teleology of universal histories in the Kantian mold. His Romantic and sociological predilections drew him to treat social progress and historical development as a contingent, context-dependent, unpredictable processes. In Mill's view, no H1 exists without its H2s. It was precisely because of this ineliminable heterogeneity that social science would "not give the laws of society in general, but the means of determining the phenomena of any given society from the particular elements or data of that society."[194] This isn't to suggest that Mill's developmentalism is entirely relativistic or that it lacks an H1 altogether, as he saw history moving in certain broad directions. As societies progressed, power would shift from individuals to masses, democracies would proliferate, equality would rise, and with it, educational levels. But in every case, these tendencies remained subject to the H2s generated by the cultural and historical particularities at the center of Mill's political thinking.

And none held greater sway over social and political life than national character. Mill's Romanticism pushed him to recognize that a society's national character – its culture – was neither incidental to it, nor would it fade away with time. Cultures were not only ineradicable features of human existence, but also invaluable to it. They were repositories of a society's collective experience, customs and history; they bound past, present and future into a community of shared fate; they imparted political stability and social cohesion; they shaped citizens to institutions, and institutions to citizens. Cultural differences, in a word, made politics worth caring about. History's sweep wouldn't pass over or iron out these differences, but would rather move through them. They also all but guaranteed the variability of historical development, as "above all, the character, that is, the opinions, feelings, and habits, of the people, though greatly the results of the state of society which precedes them, are also greatly the causes of the state of society which follows them."[195] To ignore culture's influence over history and politics wasn't just to ignore one factor among others, but the single most influential one. The contrast with Kant could scarcely be better illustrated than in Mill's conviction that it would not be possible, "setting out from the principles of human nature and from the general position of our species, to determine *a priori* the order in which human development must take place, and to predict, consequently, the general facts about history up to the present time."[196]

Altogether, Kant's and Mill's developmentalisms, liberalisms and responses to diversity diverge in philosophically substantive ways. They are not of a kind, and are ultimately irreconcilable – perhaps unsurprisingly, given Mill's reaction against the very determinism that Kant advances. They proceed from distinctive presumptions and build from them accordingly distinctive views of progress, development and difference. At best, Kant understands alterity and cultural difference as window dressing on humanity's rationalization; at worse, as headed for extinction; and most likely, as destined to take on a suitably European form, mimics inevitably short of the original.[197] By contrast, and despite his own provincialisms, Mill sees cultural differences as constitutive and valuable features of human existence. His H1 is indelibly inflected by H2s, recognizing that "different portions of mankind, under the influence of different circumstances, have developed themselves in a more or less different manner and into different forms."[198] Kant's history charts these differences' steady decline; Mill's is shaped by them.

* * *

In elaborating his critical theory of development, Thomas McCarthy traces out the monoculturalism undergirding liberal developmentalisms past and present. Development, in the many theoretical accounts he treats, is always synonymous with western modernity. A critical theory of development, by contrast, turns the analytical tools descended from western thought against its own failures and draws in historically marginalized voices. This "critical re-appropriation," as McCarthy describes it, appeals to the context-transcending nature of liberal ideals, enjoining us to "rethink putatively universal basic norms and reshape their practical and institutional embodiments to include what, in their limited historical forms, they unjustly exclude."[199] A critical theory of development endeavors to recognize the

distinctiveness of non-western social evolution to provincialize Europe, and
to replace "the idea of a single path to a single modernity with that of
a multiplicity of hybrid forms of modernization."[200]

While I'm sympathetic to the spirit of McCarthy's project, it works from the
presumption that a relatively coherent and consistent historicist impulsion
underlies liberal political thought from the early modern period onward. This
is the presumption that I want to complicate. A closer examination of Kant
and Mill shows that at a conceptual level, liberal developmentalisms are
importantly different and respond to human diversity in importantly
different ways. This does not, of course, deny the historical truth that
developmental schemas animated and sustained Eurocentrist and imperialist
projects, neither does it minimize the reprehensibility of Kant's and Mill's
views of non-Europeans, and still less, that those views shaped their moral and
political thinking. It rather pushes us to consider what we might hold on to
from ideas entangled with histories of domination. The kind of critical
reappropriation that McCarthy asks of us should consider where, exactly,
these parochialisms fit within their conceptual horizons, and what insights we
might excavate from behind them.

This pursues the intuition that what should concern us isn't Kant's and Mill's
own prejudices, but how their philosophical systems encounter and incorporate
human diversity and difference – what Charles Mills characterizes as their
liberalisms' "organizing conceptual and theoretical political frameworks."[201]
The harms of certain liberal developmentalisms lie in foreclosing the agency of
subaltern persons and peoples, in ignoring (or denying) the worth of human
diversity, and in monological notions of progress treating cultural differences as
immaturities. Not all developmentalisms, however, are equally singular in their
vision, and not all liberalisms are equally implicated in domination. To refine
our comprehension of their inner workings in no way diminishes their historical
complicity in imperialism and subjugation, but rather considers the
philosophical resources that they might nonetheless retain, against the view
that they're irreparably tainted. This is the question I want to consider in greater
detail: what contemporary liberalisms inherit from their antecedents, and what
we might reasonably carry forward from them without disregarding or over-
determining their historical and theoretical shortcomings. We turn from the
history of political thought to what it bequeaths us – from Kant's and Mill's
liberalisms to Kantian and Millian liberalisms.

NOTES

   1. Mill, *System of Logic*, 8:875.
   2. John Robson, "Civilization and Culture as Moral Concepts," in *The Cambridge
      Companion to Mill*, ed. John Skorupski (Cambridge: Cambridge University Press,
      1998), 338–371.
   3. Parekh, "Decolonizing Liberalism," 92.

4. Thomas McCarthy similarly argues for a disaggregative approach in elaborating his critical theory of global development, recognizing that aggregative conceptions of progress, intentionally or not, obfuscate the complexities and unevenness of historical development. As I emphasize in section 5.4 and in Chapter 6, Mill's developmentalism integrates this very insight, which his critics – including McCarthy – fail to recognize.

5. I pursue this argument – that we should focus less on historical thinkers' own prejudices than on where those prejudices fit within their philosophical systems – throughout this book, and elaborate it most fully in Chapter 6.

6. For an overview of the secondary literature treating Mill, race, liberalism and empire, see Bart Schultz, "Mill and Sidgwick, Imperialism and Racism," *Utilitas* 19, no. 1 (2007): 104–130. For critiques of Mill, see Bhikhu Parekh, "Liberalism and Colonialism: A Critique of Locke and Mill," in *The Decolonization of the Imagination: Culture, Knowledge and Power*, eds. Jan Nederveen Pieterse and Bhikhu Parekh (London: Zed Books, 1995), 81–98; Bhikhu Parekh, "Superior People: The Narrowness of Liberalism from Mill to Rawls," in *Times Literary Supplement*, 25 February, 1994; Parekh, "Decolonizing Liberalism"; Mehta, *Liberalism and Empire*; Mehta, "Liberal Strategies"; Jennifer Pitts, "Bentham: Legislator of the World?" in *Utilitarianism and Empire*, eds. Bart Schultz and Georgios Varouxakis (Lanham: Lexington Books, 2005), 57–92; Pitts, *Empire*; Pitts, "Savage Mind"; Eileen Sullivan, "Liberalism and Imperialism: J. S. Mill's Defense of the British Empire," *Journal of the History of Ideas* 44 (1983): 599–617; McCarthy, *Race, Empire*; Thomas R. Metcalf, *Ideologies of the Raj* (Cambridge: Cambridge University Press, 1994), ch. 2; Jahn, "Barbarian Thoughts"; Beate Jahn, "Kant, Mill and Illiberal Legacies," *International Organization* 59, no. 1 (2005): 177–207; David Theo Goldberg, "Liberalism's Limits: Carlyle and Mill on 'The Negro Question'," *Nineteenth-Century Contexts* 22 (2000): 203–216; Stephen Holmes, "Making Sense of Liberal Imperialism," in *J. S. Mill's Political Thought: A Bicentennial Reassessment*, eds. Nadia Urbinati and Alex Zakaras (Cambridge: Cambridge University Press, 2007), 319–346; D. G. Brown, "Millian Liberalism and Colonial Oppression," in *Civilization and Oppression*, ed. Catherine Wilson (Calgary: University of Calgary Press, 1999); Shiraz Dossa,"Liberal Imperialism? Natives, Muslims and Others," *Political Theory* 30, no. 5 (2002): 738–745; Robert Kurfirst, "Mill on Oriental Despotism, Including its British Variant," *Utilitas* 8, no. 1 (1996): 73–87; Homi Bhabha, *The Location of Culture* (London: Routledge, 1994); and Connolly, "Liberalism and Secularism."

For variously qualified defenses of Mill, see Varouxakis, *Mill on Nationality*; Georgios Varouxakis, "Empire, Race, Euro-Centrism: John Stuart Mill and His Critics," in Bart Schultz and Georgios Varouxakis, eds. *Utilitarianism and Empire* (Lanham: Lexington Books, 2005), 137–154; Margaret Kohn and Daniel O'Neill, "A Tale of Two Indias: Burke and Mill on Empire and Slavery in the West Indies and America," *Political Theory* 34, no. 2 (2006): 192–228; Robson, "Civilization and Culture"; Gibbons, "Liberalism and Progress"; Ronald Beiner, *Liberalism, Nationalism, Citizenship: Essays on the Problem of Political Community* (Vancouver: University of British Columbia Press, 2003); Don Habibi, *John Stuart Mill and the Ethic of Human Growth* (Springer Verlag, 2001), ch. 6; Habibi, "Moral Dimension"; Joseph J. Miller, "Chairing the Jamaica

Committee: J. S. Mill and the Limits of Colonial Authority," in *Utilitarianism and Empire*, eds. Bart Schultz and Georgios Varouxakis (Lanham: Lexington Books, 2005), 155–178; White, "Liberalism and Multiculturalism"; Menaka Philips, "Troubling Appropriations: J S Mill, Liberalism, and the Virtues of Uncertainty," *European Journal of Political Theory* 18, no. 1: (2019): 68–88; and Mark Tunick, "Tolerant Imperialism: J.S. Mill's Defense of British Rule in India," *Review of Politics* 68, no. 4 (2006): 586–611.

For analytical treatments of Mill's imperialism and international political theory that take no particular normative stance, see Duncan Bell, "Mill on the Colonies," *Political Theory* 38, no. 1 (2010): 34–64, and Varouxakis, *Liberty Abroad*.

7. Said, *Orientalism*, 7.
8. Bruce Mazlish, *James and John Stuart Mill: Father and Son in the Nineteenth Century* (New York: Basic Books, 1975), 117. See also Metcalf, *Ideologies of the Raj*, 30–31, and Javed Majeed, "James Mill's *The History of British India*: The Question of Utilitarianism and Empire," in *Utilitarianism and Empire*, eds. Bart Schultz and Georgios Varouxakis (Lanham: Lexington Books, 2005), 93–106.
9. Pitts, *Empire*, 127.
10. For variations in the Scottish Enlightenment's conjectural histories, see H. M. Höpfl, "From Savage to Scotsman: Conjectural History in the Scottish Enlightenment," *Journal of British Studies* 17, no. 2 (1978): 19–40; Bruce Buchan, "Enlightened Histories: Civilization, War and the Scottish Enlightenment," *The European Legacy* 10, no. 2 (2005): 177–92; and Aaron Garrett, "Anthropology: The 'Original' of Human Nature," in *The Cambridge Companion to the Scottish Enlightenment*, ed. Alexander Broadie (Cambridge: Cambridge University Press, 2003), 79–93.
11. Pitts, *Empire*, 130.
12. Ibid., 133.
13. Mehta, *Liberalism and Empire*, 102. Metcalf similarly argues that "[b]ehind Mill's views lay a hierarchal classification of all societies" inherited from his father (*Ideologies*, 31).
14. Pitts, *Empire*, 136. Mehta also acknowledges that the younger Mill's liberalism "is far more capacious than that of any of his contemporaries," and that "[i]n engaging with his thought, one can be confident that one is doing just that and not, as with his father, being thrust up against unreflective prejudices that masquerade as thought" (Mehta, *Liberalism and Empire*, 97). The deeper problem that I address in this chapter, however, concerns the presumption that J. S. Mill adopted his father's developmentalist framework, and not just his prejudices.
15. Pitts, *Empire*, 140.
16. Mehta, *Liberalism and Empire*, 93.
17. Pitts, *Empire*, 142. Karuna Mantena persuasively argues that J. S. Mill's conception of barbarism – unlike James Mill's – does not attribute cognitive deficits to individuals in any given society, but rather designates collective traits. See Karuna Mantena, "Mill and the Imperial Predicament," in *J. S. Mill's Political Thought: A Bicentennial Reassessment*, eds. Nadia Urbinati and Alex Zakaras (Cambridge: Cambridge University Press, 2007), 298–318.
18. Pitts, "Bentham," 79.

19. Alan Ryan describes this tendency toward unwarranted aggregation – improperly ascribed to Mill by Karl Popper, and, I argue, by more recent critics of his imperial liberalism – as "the vice of holism." See Ryan, *John Stuart Mill*, 181.

20. Ibid., 80.

21. Mehta, *Liberalism and Empire*, 101. For Étienne Balibar, this universalizing impulse – characteristic, by his reckoning, of modern humanist thought – frames social, cultural and racial differences as threats to civilizational advancement, justifying their eradication. See Étienne Balibar, "Racism and Nationalism," in *Nations and Nationalism: A Reader*, eds. Philip Spencer and Howard Wollman (New Brunswick: Rutgers University Press, 2005), 163–172.

22. Pitts, *Empire*, 141.

23. Metcalf, *Ideologies*, 34.

24. Chakrabarty, *Provincializing Europe*, 250.

25. Ibid., 23.

26. Ibid., 66.

27. Ibid., 65.

28. Ibid., 67.

29. Ibid.

30. Ibid., 254.

31. Ibid., 71.

32. Mehta, *Liberalism and Empire*, 104.

33. Ibid., 97.

34. Parekh, "Decolonizing Liberalism," 92.

35. McCarthy, *Race, Empire*, 168. For the congruence of the two Mills' views on progress, civilization and imperialism, see Kurfirst, "Oriental Despotism," 75; Pitts, *Empire*, 133; Metcalf, *Ideologies*, 31; Habibi, *Human Growth*, 189; and Mehta, *Liberalism and Empire*, 102.

36. Mill, *Autobiography*, 1:49.

37. Ibid., 1:103.

38. Martin Moir, "Introduction," in John Stuart Mill, in *The Collected Writings of John Stuart Mill, Volume XXX – Writings on India*, eds. Zawahir Moir, Martin Moir and John M. Robinson (Toronto: University of Toronto Press; London: Routledge & Kegan Paul, 1990), 30:xxiii.

39. Zastoupil, *Mill and India*, 7.

40. James Mill, "Government," reprinted from *Supplement to the Encyclopedia Britannica* (London: J. Innes, 1825), 3.

41. Ibid.

42. Ibid. 4.

43. Ibid., 17.

44. J. H. Burns, "The Fabric of Felicity: The Legislator and the Human Condition," Inaugural lecture delivered at University College London, March 2, 1947, 14 (cited in Mazlish, *James and John,* 80).

45. Zastoupil, *Mill and India*, 14.

46. James Mill, *History of British India in 6 Volumes* (London: Baldwin, Cradock and Joy, 1826), 2:134–135.

47. Zastoupil, *Mill and India*, 26. For a similar perspective on James Mill's view of India, see Javed Majeed, "James Mill's *The History of British India*: A Reevaluation," in *J. S. Mill's Encounter with India*, ed. Martin I. Moir,

Douglas M. Peers and Lynn Zastoupil (Toronto: University of Toronto Press, 1999), 53–71.

48. Zastoupil, *Mill and India*, 32. For a close examination of the Anglicist/Orientalist debate and its influence on J. S. Mill, see Penelope Carson, "Golden Casket or Pebbles and Trash? J. S. Mill and the Anglicist/Orientalist Controversy," in *J. S. Mill's Encounter with India*, eds, Martin I. Moir, Douglas M. Peers and Lynn Zastoupil (Toronto: University of Toronto Press, 1999), 149–172.

49. Eric Stokes, *The English Utilitarians and India* (Delhi: Oxford University Press, 1989), 53.

50. Zastoupil, *Mill and India*, 33.

51. For detailed accounts of Mill's disagreements with William Jones and of the *History of British India*'s role in the Anglicist/Orientalist debate, see Majeed, "Reevaluation," 53–55, and Majeed, "Utilitarianism and Empire."

52. John Stuart Mill, "Technicalities of English Law, *Morning Chronicle*, 25 September, 1823," in *The Collected Works of John Stuart Mill, Volume XXII – Newspaper Writings Part I*, eds. John M. Robson and Ann P. Robson (Toronto: University of Toronto Press; London: Routledge & Kegan Paul, 1986), 22:61.

53. John Stuart Mill, "Parliamentary Reform, *Morning Chronicle*, 3 October, 1823," in *The Collected Works of John Stuart Mill, Volume XXII – Newspaper Writings Part I*, eds. John M. Robson and Ann P. Robson (Toronto: University of Toronto Press; London: Routledge & Kegan Paul, 1986), 22:64; see also John Stuart Mill, "Securities for Good Government, *Morning Chronicle*, 25 September, 1823," in *The Collected Works of John Stuart Mill, Volume XXII – Newspaper Writings Part I*, eds. John M. Robson and Ann P. Robson (Toronto: University of Toronto Press; London: Routledge & Kegan Paul, 1986), 22:62.

54. John Stuart Mill, "Practicability of Reform in the Law, *Morning Chronicle*, 8 October, 1823," in *The Collected Works of John Stuart Mill, Volume XXII – Newspaper Writings Part I*, eds. John M. Robson and Ann P. Robson (Toronto: University of Toronto Press; London: Routledge & Kegan Paul, 1986), 22:70.

55. Moir et al., *Encounter*.

56. Berlin, "Ends of Life," 133.

57. Mill, *Autobiography*, 1:143.

58. See Mill, *Autobiography*, ch. 5; and Zastoupil, *Mill and India*, 41–50.

59. Mill, *Autobiography*, 1:138.

60. Ibid., 1:139.

61. Ibid., 1:133.

62. Ibid., 1:166–167.

63. Ibid., 1:170.

64. Capaldi, *John Stuart Mill*, 89.

65. Ibid., 85. Capaldi provides a particularly expansive examination of Romanticism's influence over Mill's moral and political philosophy.

66. Mill, *Autobiography*, 1:161.

67. Ibid.

68. Mill, "Mill to Sterling," 12:81.

69. John Stuart Mill, "Mill to John Pringle Nichol, Apr. 15, 1834," in *The Collected Works of John Stuart Mill, Volume XII – The Earlier Letters 1812–1848 Part I*, ed.

Francis E. Mineka (Toronto: University of Toronto Press; London: Routledge & Kegan Paul, 1963), 12:221.

70. Capaldi, *John Stuart Mill*, 92.

71. Zastoupil, *Mill and India*, 41.

72. Mill, *Autobiography*, 1:169.

73. Mill would in later years regret the overly critical tenor of the 1838 "Bentham," penned in the midst of his Romantic swing. Without recanting its substance, his later writings were less forceful in their rejection of Benthamic radicalism and aimed to better balance rationalism and Romanticism. See John M. Robson, "John Stuart Mill and Jeremy Bentham, with some Observations on James Mill," in *Essays in English Literature from the Renaissance to the Victorian Age*, eds. M. MacLure and F. W. Watt (Toronto: University of Toronto Press, 1964), 259–262.

74. John Stuart Mill, "Bentham," in *The Collected Works of John Stuart Mill, Volume X – Essays on Ethics, Religion and Society (Utilitarianism)*, ed. John M. Robson (Toronto: University of Toronto Press, 1969), 10:93.

75. Ibid., 10:98.

76. Ibid., 10:105. For Mill's views on national culture, affect, and social solidarity, see Varouxakis, *Mill on Nationality*, chs.1–2; and Robson, "Civilization and Culture."

77. Thomas Babington Macaulay, "Mill on Government," in *The Miscellaneous Writings of Lord Macaulay* (London: Longman, Green and Co., 1860), 1:295. For the impacts of Macaulay's critique on John Stuart Mill, see Capaldi, *John Stuart Mill*, 62–65, and Ryan, *Mill*, ch. 8.

78. Mill, *System of Logic*, 8:888–889.

79. Mill, *Autobiography*, 1:175–176.

80. Ibid., 1:177.

81. Mill, *System of Logic*, 8:840. Mill's account of self-formation has been charged with several inconsistencies, not least of which is the problem of regress. I set these aside, as my concern is with his departure from his father's view of human nature (and consequently, from his politics), not with the tenability of his moral psychology. For Mill's rejection of his father's Owenite associationism, see Collini, "The Idea of Character"; Ryan, *Mill*, 105–108; Skorupski, *John Stuart Mill*, 252–255. For the fullest account of Mill and character-formation, see Carlisle, *Writing of Character*.

82. Mill, "Coleridge," 10:132.

83. John Stuart Mill, "State of Society in America," in *The Collected Works of John Stuart Mill, Volume XVIII – Essays on Politics and Society Part I*, ed. John M. Robson (Toronto: University of Toronto Press; London: Routledge & Kegan Paul, 1977), 93. An earlier letter to d'Eichthal bears witness to the same complaint: "surely at every *present* epoch there are many things which would be good for that epoch, though not good for the being Man, at every epoch, nor perhaps at any other than that one; & whoever does not make this distinction must be a bad practical philosopher even for his own age" (John Stuart Mill, "Mill to Gustave d'Eichthal, Nov. 7, 1929," in *The Collected Works of John Stuart Mill, Volume XII – The Earlier Letters 1812–1848 Part I*, ed. Francis E. Mineka (Toronto: University of Toronto Press; London: Routledge & Kegan Paul, 1963), 12:41).

84. Mill, "Coleridge," 10:141.
85. Ibid.
86. The question of just how much – or rather, what kind of – diversity Mill envisions as shaping historical progress remains an open and vexing one for a few reasons. First, his writings contradict themselves on this front. On one hand, Mill recognized the value of Indian traditions in the Anglicist-Orientalist debate, defended negro rights and cultures in his polemic against Carlyle, and described Jewish societies as implicitly progressive, suggesting a fair degree of openness to different cultural traditions and a sensitivity to their enduring influence over social development. On the other, he persistently denigrated uncivilized peoples, defended the absorption of minorities into more civilized nations, and of course argued, in *On Liberty*, for the benefits of benevolent despotism over peoples in their "nonage." The contradiction complicates any clear assessment of his settled view. Second, Mill's thought is pervaded by the tension between his perfectionism (clearest in *Utilitarianism*) and his commitment to liberty (clearest in *On Liberty*). While the former inclines toward a narrower vision of social progress, the latter's historical fallibilism and pluralism are amenable to divergent social forms and developmental paths. Finally, it's a hard question to answer because it wasn't Mill's question at all. Mill set out neither to theorize multiple modernities nor to create a sociological record of different societies, which he only treated in the service of developing the methods and tools of "the Social Science." That he devoted most of his attention to those societies with which he was most familiar, or more directly engaged, is therefore unsurprising. Each of these points suggests that Mill's understanding of pluralism in historical development will necessarily be a matter of textual and contextual reconstruction, rather than exposition.
87. Zastoupil, *Mill and India*, 11.
88. Ibid., 13.
89. In his 1858 defense of the East India Company before Parliament, J. S. Mill noted with pride its principled regard for "the civil and religious usages of the natives" sustaining this social cohesion. See John Stuart Mill, "The Petition of the East India Company," 30:81.
90. Fred Wilson, "Psychology," 219.
91. Ibid.
92. Zastoupil, *Mill and India*, 40. For detailed examinations of the 1836 dispatch's divergence from James Mill's views on Indian education, see Lynn Zastoupil, "India, Mill, and 'Western' Culture," in *J. S. Mill's Encounter with India*, eds. Martin I. Moir, Douglas M. Peers and Lynn Zastoupil (Toronto: University of Toronto Press, 1999), 111–148, and Zastoupil, *Mill and India*, chs. 2–3. For the 1836 dispatch's relation to the Anglicist/Orientalist debate, see Carson, "Anglicist/ Orientalist Controversy."
93. John Stuart Mill, "Recent Changes in Native Education," quoted in Zastoupil, *Mill and India*, 42.
94. Zastoupil, *Mill and India*, 43.
95. John Stuart Mill, "Mill to John Morley, Nov. 4, 1865," in *The Collected Works of John Stuart Mill, Volume XVI – The Later Letters 1849–1873 Part III*, eds. Francis E. Mineka and Dwight N. Lindley (Toronto: University of Toronto Press; London: Routledge & Kegan Paul), 16:1202–1203.

96. John Stuart Mill, "Mill to Edward Lytton Bulwer, Nov. 23, 1836," in *The Collected Works of John Stuart Mill, Volume XII – The Earlier Letters 1812–1848 Part I*, ed. Francis E. Mineka (Toronto: University of Toronto Press; London: Routledge & Kegan Paul, 1963), 12:312.

97. Berlin, "Ends of Life," 140.

98. Mill, "Civilization," 18:119.

99. Ibid.

100. Ibid., 18:119.

101. Ibid., 18:120.

102. Ibid.

103. Ibid., 18:122. Mill reiterates this view – that the capacity for cooperation is the lynchpin of civilization – in *Principles of Political Economy*, 3:708, and in *Auguste Comte*, 10:312.

104. Mill, "Non-Intervention," 21:118.

105. Ibid.

106. John Stuart Mill, "The Negro Question," in *The Collected Works of John Stuart Mill, Volume XXI – Essays on Equality, Law, and Education (Subjection of Women)*, ed. John M. Robson (Toronto: Toronto University Press; London: Routledge & Kegan Paul, 1984). For Mill's denunciations of nineteenth-century biological determinism, see Robson, "Civilization and Culture"; for the development of his understanding of race, see Varouxakis, *On Nationality*, ch. 3; for the claim that his settled view is Eurocentric, rather than racist, see Varouxakis, "Empire, Race, Euro-centrism"; for the argument that, cultural or biological, Mill's account of the uncivilized remains racist, see Goldberg, "Liberalism's Limits"; and for an overview of the debates on this question, see Schultz, "Imperialism and Racism."

107. Mill, "Negro Question," 21:93.

108. *Mill, System of Logic*, 8:859.

109. Ibid.

110. Ibid.

111. For Mill's view of Jewish social order, see *Considerations*, 19:397. For his support of the Union and of the American Civil War – a "war justifiable and laudable even if it had continued to be, as it was at first, one of mere resistance to the extension of slavery, [which] is becoming, as it was easy to foresee it would, more and more a war of principle for the complete extirpation of that curse" – see John Stuart Mill, "The Civil War in the United States, *Our Daily Fare* (Philadelphia), 21 June, 1864," in *The Collected Works of John Stuart Mill, Volume XXV – Newspaper Writings Part IV*, eds. Ann P. Robson and John M. Robson (Toronto: University of Toronto Press; London: Routledge & Kegan Paul, 1986), 25:1204–1205; Varouxakis, *Liberty Abroad*; and Semmel, *Pursuit of Virtue*, ch. 3.

112. John Stuart Mill, "The Subjection of Women," in *The Collected Works of John Stuart Mill, Volume XXI – Essays on Equality, Law, and Education (Subjection of Women)*, ed. John M. Robson (Toronto: Toronto University Press; London: Routledge & Kegan Paul, 1984), 21:276.

113. Mill, *System of Logic*, 8:859.

114. Mill, "Subjection of Women," 21:340.

115. Mill, *On Liberty*, 18:273.

116. John Stuart Mill, "Guizot's Essays and Lectures on History," in *The Collected Works of John Stuart Mill, Volume XX – Essays on French History and Historians*, ed. John M. Robson (Toronto: University of Toronto; London: Routledge & Kegan Paul, 1985), 20:270. For Guizot's influence in drawing Mill away from his early, Saint-Simonian faith in the progressive power of an enlightened clerisy and toward an understanding of social progress as anchored in systemic social antagonism, see Georgios Varouxakis, "Guizot's Historical Works and J. S. Mill's Reception of Tocqueville," *History of Political Thought* 20, no. 2 (1999): 292–312. I elaborate on Mill's mature account of social development in section 5.4.

117. Mill, "Civilization," 119. Mill's rather confusing terminology is worth clarifying. His references to "civilization in the narrow sense" describe the *broad* tendencies of civilization – the wide-ranging progressive impulses that he sees as benefiting mankind. This is in contrast with the particular *iterations* of civilization – modern European and American civilizations – criticized in Mill's essay (and elsewhere).

118. Mill, "Civilization," 18:119.

119. Ibid.

120. Mill, "Coleridge," 10:123.

121. Mill, "De Tocqueville [2]," 18:198.

122. Ibid.

123. Mill makes this argument most forcefully in the fifth and final section of his series in the *Examiner* on "The Spirit of the Age." See John Stuart Mill, "The Spirit of the Age, V (Part 2)," in *The Collected Works of John Stuart Mill, Volume XXII – Newspaper Writings Part I*, eds. Ann P. Robson and John M. Robson (Toronto: University of Toronto Press; London: Routledge & Kegan Paul, 1986). This pathological state of affairs, he argues, is rooted in Britain's "national vice: the universal and all-absorbing struggle to be or to appear rich" pushing citizens to follow "a blind mechanical impulse, which renders money, and the reputation of having money, the immediate end of their actions" (John Stuart Mill, "The English National Character," in *The Collected Works of John Stuart Mill, Volume XXIII – Newspaper Writings Part II*, eds. Ann P. Robson and John M. Robson (Toronto: University of Toronto Press; London: Routledge & Kegan Paul, 1986), 23:717–727). I elaborate on Mill's critique of privatism and commercialism below, in section 5.3.4.

124. Mill, *On Liberty*, 18:265.

125. Mill, *Auguste Comte*, 10:312.

126. Mill, "De Tocqueville [2]," 18:158.

127. Mill, *Considerations*, 19:460.

128. Ibid., 19:478.

129. Mill, "De Tocqueville [2]," 18:178.

130. Ibid., 18:179.

131. Urbinati, *Athenian Polis*, 89.

132. Ibid., 76.

133. John Stuart Mill, "Representation of the People, 13 April 1866," in *The Collected Works of John Stuart Mill, Volume XXVIII – Public and Parliamentary Speeches Part I*, eds. Bruce L. Kinzer and John M. Robson (Toronto: University of Toronto Press; London: Routledge & Kegan Paul, 1988), 28:65.

134. Mill, "Rationale," 18:39. Mill also treats the distinction between delegates and representatives in *Considerations*, ch. 12, and "De Tocqueville [1]," 18:73.

135. Mill, *Considerations*, 19:468.

136. Mill, "De Tocqueville [1]," 18:80.

137. Mill, "State of Society in America," 18:101–102.

138. Mill, "De Tocqueville [2]," 18:169.

139. John Stuart Mill, "Mill to Gustave d'Eichthal, May 15, 1929," in *The Collected Works of John Stuart Mill, Volume XII – The Earlier Letters 1812–1848 Part I*, ed. Francis E. Mineka (Toronto: University of Toronto Press; London: Routledge & Kegan Paul, 1963), 12:31–32. As he puts it in another letter, rather more succinctly, "a philosophy which makes production expressly the one end of the social union, would render the only great social evil, of which there is much danger in the present state of civilization, irremediable" (Mill, "Mill to d'Eichthal, Oct. 8, 1829," 12:37).

140. Mill, "Mill to d'Eichthal, Nov. 7, 1829," 12:40. For Mill's early (and brief) championing of intellectual vangardism, see Capaldi, *John Stuart Mill*, 78, 98, 120, 170 and 210.

141. Mill, *Auguste Comte*, 10:314.

142. For Mill's view of the coexistence of civilized and barbaric tendencies within given societies, see Michael Walzer, "Mill's 'A Few Word on Non-Intervention': A Commentary," in *J. S. Mill's Political Thought: A Bicentennial Reassessment*, eds. Nadia Urbinati and Alex Zakaras (Cambridge: Cambridge University Press, 2007), 347–356.

143. Mill, *Principles of Political Economy*, 3:944.

144. Ibid.

145. Mill, "Guizot," 20:274.

146. Ibid., 20:270.

147. Mill, *Auguste Comte*, 10:288.

148. Mill, "Civilization," 18:124.

149. Mill, *Principles of Political Economy*, 3:935.

150. Mill, "Guizot," 20:271.

151. Ibid., 20:262. For Mill's consciousness of the contingency of progress, see Habibi, "Moral Dimension," and Robson, "Civilization and Culture."

152. Mill, *August Comte*, 10:308.

153. Mill, "Guizot," 20:260.

154. Ibid., 10:322.

155. Mill, *Auguste Comte*, 10:293.

156. Ibid., 10:309.

157. Ibid., 10:325.

158. For lucid examinations of Mill's philosophy of history, see Ryan, *John Stuart Mill*, ch. 10; Semmel, *Pursuit of Virtue*, ch. 4; Capaldi, *John Stuart Mill*, chs. 4–6; and Alexander, *Arnold and Mill*, ch. 2.

159. Mill, *System of Logic*, 8:912. While Mill most fully elaborates "the Social science" in the *Logic*, its contours are visible as early as 1831, when he set out to examine "*laws* of society, or laws of human nature in the social state" whose "general truths form the subject of a branch of science which may be aptly designated from the title of *social economy*"; this "science of social economy embraces every part of

man's nature, in so far as influencing the conduct or condition of man in society,"
including "in what historical order those states [of society] tend to succeed one
another" (John Stuart Mill, "On the Definition of Political Economy; and on the
Method of Investigation Proper to It," in *The Collected Works of John Stuart Mill,
Volume IV – Essays on Economics and Society Part I*, ed. John M. Robson
(Toronto: University of Toronto Press; London: Routledge & Kegan Paul,
1967), 4:320). For just a few illuminating treatments of the *System*'s moral and
social sciences, see Ryan, *John Stuart Mill*, 133–212; Wilson, "Psychology"; and
Skorupski, *John Stuart Mill*, 248–282.

160. For a view of ethology as connecting Mill's central philosophical preoccupations,
see Terence Ball, "The Formation of Character: Mill's 'Ethology' Reconsidered,"
Polity 33, no. 1 (2000): 25–48.

161. Mill, *System of Logic*, 8:861.

162. Wilson, "Psychology," 227.

163. Mill, *System of Logic*, 8:877.

164. Ibid.

165. Ibid., 8:914. For Mill's departures from the French historians on the question of
progress, see Ryan, *John Stuart Mill*, 169–188. For his "insist[ence] that even if we
had a comprehensive science of ethology, it was not possible to predict the future
unerringly," see Capaldi, *John Stuart Mill*, 76.

166. Mill, "Mill to d'Eichthal, Nov. 7, 1829," 12:43.

167. Ibid., 12:41.

168. Ibid.

169. Mill, *Auguste Comte*, 10:298.

170. Mill, *System of Logic*, 8:911.

171. Ibid., 8:898.

172. Ibid., 8:899–900.

173. Ibid., 8:912.

174. Ibid., 8:913. Mill is equally circumspect in disentangling natural and social
progress, against Comte's tendency to conflate them: "Two questions meet us at
the outset: Is there a natural evolution in human affairs? and is that evolution an
improvement?" (Mill, *Auguste Comte*, 10:315).

175. Mill, "De Tocqueville [2]," 18:191–192. Mill extends this line of criticism in
"State of Society in America": "Government is only one of a dozen causes which
have made America what she is ... It is remarkable how much of those national
characteristics which are supposed to be peculiarly the result of democracy, flow
directly from the superior condition of the people" (18:98).

176. Mill, "Mill to d'Eichthal, Oct. 8, 1829," 12:36.

177. Ibid., 12:37.

178. Parekh, "Decolonizing Liberalism," 92.

179. Mehta, *Liberalism and Empire*, 104.

180. Mill, "Mill to d'Eichthal, Nov. 7, 1829," 12:43.

181. Mill, *Principles of Political Economy*, 3:754.

182. Ibid., 3:755.

183. Ibid., 3:753–754.

184. Ibid., 3:756.

185. Mehta, *Liberalism and Empire*, 69.

186. Ibid., 68.

187. Mill, "Mill to John Morley," 16:1202.
188. Mehta, *Liberalism and Empire*, 69.
189. Bernasconi, "Unfamiliar Source."
190. Kant, VP, 9:442.
191. McCarthy, *Race, Empire*, 68.
192. Kant in fact argues against racial mixing for fear of "watering down" different races' adaptive traits, rendering them less fit for their historically given function.
193. Kant, RM, 2:441.
194. Mill, *System of Logic*, 8:899–900.
195. Ibid., 8:905.
196. Ibid., 8:915.
197. Bhabha, *Location of Culture*.
198. Mill, *System of Logic*, 8:938.
199. McCarthy, *Race, Empire*, 37.
200. Ibid., 242.
201. Mills, "Racial Liberalism," 1388.

6

Millian Liberalism

How shall man measure Progress there where the dark-faced Josie lies? How many heartfuls of sorrow shall balance a bushel of wheat? How hard a thing is life to the lowly, and yet how human and real! And all this life and love and strife and failure, – is it the twilight of nightfall or the flush of some faint-dawning day?

W. E. B. Du Bois, *The Souls of Black Folk*

Two things emerge from my reconstructions of Kant's and Mill's treatments of human difference and diversity. First, from an exegetical standpoint, we better understand their incorporations of diversity by situating them carefully, and by disentangling both thinkers' relation to empire from their accounts of non-European races and cultures. Their conflation is not only inaccurate, but anachronistic: it falls prey to Skinner's mythology of doctrines by projecting a cohesiveness – a broad-ranging openness to cultural diversity or an intractable hostility toward non-Europeans – on to Kant's and Mill's views of empire that imports contemporary measures of cultural receptivity.[1] Second, we better see their substantive philosophical departures as regards diversity. Kant's and Mill's conceptualizations of social, cultural, racial and gender-based difference are not only divergent, but incommensurable, as are their normative orientations toward them, and developmental schemas treating them.

But how exactly should their differences affect us, as contemporary interlocutors? More generally, how should we approach figures, ideas, texts and traditions of thought enmeshed with historical injustice? Should we simply move beyond liberalism, as some critics suggest, however we might go about doing that? These are particularly challenging questions that court, and even invite, misapprehensions, conceptual confusions and anachronism. That liberalism's scope has historically been severely constrained, both in theory and practice; that it coexisted with, and often sustained, racial hierarchies and imperial or colonial domination; that its emancipatory pretensions generally extended no further than Europe's shores; that its conceptual vocabularies justified the dispossession of vast swaths of humanity over centuries; that those damages continue to shape the social and political realities of millions still today – this is all incontestably true.[2] But it binds liberalism, as an intensely contested and contestable body of political thought, to domination no more necessarily than to the emancipation that its progenitors claimed for it, and that it also served in western and non-western contexts alike. What our response to these philosophical lineaments should be and what we're warranted in drawing out of them is, then, far from clear. Is liberalism implicitly connected to the imperial inequities and hierarchies alongside which it developed? Are exclusionary proclivities internal to its logic, or historically contingent?

Such questions have gained traction as liberalism's linkages to empire, historical and conceptual, have come under increasing critical scrutiny, along with its central proponents' exclusionary cast of mind. Perhaps more importantly, the line of inquiry has opened up the problem-space, as David Scott describes it, within which race and empire have gained scholarly visibility, presence and urgency.[3] Scholarship cutting across political theory, postcolonial and decolonial studies, and intellectual history has illuminated liberalism and empire's shared parentage and imbricated development, long neglected by political theory's inward-looking tendencies.

And yet, family resemblances can conceal, just as they reveal. This chapter has two broad aims. In section 6.1, I argue that common ways of conceptualizing historical wrongs and their contemporary implications are subject to misunderstandings that muddy the waters surrounding race, empire, difference and liberalism. I identify particular sources of confusion inhibiting a clear evaluation of historical injustices in the liberal tradition (as regards race and non-Europeans), one that would be neither anachronistic nor dismissive. Much of this book has focused on narrower historical, interpretive and exegetical claims surrounding Kant and Mill; here, I shift gears to make a wider conceptual claim concerning misinterpretations of liberalism. This aims at something of a ground-clearing, sketching out prevailing sites of opacity in the study of liberalism, empire and race.[4]

In section 6.2, I elaborate the conceptual resources that Kantian and Millian liberalisms hold for thinking about present-day pluralism. This aims to evaluate what we might reasonably draw out of Kant's and Mill's liberalisms for our own purposes, in light of the cautions raised in section 6.1; it educes their visions of human difference without disregarding or overstating the impacts of their prejudices. In short, I consider the utility and standpoint that each provides for thinking politically in an age of deep diversity. In this final section, I tentatively flesh out the book's normative claim: that properly understood, Millian liberalism is implicitly fallibilistic, uncertain, pluralistic and culturally inflected, providing us with a better orientation toward human difference and diversity than does Kantian liberalism. Despite Mill's own parochialisms, his liberalism remains indelibly capacious, open to the breadth of social and cultural forms marking the human condition, and self-consciously contingent. Conversely, Kantian liberalism in many ways reflects the limitations of its progenitor's monoculturalism and myopia, even if contemporary Kantians clearly have no share in them. I argue that Millian liberalism is well suited to a profoundly pluralistic world.

The critique that I undertake in section 6.1 focuses largely (but not entirely) on postcolonial theorists treating liberalism and empire, and it's an entirely sympathetic one. Many of the interpretive concerns that I raise stem from the demands of critique at a given point in time – from what David Scott describes as the "predicament of the present [that] makes up the target of our critical practice."[5] Over the last decades, postcolonial criticism has revealed the extent to which "colonial knowledge and its assumptions"[6] have shaped innumerable disciplines and fields of study. It has also pushed an entrenched and often intransigent scholarship toward "different question-answer complexes"[7] registering empire's constitutive impacts on the modern world. Its very success, however, entails that "the *demand* in the present has altered";[8] given the now-widespread recognition of liberalism's imperial associations, it falls to us to refine our critical lens. What follows in no way discounts the contributions of the critics that I engage, but rather shares in the broad ambition to consider how distinctive traditions of political thought respond to human difference in more or less inclusive ways.[9] It aims, as the aim has been throughout this book, to better understand where the problems lie.

6.1 LIBERALISMS PAST AND PRESENT

The question of how to think about race, empire and liberalism is enmeshed with larger methodological debates in the history of political thought shaped by five decades of grappling between textualists, contextualist and genealogists over what, if anything, we are warranted in extracting from historical figures and texts, and how exactly we should go about doing so.[10] These divisions have softened in a recent and more catholic scholarship resisting, as Patchen Markell puts it, "the frustrating professional conventions of academic political theory, which often represent the history of political theory and theoretical engagement with contemporary politics as separate enterprises."[11] Against this kind of "[m]ethodological tunnel vision," Jack Turner enjoins us "to think *through* the question of how to think *with* the past in a responsible manner."[12] Jeanne Morefield and John Zammito have undertaken just such careful, contextually sensitive work in the history of political thought that, for all their historical circumspection, remains firmly and self-consciously driven by presentist concerns regarding imperialism and race.[13]

This ecumenical turn suggests that our interest in liberalism's relationship to race and empire need not incur the anachronisms that Skinner alerts us to. With due care, there is little to prevent us from reading Kant, Mill, or any other historical figure for our own purposes, so long as we resist imputing those purposes – or our values, norms, interests or concerns – to them. We can (and should) work hard to discern what Kant and Mill meant, without having to restrict ourselves to that task alone. The challenges that I raise here are, then, not reducible to a contextualist antipathy toward presentism, nor to a genealogist resistance to reifying liberalism; they are not the province of any particular approach to thinking about history and political theory.

6.1.1 Western Will to Power

The first concerns the presumption, either implicit or explicit, that western political thought, or some relevant dimension of it, is internally bound to domination and exclusion. This is, of course, not an entirely a new story. Adorno and Horkheimer traced the instrumentalist rationality underlying the twentieth century's worst atrocities to the peculiarities of a bourgeois will to power stretching from antiquity to Hollywood, the inclination to dominate nature, internal and external, comprising the constitutive thread of western civilization.[14]

But for them, that civilization was entirely indiscriminate, dominating itself as much as anyone else. Contemporary critics are, rather, concerned with the more particular impulsion to tyrannize the non-west that Stuart Hall attributes to "European and then Western capitalist modernity after 1492,"[15] of which colonialism is the most direct manifestation, and the nineteenth-century's liberal imperialisms the most nakedly brazen. The problem is nothing short of what Gyan Prakash describes as "the Eurocentrism produced by the institution of the west's trajectory"[16] – or still more broadly, in Brett Bowden's estimation, the "continental chauvinism and implicit and explicit racism ... inherent to the Western canon."[17] Barbara Bush similarly tracks imperialism "from the Roman to the present-day American Empire" to derive insights into "the nature of Western hegemony."[18] Each treats "the west" as a cohesive entity underlain by an internal inclination to forcibly control the non-western world that stretches uninterrupted, if subject to local variations, throughout the modern era (and considerably earlier, in certain iterations).[19] The west is, then, inherently sloped toward violence, misrecognition and the exclusion of, in Uday Mehta's words, "the unfamiliar."[20]

While Mehta focuses on liberalism more narrowly, he nevertheless maintains that "liberals drew on and anticipated various archetypal moments of Western thought," "broad epistemological and normative commitments" tending toward the foreclosure of non-Europeans.[21] Despite his careful attention to liberalism's historical constitution, James Tully also traces "western legitimating narratives" that "describe, explain and legitimate the imperialisation of non-western countries" across a vast temporal expanse ("the various periods of western imperialism from 1492 to the present"), tracing out an exploitative proclivity whose singularity and coherence is implied by its recurrence over 600 years of western history.[22] Further attesting to its pervasiveness, this hegemonic "language of universal norms and historical processes," Tully maintains, "has been adopted and adapted in the Liberal and Marxist traditions, the social sciences, developmental studies, the policy communities of developed and developing states, international law, the League of Nations and the United Nations."[23] Dipesh Chakrabarty similarly identifies colonial historicism in both liberalism and Marxism, the domineering impulse cutting across the major currents of modern western political thought. In its broadest instantiation, the critical charge takes aim at what Andrew Sartori captures as the "deep civilizational root to the West's will-to-power over the East."[24]

The precise site of this will-to-power, however, shifts considerably from critic to critic, and is further obscured by a tendency to elide distinctive terms and ideas. Where Prakash, Bowden and Hall are centrally preoccupied with the abstract and encompassing figuration of "the west," for instance, Walter Mignolo, Enrique Dussel, Partha Chatterjee and Hall narrow in on *modernity*. For Dussel, modernity is "an essentially or exclusively European phenomenon" in which the "process of discovery and conquest is not simply of anecdotal or historical interest; it is part of the process of the constitution of modern subjectivity itself ... [and] has to do above all with the connection to Eurocentrism."[25] "Coloniality," in Mignolo's view, "is the hidden face of modernity and its very condition of possibility."[26] Chakrabarty is similarly concerned with "the phenomenon of 'political modernity' ... the genealogies of which go deep into the intellectual and even theological traditions of Europe."[27] This modernity tends to be somewhat indefinite, both in its contents and temporalization. For Dussel, Tully and Hall, it begins in 1492 (or 1415, depending on the text); Chakrabarty's modernity is indeterminate; Mehta's – or at least the relevantly "liberal" parts of it – reaches to the seventeenth century, and Mignolo's to the sixteenth; and while Thomas McCarthy observes that "[r]acism and imperialism have been basic features of the modern world order from the start,"[28] it's not clear when that might have been. This isn't just a pedantic complaint about a manifestly fluid denotation, but rather concerns what that fluidity *does* for the argument. While the concept is of course contestable, variable and intentionally under-specified, this very imprecision here serves to encapsulate vastly different harms, perpetrated by vastly different actors, at vastly different times, to vastly different ends. Modernity becomes a temporal and conceptual catch-all for the west's transgressions, vaguely agentive and yet whose more precise features, beyond a persistent Eurocentrism, remain obscure.[29] For many critics, this Eurocentrism is the binding thread connecting past and present, but the contention is often sustained by generalization, abstraction and what Frederick Cooper describes as story-plucking – "extracting tidbits from different times and places and treating them as a body independent of their historical relationship, context, or countervailing tendencies ... [to] derive a lesson that conveys a generalizable meaning."[30] Robert Stam and Ella Shohat, for instance, connect "George W. Bush's ultimatums against Iraq" with "five hundred years of colonial ultimatums, going all the way back to the Spanish *requerimiento*," bound together by a Eurocentrism that "sanitizes Western history while patronizing and even demonizing the non-West."[31] This isn't to deny the evident truth that western modernity was accompanied by Eurocentrism and political subjugation, but rather resists their explanatory over-extension and over-simplification.

Another variant conceives of the Enlightenment – or, commonly, an amorphous and wide-ranging Enlightenment "project" – as the site of domination, stretching its valorization of rationalism well beyond its historical limits to stand in as the central feature of western thought. Mehta, for example, treats liberalism's "normative commitments" – and imperial inclinations – as "anchored in a particular view of political reason, which is shared by the Enlightenment and whose disposition and self-assurance is antecedent to the encounter with the strange or the stranger."[32] If the impulsion's gravitational center remains unclear (liberalism? "archetypal moments of Western thought"? Enlightenment rationalism?), its consequences are anything but: in the empire, he avers, we witness the "vivid sense of thought that has found a *project*"[33] – the Enlightenment project. Thomas Metcalf similarly identifies liberalism's "fundamental assumptions" with the worst of the Enlightenment's hubris, Eurocentrism and monoculturalism: "liberals conceived that human nature was intrinsically the same everywhere," they "had for the most part little sympathy with established institutions," they invariably aimed to mold all persons into "autonomous, rational beings," they "never doubted that the wholesale transformation of society was not only possible but certain," and they regarded their own values as "[u]niversally valid."[34] David Scott exhorts us to abandon the "*Enlightenment project as such* in which *both* Marxism and liberal democracy have sought their futures"[35] for the same reasons: the Enlightenment carries the antipathy toward foreignness and the bullish inclination to act on it most fully displayed in modern imperialism, but hardly isolated to it. In each case, the problem lies in the historical flattening incurred by taking the west, modernity and the Enlightenment as continuous and interchangeable, all but emptying them of analytical or critical purchase, and as sufficient explanatory grounds for distinctive and complex phenomena.

6.1.2 Liberalism in/and Empire

A second set of common presumptions takes liberalism and imperialism as internally bound. While subject to considerable variations, these fall between what Duncan Bell describes as the "contingency" thesis (that liberalism's association with imperialism is historically contingent) and the "necessity" thesis (that liberalism's association with imperialism results from its internal logic).[36] As Bell observes, few commentators commit unreservedly to the necessity thesis. And yet, the force of many of their arguments – and among them, the most influential – depends on the supposition of necessity, even if it remains (often quietly) qualified. Without fully and explicitly endorsing the necessity thesis, most assume that: (a) *something* in liberalism lends itself to domination, (b) that something is shared by most (if not all) liberals, past and present, (c) it is historically continuous; and (d) only the most cautious and self-reflexive liberals are likely to avoid or resist it.

Tully's anti-imperialism, for instance, turns on a powerful critique of the Kantian liberalism – or, synonymously for him, "Kantian imperialism"[37] – shaping the contemporary global order. This liberalism animates the "historically persisting imperial character of the global relationships"[38] which Tully so perceptively illuminates. And yet, it rests on the supposition of a stable, singular liberalism enmeshed with western domination from its inception to the present day. While Tully acknowledges, in a footnote, "resources within liberalism to criticize and overcome its cultural imperialism if self-critical liberal theorists wish to do so,"[39] his larger contention – that the liberalism most clearly iterated in Kantianism embodies the western inclination to predominate structuring international relations – implicates liberalism more generally. Thomas McCarthy explicitly draws an internal, non-contingent link between liberalism and empire, arguing that it isn't just "'contexts of application' that connected liberal theory to European imperialism; that connection was already forged in its 'context of origin' ... deployed by progressive liberalism as a justification for empire from the beginning, and not by chance."[40] This same inner connection "still continue[s] to dominate it and emasculate the force of its liberal and egalitarian impulses,"[41] Bhikhu Parekh contends, and it spurs Chakrabarty's advocacy for "a radical critique and transcendence of liberalism."[42] There is, then, "a growing consensus that liberalism and aggressive international behavior not only are compatible, but are in fact causally linked."[43] This consensus carries normative implications: given inbuilt tendencies to exclusion and domination, Scott proposes that we abandon the "*presumption* that liberalism and indeed democracy (even a purportedly radical one) have any *particular* privilege among ways of organizing the political forms of our collective lives."[44]

Uday Mehta's view is worth treating in some detail, as among the most forceful, influential and – paradoxically – confusing accounts of liberalism and empire. He argues that "the exclusionary basis of liberalism ... derive[s] from its theoretical core, and the litany of exclusionary historical instances is an elaboration of this core."[45] Those exclusionary proclivities are "integral to its political vision and not peculiar amendments or modifications imposed on it ... Given liberalism's universalism, this is definitionally the case."[46] Where most critics address liberals' imperialistic designs, Mehta makes a stronger claim: he is explicitly "indifferent to the issue of authorial intent," focusing instead on the "impulse" underlying "the foundational commitments of liberalism"[47] shared by its proponents, but not particular to any of them. *Liberalism*, and not any given liberal thinker, then, is the problem. However, he goes on to narrow in on nineteenth-century British liberal imperialists. In this case, the imperial compulsion is particular to a given strand of liberalism, and not to the tradition more generally. But then, he treats "liberal involvement with the British Empire [a]s broadly coeval with liberalism itself,"[48] falling back into his original position – liberalism and empire are bedfellows from the start. Amid toggling between liberalism writ large and nineteenth-century liberalism more specifically, he also offers a qualified retreat from the full necessity thesis: "[u]rges can of course be resisted ... which is why I do not claim that liberalism *must be* imperialistic, only that the urge is *internal* to it."[49] But beyond its incompatibility with his stronger claims regarding liberalism's definitional qualities, this suggests that liberalism *is* imperialistic – authorial intention be damned – such that only the most self-conscious of liberals might resist its natural tendencies.

Critics also conjoin liberalism and empire by running liberals together, drawing associations across a range of thinkers (in spite of their frequently profound differences over race, culture and empire), often over a broad temporal expanse, to reveal liberalism's overarching antipathy toward non-liberals.[50] Tully, for instance, takes exception with "the traditions of Kant, Mill, and Spencer";[51] Parekh criticizes "the narrowness of liberalism from Mill to Rawls," projected forward (to Joseph Raz, Brian Barry, Ronald Dworkin and Michael Walzer) and backward (to Locke);[52] for McCarthy, "the mainstream of liberal thought, running from Locke through Mill to contemporary neoliberalism has continually flowed into and out of European-American imperialism";[53] and Desch treats Locke, Tocqueville and Kant as sharing in an "'imprudent vehemence' in dealing with nonliberal actors."[54] Bernard Semmel's panoramic survey of liberal imperialists includes, beyond the usual suspects, Charles Fourier, Friedrich List, Henri de Saint-Simon, Adam Smith, Auguste Comte, Lenin and many more, while Brett Bowden recovers the imperial inclination in "the vision[s] of Condorcet, Hegel, Marx, Auguste Comte, Spencer, Kant, or some other theorist."[55]

6.1.3 Liberalism, Historicism, Developmentalism

Finally – and still more narrowly – commentators take aim at the historicist developmentalism binding liberalism, imperialism and domination. The exposition and critique of "stadial, developmentalist metanarratives of historical progress in which societies of the global North-West are construed as more civilized, superior, and/or advanced than the rest of the world" is, Jakeet Singh observes, "one of the primary tenets of postcolonial and decolonial thought,"[56] and has been taken up by scholarship in intellectual history, political theory, critical theory, history, cultural studies, anthropology and beyond. This has illuminated the historicism sustaining European ascendency over the non-European world, arguing that developmentalism: (a) anchors western hegemony by framing the space – political, moral and intellectual – between Europeans and non-Europeans; (b) recurs consistently, although in appropriately updated tropes, from the early modern period up to the present day; and (c) is woven into liberalism's fabric. "[T]hrough all the alterations and variations that take us from Enlightenment philosophies of history to contemporary theories of social and cultural development," McCarthy holds, "in all the major developmental theorists ... the main lines of development, at least in the modern period, run through the West and from there outward to the rest of the world."[57] Tully and Mehta similarly treat "developmentalism as an integral feature of liberalism"[58] and Enrique Dussel sketches out "the connection of Eurocentrism with the concomitant 'fallacy of developmentalism'."[59] In each case, liberals take "historical time as a measure of the cultural distance (at least in institutional development) that was assumed to exist between the West and the non-West."[60] Historicist and developmental frameworks are, then, at the root of liberalism's intractable closure to human difference (conceptually) and imperialist proclivities (politically).

6.1.4   Revisiting Liberalism and Empire

Each of these lines of criticism is invaluable in illuminating the theoretical foundations and historical realities of European imperial and colonial depredations throughout the modern era. They elucidate the broad movements of a half-millennium of political domination and empire's constitutive role in forming global legal, political and economic realities. They show the pervasiveness, insidiousness and tenacity of Eurocentrism, its capacity to reconcile the promise of liberty, equality and freedom with practices of violence, exclusion and hierarchy, and its persistence in neocolonialisms that continue to retain the Global South in systemic subjugation to the Global North.[61] But they also lapse into simplifications that over-determine liberalism's connectedness to domination. For all of their critical acuity, these strains of argument share in what Sartori describes as the "vague sense that Western universalism ... is at root a 'civilizational' affair, part of the West's constitutive cultural legacy," and that liberalism's "immanent aggression ... stand[s] in metonymic subordination to a more general tendency toward aggressively universalistic abstraction in the Western tradition."[62] The extension is problematic in several ways.

First is a tendency toward generalization that elides salient conceptual and historical distinctions, dissolving differences between thinkers (e.g. Locke, Kant, Mill, Spencer, Tocqueville, Raz, Rawls, Dworkin), eras (tracing the imperial impulse from ancient Rome to the present day), conceptual frameworks (conflating liberalism, rationalism, Enlightenment, modernity and the west), social and political contexts (subsumed under a broad-ranging Europe) and philosophies (subsumed under an equally broad-ranging liberalism).[63] These vanish under the umbrella of a "west" whose movements and counter-currents are reduced to cosmetic flourishes papering over an all-encompassing civilizational drive to domination. Such critics, Frederick Cooper notes, "write with little apparent misgivings about a phenomenon labeled colonial, appearing in many places and times ... abstracted from context and process,"[64] leaving us with "a colonial project vaguely situated between 1492 and the 1970s, of varying contents and significance, alongside an equally a-temporal 'post-Enlightenment' Europe, missing the struggles that reconfigured possibilities and constraints across this period."[65] Beyond obfuscating the complexities of colonial conditions, this narrative selectiveness fixes colonizer and colonized, dominator and dominated, and west and non-west into "immutable categories," rather than treating them as variable, contested and historically constituted concepts.

These modes of critique are also prone to what Cooper describes as time-flattening, the "assumption that a certain essence characterizes a long period of time, passing over the conflict and change within it," leading "a wide range of scholars to attribute practices and discourses to the fact of modernity, often elided with post-Enlightenment rationalism, bourgeois equality, and liberalism."[66] The "epochal fallacy"[67] hides the ideational variations within these imaginaries: the west, modernity, Enlightenment and liberalism were entwined with conservatism, Romanticism, evolutionism, Marxism and republicanism, to name just a few of the many ideologies shaping modern political thought. It not only fails to register "how badly the tale of progress fits the political, intellectual and cultural history of this continent, but the extent to which even such constructs ... were not some essence of 'the West', but products of struggle."[68] The presumption of Europe's single-minded drive to domination glosses over the rifts, divisions, challenges and heterodoxies both permeating and resisting imperialist projects and logics. Imputing that uniformity of purpose to liberalism, more narrowly, also conceals both non-liberal (republican, nationalist, etc.) arguments for empire and liberal arguments against it.[69] We should, then, be wary of the "occlusion that results from turning the centuries of European colonialization overseas into a critique of Enlightenment, democracy, or modernity."[70]

Oversimplification also reduces our sensitivity to the political capacities, resources and agency standing against unjust power, historically and in the present; it is depoliticizing in that "ahistorical history encourages an apolitical politics."[71] The chimera of a monolithic west "carr[ies] the suggestion that we already know very well what the oppressive coordinates of that legacy are"[72] rather than undertaking the political work of identifying them in a more determinate way, and of engaging those supposedly rendered voiceless by them (a conceit that global intellectual historians have complicated).[73] Reifying the west not only "give[s] excessive weight to the determining power of agentless abstractions,"[74] but also turns a blind eye to colonial subjects' responses to fractious and disputed political authorities. Far from being passive recipients or supine objects of imperial hegemony, colonial actors asserted their agency by integrating, synthesizing, adopting, adapting and rejecting metropolitan ideas, relations and structures across a wide range of colonial contexts.[75] Overly broad critiques are also depoliticizing in a second sense: they fail to identify the relevant site of domination, blurring the nature of the problems that should concern us. Locke, Kant, Mill and innumerable others held abhorrent and problematic views of non-Europeans; but they are not at all the same problems, neither do they carry the same moral and political implications. Submerging them under a singular Eurocentrism conceals their distinctive harms and diminishes our capacity to recognize and respond to them.

Excessively broad critiques of liberalism also neglect the differences demarcating distinctive liberalisms drawn to light by recent scholarship. Jennifer Pitts, for instance, chronicles liberalism's "turn to empire" at the hinge of the eighteenth and nineteenth centuries, and Karuna Mantena traces fluctuations in liberal justifications for empire following the 1857 Sepoy Rebellion, both showing marked shifts across 18th-20th century liberalisms and their visions of race and empire.[76] Sankar Muthu's exposition of eighteenth-century anti-imperialists similarly troubles the neat equation of liberalism, Enlightenment and domination.[77] The thinkers he treats are not alone: even at high point of nineteenth century liberal imperialism, liberals expressly opposed imperialist and colonial expansionism. Herbert Spencer, the late nineteenth century's preeminent liberal thinker, was a vociferous opponent of empire, castigating "these deeds of blood and rapine, for which European nations in general have to blush, [which] are mainly due to the carrying on of colonization,"[78] the inevitable result of "that concentration of power which is the concomitant of Imperialism."[79] Liberalism has, also, advanced freedom and political emancipation in colonial contexts, providing a conceptual vocabulary, Christopher Bayly has demonstrated, for India's early independence movement. "Indian liberal ideas," he argues, "were foundational to all forms of Indian nationalism,"[80] "a broad field on which Indians and other South Asians began ... to resist colonial rule."[81] In India, liberalism animated colonial policy and also stood against it: as a set of conceptual commitments, it remains no more tied to domination than to the liberation it helped to advance. Liberalism thus resists generalization because, historically and currently, it is marked by ruptures, competing and sometimes-incompatible ideals, and an accordingly wide range of social, political and moral aspirations – some in tension, others in contradiction. There is no center to liberalism that we might fix to either domination or emancipation, and no attempt to burrow down to its "essential" features is likely to succeed. It is mutable, elusive and protean, just as any other comparably complex theoretical assemblage. The monolithism implied by the critical charge is, then, distorting.

Finally, without minimizing the evidently problematic and hierarchizing features of historicist thinking, liberal developmentalisms (as well as non-liberal ones) are subject to important variations, framing the relationship between west and non-west in distinctive ways.[82] As we have seen, Kant's teleological history shares little with Mill's social scientific account of civilizational advancement. Pitts also differentiates the Scottish Enlightenment's conjectural histories from their nineteenth-century articulations, the former abstaining from the evaluative judgments of non-Europeans that would become characteristic. Developmentalisms within the Scottish Enlightenment, still further, diverged considerably: where Adam Smith's four-stages theory was materialist, economic and stringently agnostic regarding the moral character of differently situated societies, Lord Kames's historicism countenanced a polygenetic racial hierarchy. Finally, developmental frameworks extend well beyond their Eurocentric embodiments. At the turn of the twentieth century, for instance, liberal and non-liberal thinkers drew on historicist frameworks to resist colonial rule. Indian anti-imperialists such as Shyamji Krishnavarma, Surendranath Banerjee and Aurobindo Ghose marshaled sophisticated developmental arguments to counter British power, criticize its justifications and advance Indian independence.[83] Developmentalisms thus have a malleability poorly captured by their subsumption under a uniform Eurocentrism.

6.2   KANTIAN AND MILLIAN LIBERALISMS

How, then, should we think about these traditions of political thought? How should we disentangle Kant's and Mill's liberalisms from Kantian and Millian liberalisms? What political vision might we reasonably draw out of them, without bracketing, neglecting or minimizing their shortcomings?

Bhikhu Parekh offers one possible answer, and a fairly typical one worth considering for its representativeness. "To be a Millian liberal," he stipulates, "is to take a condescending and paternalistic view of non-liberal societies."[84] But this simply conflates Mill's liberalism with the Millian liberalism that we might draw out of him, extending Mill's own condescension and paternalism to a long line of thinkers "deeply apprehensive about the future of liberalism."[85] The association is unwarranted: nothing in Mill's response to cultural difference broadly commits Millian liberals to his prejudiced assessments of non-Europeans more narrowly. Kant's and Mill's liberalisms – their own moral and political doctrines – can surely be distinguished from the political possibilities descended, derived or sparked by them.

Ultimately, the question boils down to how problematic historical texts, thinkers and ideas might illuminate our political present, if at all. For Thomas McCarthy, "the resources required to reconstruct our traditions of social and political thought can be wrested from those traditions, provided they are critically appropriated and opened to contestation by their historical 'others'."[86] But we also need not be so direct. Patchen Markell helpfully suggests that we "mine earlier texts in order to reconstruct some piece of theoretical apparatus that might be useful in the present," as one possibility, or "treat history … as the first-personal medium of contemporary political experience, asking what configurations of past (and future) accompany our sense of the present as a certain kind of 'now'."[87] Drawing on W. E. B. Du Bois's reflections on the "present-past," Jack Turner notes that the line between "past and present is an open, political question, and that ... [t]he relation of past and present is a matter of interpretive judgment."[88] "To think historically," he maintains, "means making judgments about what is required to interpret the present, to make it productively strange, productively unfamiliar, so that we may decide if we need something new."[89] There are, then, different ways that historical antecedents might awaken or sensitize us to moral, ethical and political possibilities in the present. Our political insights are not tethered to the strictures and commitments of the figures that might stimulate them, much less their prejudices. We can, rather, take them up more obliquely, as angles of political reflection or insight, or as imparting a given tenor for thinking politically. As Kwame Anthony Appiah suggests, they "provide heat, not light,"[90] a practical orientation toward what we might do as political agents in a pluralistic world, rather than normative rules telling us what we must. They can, in a word, open political horizons and incline us toward given political sensibilities.

How, then, should we understand Kantian and Millian liberalisms, and the horizons that they might open up? Given the cautions enumerated, concerning tenuous linkages binding past and present, I do not take Kantian and Millian liberalisms as set bodies of doctrine, as we might get from Kant and Mill themselves. They are, rather, orientations to politics – dispositions toward thinking about plurality and the political. They're not *things*; they're not fixed or constitutive; they do not go all the way down. They do not bind their adherents or commit them to theoretical tools or vocabularies ineluctably enmeshed with domination, or with much of anything else. Kantian and Millian liberalisms are, rather, tendencies: they are distinctive ways of envisioning diversity immanent in liberalism – wide tent that it is – that pull in radically divergent and even opposing directions. What's of interest is their *bearing* toward difference: how they position our thinking toward diversity, and toward the tasks of political theory more generally. Kantian and Millian liberalisms make manifest inclinations toward pluralism instantiated not only in Kant's and Mill's own thought, but in those of other liberals; they are not unique to them, even if Kant and Mill give them particularly rich articulations (the very reason for focusing on them). But this ties neither Millians nor Kantians to either thinker's parochialisms. To treat broad, flexible and variable theoretical assemblages as implicitly denigrating is to lapse into the conceptual murk and anachronism that I have tried to resist. Neo-Kantians are, then, no more committed to Kant's bigotries than Millians are to Mill's. Given the multifarious ways that historical thinkers might be brought to bear on contemporary circumstances, it is untenable to treat liberalism – Kantian, Millian or other – as constitutively bound to its historical limitations, or as constitutively antipathetic to non-liberals.

This is because the conceptual tools shaping Kant's and Mill's responses to cultural/racial/gender-based pluralism are themselves inexorably ambivalent (which isn't to suggest that they don't have their leanings).[91] Kant's moral universalism is both emancipatory, as a difference-blind egalitarianism, and exclusionary, advancing a Eurocentric ideal of moral personhood. Mill's consciousness of the cultural facets of politics registers social difference, and also justifies a colonial rule of difference. As Judith Butler observes, the theoretical frameworks and languages articulating liberal ideals are not exhausted by any particular configuration, but are always incomplete, exceeding any possible singularity, and thus invite political work. "[E]xposing the parochial and exclusionary character of a given historical articulation of universality," she argues, "is part of the project of extending and rendering substantive the notion of universality itself"; these are the "contestations crucial to the continuing elaboration of the universal itself, and it would be a mistake to foreclose them."[92] Moral universalism, democracy, developmentalism, equality, liberty, self-determination, autonomy: these are malleable ideals that can and have been understood and operationalized through a wide range of practices, some gravely unjust, others freedom-enhancing. As Tully notes, drawing on Wittgenstein, "there is neither an essential set of necessary and sufficient criteria for the correct use of such concepts nor a calculus for their application in particular cases"; "[i]t is almost always possible," then, to "argue that the term can be extended in an unexpected and unpredictable way."[93]

This fluidity suggests that liberalism is neither committed nor reducible to any one of its historical forms, and that those forms are themselves fundamentally unfixed. The range of interpretive lives lived by Locke's defense of property, to illustrate the point, is a veritable palimpsest of liberalism's fluctuating fortunes: for long, a wellspring of the labor theory of value central to liberal justifications for private property; in the 1960s, the target of C. B. McPherson's critique of possessive individualism, tying liberalism to rapacious, market-driven capitalism;[94] in the 1990s and 2000s, connected to colonial expropriations of Indigenous land, exposing liberalism's imperial underbelly;[95] and recently recovered in Bengali resistance movements by global intellectual historians examining non-western liberalisms.[96] From champion of liberty, to imperial administrator, to guiding light of Indian liberalism, Mill's reception has been comparably varied.[97] Liberalism's conceptual vocabularies, like those of other ideological persuasions, are shackled to domination or liberation only awkwardly. "Since the use of concepts with complex histories 'is not everywhere circumscribed by rules'," Tully holds, "'the extension of the concept is *not* closed by a frontier'."[98]

Kantian and Millian liberalisms are, then, neither tied to any particular view of race, culture or diversity, nor integrally hostile toward non-Europeans. As Amanda Anderson observes, "the history of liberalism, as both a philosophy and a literary topos, is richer, and more amenable to interpretive challenges and complexity, than many of the current critiques allow."[99] To conceptualize Millian liberalism is not to propose a radically new or distinctive liberalism clear of imperial, racial or cultural domination. It is, rather, to excavate an outlook implicit in certain strands of liberalism particularly receptive to human variation, while remaining conscious of the parochialisms with which it has coexisted. Kantian liberalism, conversely, is not explicitly ill-disposed toward racial and cultural difference, but draws on a theoretical lexicon less attuned to cultural heterogeneity, less sensitive to diverse registers of harm, injustice and occlusion, and more tilted toward certain forms of monoculturalism. The point in both cases is less to fix their commitments – to stipulate what Kantians and Millians *must* be or believe – than to consider their positioning toward diversity, and how they respond to it. While this might seem unsatisfyingly under-specified, it is by design, informed by my resistance to unwarranted over-determinations of liberalism, the west, modernity, and Kant's and Mill's moral and political philosophies.

These cautions do not, however, imply Kantian and Millian liberalisms' complete plasticity. Each inclines in particular ways, and Millian liberalism, in my view, encounters such differences more generatively than the critical stance allows. As Kwame Anthony Appiah observes, and as I have argued, Millian liberalism is essentially amenable to the claims of culture: it understands human beings as inherently cultural and prizes national character and social plurality. It is animated by the conviction, Richard White argues, "that other cultures are to be valued because they represent different ways of promoting human flourishing," and so, that we ought "to celebrate cultural diversity and to affirm that we usually have something to learn from other cultures."[100] Despite Mill's small-minded assessments of non-Europeans, the Millian account of social, political and historical advancement is shaped by the ineliminable fact of diversity. His political philosophy's central advance over eighteenth-century rationalism and nineteenth-century radicalism was precisely its appreciation of political life's cultural dimensions, and he criticized political theories deriving "the general principle of the government" from "large and sweeping practical maxims"[101] for disregarding them. His valuation of the social sciences reflects the same sensitivity to cultural pluralism: by conceptualizing progress through the interaction of generalized empirical laws and mutable social phenomena, the "inverse deductive method"[102] captures the idiosyncratic and varied nature of development. This structures his moral and political arguments: *because* cultures formed human existence; *because* they were shaped by sociological and historical contingencies; *because* they sustained social cohesion; and *because* they contained a people's identity, any viable political theory was bound to incorporate them. Millian liberalism thus treats distinctive ways of life and cultural practices as endemically political, rather than as secondary to preordained political ends, or as destined to fade through social rationalization. It is structurally antipathetic to convergent or monocultural accounts of progress and modernization, recognizing that cultural character conditions institutional life, political systems and developmental pathways.

Millian liberalism is also innately fallibilistic and anchored in an open-ended ideal of self-development, rather than in a priori political principles. We need only recall *On Liberty*'s central argument – that liberty enables continual self-criticism, revision and improvement – to recognize what Menaka Philips describes as the deep uncertainty characterizing Mill's political thought.[103] If every era's verities are invalidated by the next, Mill argues, political life cannot consist in uncovering eternal or transcultural rules of government. History reveals that the truth on any given matter is invariably split between conventional wisdom and heretics, and every society's articles of faith become the object of its successors' ridicule, bewilderment or consternation. This is because we place "implicit trust on the infallibility of 'the world' in general," forgetting that "the world, to each individual, means the part of it with which he comes in contact; his party, his sect, his church, his class of society." For Mill then, "ages are no more infallible than individuals; every age having held many opinions which subsequent ages have deemed not only false but absurd; and it is as certain that many opinions, now general, will be rejected by future ages, as it is that many, once general, are rejected by the present."[104] This fallibilism shapes the Millian understanding of progress as unfixed, provisional and erratic, and of the nature and tasks of politics more generally.[105] History moves us toward neither moral perfection nor predetermined social and political institutions, as the certainties sustaining them are unvaryingly partial and incomplete, the half-truths of a given people and place.

Mill's fallibilism is central to his political vision, stretching back to his early years and molding many of his most celebrated arguments. In an 1829 letter, 30 years prior to *On Liberty*'s publication, he lamented that in every age, era and state of civilization, "one hardly meets with a single man who does not habitually think & talk as if whatever was good or bad for one portion of these countries or of these individuals was good or bad for all the other portions." "The great instrument for the improvement of man," he concludes, "is to supply them with the other half of the truth, one side of which they have only ever seen," the half always buried in unconventional and unpopular heterodoxies. "[N]ot errors but half-truths," he saw, "are the bane of human improvement."[106] The Millian valuation of liberty rests on these anti-foundationalist grounds: liberty's good is not intrinsic, as libertarian readings suggest, but rather lies in carving out the space for the disagreement and dissent enabling social progress. "[T]he only unfailing and permanent source of improvement is liberty," Mill argues, "since by it there are as many possible independent centres of improvement as there are individuals."[107] Historical circumspection imparts a philosophical modesty to the Millian defense of liberty, and to its political approach more broadly: if the passage of time persistently invalidates political certainties, our best recourse is to safeguard the liberties allowing individual and collective self-development, rather than seeking a firmer set of certainties. That Mill restricted those liberties to societies beyond their nonage, again, does not bind Millian liberals to do the same.

Millian liberalism understands us, then, as neither closing in on a fixed set of political principles, nor on rationalized political institutions; it is predicated on no static account of human nature or human goods; it advances no conception of political life on which we might expect societies to converge; and it does not treat the ends of government as singular, or as speculatively determinable. If "[g]overnment exists for all purposes whatever that are for man's good," as Mill holds, "[t]he united forces of society never were, nor can be, directed to one single end, nor is there ... any reason for desiring that they should."[108] Millian liberalism preserves the conditions securing "the permanent interests of man as a progressive being"[109] – the conditions, given Mill's fallibilism, for constant, ongoing self-reflection and self-improvement in accordance with a people's cultural character. Mill believed that "government altogether being only a means, the eligibility of the means must depend on their adaptation to the end," such that "the proper functions of a government are not a fixed thing, but different in different states of society."[110] Millian liberalism likewise resists adjudicating political doctrines in abstraction from a people's social, political and historical circumstances, and more generally, conceiving of political theory in such terms. If "[h]uman nature is not a machine to be built after a model, and set to do exactly the work prescribed for it, but a tree, which requires to grow and develop itself on all sides, according to the tendency of the inward forces which make it a living thing,"[111] we should not approach the political institutions surrounding it as settled in advance. The Millian view thus stands apart from the Kantian one in its recognition that "there are no absolute truths in the political art."[112] It is "free from the error of considering any practical rule or doctrine that can be laid down in politics as universal and absolute,"[113] or more generally, from treating the aim of political thinking as securing or uncovering any such rules or doctrines. It belongs to what Amanda Anderson characterizes as a tradition of bleak liberalism riven by "doubts about its own project," which remains always "an unfinished project."[114]

This anti-foundationalism also inflects Millian liberalism's resistance to social and political determinism, displayed with particular lucidity in Mill's trenchant critique of women's subordination. Women's domination rests on the canard that "that the *nature* of the two sexes adapts them to their present function and position";[115] their inequality represents "the primitive state of slavery lasting on."[116] Beyond the naked injustice of differentiating rights on a naturalistic basis – grounded, still further, in an equally unjustifiable physical dominance – such claims are themselves untenable as the "character" of either sex is unknowable outside of their historical relation of domination. While Kantian and Millian liberalisms likewise oppose unequal rights, the Millian view recognizes and resists their naturalistic basis and is attuned to their historical constitution and social entrenchment. It cleaves to a skepticism undermining the deterministic pretentions sustaining liberals' (and others') defenses of women's and minorities' disenfranchisement.

This attentiveness to political systems' social implications and social valences similarly informs Mill's sharp admonishments, in the final section of *On Liberty*, against using liberty to shield the abuse of women and children. Social justice, in the Millian view, imposes substantive limitations on the liberty principle. "The State, while it respects the liberty of each in what specially regards himself, is bound to maintain a vigilant control over his exercise of any power which it allows him to possess over others" – an obligation, Mill notes, that "is almost entirely disregarded in the case of the family relations," and more particularly, in "[t]he almost despotic power of husbands over wives."[117] Far from defending the rigid public/private divide yielded by simplistic interpretations of the liberty principle (and central to many liberalisms), Mill is acutely conscious of its pernicious potentialities, particularly as regards more vulnerable classes of citizens, which feminist scholarship has in the intervening years greatly illuminated.[118] Millian liberalism thus defends women's rights (as do Kantian liberalisms, even if Kant did not); but more profoundly, it registers social and historical asymmetries of power perpetuating harms neglected by systems of law and justice – and particularly, by neo-Kantian neutralism.[119] It identifies the social inequities that coexist with formally egalitarian regimes by falling beneath the ambit of law, most often experienced by minority populations poorly represented and poorly defended by difference-blind egalitarianism.[120] Mill astutely perceived that society itself "practises a social tyranny more formidable than many kinds of political oppression, since, though not usually upheld by such extreme penalties, it leaves fewer means of escape, penetrating much more deeply into the details of life, and enslaving the soul itself."[121] Millian liberalism's sensitivity to the harms of social conditioning, historical inequality and customary practices captures these more insidious forms of injustice, and treats them as remediable by state intervention. The Millian defense of liberty thus endeavors to shelter citizens from sub-legal forms of oppression ("the tyranny of the prevailing opinion and feeling") as much as from the domination of political majorities ("acts of the public authorities").[122]

Not unrelatedly, Millian liberalism integrates core arguments and insights of the capabilities approach pioneered by Amartya Sen and Martha Nussbaum: that justice concerns the well-being of citizens – their real capacity to live fulsome, self-directed and self-actualizing lives – and not just their equal rights, understood strictly as opportunity-concepts.[123] Mill's moral, political, psychological and economic writings revolve around the common practical-normative aim of enabling citizens to realize and develop themselves. From treating government as fostering citizens' "active" faculties (in *Considerations* and *Utilitarianism*), to resisting laissez-faire market boosterism and advocating economic redistribution to advance the working class (in *Principles of Political Economy*), to championing widespread education (in *On Liberty*), to analyzing the formation (in the *System of Logic*) and deformations (in the *Subjection of Women*) of human character, Mill's thought is intrinsically attuned to human flourishing and responsive to its impediments. As we have seen, Mill's liberalism raises social and political ends over the analytical rigidity characterizing Kant's and many neo-Kantian liberalisms; Millian liberalism inherits this practical orientation and is likewise more concerned with citizens' capabilities to satisfy their goods and ambitions than with furnishing first principles governing any and all liberal polities. Millian liberalism, then (a) takes citizens' capacities for self-fulfillment as a central object of concern, (b) recognizes the legal and sub-legal social barriers and pressures hampering them, and (c) understands the task of social and political institutions as redressing them. It does not conceive of justice in terms of ideal-type rights and institutional arrangements abstracted from social and historical realities, or as adequately realized through opportunity rights and blind equalities often associated with liberal neutralism and fairness.

Finally, Millian liberalism is necessarily self-reflexive. Despite its inclination toward valuing diversity and difference, Mill's liberalism evidently and egregiously fails to do so at points. This serves as a cautionary tale: for all of its implicit openness to cultural pluralism, Mill's liberalism remains shot through with chauvinisms, inequalities and exclusions. Particular liberalisms' conceptual frames may push in certain directions, but they remain pliable, sustaining both liberalism's open-endedness and its constant possibility of failure. Mill's deficiencies are an important reminder for Millian liberalism: whatever their progressive tendencies, all liberalisms, like all political philosophies, court domination, injustice and intolerance. As an effort to reconstruct the best of Mill's liberalism without neglecting its limitations, Millian liberalism strives to be acutely conscious of, and vigilant toward, its own shortcomings and blind spots.

What, then, of Kantian liberalism?

As I have argued, the Kantian orientation leaves little conceptual space to acknowledge the internal value of diversity: non-European cultures are legible only as immature, irrational and aberrant, and non-European races, as instruments of a purposive natural history anchored by humanity's moralization. Kant's frequent invocations of morally salient racial characteristics (Negroes' cognitive ceiling, Amerindians' developmental stuntedness, etc.) are certainly troubling, but the teleological framework shaping his response to pluralism more broadly is the real problem, suffocating any possibility of envisioning human diversity in terms that might register its worth. If we take Kant's full theorization of our moral nature, as he laid it out – incorporating both our transcendental freedom as rational beings and our lifelong moral evolution as phenomenal ones – it appears difficult to uncouple his moral system's egalitarian pretensions from its limitations. A simple way of mapping the distinction between Kant and Mill on this front is this. If we remove Mill's parochial assessments of given cultural groups – Indians, Basques, the Chinese and so on – from his account of human development, its philosophical coherence remains and its structure is unaffected. If we do the same for Kant, his theorization of our moral nature and moral progress lapses into unintelligibility. The movement from nature to freedom is, for Kant, *precisely* humanity's evolution from unenlightened, "raw," non-European social forms to the cultured civilizations cradling the dominion of reason. That movement *is* our moral and political vocation, and is incoherent outside of its racial and culturalist presumptions. We can certainly extricate or bracket that developmentalism from the moral theory inspiring neo-Kantians, but it's unclear how Kantian such a liberalism remains. "If we lift Kant's concept of the person out of his system," Anthony La Vopa reflects, "what gives it philosophical cogency?"[124]

It's also unclear how successful this bracketing is. Without reproducing his chauvinisms, Kant's closure to pluralism nonetheless shades and reverberates in neo-Kantian liberalisms. Kennan Ferguson observes that Rawls, for instance, takes social diversity as liberalism's central challenge, an obstacle that a well-calibrated theory of justice mitigates. Pluralism is a "fact," and "liberalism's responsibility is to deal most humanely with the difficulties this fact engenders."[125] From the Rawlsian standpoint, diversity is an impediment to liberal political stability to be endured (at least, in its "reasonable" forms), reflecting Kantianism's "idealistic monism"[126] and "the absolutism demanded by Kantian ... thought."[127] Kant, we have seen, treats social differences as remainders, irrationalities transcended in a civilized, well-governed republic. While Rawls's liberalism has no share in those prejudices, it reflects its bearing: it seeks to contain, domesticate or expulse forms of difference depicted as threats to social order and liberal government. Pluralism remains "a necessary evil, an unfortunate aspect of the human condition that often necessitates amelioration" through legal or institutional measures aiming at "the camouflage or dissolution of disagreement."[128] Like Kant, Kantian liberalism is indisposed toward heterogeneity, which it incorporates through an institutionalism "that can either negotiate the claims and counterclaims that plurality creates, or that can declare certain of these claims alien to civil society and prohibit them."[129] Rawls ultimately encounters diversity as a problem to be managed and enclosed – to be tolerated by liberal institutions that, in Wendy Brown's words, regulate aversion.[130] Kantian liberalism has little capacity to see the worth of different ways of living and being, treating them as private matters whose thorny edges, in the best possible case, might be sufficiently dulled to avoid chipping away at liberalism's fragile social and political consensus.

William Connolly elucidates further conceptual impoverishments bequeathed from Kant to Kantian liberalism. For Connolly, the apodictic certainty that Kant claims for the moral law's authority, along with its impulsions to unity, systematicity and universality, are recast in "Kantian, neo-Kantian, and secular drives to simplicity and singularity in public life [that] do not cope subtly enough with the complexity and multifaceted character of actually existing ethical issues."[131] The trouble lies in Kantian liberalism's ambition to "secure the Kantian effect by Kantian and/or non-Kantian means"[132] – that is, to narrowly circumscribe the liberal public sphere's boundaries, securing it from the heterodoxies of ethics, religion, non-rationalist speech and "comprehensive doctrines." This widespread tendency and neo-Kantianism's spread more generally produce at least two problems, both closing it to difference and diversity.

First, Kantianism's overwhelming preponderance since the 1970s has contracted our vision, eclipsing the diverse theoretical vantage points – "the pre-Kantian philosophies of Epicurianism, Spinozism, and Humeanism,"[133] or the Millianism that I have elaborated – which might widen our moral and political horizons. Debates surrounding Kantian liberalisms' internecine minutiae have diminished the scope of political theory, thinning the theoretical resources and perspectives available to us. Second, the neo-Kantian public sphere excludes forms of discourse often employed by minority and subaltern populations, making it not just unresponsive to their concerns, but also unconscious of the registers of injustice to which they are subject. "Rational" and "reasonable" speech are neither neutral nor commonly shared across cultures; they presuppose a familiarity and ease with modes of discourse rooted in specific social, philosophical, educational and ideational backgrounds. As Iris Marion Young observes, "neutral, universal, and dispassionate expression actually carries the rhetorical nuances of particular situated social positions and relations,"[134] alienating groups whose racial, cultural, religious, sexual and/or gender-related orientations set them outside of public reason's normative universe. The neo-Kantian public sphere is thus unreceptive to marginalized citizens' often "heteronomous" claims for justice precisely because of its constrained notion of linguistic competence, the de-transcendentalized inheritance of Kant's own universalistic – and ultimately insular – notion of reason. The Kantian "temptation to purity"[135] – moral and metaphysical in Kant's case, institutional and linguistic in neo-Kantians' – renders voices outside its sphere of intelligibility inaudible and runs through its "theories of morality, ranging from the Kantian model of command through the Habermasian model of deliberative ethics and the Rawlsian model of justice."[136] Kantian liberalism tends toward a cultural shortsightedness not identical, but nonetheless analogous, to Kant's: it has difficulty stepping out of its own skin to see lifeworlds and languages beyond its over-confident normative bubble.

These limitations also emerge in neo-Kantian theories of global justice, which, following their point of origin, fold "an element of European superiority and dogmatism into cosmopolitanism."[137] The moral certainty and normative authority underpinning Kant's philosophy of right generates cosmopolitanisms and visions of international order that cope poorly with cultural difference. Charles Beitz, for instance, defends an explicitly parochial account of universal human rights whose violation, he argues, warrants international (western) intervention. Echoing Kant in certain regards and exceeding him in others, Beitz justifies "paternalistic interference" into recalcitrant states on the basis of "what it would be rational for people to want if they were in possession of full information and able to reason freely."[138] As Connolly sees it, and as Beitz's view appears to confirm, "Kantian cosmopolitanism cannot tolerate plural sources of morality," which, in an age of deep plurality, "throws into question the model of cosmopolitanism derived from it."[139] This model's congenital idealism and monism, along with its faith in the indisputability of select core rights, also surface in Rawls's schematization of liberal, decent and variously indecent peoples.[140] As he stipulates quite directly, the function of human rights in his cosmopolitanism is precisely to "set a moral limit to pluralism among peoples"[141] – to delimit acceptable and unacceptable forms of plurality on the basis of a preordained normative standard. The problem here doesn't relate to Kant's closed-mindedness toward non-Europeans, but rather concerns the narrowness of his conceptualization of right, parroted as universal and echoed in contemporary cosmopolitanisms. The problem is at the center of his cosmopolitanism, with the philosophical apparatus itself, and not with its externalities. It lies in an overconfident moral order transmuted, in neo-Kantian cosmopolitanisms, into a fixed set of rights whose particularistic foundations – the product of a specific philosophical, cultural and political tradition – do little to shake their claim to universalism. These cosmopolitanisms "carry within them elements of a dogmatic Western imperialism still in need of reconstruction," which, Connolly argues, requires that they "relinquish the demand that all reasonable people in all cultures must actually or implicitly recognize the logic of morality in the same way Kant did. Or even as neo-Kantian universalists do ... this cultural particularism can no longer pretend to set the universal matrix of cosmopolitanism itself."[142]

Kantian liberalism isn't just inflected by Kant's substantive views, but also by his methods. It inherits his understanding of moral and political theory's task, and its antipathy toward the messy, heteronomous and *political* features of political life. Kant imparts a particular way of thinking about ethics and politics that sidesteps the dreck of phenomenality: our duties are, of course, determined a priori, derived from our nature as rational, purposive, end-setting beings with a capacity for autonomous self-determination. Political entitlements and obligations are generated by the innate right of humanity (freedom), and strictly exclude any consideration relating to our embodied selves. The heteronomous features of human life, then – race, culture, gender, class – have no place in Kant's account of right. They don't belong to the political calculus, falling outside of what we're trying to *do* when thinking about politics, justice and right. For Kant, ethical and political thought set aside sensibility in order to divine the transcendental grounds of rights and duties: both the spirit of the law (applied internally, the basis of practical ethics) and its letter (applied externally, the basis of right) are determined free from corporeal admixture, in strict isolation from questions of application treated by moral psychology and pragmatic anthropology.

This orientation toward the work of political theory – fixing principles of justice in abstraction from social realities – shapes neo-Kantian analytic liberalism, and is particularly clear in its central figure, Rawls. Rawlsian liberalism's basic approach adopts Kant's conception of moral and political thinking by bracketing a people's sociological, historical and cultural character to determine the precepts governing a just liberal order. Those non-ideal features are deferred to a later stage of "application" in which the veil of ignorance is progressively lifted to reveal the substance of social and political life, but have no part in settling principles of justice – the real work of political theory. "The reason for beginning with ideal theory," Rawls maintains, "is that it provides, I believe, the only basis for the systematic grasp of these more pressing problems ... that we are faced with in everyday life," best adjudicated by higher-order, self-standing "principles of justice that would regulate a well-ordered society."[143] This stance is shared by other neo-Kantians, such as Adam Swift, convinced that "we need fundamental, context-independent normative philosophical claims to guide political action even in nonideal circumstances."[144] As with Kant, then, Kantian liberals understand political theory as developing a priori dicta for just polities whose more particular contours are concerns for another time and for other people (not, presumably, philosophers).[145] And as with Kant, this framing of the kinds of things preoccupying liberal political theory renders racial and cultural diversity invisible. To think politically is precisely to work through principles of justice preceding the mere "facts" of racial, cultural and social pluralism. In Kantian liberalism, McCarthy notes, "there is no longer any attempt to justify or accommodate racial subordination within a putatively universalistic framework. Instead, the treatment of this persistent feature of the messy political reality we inhabit tends to be consigned to the province of 'nonideal theory'."[146] The Rawlsian framework isolates gender, race and class from liberalism's theoretical core, a secondary set of concerns that primary principles accommodate, rather than constitutive matters of justice and politics.

And as Charles Mills points out, ideal theory's myopia is hardly innocent, willfully obfuscating the inequities faced by subordinated populations by abstracting away from the circumstances sustaining systemic disenfranchisement.[147] Kantian liberalism in the Rawlsian vein, Mills argues: (a) advances an ideal-type social ontology that neglects long-term, structural domination, (b) naturalizes particular social and political capacities, neglecting their ties to privilege, (c) disregards historical oppressions and their ongoing impacts, (d) assumes idealized social institutions (the family, the economy, the legal system and so on) whose enduring internal biases evaporate, (e) ignores cognitive barriers incurred by social repression, imputing an unproblematic "rationality" and "reasonability" to all citizens and (f) presumes strict compliance with principles of justice.[148] These questionable premises have set the parameters for four decades' worth of ideal theory whose deficits have become entrenched in Anglo-American liberalism. Neo-Kantian ideal theory is, then, "really an *ideology*, a distortional complex of ideas, values, norms, and beliefs that reflects the nonrepresentative interests and experiences of a small minority of the national population – middle-to-upper-class white males – who are hugely *over-represented* in the professional philosophical population."[149] It is a mode of theorizing that cannot and does not capture injustices faced by women and racialized subjects, much less redress them. As Mills astutely observes, women's (justice-based) interests are not served by treating the family in ideal terms shelving its historically constituted and ongoing patriarchal features as "non-ideal," any more than it serves African Americans' (justice-based) interests to discount centuries of white supremacy shaping American institutions.[150] If ideal theory displaces social and political oppressions affecting marginalized populations, pitching its field of analysis at a level of abstraction insensible to them, it is difficult to see how it advances justice. Pervasive, systemic race- and gender-based discriminations obscured by Kantian liberalism's apriorism comprise the *substance* of injustice, not anomalies or irregularities that a right-minded liberalism, derived from sufficiently Archimedean principles, might iron out. If Mill and Mills show us anything, it's that political theory requires historical circumspection; in Kantian liberalism, however, an "idealized model is being represented as capturing the actual reality ... this misrepresentation has been disastrous for an adequate understanding of the real structures of oppression and exclusion that characterize the social and political order. The opting for 'ideal' theory has served to rationalize the status quo."[151]

While Mills retains a faith in the possibility of Kantianism's salvation, Carole Pateman treats contractarianism – characteristic of Kantian liberalism, but not exclusive to it – as implicitly problematic. Rawls's contractarian heuristic models what neutral representatives in the original position would select as principles of justice for a liberal polity, drawing "solely upon basic intuitive ideas that are embedded in the political institutions of a constitutional democratic regime and the public traditions of their interpretation."[152] Rawls's contract, then, like Kant's, turns on an "idea of reason" – metaphysical in the latter case, rooted in the liberal tradition in the former. But given this framing, Pateman points out, "Rawls' task is to find a picture of an original position that will confirm 'our' intuitions about existing institutions, which include patriarchal relations of subordination."[153] Far from being neutral, the liberal "common sense" underpinning the Rawlsian contract incorporates sexist norms and presumptions encoded in the public reason and institutional life of historically male-dominated societies. Without lapsing into the naked sexism of its classical formulations, "[c]ontemporary contract theorists implicitly follow their example [which] goes unnoticed because they subsume feminine beings under the apparently universal, sexually neuter category of the 'individual'."[154] This is the exact trapping of both thinkers' impartiality-by-abstraction, as "Rawls, of course, like Kant before him, inevitably introduces real, embodied male and female beings in the course of his argument."[155] These emerge, for example, in the "heads of families"[156] represented in the original position, or in the particular sexual, gender and family relations assumed by the polity's intergenerational reproduction. Rawls's polity, like Kant's republic, is wedded to patriarchal institutions whose partialities are covered over by their shared appeal to rationalism and neutrality. For Pateman, the social contract's internal logic is also itself dominating by depicting human beings as atomistic monads holding proprietary/property rights over their own bodies. Political society, in this view, is an association of private agents connected by imbricated contractual obligations, which form the basis of social relations. As these are based on domination – I transfer to you, for a time and a price, rights over my body or labor – Pateman reasons, the social contract models an inexorably exploitative politics. Rather than founding a just social order, it enables overlapping relations of domination – and more often than not, historically and in the present, relations of sexual and racial domination.[157]

For Robert Nichols, contractarianism's argumentative form is connected to the dispossession of indigenous peoples. "[S]ocial contract theory," he argues, "has served as a primary justificatory device for ... an expropriation and usurpation contract whereby the constitution of the ideal civil society is premised upon the extermination of indigenous peoples and/or the displacement of them from their lands."[158] The "settler contract," in Nichols' recasting, "serves to displace questions of the historical instantiation of actual political societies and domains of sovereignty and, as such, has served and continues to serve the function of justifying ongoing occupation of settler societies in indigenous territory."[159] The move to idealization and abstraction plays a "strategic function in relieving the burden of the historical inheritance of conquest,"[160] erasing the traces of concrete imperial violence alongside which contractarianism evolved. The contractual scenario's artifice vaporizes the realities of colonial domination; where is the harm, after all, in occupying what Locke so artfully termed the "vacant places of *America*"?[161] Contemporary contractarians such as Rawls, Nozick and Waldron extend the logic, bowdlerizing indigenous claims to sovereignty by adjudicating them as property relations *within* western legal, political and normative frameworks, rather than as disputes *between* independent nations. The problem is not, of course, exclusive to Kantian liberalism, and neither does it commit Kantian liberals to any particular course of action. But it speaks to its orientation, representing yet another way that it fails to capture the concerns of, and harms to, marginalized and non-western populations.

Finally, the Kantian-Rawlsian portrayal of liberalism as endemic to an enclosed and inward-looking west casts it in particularly emaciated terms.

Rawls quite self-consciously treats liberalism's values and commitments – autonomy, liberty, toleration, individualism – as the particular provenance of a western, liberal democratic heritage. But the presumption of their inherency in a self-standing western European and Christian "tradition" takes them as emanating from strictly inter-European exchanges, neglecting their transnational entanglements through colonialism, empire, global commerce, international legal orders and so on, and as the exclusive purview of the West. This obscures liberalism's internationalism: liberal ideals developed neither solely in Europe, nor from Europeans in isolation from the rest of the world. Postcolonial scholars have long recognized its multi-valent and outward-facing constitution, and global intellectual historians have further de-parochialized it by uncovering its articulations and resonances in a wide range of non-western contexts.[162] Echoing Kant's presumptions, the Rawlsian supposition of liberalism's innately Euro-American character disregards its variable and transnational composition, reinforcing the reductive misperception of its principles and ideals as specifically western.

Kantian liberalism, then, comprises an altogether narrow vision of what liberal political thought is, what it should be, and what it might aim at. Liberalism is a capacious, inconclusive and multifaceted tradition of moral and political theory, as deep as it is wide. It does not necessarily eschew eudaimonism or perfectionism, as its strictly neutralist proponents insist it should, but can, and frequently does, advance substantive views on particular ways of being – it makes space for public virtue. It can also, and frequently does, register the depth and worth of social, cultural and political plurality. It values individuals and individualism without treating them as unencumbered or as rational egoists, and it is not reducible to market-driven proto-neoliberalism. In its more fruitful instantiations, it does not submit to convergent historicisms fixing social and political futures, and it need not be monocultural, even if many of its prevalent articulations, historically and today, have been (and continue to be).

What we lose in a world dominated by neo-Kantianism, in short, is liberalism's richness – the profundity and variability of a body of ideas poorly captured by the single-minded ambition to root out the right principles of justice. Kantianism's preponderance has reduced liberalism to little more than analytical chair-shuffling on the deck of the Rawlsian ship, when it is so much fuller a repository for political reflection. Millian liberalism, then, also widens the terms of liberalism itself – our view of what liberalism is, and might be. It understands political thinking differently. Millian liberalism joins the realist turn in political theory's resistance to neo-Kantian approaches, harboring a methodological antipathy toward conceiving of it in terms of ideal theory, or as applied moral philosophy.[163] Liberalism is not contained by the Kantian framework bequeathed by Rawls, and neither should we limit ourselves to its terms, premises and ambitions, all of which Millian liberalism emphatically rejects.

In an effort to decolonize the foundations critical theory, Amy Allen reflects on the ideal of progress central to the dispossession, colonization and subjugation of non-Europeans throughout the modern era, and still today. Historicism remains a central feature of our political imagination; it's difficult to envision what a politics might look like entirely shorn of it. Instead, Allen proposes a more tentative, self-critical and contingent version. A non-dominating ideal of progress, she argues, is

understood in contingent rather than necessary, disaggregated rather than total, and postmetaphysical rather than metaphysical terms. To say that progress is contingent is to say that whether or not any particular culture or society will in fact progress is a matter of contingent historical circumstances, and that regressions are always also possible. To say that it is disaggregated is to say that progress in one domain – say, the economic or technical-scientific sphere – can occur simultaneously with regress in another – say, the cultural or political sphere. To say that progress is understood in postmetaphysical terms is to say that the conception of the end toward which progress aims is understood in a deflationary, fallibilistic and de-transcendentalized way, as a hypothesis about some fundamental features of human sociocultural life – the role that mutual understanding plays in language, or that mutual recognition plays in the formation of identity – that stands in need of empirical confirmation.[164]

Mill's liberalism did not, of course, treat progress and difference in these exact terms. But it was an awful lot closer than we might have expected, and still more so in Millian liberalism.

NOTES

1. Skinner, "Meaning and Understanding."
2. For an incisive overview of these and other historical injustices and their contemporary legacies, see James Tully, "On Global Citizenship," in *On Global Citizenship: James Tully in Dialogue* (London: Bloomsbury Academic, 2014), 3–102.
3. David Scott, "The Social Construction of Postcolonial Studies," in *Postcolonial Studies and Beyond*, eds. Ania Loomba, Suvir Kaul, Matti Bunzl and Antoinette Burton (Durham, Duke University Press, 2005), 392. For Scott's fuller elaboration of problem-spaces, see David Scott, *Conscripts of Modernity: The Tragedy of Colonial Enlightenment* (Durham: Duke University Press, 2004).
4. I focus here on the literature treating liberalism and empire specifically. For a comprehensive survey of political thought and empire more generally, see Jennifer Pitts, "Political Theory of Empire and Imperialism," *Annual Review of Political Science* 13 (2010): 211–235.
5. Scott, "Social Construction," 391.
6. Ibid., 391–392.
7. Ibid.
8. Ibid., 391.

9. For a fuller rejection of postcolonial theory (focused on the Subaltern Studies Collective), see Chibber, *Specter of Capitalism*; for a forceful and persuasive rejoinder, see Partha Chatterjee's rebuttal: www.youtube.com/watch? v=xbM8HJrxSJ4.

10. For just a few seminal contextualist arguments, see Skinner, "Meaning and Understanding"; John Dunn, "The Identity of the History of Ideas," *Philosophy* 43, no. 164 (1968): 85–104; and Pocock, "History of Political Thought." For a range of textualist views, see Leo Strauss, "Persecution and the Art of Writing," *Social Research* 8, no. 4 (1941): 488–504; Jeremy Waldron, "What Plato Would Allow," *Nomos* 37 (1995): 138–178; and Ronald Beiner, "Textualism: An Anti-Methodology," in *Political Theory: The State of the Discipline*, ed. Evangelia Sembou (Newcastle upon Tyne: Cambridge Scholars, 2013), 22–35. For the fountainhead of genealogical-Foucaultian approaches to history, politics and empire, see Said, *Orientalism*.

11. Patchen Markell, "Unexpected Paths: On Political Theory and Method," *Theory & Event* 19, no. 1 (2016).

12. Jack Turner, "Thinking Historically," *Theory & Event* 19, no. 1 (2016). For lucid reflections on historical scholarship in political theory, see contributions to this issue of *Theory & Event* by Jeanne Morefield, Keally McBride and Samuel Moyn.

13. Zammito, *Birth of Anthropology*, 13; Morefield, *Empires without Imperialism*, 23–25.

14. Max Horkheimer and Theodor W. Adorno, *Dialectic of Enlightenment: Philosophical Fragments* (Stanford: Stanford University Press, 2002).

15. Stuart Hall, "When Was 'the Postcolonial'? Thinking at the Limit," in *The Post-Colonial Question: Common Skies, Divided Horizons*, eds. I. Chambers and L. Curtis (London: Routledge, 1996), 249.

16. Gyan Prakash, "Postcolonial Criticism and Indian Historiography," *Social Text* 31/32 (1992): 8.

17. Bowden, "The Ebb and Flow," 93. For a similar argument regarding racism's constitutive place in western and liberal political thought, see David Theo Goldberg, *Racist Culture: Philosophy and the Politics of Meaning* (Malden: Wiley-Blackwell, 1993).

18. Barbara Bush, *Imperialism and Postcolonialism* (Harlow: Pearson Education, 2006), 3–4.

19. Against this, Georgios Varouxakis traces the origins of "the west," as a specific sociopolitical concept, to Auguste Comte's inward-looking reflections on the future of European, American and Australian social organization, which in fact sought to "abolish empires of conquest," along with "all forceful interference in the affairs of other countries or civilizations" (Georgios Varouxakis, "The Godfather of 'Occidentality': Auguste Comte and the Idea of 'the West'," *Modern Intellectual History*, doi: 10.1017/S1479244317000415).

20. Mehta, *Liberalism and Empire*, 104.

21. Ibid., 25.

22. James Tully, "Lineages of Contemporary Imperialism," in *Lineages of Empire: The Historical Roots of British Imperial Thought*, ed. Duncan Kelly (Oxford: Oxford University Press, 2009), 8–10.

23. James Tully, *Public Philosophy in a New Key, Vol. II: Imperialism and Civic Freedom* (Cambridge: Cambridge University Press, 2008), 149.

24. Andrew Sartori, "The British Empire and Its Liberal Mission," *The Journal of Modern History* 78, no. 3 (2006): 626.
25. Dussel, "Eurocentrism and Modernity," 65–67. For Dussel's fuller critique of Eurocentrism and development, see his *Philosophy of Liberation*.
26. Walter Mignolo, "The Many Faces of Cosmo-polis: Border Thinking and Critical Cosmopolitanism," *Public Culture* 12, no. 3 (2000): 722. For a fuller argument treating coloniality as the root of modernity (and not the other way around), see Aníbal Quijano, "Coloniality and Modernity/Rationality," *Cultural Studies* 21 (2007): 168–178, and Aníbal Quijano, "Coloniality of Power, Eurocentrism, and Latin America," *Neplanta: Views from South* 1 (2000): 533–580.
27. Chakrabarty, *Provincializing Europe*, 4.
28. McCarthy, *Race, Empire*, 1.
29. For an example of treating modernity as agentive, see Janet Conway and Jakeet Singh, "Radical Democracy in Global Perspective: Notes from the Pluriverse," *Third World Quarterly* 32, no. 4 (2011): 690, and Partha Chatterjee, *The Nation and Its Fragments: Colonial and Postcolonial Histories* (Princeton: Princeton University Press, 1993).
30. Frederick Cooper, *Colonialism in Question: Theory, Knowledge, History* (Berkeley: University of California Press, 2005), 17.
31. Robert Stam and Ella Shohat, "Travelling Multiculturalism," in *Postcolonial Studies and Beyond*, eds. Ania Loomba, Suvir Kaul, Matti Bunzl and Antoinette Burton (Durham: Duke University Press, 2005), 298. Antony Anghie similarly ties Bush's bluster to "the rhetoric used by Vitoria to justify the Spanish conquest of the Indians"; see Antony Anghie, "The Evolution of International Law: Colonial and Postcolonial Realities," *Third World Quarterly* 27, no. 5 (2006): 750.
32. Mehta, *Liberalism and Empire*, 25–26.
33. Ibid., 12.
34. Metcalf, *Ideologies*, 29.
35. David Scott, *Refashioning Futures: Criticism After Postcoloniality* (Princeton: Princeton University Press, 1999), 155.
36. Bell, *Reordering the World*, 21.
37. Tully, *Public Philosophy*, 143.
38. Ibid., 6.
39. Ibid., 34.
40. McCarthy, *Race, Empire*, 179.
41. Parekh, "Liberalism and Colonialism," 97.
42. Chakrabarty, *Provincializing Europe*, 42.
43. Michael C. Desch, "Benevolent Cant? Kant's Liberal Imperialism," *Review of Politics* 73, no. 4 (2011): 655.
44. Scott, *Refashioning Futures*, 156.
45. Mehta, *Liberalism and Empire*, 48; and Mehta, "Liberal Strategies of Exclusion," 429.
46. Mehta, *Liberalism and Empire*, 47.
47. Ibid.
48. Ibid., 4.
49. Ibid., 20.

50. Another variant takes one liberal – Kant for McCarthy and Tully, Mill for Mehta and Parekh – to exemplify liberalism's central deficit or exclusionary impulse and extends it to the liberal tradition more generally.

51. Tully, "Lineages," 27.

52. Parekh, "Superior People," "Decolonizing Liberalism" and "Liberalism and Colonialism."

53. McCarthy, *Race, Empire*, 169.

54. Desch, "Benevolent Cant," 649–650.

55. Bernard Semmel, *The Liberal Ideal and Demons of Empire: Theories of Empire from Adam Smith to Lenin* (Baltimore: Johns Hopkins University Press, 1993); Brett Bowden, *The Empire of Civilization: The Evolution of an Imperial Idea* (Chicago: University of Chicago Press, 2009), 74.

56. Singh, "Colonial Pasts." For an overview of postcolonial critiques of developmentalism, see Duncan Ivison, *Postcolonial Liberalism* (Cambridge: Cambridge University Press, 2002).

57. McCarthy, "Multicultural Cosmopolitanism," 95.

58. Mehta, *Liberalism and Empire*, 199; Tully, *Public Philosophy*, 16.

59. Dussel, "Eurocentrism and Modernity," 67.

60. Chakrabarty, *Provincializing Europe*, 7.

61. For just a few critiques of neocolonialism, see Dussel, *Philosophy of Liberation*; Tully, *Public Philosophy*; and Anghie, *Imperialism and Sovereignty*.

62. Sartori, "British Empire," 626–627. For a more focused analysis of western philosophies' colonial underpinnings, see Burke Hendrix, "The Political Dangers of Western Philosophical Approaches," in *The Oxford Handbook of Indigenous Peoples' Politics*, eds. Jose Antonio Lucero, Dale Turner and Donna Lee VanCott (published online January 2013, doi: 10.1093/oxfordhb/9780195386653.001.0001).

63. For a sweeping analysis of liberalism predicated on almost all such elisions, see Losurdo, *Liberalism: A Counter-History*. For a comprehensive account of empire's conceptual complexities, see Bell, *Reordering the World*.

64. Frederick Cooper, "Postcolonial Studies and the Study of History," in *Postcolonial Studies and Beyond*, eds. Ania Loomba, Suvir Kaul, Matti Bunzl and Antoinette Burton (Durham: Duke University Press, 2005), 405.

65. Cooper, *Colonialism in Question*, 4.

66. Cooper, "Study of History," 406.

67. Cooper, *Colonialism in Question*, 19.

68. Cooper, "Study of History," 407.

69. For non-liberal justifications of nineteenth-century British imperialism, see Bell, *Reordering the World*.

70. Cooper, *Colonialism in Question*, 17.

71. Cooper, "Study of History," 412.

72. Ann Laura Stoler and Frederick Cooper, "Between Metropole ande Colony: Rethinking a Research Agenda," in *Tensions of Empire: Colonial Cultures in a Bourgeois World* (Berkeley: University of California Press, 1997), 33.

73. For a few such recent works in global intellectual history, see Samuel Moyn and Andrew Sartori, eds., *Global Intellectual History* (Columbia: Columbia University Press, 2015); Shruti Kapila, ed., *An Intellectual History for India* (Cambridge:

Cambridge University Press, 2010); Andrew Sartori, *Liberalism in Empire: An Alternative History* (Berkeley: University of California Press, 2014); Murad Idris, *War for Peace: Genealogies of a Violent Ideal in Western and Islamic Thought* (New York: Oxford University Press, 2018); and Bayly, *Recovering Liberties*. For a lucid treatment of "alternative visions of the universal" developed by non-Europeans in colonial contexts, see Adom Getachew, "Universalism after the Post-Colonial Turn: Interpreting the Haitian Revolution," *Political Theory*, doi: 10.1177/0090591716661018.

74. Cooper, *Colonialism in Question*, 25.
75. For an examination of colonial subjects' agency across a wide range of contexts, see Burke A. Hendrix and Deborah Baumgold, eds., *Colonial Exchanges: Political Theory and the Agency of the Colonized* (Manchester: Manchester University Press, 2017).
76. Pitts, *Empire*; Mantena, *Alibis of Empire*.
77. Muthu, *Enlightenment Against Empire*.
78. Herbert Spencer, *Social Statics: Or, the Conditions Essential to Human Happiness Specified, and the First of them Developed* (London: John Chapman, 1860), 368.
79. Herbert Spencer, *Facts and Comments* (New York: D. Appleton and Co., 1902), 167.
80. Bayly, *Recovering Liberties*, 1.
81. Ibid., 343.
82. For a careful examination of the diversity of nineteenth-century historicisms responding to liberal imperialism's contradictions, see Theodore Koditschek, *Liberalism, Imperialism, and the Historical Imagination: Nineteenth-Century Visions of a Greater Britain* (Cambridge: Cambridge University Press, 2011).
83. For developmentalist arguments in Indian anti-imperialism, see Inder S. Marwah, "Provincializing Progress: Developmentalism and Anti-Imperialism in Colonial India," *Polity*, forthcoming.
84. Parekh, "Decolonizing Liberalism," 92.
85. Ibid., 94.
86. McCarthy, *Race, Empire*, 14.
87. Markell, "Unexpected Paths."
88. Turner, "Thinking Historically."
89. Ibid.
90. Appiah, *Ethics of Identity*, xvii.
91. Charles Mills's theorization of a "black radical liberalism" similarly pursues the conviction that these conceptual tools (and traditions of thought), "[f]ar from being monolithic ... should be regarded as a general category extending over many different variants," some advancing non-dominating politics (Charles W. Mills, "Black Radical Kantianism," *Res Philosophica* 95 (2018): 2).
92. Butler, *Excitable Speech*, 89.
93. Tully, "Global Citizenship," 4–5.
94. C. B. McPherson, *The Political Theory of Possessive Individualism: Hobbes to Locke* (Oxford: Clarendon Press, 1962).
95. See Barbara Arneil, *John Locke and America: The Defence of English Colonialism* (Oxford: Clarendon Press, 1996); Barbara Arneil, "The Wild Indian's Venison: Locke's Theory of Property and English Colonialism in America," *Political Studies* 44, no. 1 (1996): 60–74; David Armitage, "John Locke, Carolina, and the Two

Treatises of Government," *Political Theory* 32, no. 5 (2004): 602–627; Duncan Ivison, "Locke, Liberalism and Empire," in *The Philosophy of John Locke: New Perspectives*, ed. Peter R. Anstey (London: Routledge, 2003): 86–105; and James Tully, *An Approach to Political Philosophy: Locke in Contexts* (Cambridge: Cambridge University Press, 1993).

96. Sartori, *Liberalism in Empire*.
97. Bayly, *Recovering Liberties*.
98. Tully, "Global Citizenship," 5.
99. Anderson, *Bleak Liberalism*, 9.
100. White, "Liberalism and Multiculturalism," 205.
101. Mill, *System of Logic*, 8:946–947.
102. Ibid., 8:911.
103. Philips, "Troubling Appropriations."
104. Mill, *On Liberty*, 18:230.
105. Mill's recognition of the contingency of moral and political truths is articulated particularly clearly in his critique of he who "devolves upon his own world the responsibility of being in the right against the dissentient worlds of other people; and it never troubles him that mere accident has decided which of these numerous worlds is the object of his reliance, and that the same causes which make him a Churchman in London, would have made him a Buddhist or a Confucian in Pekin" (Mill, *On Liberty*, 18:230).
106. Mill, "Mill to d'Eichthal, Nov. 7, 1829," 12:41–42.
107. Mill, *On Liberty*, 18:272.
108. Mill, "Mill to d'Eichthal, Oct. 8, 1829," 12:36.
109. Mill, *On Liberty*, 18:224.
110. Mill, *Considerations*, 19:383.
111. Mill, *On Liberty*, 18:263.
112. Mill, *Auguste Comte*, 10:303.
113. Ibid., 10:323.
114. Anderson, *Bleak Liberalism*, 22.
115. Mill, "Subjection of Women," 21:276.
116. Ibid., 21:264.
117. Mill, *On Liberty*, 18:301. Mill was acutely conscious and deeply critical of such abuses of the ideal of liberty. "When we compare the strange respect of mankind for liberty, with their strange want of respect for it," he observes acidly, "we might imagine that a man had an indispensable right to do harm to others" (*On Liberty*, 18:304–305).
118. While the feminist literature criticizing the public/private divide is far too expansive to list here, see, for a seminal articulation, Carole Pateman, "Feminist Critiques of the Public/Private Dichotomy," in *Public and Private in Social Life*, eds. Stanley I. Benn and G. F. Gaus (London: St. Martin's Press, 1983).
119. The literature on liberal neutrality/neutralism is also too expansive to list here; for a synoptic view, see Will Kymlicka, "Liberal Individualism and Liberal Neutrality," *Ethics* 99, no. 4 (1989): 883–905.
120. For multiculturalist critiques of difference-blind egalitarianism, see Will Kymlicka, *Multicultural Citizenship: A Liberal Theory of Minority Rights* (Oxford: Oxford University Press, 1995); and Charles Taylor, *Multiculturalism and the Politics of Recognition* (Princeton: Princeton University Press, 1992). For Kantian

liberalism's insensitivity to "incipient" minority voices, see Connolly, *Ethos of Pluralization* and *Secularist*.

121. Mill, *On Liberty*, 18:220.

122. Ibid., 18:219–220.

123. For founding works in the capabilities approach, see Martha Nussbaum, *Women and Human Development: The Capabilities Approach* (Cambridge: Cambridge University Press, 2000); Martha Nussbaum, *Creating Capabilities* (Cambridge: Harvard University Press, 2011); Amartya Sen, *Development as Freedom* (New York: Knopf, 1999); and Amartya Sen, *Commodities and Capabilities* (Amsterdam: North-Holland, 1985).

124. La Vopa, "Thinking About Marriage," 33–34.

125. Kennan Ferguson, *William James: Politics in the Pluriverse* (Lanham: Rowman & Littlefield, 2007), 10.

126. Ibid., 3.

127. Ibid., xxii.

128. Ibid., 5.

129. Ibid., 10.

130. Wendy Brown, *Regulating Aversion: Tolerance in the Age of Identity and Empire* (Princeton: Princeton University Press, 2008).

131. Connolly, *Secularist*, 11.

132. Ibid., 33.

133. Ibid., 32.

134. Iris M. Young, *Inclusion and Democracy* (Oxford: Oxford University Press, 2002), 63.

135. Connolly, *Secularist*, 178.

136. Connolly, *Neuropolitics*, 84.

137. Ibid., 180.

138. Charles Beitz, "Human Rights as a Common Concern," *American Political Science Review* 95, no. 2 (2001): 279.

139. Connolly, *Neuropolitics*, 181–182.

140. John Rawls, *The Law of Peoples: With "The Idea of Public Reason Revisited"* (Cambridge: Harvard University Press, 2008).

141. John Rawls, "The Law of Peoples," *Critical Inquiry* 20 (1993): 59.

142. Connolly, *Neuropolitics*, 183–184.

143. Rawls, *Theory of Justice*, 8.

144. Adam Swift, "The Value of Philosophy in Nonideal Circumstances," *Social Theory and Practice* 34, no. 3 (2008): 363.

145. While Rawls long acknowledged the need to address "urgent" non-ideal questions, why, Charles Mills pithily asks, "in the thirty-plus years up to his death, was he still at the beginning? Why was this promised shift of theoretical attention endlessly deferred, not just in his own writings but in the vast majority of his followers?" (C. W. Mills, "Ideal Theory as Ideology," in *Moral Psychology: Feminist Ethics and Social Theory*, eds. Peggy DesAutels and Margaret Urban Walker (Lanham: Rowman & Littlefield Publishers, 2004), 179). For Mills's sketch of how the Rawlsian contract might be adjusted to advance racial equality, see Charles W. Mills, "Racial Equality," in *The Equal Society: Essays on Equality in Theory and Practice*, ed. George Hull (Lanham: Lexington Books, 2015).

146. McCarthy, *Race, Empire*, 27.
147. To be clear, Mills doesn't suggest that neo-Kantians are themselves *intentionally* closed to these registers of injustice, but rather that they labor under an ideology that conceals them by naturalizing their own privileged position.
148. Mills, "Ideal Theory," 168–169.
149. Ibid., 172.
150. Ibid.
151. Ibid., 181; see also Mills's "Racial Liberalism," 1384–1385. For his now-classic critique of the white supremacy embedded in Rawls's contractarianism, see Charles Mills, *The Racial Contract* (Ithaca: Cornell University Press, 1997). For his updated and far-reaching examination of the racial foundations of liberalism, see Charles Mills, *Black Rights/White Wrongs: The Critique of Racial Liberalism* (Cambridge: Oxford University Press, 2017).
152. John Rawls, "Justice as Fairness: Political not Metaphysical," *Philosophy and Public Affairs* 14, no. 3 (1985): 238.
153. Carole Pateman, *The Sexual Contract* (Stanford: Stanford University Press, 1988), 42.
154. Ibid., 42.
155. Ibid., 43.
156. Rawls, *Theory of Justice*, 111.
157. Carole Pateman and C. W. Mills, *Contract and Domination* (Cambridge: Polity Press, 2007).
158. Robert Nichols, "Indigeneity and the Settler Contract Today," *Philosophy and Social Criticism* 39, no. 2 (2013): 168.
159. Ibid., 169.
160. Ibid.
161. John Locke, *Two Treatises of Government*, ed. Peter Laslett (Cambridge: Cambridge University Press, 1960), 293.
162. See references in fn. 73.
163. For a programmatic view of realist political theory, see Raymond Geuss, *Philosophy and Real Politics* (Princeton: Princeton University Press, 2008). For an overview of its players, themes and insights, see articles by William A. Galston, Matt Sleat, Mark Philp, Richard Bellamy, Richard North, Glen Newey, John Horton and Enzo Rossi in *European Journal of Political Theory* 9, no. 4 (2010).
164. Allen, *End of Progress*, 9.

7

Epilogue

[T]he relative freedom which we enjoy depends on public opinion. The law is no protection. Governments make laws, but whether they are carried out, and how the police behave, depends on the general temper in the country. If large numbers of people are interested in freedom of speech, there will be freedom of speech, even if the law forbids it; if public opinion is sluggish, inconvenient minorities will be persecuted, even if laws exist to protect them.

George Orwell, "Freedom of the Park"

It's a funny time to be writing about liberalism, at a point when few people on the left or right, academic and non-academic, seem to want anything to do with it. If this isn't a moment of crisis for liberalism, it's certainly a crisis of confidence, a low ebb of public and scholarly receptivity to a set of ideas that, for many, land somewhere between irrelevant and bankrupt. On the academic left, critics have drawn out a wide range of harms associated with liberal ideas, texts and thinkers. Most obvious are its associations with empire, colonialism and neocolonialism. As Indigenous peoples' rights gladly gain greater visibility and urgency, liberalism, as the historical and conceptual context often surrounding their longstanding (and ongoing) denial, appears increasingly untenable.[1]

Others writing in the wake of Foucault's 1978–1979 lectures on the birth of biopolitics treat neoliberalism as either identical to liberalism, or as its inevitable outcome – the fullest realization of a world shaped by and to *homo economicus.*[2] Foucault limns the eighteenth-century shift from juridical to economic modes of governmentality – from raison d'état to political economy – constituting liberalism, tracing the imbrications of economic rationality, civil society and political structures. From the Physiocrats through German postwar ordoliberalism and into the present, in liberal orders the economy becomes a self-standing sphere of veridiction encompassing all social and political relations. As colonialism's impacts increasingly come to light, and as the creep of market logic eclipses liberalism's social orientation, both lines of criticism are compelling.

On the popular left, critics denounce a hubristic and overconfident ideology whose moralistic posturing blithely disregards the lived realities of the majority it leaves behind, as the gap widens between cadres of globe-trotting elites and the denizens of fly-over states only too glad to hand them their comeuppance. It's by now a commonplace to acknowledge retrenchments against internationalism, multilateralism and their cognates by citizens excluded from liberalism's largesse, yet judged atavistic for failing to take an appropriately cosmopolitan view. The resulting resentments, William Connolly and Steven White have warned us for years, were entirely predictable.[3] It is, then, unsurprising that scholarly attention has increasingly turned toward decidedly non-liberal political tendencies – namely, fascism and populism.[4] That hard-nosed turn is equally manifest in the growing appeal of explicitly anti-liberal politics (Brexit, the election of Donald Trump, ascendant far-right parties in France, Belgium, Denmark, Poland, Hungary, Austria, Italy, Switzerland and beyond) and political strongmen (Recep Tayyip Erdoğan, Jean-Marie and Marine Le Pen, Viktor Orbán, Jair Bolsonaro, Trump). Liberalism, quite clearly, is on its heels. So why think about it?

It may be at this point, when liberalism's lights are dimmed and its inclinations toward triumphalism chastened, that we can better see its goods, though this requires some circumspection. The standard liberal solution to liberalism's failures, Michael Goodhart and Jeanne Morefield point out, is to prescribe more liberalism (a standpoint they pithily capture as TINA – "there is no alternative"),[5] attributing its failures, as Kant once did, to its state of incompletion. We just need to break down those last few recalcitrants, the story goes, for liberalism to deliver on its promises. Goodhart and Morefield are entirely right to push back: there certainly *are* alternatives to liberalism. But it's worth remembering, too, that there also are alternatives *in* liberalism. This doesn't suggest that liberalism is the right way (much less the only way) to pursue progressive politics, but rather resists the view that it can't be by recovering variants moving us to think critically, self-reflexively and politically.

Millian liberalism comprises just such a standpoint, and one that might elucidate our contemporary condition's illiberality, as Mill understood liberal democracy's dangers all too well. As we have seen, Mill did not treat – forgiving his language – civilization and barbarism as separate, distinct states, the one following the other in a seamless transition underwritten by teleological fiat. He lucidly saw, rather, that regressive impulses remain in any sociological state, needing only the right circumstances to tilt one way or the other. Unchecked, he reminds us, liberal democracies fall into the darkest despotism, their majoritarian bullishness, if encouraged, running roughshod over minorities through law and public opinion. Small-minded nationalism and provincialism are neither liberal anomalies nor externalities, but rather its entrenched and ever-present dangers.

Mill's prescience holds a lesson. If liberality and insularity coexist in perpetuity, we are bound to remain alert to the worse facets of our democratic lives, systems and institutions. Our tendencies to domination, narrowness and exclusion are always just a hair's breadth away, and always turn against the most vulnerable among us. The danger lies in the opposing view, that progress means moving from one social condition to a qualitatively different one – to a post-racial, post-sexist, post-national or postcolonial society that runs no risk of backsliding. It lies in that excess of confidence suggesting that liberal democracy has superseded or transcended – moved past – its limitations, rather than concertedly containing them. Our propensities to generosity and receptivity sit cheek by jowl with those to exclusion, othering and contempt. They may recede, they may wane, but they do not vanish, and the work of democratic public life is to create conditions fostering the former and dampening the latter.

Mill also reminds us of the public-mindedness and civic formation comprising that democratic work, political virtues today in short supply. Democracy depends on public spirit – on an ethos of inclusiveness, engagement and civic care binding citizens to one another and to their institutions. Without it, we fall prey to what Judith Shklar describes as passive injustice, the "specifically civic failure to stop private and public acts of injustice" whose prevention she and Mill both take as "the obligation of citizens of constitutional democracies."[6] Passive injustice captures the dispositional deficits to which democrats are prone with respect to our informal citizenly duties: the habituated neglect of civil responsibilities, treating laws and institutions as inviting acquiescence rather than engagement, the willingness to tolerate small acts of everyday injustice. Democracy works not because of its machinery, but because of its conscience; a passively unjust citizenry is one that doesn't *care* enough about social and political fairness. Despite the century and a quarter separating them, Mill and Shklar share in this liberal-democratic sensitivity. Where Mill regards as democratically unfit

[a] people who are more disposed to shelter a criminal than to apprehend him; who . . . will perjure themselves to screen the man who has robbed them, rather than take trouble or expose themselves to vindictiveness by giving evidence against him; who . . . if a man poniards another in the public street, pass by on the other side, because it is the business of the police to look to the matter, and it is safer not to interfere in what does not concern them,

Shklar sees that "[a]s citizens, we are passively unjust . . . when we do not report crimes, when we look the other way when we see cheating and minor thefts, when we tolerate political corruption, and when we silently accept laws that we regard as unjust, unwise, or cruel."[7]

Passive injustice is, also, a specifically liberal-democratic problem, annexed "to our public roles and their political context – citizenship in a constitutional democracy."[8] In this, Mill and Shklar elicit liberalism's republican tenors, the democratic socialization cultivating public-minded affects, dispositions and habits. Shklar's concerns dovetail with Mill's account of democratic character: citizens who don't care about public life invite injustice into it, failing to live up to their elementary civic duties. True democratic citizenship "finds its glory not simply in the right to political participation but in the democracy of everyday life, in the habits of equality, and the mutuality of ordinary obligations between citizens."[9] All too often, we paint democracy through rights, obligations and institutional arrangements, but its center, for Shklar, lies in its constitutive compassion, the "ineradicable social emotion"[10] provoked by injustice. "[W]ithout this ability to feel the pain of unjust slights, both one's own and other people's," she cogently argues, "the sense of injustice would not be, as it is, the core of the modern democratic political sensibility."[11]

This is the climate of democratic incivility and passive injustice we've come to inhabit. It's a world in which a presidential candidate wears tax evasion as a badge of pride, as though defaulting on basic democratic reciprocity were a sign of acumen; in which this kind of failure of public conscience is rampant, as the Panama Papers revealed, surprising no one; in which denigrating women is acceptable, because it's not against the law; in which undermining citizens' confidence in their political institutions passes for electioneering; in which race-baiting and pandering to public insecurities is par for the course; in which truth and the accountability it ought to entail gives way to what Stephen Colbert has so artfully termed "truthiness"; in which social media, once hailed as enhancing civic capacities, serves to undermine them. It's a world in which the democratic ethos is withered and emaciated, marked by passive injustice denigrating those values – mutuality, fair-mindedness, equality and respect – that sustain a healthy public life. It's a world that not only fails to encourage citizens to "feel the pain of unjust slights," but treats them as fair game. None of this is illegal, but it isn't just either. It shows that liberal democracy can fail while succeeding, and that institutions and laws shelter precious little when the general temper of the country, as Orwell put it, is pervasively illiberal.

Why, then, should we care about liberalism, as many of the world's liberal democracies slope toward injustice? The answer isn't always clear – because of liberalism's mutability, because of its slipperiness, because of its ugliness. But these days, it might be just a little clearer, as we glimpse the implications of abandoning its guiding commitments to individual liberties, a free press, universal rights, political inclusiveness, moral equality, mutual respect and toleration. We can see how their diminishment leaves us worse off, and that despite their many and pronounced failures, we have good reasons to want to pursue certain liberal ambitions. As many of its loftier goals come under attack – recognizing all persons' moral equality, encouraging autonomy and self-direction, resisting intolerance and self-enclosure, guarding against strong-armed politics and authoritarianism – we can perhaps better see their value.

Against this encroaching reclusiveness, against the invocation of spectral bogeymen within and beyond borders, against the denigration of people and peoples, against the scapegoating of difference and diversity, we can better see the best parts of what liberalisms can be, and why they might matter. Liberalism is, of course, by no means the only way of seeking out and realizing these aspirations, but it is one through which they *have* been realized, to the degree that they've been realized, in recent years. When those ideals are drained from our social and political lives, as they have to a great degree been as of late, we better see why liberalism remains worth talking about, and why its better impulses remain worth pursuing.

NOTES

1. For incisive and forceful rejections of liberal approaches to Indigenous justice, see Coulthard, *Red Skin*; Taiaiake Alfred and Jeff Corntassel, "Being Indigenous: Resurgences against Contemporary Colonialism," *Government and Opposition* 40 (2005): 597–614; Gerald Taiaiake Alfred, "Colonialism and State Dependency," *Journal of Aboriginal Health* 5 (2009): 42–60; and Gerald Taiaiake Alfred, "Restitution Is the Real Pathway to Justice for Indigenous Peoples," in *Response, Responsibility and Renewal: Canada's Truth and Reconciliation Journey*, eds. Gregory Younging, Jonathan Dewar and Mike Gagné (Ottawa: Aboriginal Healing Foundation, 2009), 179–187.

2. Michel Foucault, *Naissance de la biopolitique: Cours au College de France (1978–1979)* (Paris: Seuil, 2004). For a sophisticated application of Foucault's analysis to contemporary neoliberalism, see Wendy Brown, *Undoing the Demos: Neoliberalism's Stealth Revolution* (Cambridge MA: MIT Press, 2015). For an argument closely tying liberalism and neoliberalism, see Michael Goodhart and Jeanne Morefield, "Reflection Now! Critique and Solidarity in the Trump Era," *Theory & Event* 20 (2017): 68–85. For the same linkage in the popular press, see Martin Kettle, "Brexit Was a Revolt against Liberalism. We've Entered a New Political Era," *Guardian*, September 15, 2016. For a rejoinder disentangling liberalism and neoliberalism, see David Boyle, "Liberalism Is Still Alive – It's Neoliberalism That's the Problem," *Guardian*, October 3, 2016. For a scholarly rebuttal of neoliberalism's elision with liberalism, arguing that "many of the more considered analyses of neoliberal theory and practice actually invoke forms of liberalism as a counter-ideal" (43), see Anderson, *Bleak Liberalism*.

3. See Connolly, *Ethos of Pluralization*; and White, *Late-Modern Citizen*.

4. For recent analyses of contemporary populism, see Jan-Werner Müller, *What is Populism?* (Philadelphia: University of Pennsylvania Press, 2016) and Cas Mudde and Cristobal Rovira Kaltwasser, *Populism: A Very Short Introduction* (New York: Oxford University Press, 2017). For populism and fascism in the context of Donald Trump's election, see *Theory & Event* 20, no. 1 (January 2017; supplement). For the relationship of liberalism, neoliberalism and populism, see Alessandro Ferrara, "Can Political Liberalism Help Us Rescue 'the People' from Populism?"; Volker Paul, "Populism and the Crisis of Liberalism"; Michael J. Sandel, "Populism,

Liberalism, and Democracy"; Albena Azmanova, "The Populist Catharsis: On the Revival of the Political"; Cemil Boyraz, "Neoliberal Populism and Governmentality in Turkey: The Foundation of Communication Centers During the AKP Era"; Akeel Bilgrami, "Reflections on Three Populisms"; and Lisa Anderson, "Bread, Dignity and Social Justice: Populism in the Arab World," all in *Philosophy & Social Criticism* 44, no. 4 (May 2018).

5. Goodhart and Morefield, "Reflection Now," 71.
6. Shklar, *Faces*, 6.
7. Mill, *Considerations*, 19:377; Shklar, *Faces*, 6.
8. Shklar, *Faces*, 41.
9. Ibid., 43.
10. Ibid., 86.
11. Ibid.

Bibliography

Alexander, Edward. *Matthew Arnold and John Stuart Mill*. London: Routledge, 2012.

Alfred, Gerald Taiaiake. "Colonialism and State Dependency." *Journal of Aboriginal Health* 5 (2009): 42–60.

"Restitution Is the Real Pathway to Justice for Indigenous Peoples." In *Response, Responsibility and Renewal: Canada's Truth and Reconciliation Journey*, eds. Gregory Younging, Jonathan Dewar and Mike Gagné, 179–187. Ottawa: Aboriginal Healing Foundation, 2009.

Alfred, Taiaiake, and Jeff Corntassel. "Being Indigenous: Resurgences against Contemporary Colonialism." *Government and Opposition* 40 (2005): 597–614.

Allen, Amy. *The End of Progress: Decolonizing the Normative Foundations of Critical Theory*. New York: Columbia University Press, 2016.

Allison, Henry. *Kant's Theory of Freedom*. Cambridge: Cambridge University Press, 1990.

"Kant on Freedom: A Reply to My Critics." *Inquiry* 36, no. 4 (1993): 443–464.

Idealism and Freedom: Essays on Kant's Theoretical and Practical Philosophy. Cambridge: Cambridge University Press, 1996.

Kant's Theory of Taste: A Reading of the Critique of Aesthetic Judgement. Cambridge: Cambridge University Press, 2001.

Ameriks, Karl. "The Purposive Development of Human Capacities." In *Kant's "Idea for a Universal History with a Cosmopolitan Aim": A Critical Guide*, eds. Amélie Oksenberg Rorty and James Schmidt, 46–67. Cambridge: Cambridge University Press, 2009.

Anderson, Amanda. *Bleak Liberalism*. Chicago: University of Chicago Press, 2016.

Anderson, Lisa. "Bread, Dignity and Social Justice: Populism in the Arab World." *Philosophy & Social Criticism* 44 (2018): 478–490.

Anderson-Gold, Sharon. *Unnecessary Evil: History and Moral Progress in the Philosophy of Immanuel Kant*. Albany: State University of New York Press, 2001.

Anghie, Antony. *Imperialism, Sovereignty and the Making of International Law*. Cambridge: Cambridge University Press, 2004.

"The Evolution of International Law: Colonial and Postcolonial Realities." *Third World Quarterly* 27, no. 5 (2006): 739–753.

Appiah, Kwame Anthony. *The Ethics of Identity*. Princeton: Princeton University Press, 2005.

Aristotle. *The Politics of Aristotle*, ed. and trans. Ernest Barker. New York: Oxford University Press, 1958.

Armitage, David. "The Fifty Years' Rift: Intellectual History and International Relations." *Modern Intellectual History* 1, no. 1 (2004): 97–109.

"John Locke, Carolina, and the Two Treatises of Government." *Political Theory* 32, no. 5 (2004): 602–627.

Arneil, Barbara. *John Locke and America: The Defence of English Colonialism*. Oxford: Clarendon Press, 1996.

"The Wild Indian's Venison: Locke's Theory of Property and English Colonialism in America." *Political Studies* 44, no. 1 (1996): 60–74.

"Disability, Self-Image and Modern Political Theory." *Political Theory* 37, no. 2 (2009): 218–242.

Arneil, Barbara, and Nancy Hirschmann, eds. *Disability and Political Theory*. Cambridge: Cambridge University Press, 2016.

Arneson, Richard J. "Democracy and Liberty in Mill's Theory of Government." *Journal of the History of Philosophy* 20, no. 1 (1982): 43–64.

"Rawls versus Utilitarianism in the Light of *Political Liberalism*." In *The Idea of a Political Liberalism: Essays on Rawls*, eds. Victoria Davion and Clark Wolf, 231–252. Lanham: Rowman & Littlefield, 1999.

Azmanova, Albena. "The Populist Catharsis: On the Revival of the Political." *Philosophy & Social Criticism* 44 (2018): 399–411.

Balibar, Étienne. "Difference, Otherness, Exclusion." *Parallax* 11, no. 1 (2005): 19–34.

"Racism and Nationalism." In *Nations and Nationalism: A Reader*, eds. Philip Spencer and Howard Wollman, 163–172. New Brunswick: Rutgers University Press, 2005.

Ball, Terence. "The Formation of Character: Mill's 'Ethology' Reconsidered." *Polity* 33, no. 1 (2000): 25–48.

Bellamy, Richard. "Dirty Hands and Clean Gloves: Liberal Ideals and Real Politics." *European Journal of Political Theory* 9, no. 4 (2010): 412–430.

Bannerji, Himani. *Dark Side of the Nation: Essays on Multiculturalism, Nationalism and Gender*. Toronto: Canadian Scholars' Press, 2000.

Baum, Bruce. *Rereading Power and Freedom in J. S. Mill*. Toronto: University of Toronto Press, 2000.

"J. S. Mill and Liberal Socialism." In *J. S. Mill's Political Thought: A Bicentennial Reassessment*, eds. Nadia Urbinati and Alex Zakaras, 98–123. Cambridge: Cambridge University Press, 2007.

"Decolonizing Critical Theory." *Constellations* 22, no. 3 (2015): 420–434.

Baxley, Anne Margaret. "Autocracy and Autonomy." *Kant-Studien*, 94 (2003): 1–23.

Bayly, C. A. *Recovering Liberties: Indian Thought in the Age of Liberalism and Empire*. Cambridge: Cambridge University Press, 2011.

Baynes, John Kenneth. "Kant on Property Rights and the Social Contract." *The Monist* 72 (1989): 433–453.

Beck, Lewis W. "Kant and the Right of Revolution." *Journal of the History of Ideas* 32, no. 3 (1971): 411–422.
"Five Concepts of Freedom in Kant." In *Philosophical Analysis and Reconstruction: A Festrschrift to Stephan Körner*, ed. Jan J. T. Srzednicki. Dordrecht: Martinus Nijhoff, 1987.
Beitz, Charles. "Human Rights as a Common Concern." *American Political Science Review* 95, no. 2 (2001): 269–282.
Berlin, Isaiah. "John Stuart Mill and the Ends of Life." In *Mill's On Liberty in Focus*, eds. John Gray and G. W. Smith, 131–161. London: Routledge, 2015.
Beiner, Ronald. *Liberalism, Nationalism, Citizenship: Essays on the Problem of Political Community*. Vancouver: University of British Columbia Press, 2003.
"Paradoxes in Kant's Account of Citizenship." In *Responsibility in Context: Perspectives*, ed. Gorana Ognjenovic, 19–34. Dordrecht: Springer, 2010.
"Textualism: An Anti-Methodology." In *Political Theory: The State of the Discipline*, ed. Evangelia Sembou, 22–35. Newcastle upon Tyne: Cambridge Scholars Press, 2013.
Bell, Duncan. "Mill on the Colonies." *Political Theory* 38, no. 1 (2010): 34–64.
"What Is Liberalism?" *Political Theory* 42, no. 6 (2014): 682–715.
Reordering the World: Essays on Liberalism and Empire. Princeton: Princeton University Press, 2016.
Bentham, Jeremy. *An Introduction to the Principles of Morals and Legislation*. Oxford: Clarendon Press, 1907.
Berkowitz, Peter. "Mill: Liberty, Virtue, and the Discipline of Individuality." In *Mill and the Moral Character of Liberalism*, ed. Eldon J. Eisenach, 13–48. University Park: Pennsylvania State University Press, 1998.
Benhabib, Seyla. *Another Cosmopolitanism: Hospitality, Sovereignty and Democratic Iterations*. New York: Oxford University Press, 2006.
Bernasconi, Robert. "Who Invented the Concept of Race? Kant's Role in the Enlightenment Construction of Race." In *Race*, 11–36. Malden: Blackwell Publishers, 2001.
"Kant as an Unfamiliar Source of Racism." In *Philosophers on Race: Critical Essays*, eds. Julie K. Ward and Tommy Lee Lott, 145–166. Oxford: Blackwell, 2002.
"Kant's Third Thoughts on Race." In *Reading Kant's Geography*, eds. Stuart Elden and Eduardo Mendieta, 291–318. New York: State University of New York Press, 2011.
Bhabha, Homi. *The Location of Culture*. New York: Routledge, 1994.
Biagini, E. F. "Neo-Roman Liberalism: 'Republican' Values and British Liberalism, ca. 1860–1875." *History of European Ideas* 29, no. 1 (2003): 55–72.
Bilgrami, Akeel. "Reflections on Three Populisms." *Philosophy & Social Criticism* 44 (2018): 453–462.
Bowden, Brett. "The Ebb and Flow of Peoples, Ideas and Innovations: Towards a Global History of Political Thought." In *Western Political Thought in Dialogue with Asia*, eds. Takashi Shōgimen and Cary J. Nederman, 87–108. Lanham: Lexington Books, 2008.
The Empire of Civilization: The Evolution of an Imperial Idea. Chicago: University of Chicago Press, 2009.
Boyle, David. "Liberalism Is Still Alive – It's Neoliberalism That's the Problem." *Guardian*, October 3, 2016.

Boyraz, Cemil. "Neoliberal Populism and Governmentality in Turkey: The Foundation of Communication Centers during the AKP Era." *Philosophy & Social Criticism* 44 (2018): 437–452.

Boxill, Bernard R. *Race and Racism.* Oxford: Oxford University Press, 2001.

Boxill, Bernard R., and Thomas Hill, "Kant and Race." In *Race and Racism,* 448–471. Oxford: Oxford University Press, 2001.

Brandt, Reinhard. "The Guiding Idea of Kant's Anthropology and the Vocation of the Human Being." In *Essays on Kant's Anthropology,* eds. Brian Jacobs and Patrick Kain, 85–104. Cambridge: Cambridge University Press, 2003.

"The Vocation of the Human Being," in *Essays on Kant's Anthropology,* eds. Brian Jacobs and Patrick Kain, 85–104. Cambridge: Cambridge University Press, 2003.

Brown, D. G. "Millian Liberalism and Colonial Oppression." *Canadian Journal of Philosophy* 29 (1999): 79–97.

Brown, Wendy. *Regulating Aversion: Tolerance in the Age of Identity and Empire.* Princeton: Princeton University Press, 2008.

Undoing the Demos: Neoliberalism's Stealth Revolution. Cambridge, MA: MIT Press, 2015.

Buchan, Bruce. "Enlightened Histories: Civilization, War and the Scottish Enlightenment." *The European Legacy* 10, no. 2 (2005): 177–192.

Burns, J. H. "J. S. Mill and Democracy, 1829–61." *Political Studies* 5, no. 2 (1957): 158–175.

Bush, Barbara. *Imperialism and Postcolonialism.* Harlow: Pearson Education, 2006.

Butler, Judith. *Excitable Speech: A Politics of the Performative.* New York: Routledge, 1997.

Capaldi, Nicholas. "The Libertarian Philosophy of John Stuart Mill." *Reason Papers* 9 (1983): 3–19.

John Stuart Mill: A Biography. Cambridge: Cambridge University Press, 2004.

Carlisle, Janice. *John Stuart Mill and the Writing of Character.* Athens: University of Georgia Press, 1991.

"Mr. John Stuart Mill, M.P., and the Character of the Working Classes." In *Mill and the Moral Character of Liberalism,* ed. Eldon Eisenach, 143–168. University Park: Pennsylvania State University Press, 1998.

Carson, Penelope. "Golden Casket or Pebbles and Trash? J. S. Mill and the Anglicist/ Orientalist Controversy." In *J. S. Mill's Encounter with India,* eds. Martin I. Moir, Douglas M. Peers and Lynn Zastoupil, 149–172. Toronto: University of Toronto Press, 1999.

Caswell, Matthew. "Kant's Conception of the Highest Good, the *Gesinnung,* and the Theory of Radical Evil." *Kant Studien* 97, no. 2 (2006): 184–209.

Chakrabarty, Dipesh. *Provincializing Europe: Postcolonial Thought and Historical Difference.* Princeton: Princeton University Press, 2000.

Chatterjee, Partha. *The Nation and Its Fragments: Colonial and Postcolonial Histories.* Princeton: Princeton University Press, 1993.

Chibber, Vivek. *Postcolonial Theory and the Specter of Capital.* London: Verso, 2013.

Ciccariello-Maher, George. *Decolonizing Dialectics.* Durham: Duke University Press, 2017.

Cobbe, Frances Power. "Criminals, Idiots, Women and Minors." Fraser's Magazine for Town and Country 78 (1868): 1–27.

Cohen, Alix. "Kant on Epigenesis, Monogenesis and Human Nature: The Biological Premises of Anthropology." *Studies in History and Philosophy of Biological and Biomedical Sciences* 37 (2006): 675–693.

Kant and the Human Sciences: Biology, Anthropology and History. London: Palgrave Macmillan, 2009.

ed. *Kant's Lectures on Anthropology: A Critical Guide.* Cambridge: Cambridge University Press, 2014.

"Kant on the Moral Cultivation of Feelings." In *Thinking about the Emotions: A Philosophical History*, eds. Alix Cohen and Robert Stern, 172–183. Oxford: Oxford University Press, 2017.

"Rational Feelings." In *Kant and the Faculty of Feeling*, eds. K. Sorensen and D. Williamson, 9–24. Cambridge: Cambridge University Press, 2018.

"Kant on Moral Feelings, Moral Desires and the Cultivation of Virtue." In *Begehren/Desire*, eds. Sally Sedgwick and Dina Emundts, 3–18. Berlin: De Gruyter, 2018.

Coleridge, Samuel Taylor. "On the Constitution of Church and State." In *The Collected Works of Samuel Taylor Coldridge, Volume 10: On the Constitution of Church and State*, ed. John Colmer. Princeton: Princeton University Press, 2015.

Collini, Stefan. "The Idea of Character in Victorian Political Thought." *Transactions of the Royal Historical Society* 35 (1985): 29–50.

Public Moralists: Political Thought and Intellectual Life in Britain. Oxford, Clarendon Press, 1993.

Connolly, William. *The Ethos of Pluralization.* Minneapolis: University of Minnesota Press, 1995.

Why I Am Not a Secularist. Minneapolis: University of Minnesota Press, 1999.

Neuropolitics: Thinking, Culture, Speed. Minneapolis: University of Minnesota Press, 2002.

Capitalism and Christianity, American-Style. Durham: Duke University Press, 2008.

Conway, Janet, and Jakeet Singh, "Radical Democracy in Global Perspective: Notes from the Pluriverse." *Third World Quarterly* 32, no. 4 (2011).

Cooper, Frederick. *Colonialism in Question: Theory, Knowledge, History.* Berkeley: University of California Press, 2005.

"Postcolonial Studies and the Study of History." In *Postcolonial Studies and Beyond*, eds. Ania Loomba, Suvir Kaul, Matti Bunzl and Antoinette Burton, 401–422. Durham: Duke University Press, 2005.

Cooper, Frederick, and Ann Laura Stoler, eds. *Tensions of Empire: Colonial Cultures in a Bourgeois World.* Berkeley: University of California Press, 1997.

Cooke, Vincent M. "Kant, Teleology, and Sexual Ethics." *International Philosophical Quarterly* 31, no. 1 (1991): 3–13.

Coulthard, Glen. *Red Skin, White Masks: Rejecting the Colonial Politics of Recognition.* Minneapolis: University of Minnesota Press, 2014.

Cowling, Maurice. *Mill and Liberalism.* Cambridge: Cambridge University Press, 1990.

Cummiskey, David. "Justice and Revolution in Kant's Political Philosophy." In *Rethinking Kant, Volume I*, ed. Pablo Muchnik, 217–240. Newcastle upon Tyne: Cambridge Scholars Publishing, 2008.

Denis, Lara. "Individual and Collective Flourishing in Kant's Philosophy." *Kantian Review* 13, no. 1 (2008): 82–115.

Desch, Michael C. "Benevolent Cant? Kant's Liberal Imperialism." *Review of Politics* 73, no. 4 (2011): 649–656.

Devigne, Robert. *Reforming Liberalism: J. S. Mill's Use of Ancient, Religious, Liberal, and Romantic Moralities*. New Haven: Yale University Press, 2006.

Dhamoon, Rita. *Identity/Difference Politics: How Difference Is Produced and Why It Matters*. Vancouver: UBC Press, 2009.

Donner, Wendy. *The Liberal Self: John Stuart Mill's Moral and Political Philosophy*. New York: Cornell University Press, 1991.

"Mill's Utilitarianism." In *The Cambridge Companion to Mill*, ed. John Skorupski, 255–292. Cambridge: Cambridge University Press, 1998.

"John Stuart Mill on Education and Democracy." In *J. S. Mill's Political Thought: A Bicentennial Reassessment*, eds. Nadia Urbinati and Alex Zakaras, 250–276. Cambridge: Cambridge University Press, 2007.

"John Stuart Mill and Virtue Ethics." In *John Stuart Mill: Thought and Influence – The Saint of Rationalism*, eds. Georgios Varouxakis and Paul Kelly, 84–98. London: Routledge, 2010.

Donner, Wendy and Richard A. Fullerton. *Mill*. Malden: Wiley-Blackwell, 2009.

Dossa, Shiraz. "Liberal Imperialism? Natives, Muslims and Others." *Political Theory* 30, no. 5 (2002): 738–745.

Du Bois, W. E. B. *The Souls of Black Folk*. London: Penguin, 1996.

Duncan, Graeme. *Marx and Mill: Two Views of Social Conflict and Social Harmony*. Cambridge: Cambridge University Press, 1973.

Dunn, John. "The Identity of the History of Ideas." *Philosophy* 43, no. 164 (1968): 85–104.

Dussel, Enrique. *Philosophy of Liberation*. Maryknoll: Orbis Books, 1985.

"Eurocentrism and Modernity." *Boundary 2* 20, no. 3 (1993): 65–76.

Eggleston, Ben, Dale Miller and David Weinstein, eds. *John Stuart Mill and the Art of Life*. Oxford: Oxford University Press, 2011.

Ellis, Elisabeth. *Kant's Politics: Provisional Theory for an Uncertain World*. New Haven: Yale University Press, 2005.

"Citizenship and Property Rights: A New Look at Social Contract Theory." *The Journal of Politics* 68, no. 3 (2006): 544–555.

Elshtain, Jean Bethke. *Meditations on Modern Political Thought: Masculine/Feminine Themes from Luther to Arendt*. New York: Praeger, 1986.

Engelmann, Stephen G. "Mill, Bentham, and the Art and Science of Government." *Revue d'études Benthamiennes* 4 (2008).

Engstrom, Stephen. "The Concept of the Highest Good in Kant's Moral Theory." *Philosophy and Phenomenological Research* 52, no. 4 (1992): 747–780.

Eze, Emmanuel Chukwudi. "The Color of Reason: The Idea of 'Race' in Kant's Anthropology." In *Anthropology and the German Enlightenment: Perspectives on Humanity*, ed. Katherine M. Faull, 201–241. Lewisburg: Bucknell University Press, 1995.

Ferguson, Kennan. *William James: Politics in the Pluriverse*. Lanham: Rowman & Littlefield, 2007.

Ferguson, Niall. *Empire: How Britain Made the Modern World*. London: Penguin, 2004.

Ferrara, Alessandro. "Can Political Liberalism Help Us Rescue 'the People' from Populism?" *Philosophy & Social Criticism* 44 (2018): 463–477.

Finlay, Graham. "Power and Development: John Stuart Mill and Edmund Burke on Empire." In *Postcolonialism and Political Theory*, ed. Nalini Persram, 57–75. Lanham: Lexington Books, 2007.

Fisher, Mark. "Metaphysics and Physiology in Kant's Attitudes Towards Theories of Preformation." In *Kant's Theory of Biology*, eds. Eric Watkins and Ina Goy, 25–42. Boston: De Gruyter, 2014.

Flikschuh, Katrin. *Kant and Modern Political Philosophy*. Cambridge: Cambridge University Press, 2008.

"Reason, Right and Revolution: Kant and Locke." *Philosophy and Public Affairs* 36, no. 4 (2008): 375–404.

Flikschuh, Katrin, and Lea Ypi, eds. *Kant and Colonialism: Historical and Critical Perspectives*. New York: Oxford University Press, 2014.

Foucault, Michel. *Naissance de la biopolitique: Cours au College de France (1978–1979)*. Paris: Seuil, 2004.

"What Is Enlightenment?" In *The Politics of Truth*, eds. Sylvère Lotringer and John Rajchman, 97–120. Los Angeles: Semiotext(e), 2007.

Formosa, Paul. "All Politics Must Bend Its Knee Before Right." *Social Theory and Practice* 34, no. 2 (2008):157–181.

Frierson, Patrick. *Freedom and Anthropology in Kant's Moral Philosophy*. Cambridge: Cambridge University Press, 2003.

"Kant's Empirical Account of Human Action." *Philosophers' Imprint* 5, no. 7 (2005): 1–34.

"Character and Evil." *Journal of the History of Philosophy* 44, no. 4 (2006): 623–634.

Fukuyama, Francis. *The End of History and the Last Man*. New York: Free Press, 2006.

Galston, William A. "Moral Personality and Liberal Theory: John Rawls's 'Dewey Lectures'." *Political Theory* 10, no. 4 (1982): 492–519.

Liberal Pluralism: The Implications of Value Pluralism for Political Theory and Practice. Cambridge: Cambridge University Press, 2002.

"Realism in Political Theory." *European Journal of Political Theory* 9, no. 4 (2010): 385–411.

Garrett, Aaron. "Anthropology: the 'Original' of Human Nature." In *The Cambridge Companion to the Scottish Enlightenment*, ed. Alexander Broadie. Cambridge, Cambridge University Press, 2003.

Gaus, Gerald and Shane Cortland, "Liberalism." *Stanford Encyclopedia of Philosophy*, December 22, 2014, http://plato.stanford.edu/entries/liberalism/.

Getachew, Adom. "Universalism after the Post-Colonial Turn: Interpreting the Haitian Revolution." *Political* Theory, doi: 10.1177/0090591716661018.

Geuss, Raymond. *Philosophy and Real Politics*. Princeton: Princeton University Press, 2008.

Gibbons, John. "J. S. Mill, Liberalism, and Progress." In *Victorian Liberalism: Nineteenth-Century Political Thought and Practice*, ed. Richard Bellamy, 91–109. London: Routledge, 1989.

Goldberg, David Theo. *Racist Culture: Philosophy and the Politics of Meaning*. Malden: Wiley-Blackwell, 1993.

"Liberalism's Limits: Carlyle and Mill on 'The Negro Question'." *Nineteenth-Century Contexts* 22 (2000): 203–216.

Goodhart, Michael, and Jeanne Morefield. "Reflection Now! Critique and Solidarity in the Trump Era." *Theory & Event* 20 (2017): 68–85.

Gray, John, *Mill on Liberty: A Defence*. London: Routledge, 1996.

"Mill's Conception of Happiness and the Theory of Individuality." In *J. S. Mill's On Liberty in Focus*, eds. John Gray and G. W. Smith (London: Routledge, 2015).

Grcic, Joseph. "Kant on Revolution and Economic Inequality." *Kant-Studien* 77, no. 4 (1986): 447–457.

Guyer, Paul. *Kant on Freedom, Law, and Happiness*. Cambridge: Cambridge University Press, 2000.

"Kant's Deductions of the Principles of Right." In *Kant's Metaphysics of Morals: Interpretative Essays*, ed. Mark Timmons, 23–64. Oxford: Oxford University Press, 2002.

"Beauty, Systematicity, and the Highest Good: Eckart Förster's Kant's Final Synthesis." *Inquiry* 46, no. 2 (2003): 195–214.

Kant's System of Nature and Freedom: Selected Essays. Oxford: Oxford University Press, 2005.

"The Obligation to Be Virtuous: Kant's Conception of the *Tugendverpflichtung*." *Social Philosophy & Policy* 27, no. 2 (2010): 206–232.

Haakonssen, Knud. *Traditions of Liberalism: Essays on John Locke, Adam Smith and John Stuart Mill*. St. Leonards: Center for Independent Studies, 1988.

Habermas, Jürgen. *Between Facts and Norms: Contributions to a Discourse Theory of Law and Democracy*. Cambridge: MIT Press, 1996.

"Kant's Idea of Perpetual Peace: At Two Hundred Years' Historical Remove." In *The Inclusion of the Other*, eds. Ciaran Cronin and Pablo de Greiff, 165–202. Cambridge: MIT Press, 1998.

The Postnational Constellation, ed. and trans. Max Pensky. Cambridge: MIT Press, 2001.

Habibi, Don. "The Moral Dimension of J. S. Mill's Colonialism." *Journal of Social Philosophy* 30, no. 1 (1999): 125–146.

John Stuart Mill and the Ethic of Human Growth. Dordrecht: Kluwer Academic Publishing, 2001.

Hall, Stuart. "When Was 'the Postcolonial'? Thinking at the Limit." In *The Post-Colonial Question: Common Skies, Divided Horizons*, eds. I. Chambers and L. Curtis, 242–260. London: Routledge, 1996.

Hamburger, Joseph. *John Stuart Mill on Liberty and Control*. Princeton: Princeton University Press, 1999.

von Hayek, Friedrich A. "Liberalism." In *New Studies in Philosophy, Politics, Economics, and the History of Ideas*, 119–151. Chicago: University of Chicago Press, 1978.

von Mises, Ludwig. *Liberalism in the Classical Tradition*, trans. Ralph Raico. New York: Foundation for Economic Education, 1985.

The Counter-Revolution of Science: Studies on the Abuse of Reason. Indianapolis: Liberty Press, 1979.

Hedrick, Todd. "Race, Difference, and Anthropology in Kant's Cosmopolitanism." *Journal of the History of Philosophy* 46 (2008): 245–268.

Hendrix, Burke. "The Political Dangers of Western Philosophical Approaches." In *The Oxford Handbook of Indigenous Peoples' Politics*, eds. Jose

Antonio Lucero, Dale Turner and Donna Lee VanCott. Published online January 2013, doi: 10.1093/oxfordhb/9780195386653.001.0001.

Hendrix, Burke, and Deborah Baumgold, eds. *Colonial Exchanges: Political Theory and the Agency of the Colonized*. Manchester: Manchester University Press, 2017.

Herman, Barbara. *The Practice of Moral Judgment*. Cambridge: Harvard University Press, 1993.

"A Cosmopolitan Kingdom of Ends." In *Reclaiming the History of Ethics: Essays for John Rawls*, eds. Andrews Reath, Barbara Herman and Christine Korsgaard, 187–213. Cambridge: Cambridge University Press, 1997.

"Training to Autonomy." In *Philosophers on Education: New Historical Perspectives*, ed. Amélie Oksenberg Rorty, 255–272. London: Routledge, 1998.

Höffe, Otfried. *Kant's Cosmopolitan Theory of Law and Peace*. Cambridge: Cambridge University Press, 2006.

Holmes, Stephen. "Making Sense of Liberal Imperialism." In *J. S. Mill's Political Thought: A Bicentennial Reassessment*, eds. Nadia Urbinati and Alex Zakaras, 319–346. Cambridge: Cambridge University Press, 2007.

Höpfl, H. M. "From Savage to Scotsman: Conjectural History in the Scottish Enlightenment." *Journal of British Studies* 17, no. 2 (1978): 19–40.

Horkheimer, Max, and Theodor W. Adorno. *Dialectic of Enlightenment: Philosophical Fragments*. Stanford: Stanford University Press, 2002.

Horton, John. "Realism, Liberal Moralism and a Political Theory of Modus Vivendi." *European Journal of Political Theory* 9, no. 4 (2010): 431–448.

Hospers, John. *Libertarianism: A Political Philosophy for Tomorrow*. Los Angeles: Nash Publishing, 1971.

Huneman, Philippe, ed. *Understanding Purpose: Kant and the Philosophy of Biology*. Rochester: University of Rochester Press, 2007.

Idris, Murad. *War for Peace: Genealogies of a Violent Ideal in Western and Islamic Thought*. New York: Oxford University Press, 2018.

Ignatieff, Michael. "The American Empire; the Burden." *New York Times Magazine*, January 5, 2003.

Empire Lite: Nation-Building in Bosnia, Kosovo, Afghanistan. Toronto: Penguin Canada, 2006.

Ingram, James. *Radical Cosmopolitics: The Ethics and Politics of Democratic Universalism*. New York: Columbia University Press, 2013.

Ivison, Duncan. *Postcolonial Liberalism*. Cambridge: Cambridge University Press, 2002.

"Locke, Liberalism and Empire." In *The Philosophy of John Locke: New Perspectives*, ed. Peter R. Anstey, 86–105. London: Routledge, 2003.

Jacobs, Brian. "Kantian Character and the Problem of a Science of Humanity." In *Essays on Kant's Anthropology*, eds. Brian Jacobs and Patrick Kain, 105–134. Cambridge: Cambridge University Press, 2003.

Jacobs, Brian and Patrick Kain, eds. *Essays on Kant's Anthropology*. Cambridge: Cambridge University Press, 2003.

Jahn, Beate. "Barbarian Thoughts: Imperialism in the Philosophy of John Stuart Mill." *Review of International Studies*, 31 (2005): 599–618.

"Kant, Mill and Illiberal Legacies." *International Organization* 59, no. 1 (2005): 177–207.

Justman, Stewart. *The Hidden Text of Mill's Library*. Lanham: Rowman & Littlefield, 1990.

Kant, Immanuel. *Critique of Pure Reason*, trans. Norman Kemp Smith. London: Macmillan and co, 1953.

Critique of Judgment, ed. and trans. Werner S. Pluhar. Indianapolis: Hackett Publishing Co., 1987.

"An Answer to the Question: What Is Enlightenment?" In *Practical Philosophy*, ed. Mary J. Gregor, 311–352. Cambridge: Cambridge University Press, 1996.

Critique of Practical Reason. In *Practical Philosophy*, ed. Mary J. Gregor, 133–272. Cambridge: Cambridge University Press, 1996.

Groundwork of The Metaphysics of Morals. In *Practical Philosophy*, ed. Mary J. Gregor, 37–108. Cambridge: Cambridge University Press, 1996.

The Metaphysics of Morals. In *Practical Philosophy*, ed. and trans. Mary J. Gregor, 353–604. Cambridge: Cambridge University Press, 1996.

"On the Common Saying: That May Be Correct in Theory, but It Is of No Use in Practice." In *Practical Philosophy*, ed. Mary J. Gregor, 273–310. Cambridge: Cambridge University Press, 1996.

Practical Philosophy, ed. and trans. Mary J. Gregor. Cambridge: Cambridge University Press, 1996.

"Toward Perpetual Peace." In *Practical Philosophy*, ed. Mary J. Gregor, 311–352. Cambridge: Cambridge University Press, 1996.

Lectures on Ethics, eds. Peter Heath and J. B. Schneewind. Cambridge: Cambridge University Press, 2001.

Anthropology from a Pragmatic Point of View, ed. Robert B. Louden. New York: Cambridge University Press, 2006.

Religion within the Boundaries of Mere Reason: And Other Writings, eds. Allen W. Wood and George di Giovanni. Cambridge: Cambridge University Press, 2006.

Anthropology, History, and Education, eds. Günter Zöller and Robert B. Louden. Cambridge: Cambridge University Press, 2007.

"Conjectural Beginning of Human History." In *Anthropology, History, and Education*, eds. Günter Zöller and Robert B. Louden, 160–175. Cambridge: Cambridge University Press, 2007.

"Determination of the Concept of a Human Race." In *Anthropology, History, and Education*, eds. Günter Zöller and Robert B. Louden, 143–159. Cambridge: Cambridge University Press, 2007.

"Essays Regarding the *Philanthropium*." In *Anthropology, History, and Education*, eds. Günter Zöller and Robert B. Louden, 98–104. Cambridge: Cambridge University Press, 2007.

"Idea for a Universal History with a Cosmopolitan Aim." In *Anthropology, History, and Education*, eds. Günter Zöller and Robert B. Louden, 107–120. Cambridge: Cambridge University Press, 2007.

"Lectures on Pedagogy." In *Anthropology, History, and Education*, eds. Günter Zöller and Robert B. Louden, 434–485. Cambridge: Cambridge University Press, 2007.

"Observations on the Feeling of the Beautiful and Sublime." In *Anthropology, History, and Education*, eds. Günter Zöller and Robert B. Louden, 18–62. Cambridge: Cambridge University Press, 2007.

"Of the Different Races of Human Beings." In *Anthropology, History, and Education*, eds. Günter Zöller and Robert B. Louden, 82–97. Cambridge: Cambridge University Press, 2007.

"On the Use of Teleological Principles in Philosophy." In *Anthropology, History, and Education*, eds. Günter Zöller and Robert B. Louden, 192–218. Cambridge: Cambridge University Press, 2007.

"Review of J. G. Herder's *Ideas for the Philosophy of the History of Humanity*. Parts 1 and 2." In *Anthropology, History, and Education*, eds. Günter Zöller and Robert B. Louden, 121–142. Cambridge: Cambridge University Press, 2007.

"Anthropology Busolt." In *Lectures on Anthropology*, eds. Allen W. Wood and Robert B. Louden, 511–524. Cambridge: Cambridge University Press, 2012.

"Anthropology Friedländer." In *Lectures on Anthropology*, eds. Allen W. Wood and Robert B. Louden, 37–255. Cambridge: Cambridge University Press, 2012.

"Anthropology Mrongovius." In *Lectures on Anthropology*, eds. Allen W. Wood and Robert B. Louden, 339–509. Cambridge: Cambridge University Press, 2012.

"Anthropology Parow." In *Lectures on Anthropology*, eds. Allen W. Wood and Robert B. Louden, 27–36. Cambridge: Cambridge University Press, 2012.

"Anthropology Pillau." In *Lectures on Anthropology*, eds. Allen W. Wood and Robert B. Louden, 257–278. Cambridge: Cambridge University Press, 2012.

Lectures on Anthropology, eds. Allen W. Wood and Robert B. Louden. Cambridge: Cambridge University Press, 2012.

"*Menschenkunde*." In *Lectures on Anthropology*, eds. Allen W. Wood and Robert B. Louden, 281–333. Cambridge: Cambridge University Press, 2012.

Physical Geography. In *Natural Science*, ed. Eric Watkins, 434–678. Cambridge: Cambridge University Press, 2012.

Kapila, Shruti, ed. *An Intellectual History for India*. Cambridge: Cambridge University Press, 2010.

Kateb, George. "A Reading of *On Liberty*." In *On Liberty*, eds. David Bromwich and George Kateb, 28–66. New Haven: Yale University Press, 2003.

Kelly, Paul, and Georgios Varouxakis. "John Stuart Mill's Thought and Legacy: A Timely Reappraisal." In *John Stuart Mill: Thought and Influence – The Saint of Rationalism*, eds. Georgios Varouxakis and Paul Kelly. London: Routledge, 2010.

Kersting, Wolfgang. "Politics, Freedom and Order: Kant's Political Philosophy." *The Cambridge Companion to Kant*, 342–366. Cambridge: Cambridge University Press, 1992.

Kettle, Martin. "Brexit Was a Revolt against Liberalism. We've Entered a New Political Era." *Guardian*, September 15, 2016.

Kinzer, Bruce L., Ann P. Robson, and John M. Robson, *A Moralist In and Out of Parliament: John Stuart Mill at Westminster, 1865–1868*. Toronto: University of Toronto Press, 1992.

Kleingeld, Pauline. "The Problematic Status of Gender-Neutral Language in the History of Philosophy: The Case of Kant." *The Philosophical Forum* XXV (1993): 134–150.

"What Do the Virtuous Hope For? Re-Reading Kant's Doctrine of the Highest Good." In *Proceedings of the Eighth International Kant Congress*, ed. Hoke Robinson, 91–112. *Memphis*: Marquette University Press, 1995.

"Kant's Cosmopolitan Law: World Citizenship for a Global Order." *Kantian Review* 2 (1998): 72–90.

"Kant, History, and the Idea of Moral Development." *History of Philosophy Quarterly* 16, no. 1 (1999): 59–80.

"Kantian Patriotism." *Philosophy & Public Affairs* 29, no. 4 (2000): 313–341.

"Kant's Second Thoughts on Race." *The Philosophical Quarterly* 57, no. 226 (2007): 573–592.

Kant and Cosmopolitanism: The Philosophical Ideal of World Citizenship. Cambridge: Cambridge University Press, 2013.

"Debunking Confabulation: Emotions and the Significance of Empirical Psychology for Kantian Ethics." In *Kant on Emotion and Value*, ed. A. Cohen, 146–165. Basingstoke: Palgrave Macmillan, 2014.

"Kant's Second Thoughts on Colonialism." In *Kant and Colonialism: Historical and Critical Perspectives*, eds. Katrin Flikschuh and Lea Ypi, 43–67. Oxford: Oxford University Press, 2014.

Klinger, Cornelia. "The Concepts of the Sublime and the Beautiful in Kant and Lyotard." In *Feminist Interpretations of Immanuel Kant*, ed. Robin May Schott, 191–211. University Park: Pennsylvania State University Press, 1997.

Koditschek, Theodore. *Liberalism, Imperialism, and the Historical Imagination: Nineteenth-Century Visions of a Greater Britain.* Cambridge: Cambridge University Press, 2011.

Kofman, Sarah. "The Economy of Respect: Kant and Respect for Women." *Social Research* 49, no. 2 (1982): 383–404.

Kohn, Margaret and Daniel O'Neill. "A Tale of Two Indias: Burke and Mill on Empire and Slavery in the West Indies and America." *Political Theory* 34, no. 2 (2006): 192–228.

Korsgaard, Christine. "Taking the Law into Our Own Hands: Kant on the Right to Revolution." In *The Constitution of Agency: Essays on Practical Reason and Moral Psychology*, 233–262. Oxford: Oxford University Press, 2008.

"Natural Motives and the Motive of Duty: Hume and Kant on Our Duties to Others." *Contemporary Readings in Law and Social Justice* 1, no. 2 (2009): 9–36.

Kuehn, Manfred. *Kant: A Biography.* Cambridge: Cambridge University Press, 2001.

"Introduction." In *Anthropology from a Pragmatic Point of View* by Immanuel Kant, ed. Robert B. Louden, viii–xxix. Cambridge: Cambridge University Press, 2006.

Kurfirst, Robert. "Mill on Oriental Despotism, Including Its British Variant." *Utilitas*, 8 no. 1 (1996): 73–87

Kymlicka, Will. "Liberal Individualism and Liberal Neutrality." *Ethics* 99, no. 4 (1989): 883–905.

Multicultural Citizenship: A Liberal Theory of Minority Rights. Oxford: Oxford University Press, 1995.

La Vopa, Anthony J. "Thinking about Marriage: Kant's Liberalism and the Peculiar Morality of Conjugal Union." *The Journal of Modern History* 77, no. 1 (2005): 1–34.

Larmore, Charles. "Political Liberalism." *Political Theory* 18, no. 3 (1990): 339–360.

The Morals of Modernity. Cambridge: Cambridge University Press, 1996.

Larrimore, Mark. "Sublime Waste: Kant on the Destiny of the 'Races'." *Canadian Journal of Philosophy* 25 (1999): 99–125.

"Antinomies of Race: Diversity and Destiny in Kant." *Patterns of Prejudice* 42, nos. 4–5 (2008): 341–363.

Laski, Harold. *The Rise of Liberalism: The Philosophy of a Business Civilization.* New York: Harper and Brothers, 1936.

Levin, Michael. *J. S. Mill on Civilization and Barbarism.* London: Routledge, 2004.

Livingston, Alexander. "Moralism and Its Discontents." *Humanity: An International Journal of Human Rights, Humanitarianism and Development* 7, no. 3 (2016): 499–522.

Locke, John. *Two Treatises of Government,* ed. Peter Laslett. Cambridge: Cambridge University Press, 1960.

Losurdo, Domenico. *Liberalism: A Counter-History.* London: Verso, 2011.

Louden, Robert B. *Kant's Impure Ethics: From Rational Beings to Human Beings.* New York: Oxford University Press, 2000.

"The Second Part of Morals." In *Essays on Kant's Anthropology,* eds. Brian Jacobs and Patrick Kain, 60–84. Cambridge: Cambridge University Press, 2003.

"General Introduction." In *History, Anthropology, Education* by Immanuel Kant, eds. Günter Zöller and Robert B. Louden, 1–17. Cambridge: Cambridge University Press, 2007.

"Introduction." In *Lectures on Pedagogy* by Immanuel Kant, eds. Günter Zöller and Robert B. Louden, 434–436. Cambridge: Cambridge University Press, 2007.

MacIntyre, Alasdair C. *After Virtue: A Study in Moral Theory.* Notre Dame: University of Notre Dame Press, 2007.

Macaulay, Thomas Babington. "Mill on Government." In *The Miscellaneous Writings of Lord Macaulay.* Vol. 1, 282–323. London: Longman, Green and Co., 1860.

Majeed, Javed. "James Mill's *The History of British India*: A Reevaluation." In *J. S. Mill's Encounter with India,* eds. Martin I. Moir, Douglas M. Peers and Lynn Zastoupil, 53–71. Toronto: University of Toronto Press, 1999.

"James Mill's *The History of British India*: The Question of Utilitarianism and Empire." In *Utilitarianism and Empire,* eds. Bart Schultz and Georgios Varouxakis, 93–106. Lanham: Lexington Book, 2005.

Mantena, Karuna. "Mill and the Imperial Predicament." In *J. S. Mill's Political Thought: A Bicentennial Reassessment,* eds. Nadia Urbinati and Alex Zakaras, 298–318. Cambridge: Cambridge University Press, 2007.

Alibis of Empire: Henry Maine and the Ends of Liberal Imperialism. Princeton: Princeton University Press, 2010.

Markell, Patchen. "Unexpected Paths: On Political Theory and Method." *Theory & Event* 19, no. 1 (2016).

Marwah, Inder S. "Bridging Nature and Freedom? Kant, Culture and Cultivation." *Social Theory and Practice* 38, no. 3 (2012): 385–406.

"*Elateres Motiva*: From the Good Will to the Good Human Being." *Kantian Review,* 18 no. 3 (2013): 413–437.

"Liberal Theory." In *The Encyclopedia of Political Thought,* eds. Michael T. Gibbons, Diana Coole, Elisabeth Ellis and Kennan Ferguson, 2134–2139. Malden: Wiley-Blackwell, 2014.

"Rethinking Resistance: Spencer, Krishnavarma and *The Indian Sociologist.*" In *Colonial Exchanges: Political Theory and the Agency of the Colonized,* eds. Burke Hendrix and Deborah Baumgold, 43–72. Manchester: Manchester University Press, 2017.

"Provincializing Progress: Developmentalism and Anti-Imperialism in Colonial India." *Polity*, forthcoming 2019.

Mazlish, Bruce. *James and John Stuart Mill: Father and Son in the Nineteenth Century.* New York: Basic Books, 1975.

McCarthy, Thomas. "Multicultural Cosmopolitanism: Remarks on the Idea of Universal History." In *Letting Be: Fred Dallmayr's Cosmopolitical Vision*, ed. Stephen Schneck, 88–113. Notre Dame: University of Notre Dame Press, 2006.

Race, Empire, and the Idea of Human Development. Cambridge: Cambridge University Press, 2009.

McPherson, C. B. *The Political Theory of Possessive Individualism: Hobbes to Locke.* Oxford: Clarendon Press, 1996.

Meadowcroft, James. "The New Liberal Conception of the State." In *The New Liberalism: Reconciling Liberty and Community*, eds. Abital Simonhy and David Weinstein, 115–136. Cambridge: Cambridge University Press, 2001.

Mehta, Uday Singh. "Liberal Strategies of Exclusion." *Politics and Society* 18, no. 4 (1990): 427–454.

Liberalism and Empire: A Study in Nineteenth Century British Liberal Thought. Chicago: University of Chicago Press, 1999.

Mendieta, Eduardo. "Geography Is to History as Woman Is to Man: Kant on Sex, Race, and Geography." In *Reading Kant's Geography*, eds. Stuart Elden and Eduardo Mendieta, 345–368. Albany: SUNY Press, 2011.

Mensch, Jennifer. *Kant's Organicism: Epigenesis and the Development of Critical Philosophy.* Chicago: University of Chicago Press, 2013.

"From Crooked Wood to Moral Agency: On Anthropology and Ethics in Kant." *Estudos Kantianos* 2, no. 1 (2014): 185–203.

"What's Wrong with Inevitable Progress? Notes on Kant's Anthropology Today." *Cogent Arts and Humanities* 4 (2017).

"Kant and the Skull Collectors: German Anthropology from Blumenbach to Kant." In *Kant and His German Contemporaries. Volume 1, Logic, Mind, Epistemology, Science and Ethics*, eds. W. Dyck and F. Wunderlich, 192–210. Cambridge: Cambridge University Press, 2018.

Metcalf, Thomas R. *Ideologies of the Raj.* Cambridge: Cambridge University Press, 1994.

Mendus, Susan. "Kant: 'an Honest but Narrow-Minded Bourgeois'?" In *Essays on Kant's Political Philosophy*, ed. Howard Williams, 166–190. Cardiff: University of Wales Press, 1992.

Mignolo, Walter. "The Many Faces of Cosmo-polis: Border Thinking and Critical Cosmopolitanism." *Public Culture* 12, no. 3 (2000): 721–748.

Mill, James. "Government", Reprinted from *Supplement to the Encyclopedia Britannica*. London: J. Innes, 1825.

History of British India in 6 Volumes. London: Baldwin, Cradock and Joy, 1826.

"An Essay on Government." In *Utilitarian Logic and Politics: James Mill's "Essay on Government," Macaulay's Critique, and the Ensuing Debate*, eds. Jack Lively and J. C. Rees, 53–96. Oxford: Clarendon Press, 1978.

Mill, John Stuart. "Mill to Edward Lytton Bulwer, Nov. 23, 1836." In *The Collected Works of John Stuart Mill, Volume XII – The Earlier Letters 1812–1848 Part I*, eds.

Francis E. Mineka. Toronto: University of Toronto Press; London: Routledge & Kegan Paul, 1963.

"Mill to Gustave d'Eichthal, Oct. 8 1829." In *The Collected Works of John Stuart Mill, Volume XII – The Earlier Letters 1812–1848 Part I*, ed. Francis E. Mineka. Toronto: University of Toronto Press; London: Routledge & Kegan Paul, 1963.

"Mill to John Sterling, Oct. 20–22, 1831." In *The Collected Works of John Stuart Mill, Volume XII – The Earlier Letters 1812–1848 Part I*, ed. Francis E. Mineka. Toronto: University of Toronto Press; London: Routledge & Kegan Paul, 1963.

"Mill to Gustave d'Eichthal, Oct. 8, 1829." In *The Collected Works of John Stuart Mill, Volume XII – The Earlier Letters 1812–1848 Part I*, ed. Francis E. Mineka. Toronto: University of Toronto Press; London: Routledge & Kegan Paul, 1963.

"Mill to Gustave d'Eichthal, Nov. 7, 1829." In *The Collected Works of John Stuart Mill, Volume XII – The Earlier Letters 1812–1848 Part I*, ed. Francis E. Mineka. Toronto: University of Toronto Press; London: Routledge & Kegan Paul, 1963.

"Mill to Gustave d'Eichthal, May 15, 1829." In *The Collected Works of John Stuart Mill, Volume XII – The Earlier Letters 1812–1848 Part I*, ed. Francis E. Mineka. Toronto: University of Toronto Press; London: Routledge & Kegan Paul, 1963.

"Mill to John Pringle Nichol, Apr. 15, 1834." In *The Collected Works of John Stuart Mill, Volume XII – The Earlier Letters 1812–1848 Part I*, eds. Francis E. Mineka. Toronto: University of Toronto Press; London: Routledge & Kegan Paul, 1963.

Principles of Political Economy. In *The Collected Works of John Stuart Mill, Volume III – Principles of Political Economy Part II*, ed. John M. Robson. Toronto: University of Toronto Press; London: Routledge & Kegan Paul, 1965.

"On the Definition of Political Economy; and on the Method of Investigation Proper to It." In *The Collected Works of John Stuart Mill, Volume IV – Essays on Economics and Society Part I*, ed. John M. Robson. Toronto: University of Toronto Press; London: Routledge & Kegan Paul, 1967.

August Comte and Positivism. In *The Collected Works of John Stuart Mill, Volume X – Essays on Ethics, Religion and Society (Utilitarianism)*, ed. John M. Robson. Toronto: University of Toronto Press; London: Routledge & Kegan Paul, 1969.

"Bentham." In *The Collected Works of John Stuart Mill, Volume X – Essays on Ethics, Religion and Society (Utilitarianism)*, ed. John M. Robson. Toronto: University of Toronto Press, 1969.

"Coleridge." In *The Collected Works of John Stuart Mill, Volume X – Essays on Ethics, Religion and Society (Utilitarianism)*, ed. John M. Robson. Toronto: University of Toronto Press, 1969.

Utilitarianism. In *The Collected Works of John Stuart Mill, Volume X – Essays on Ethics, Religion and Society (Utilitarianism)*, ed. John M. Robson. Toronto: University of Toronto Press, London: Routledge & Kegan Paul, 1969.

"Mill to George Cornewall Lewis, March 20, 1859." In *The Collected Works of John Stuart Mill, Volume XV – The Later Letters 1849–1873 Part II*, eds. Francis E. Mineka and Dwight N. Lindley. Toronto: University of Toronto Press; London: Routledge & Kegan Paul, 1972.

"Mill to Henry Jones." In *The Collected Works of John Stuart Mill, Volume XVI – The Later Letters 1849–1873 Part III*, eds. Francis E. Mineka and Dwight N. Lindley. Toronto: University of Toronto Press; London: Routledge & Kegan Paul, 1972.

"Mill to John Morley, Nov. 4, 1865." In *The Collected Works of John Stuart Mill, Volume XVI – The Later Letters 1849–1873 Part III*, eds. Francis E. Mineka and Dwight N. Lindley. Toronto: University of Toronto Press; London: Routledge & Kegan Paul, 1972.

A System of Logic Ratiocinative and Inductive: Being a Connected View of the Principles of Evidence and the Methods of Scientific Investigation. In *The Collected Works of John Stuart Mill, Volume VIII – A System of Logic Part II*, ed. John M. Robson. Toronto: University of Toronto Press; London: Routledge & Kegan Paul, 1974.

Considerations on Representative Government. In *The Collected Works of John Stuart Mill, Volume XIX – Essays on Politics and Society Part II*, ed. John M. Robson. Toronto: University of Toronto Press; London: Routledge & Kegan Paul, 1977.

"Civilization." In *The Collected Works of John Stuart Mill, Volume XVIII – Essays on Politics and Society Part I (On Liberty)*, ed. John M. Robson. Toronto: University of Toronto Press; London: Routledge & Kegan Paul, 1977.

"De Tocqueville on Democracy in America [1]." In *The Collected Works of John Stuart Mill, Volume XVIII – Essays on Politics and Society Part I (On Liberty)*, ed. John M. Robson. Toronto: University of Toronto Press; London: Routledge & Kegan Paul, 1977.

"De Tocqueville on Democracy in America [2]." In *The Collected Works of John Stuart Mill, Volume XVIII – Essays on Politics and Society Part I (On Liberty)*, ed. John M. Robson. Toronto: University of Toronto Press; London: Routledge & Kegan Paul, 1977.

On Liberty. In *The Collected Works of John Stuart Mill, Volume XVIII – Essays on Politics and Society Part 1 (On Liberty)*, ed. John M. Robson. Toronto: University of Toronto Press; London: Routledge & Kegan Paul, 1977.

"Rationale of Representation." In *The Collected Works of John Stuart Mill, Volume XVIII – Essays on Politics and Society Part I (On Liberty)*, ed. John M. Robson. Toronto: University of Toronto Press; London: Routledge & Kegan Paul, 1977.

"State of Society in America." In *The Collected Works of John Stuart Mill, Volume XVIII – Essays on Politics and Society Part I*, ed. John M. Robson. Toronto: University of Toronto Press; London: Routledge & Kegan Paul, 1977.

"Thoughts on Parliamentary Reform." In *The Collected Works of John Stuart Mill, Volume XIX – Essays on Politics and Society Part II*, ed. John M. Robson. Toronto: University of Toronto Press; London: Routledge & Kegan Paul, 1977.

Autobiography. In *The Collected Works of John Stuart Mill, Volume I – Autobiography and Literary Essays*, eds. John M. Robson and Jack Stillinger. Toronto: University of Toronto Press; London: Routledge & Kegan Paul, 1981.

"A Few Words on Non-Intervention." In *The Collected Works of John Stuart Mill, Volume XXI – Essays on Equality, Law, and Education (Subjection of Women)*, ed. John M. Robson. Toronto: University of Toronto Press; London: Routledge & Kegan Paul, 1984.

"Inaugural Address Delivered to the University of St. Andrews 1867." In *The Collected Works of John Stuart Mill, Volume XXI – Essays on Equality, Law, and Education*, ed. John M. Robson. Toronto: University of Toronto Press; London: Routledge & Kegan Paul, 1984.

"The Subjection of Women." In *The Collected Works of John Stuart Mill, Volume XXI – Essays on Equality, Law, and Education (Subjection of Women)*, ed. John M. Robson. Toronto: University of Toronto Press; London: Routledge & Kegan Paul, 1984.

"Vindication of the French Revolution of February 1848–1849." In *The Collected Works of John Stuart Mill, Volume XX – Essays on French History and Historians*, ed. John M. Robson. Toronto: University of Toronto Press; London: Routledge & Kegan Paul, 1985.

"Municipal Institutions *The Examiner*, 11 Aug. 1833." In *The Collected Works of John Stuart Mill, Volume XIII – Newspaper Writings Part II*, eds. Ann P. Robson and John M. Robson. Toronto: University of Toronto Press; London: Routledge & Kegan Paul, 1986.

"Romilly's Public Responsibility and the Ballot Reader." In *The Collected Works of John Stuart Mill, Volume XXV – Newspaper Writings Part IV*, eds. Ann P. Robson and John M. Robson. Toronto: University of Toronto Press; London: Routledge & Kegan Paul, 1986.

"The Spirit of the Age, III." In *The Collected Works of John Stuart Mill, Volume XXII – Newspaper Writings Part I*, eds. Ann P. Robson and John M. Robson. Toronto: University of Toronto Press; London: Routledge & Kegan Paul, 1986.

"James Mill's *Analysis of the Phenomena of the Human Mind*." In *The Collected Works of John Stuart Mill, Volume XXXI – Miscellaneous Writings*, ed. John M. Robson. Toronto: University of Toronto Press; London: Routledge & Kegan Paul, 1989.

"The Petition of the East India Company." In *The Collected Works of John Stuart Mill, Volume XXX – Writings on India*, eds. John M. Robson, Martin Moir, and Zawahir Moir. Toronto: University of Toronto Press; London: Routledge & Kegan Paul, 1990.

"The Negro Question." In *The Collected Works of John Stuart Mill, Volume XXI – Essays on Equality, Law, and Education (Subjection of Women)*, ed. John M. Robson. Toronto: Toronto University Press; London: Routledge & Kegan Paul, 1984.

"Guizot's Essays and Lectures on History." In *The Collected Works of John Stuart Mill, Volume XX – Essays on French History and Historians*, ed. John M. Robson. Toronto: University of Toronto; London: Routledge & Kegan Paul, 1985.

"Michelet's History of France." In *The Collected Works of John Stuart Mill, Volume XX – Essays on French History and Historians*, ed. John M. Robson. Toronto: University of Toronto; London: Routledge & Kegan Paul, 1985.

"The Civil War in the United States, *Our Daily Fare*, 21 June, 1864." In *The Collected Works of John Stuart Mill, Volume XXV – Newspaper Writings Part IV*, eds. Ann P. Robson and John M. Robson. Toronto: University of Toronto Press; London: Routledge & Kegan Paul, 1986.

"The English National Character." In *The Collected Works of John Stuart Mill, Volume XXIII – Newspaper Writings Part II*, eds. Ann P. Robson and John M. Robson. Toronto: University of Toronto Press; London: Routledge & Kegan Paul, 1986.

"Parliamentary Reform, *Morning Chronicle*, 3 October, 1823" In *The Collected Works of John Stuart Mill, Volume XXII – Newspaper Writings Part I*, eds.,

John M. Robson, and Ann P. Robson. Toronto: University of Toronto Press; London: Routledge & Kegan Paul, 1986.

"Practicability of Reform in the Law, *Morning Chronicle*, 8 October, 1813." In *The Collected Works of John Stuart Mill, Volume XXII – Newspaper Writings Part I*, eds., John M. Robson, and Ann P. Robson. Toronto: University of Toronto Press; London: Routledge & Kegan Paul, 1986.

"Securities for Good Government, *Morning Chronicle*, 25 September, 1823." In *The Collected Works of John Stuart Mill, Volume XXII – Newspaper Writings Part I*, eds. John M. Robson, and Ann P. Robson. Toronto: University of Toronto Press; London: Routledge & Kegan Paul, 1986.

"The Spirit of the Age, V (Part 2)." In *The Collected Works of John Stuart Mill, Volume XXII – Newspaper Writings Part I*, eds. Ann P. Robson and John M. Robson. Toronto: University of Toronto Press; London: Routledge & Kegan Paul, 1986.

"Technicalities of English Law, *Morning Chronicle*, 25 September, 1823." In *The Collected Works of John Stuart Mill, Volume XXII – Newspaper Writings Part I*, eds. John M. Robson, and Ann P. Robson. Toronto: University of Toronto Press; London: Routledge & Kegan Paul, 1986.

"Representation of the People, 13 April 1866." In *The Collected Works of John Stuart Mill, Volume XXVIII – Public and Parliamentary Speeches Part I*, eds. Bruce L. Kinzer and John M. Robson, 74–75. Toronto: University of Toronto Press; London: Routledge & Kegan Paul, 1988.

Millgram, Elijah. "Liberty, the Higher Pleasures, and Mill's Missing Science of Ethnic Jokes." *Social Philosophy and Policy*, 26, no. 1 (2009): 326–353.

"Mill's Incubus." In *John Stuart Mill and the Art of Life*, eds. Ben Eggleston, Dale E. Miller and David Weinstein, 169–191. Oxford: Oxford University Press, 2011.

Mills, C. W. *The Racial Contract*. Ithaca: Cornell University Press, 1997.

"Ideal Theory as Ideology." In *Moral Psychology: Feminist Ethics and Social Theory*, eds. Peggy DesAutels and Margaret Urban Walker, 163–181. Lanham: Rowman & Littlefield Publishers, 2004.

"Racial Liberalism." *PMLA* 123 (2008): 1380–1397.

"Kant's *Untermenschen*." In *Race and Racism in Modern Philosophy*, ed. Andrew Valls, 169–193. Ithaca: Cornell University Press, 2005.

"Kant and Race, *Redux*." *Graduate Faculty Philosophy Journal* 35, nos. 1–2 (2014): 125–157.

"Racial Equality." In *The Equal Society: Essays on Equality in Theory and Practice*, ed. George Hull, 43–72. Lanham: Lexington Books, 2015.

"Decolonizing Western Political Philosophy." *New Political Science* 37, no. 1 (2015): 1–24.

Black Rights/White Wrongs: The Critique of Racial Liberalism. Cambridge: Oxford University Press, 2017.

"Black Radical Kantianism." *Res Philosophica* 95 (2018): 1–33.

Mikkelsen, Jon M., ed. and trans. *Kant and the Concept of Race: Late Eighteenth-Century Writings*. Albany: State University of New York Press, 2013.

Miller, Dale E. "John Stuart Mill's Civic Liberalism." *History of Political Thought* 21, no. 1 (2000): 88–113.

John Stuart Mill: Moral, Social and Political Thought. Cambridge: Polity Press, 2010.

"The Place of Plural Voting in Mill's Conception of Representative Government." *The Review of Politics* 77, no. 3 (2015): 399–425.

Miller, James. *The Passion of Michel Foucault*. London: Flamingo, 1993.

Miller, Joseph J. "J. S. Mill on Plural Voting, Competence and Participation." *History of Political Thought* 24, no. 4 (2003): 647–667,

"Chairing the Jamaica Committee: J. S. Mill and the Limits of Colonial Authority." In *Utilitarianism and Empire*, eds. Bart Schultz and Georgios Varouxakis, 155–178. Lanham: Lexington Books, 2005.

Moir, Martin. "Introduction." In John Stuart Mill, *The Collected Writings of John Stuart Mill, Volume XXX – Writings on India*, eds. Zawahir Moir, Martin Moir and John M. Robinson. Toronto: University of Toronto Press; London: Routledge & Kegan Paul, 1990.

Moir, Martin, Douglas M. Peers and Lynn Zastoupil, eds, *J. S. Mill's Encounter with India*. Toronto: University of Toronto Press, 1999.

Morefield, Jeanne. *Empires without Imperialism: Anglo-American Decline and the Politics of Deflection*. Oxford: Oxford University Press, 2014.

Morley, John. *The Life of William Ewart Gladstone*. London: Macmillan, 1903.

Moyn, Samuel, and Andrew Sartori, eds. *Global Intellectual History*. New York: Columbia University Press, 2015.

Mudde, Cas, and Cristobal Rovira Kaltwasser. *Populism: A Very Short Introduction*. New York: Oxford University Press, 2017.

Mulholland, Leslie A. *Kant's System of Rights*. New York: Columbia University Press, 1990.

Müller, Jan-Werner. *What Is Populism?* Philadelphia: University of Pennsylvania Press, 2016.

Munzel, G. Felicitas. *Kant's Conception of Moral Character: The "Critical" Link of Morality, Anthropology, and Reflective Judgment*. Chicago: Chicago University Press, 1999.

"Indispensable Education of the Being of Reason and Speech." In Kant's *Lectures on Anthropology: A Critical Guide*, ed. A. Cohen, 172–190. Cambridge: Cambridge University Press, 2014.

Murray, Charles. *What It Means to Be a Libertarian*. New York: Broadway Books, 1997.

Muthu, Sankar. *Enlightenment against Empire*. Princeton: Princeton University Press, 2003.

"Conquest, Commerce, and Cosmopolitanism in Enlightenment Political Thought." In *Empire and Modern Political Thought*, ed. Sankar Muthu, 199–231. Cambridge: Cambridge University Press, 2012.

Newey, Glen. "Two Dogmas of Liberalism." *European Journal of Political Theory* 9, no. 4 (2010): 449–465.

North, Richard. "Political Realism: Introduction." *European Journal of Political Theory* 9, no. 4 (2010): 381–384.

Nichols, Robert. "Indigeneity and the Settler Contract Today." *Philosophy and Social Criticism* 39, no. 2 (2013): 165–186.

Nussbaum, Martha. *Women and Human Development: The Capabilities Approach*. Cambridge: Cambridge University Press, 2000.

"Mill on Happiness: The Enduring Value of a Complex Critique." In *Utilitarianism and Empire*, eds. Bart Schultz and Georgios Varouxakis, 107–124. Lanham: Lexington Books, 2005.

Creating Capabilities. Cambridge: Harvard University Press, 2011.

O'Connell, Eoin. "Happiness Proportioned to Virtue: Kant and the Highest Good." *Kantian Review* 17, no. 2 (2012): 257–279.

Okin, Susan Moller. "Women and the Making of the Sentimental Family." *Philosophy & Public Affairs* 11, no. 1 (1982): 65–88.

Olsen, Mark. "Foucault and Critique: Kant, Humanism and the Human Sciences." In *Futures of Critical Theory: Dreams of Difference*, eds. Michael Peters, Mark Olsen and Colin Lankshear, 73–102. Lanham: Rowman and Littlefield, 2003.

Orwell, George. "Freedom of the Park." *Tribune*, December 7, 1945.

Parekh, Bhikhu. "Decolonizing Liberalism A Critique of Locke and Mill." In *The End Of "Isms"? Reflections on the Fate of Ideological Politics after Communism's Collapse*, ed. Alexander Shtromas, 85–103. Oxford: Blackwell, 1994.

"Superior People: The Narrowness of Liberalism from Mill to Rawls." *Times Literary Supplement*, February 25, 1994.

"Liberalism and Colonialism." In *The Decolonization of the Imagination: Culture, Knowledge and Power*, eds. Jan Nederveen Pieterse and Bhikhu Parekh, 81–98. London: Zed Books, 1995.

Pateman, Carole. "Feminist Critiques of the Public/Private Dichotomy." In *Public and Private in Social Life*, eds. Stanley I. Benn and G. F. Gaus, 281–303. London: St Martin's Press, 1983.

The Sexual Contract. Stanford: Stanford University Press, 1988.

Pateman, Carole, and C. W. Mills. *Contract and Domination.* Cambridge: Polity Press, 2007.

Paul, Volker. "Populism and the Crisis of Liberalism." *Philosophy & Social Criticism* 44 (2018): 346–352.

Philips, Menaka. "Troubling Appropriations: J. S. Mill, Liberalism, and the Virtues of Uncertainty." *European Journal of Political Theory* 18 (1) 2019: 68–88.

Pitts, Jennifer. *A Turn to Empire: The Rise of Imperial Liberalism in Britain and France.* Princeton: Princeton University Press, 2005.

"Bentham: Legislator of the World?" In *Utilitarianism and Empire*, eds. Bart Schultz and Georgios Varouxakis, 57–92. Lanham: Lexington Books, 2005.

"Political Theory of Empire and Imperialism." *Annual Review of Political Science*, 13 (2010): 211–235.

"Empire, Progress and the 'Savage Mind'." In *Colonialism and Its Legacies*, eds. Jacob Levy and Iris Marion Young. Lanham: Lexington Books, 2011.

Philp, Mark. "What Is to Be Done? Political Theory and Political Realism." *European Journal of Political Theory* 9, no. 4 (2010): 466–484.

Pippin, Robert B. "Mine and Thine? The Kantian State." In *The Cambridge Companion to Kant and Modern Philosophy*, ed. Paul Guyer, 416–446. Cambridge: Cambridge University Press, 2006.

Plato, *The Republic*, trans. G. M. A. Grube. Indianapolis: Hackett Publishing Co., 1992.

Pocock, J. G. A. "The History of Political Thought: A Methodological Enquiry." In *Philosophy, Politics and Society*, eds. Peter Laslett and W. G. Runciman. New York: Barnes and Noble, 1962.

Pogge, Thomas W. "Is Kant's *Rechtslehre* a 'Comprehensive Liberalism'?" In *Kant's Metaphysics of Morals: Interpretative Essays*, ed. Mark Timmons, 133–158. Oxford: Oxford University Press, 2002.

Prakash, Gyan. "Postcolonial Criticism and Indian Historiography." *Social Text* 31/32 (1992): 8–19.

Quijano, Aníbal. "Coloniality of Power, Eurocentrism, and Latin America." *Neplanta: Views from South* 1 (2000): 533–580.

"Coloniality and Modernity/Rationality." *Cultural Studies* 21 (2007): 168–178.

Rancière, Jacques. *Disagreement: Politics and Philosophy.* Minneapolis: University of Minnesota Press, 1999.

Rasmussen, Dennis. *The Pragmatic Enlightenment: Recovering the Liberalism of Hume, Smith, Montesquieu and Voltaire.* New York: Cambridge University Press, 2013.

Rawls, John. "Justice as Fairness: Political Not Metaphysical." *Philosophy and Public Affairs* 14, no. 3 (1985): 223–251.

"The Law of Peoples." *Critical Inquiry* 20 (1993).

A Theory of Justice: Revised Edition. Cambridge: Harvard University Press, 1999.

Political Liberalism. New York: Columbia University Press, 2005.

The Law of Peoples: with "The Idea of Public Reason Revisited." Cambridge: Harvard University Press, 2008.

Reaths, Andrews, *Agency and Autonomy in Kant's Moral Theory: Selected Essays.* New York: Oxford University Press, 2006.

Richards, Robert J. "Kant and Blumenbach on the *Bildungstrieb*: A Historical Misunderstanding." *Studies in History and Philosophy of Science Part C* 31, no. 1 (2000): 11–32.

Riley, Jonathan. "Mill's Neo-Athenian Model of Liberal Democracy." In *J. S. Mill's Political Thought: A Bicentennial Reassessment*, eds. Nadia Urbinati and Alex Zakaras, 221–249. Cambridge: Cambridge University Press, 2007.

Riley, Patrick. *Kant's Political Philosophy.* Totowa: Rowman & Littlefield, 1983.

Ripstein, Arthur. *Force and Freedom: Kant's Legal and Political Philosophy.* Cambridge: Harvard University Press, 2009.

Robson, John M. "John Stuart Mill and Jeremy Bentham, with some Observations on James Mill." In *Essays in English Literature from the Renaissance to the Victorian Age*, eds. M. MacLure and F. W. Watt, 259–262. Toronto: University of Toronto Press, 1964.

The Improvement of Mankind: The Social and Political Thought of John Stuart Mill. Toronto: University of Toronto Press, 1968.

"Civilization and Culture as Moral Concepts." In *The Cambridge Companion to Mill*, ed. John Skorupski, 338–371. Cambridge: Cambridge University Press, 1998.

Rorty, Amélie Oksenberg, and James Schmidt, eds. *Idea for a Universal History with a Cosmopolitan Aim: A Critical Guide.* Cambridge: Cambridge University Press, 2009.

Rosen, Allen D. *Kant's Theory of Justice.* Ithaca: Cornell University Press, 1996.

Rosen, Fred. "Method of Reform: J. S. Mill's Encounter with Bentham and Coleridge." In *J. S. Mill's Political Thought: A Bicentennial Reassessment*, eds. Nadia Urbinati and Alex Zakaras, 124–144. Cambridge: Cambridge University Press, 2007.

Rossi, Enzo. "Reality and Imagination in Political Theory and Practice: On Raymond Geuss's Realism." *European Journal of Political Theory* 9, no. 4 (2010): 504–512.

Rumsey, Jean P. "The Development of Character in Kantian Moral Theory." *Journal of the History of Philosophy* 27, no. 2 (1989): 247–265.

"Re-Visions of Agency in Kant's Moral Theory." In *Feminist Interpretations of Immanuel Kant*, ed. Robin May Schott, 125–144. University Park: Pennsylvania State University Press, 1997.

Ryan, Alan. *John Stuart Mill.* London: Rouledge & Kegan Paul, 1974.

The Making of Modern Liberalism. Princeton: Princeton University Press, 2012.

"John Stuart Mill's Art of Living." In *J. S. Mill's On Liberty in Focus*, eds. John Gray and G. W. Smith, 162–168. London: Routledge, 2015.

Said, Edward W. *Orientalism*. New York: Pantheon Books, 1978.

Sandel, Michael. "Populism, Liberalism, and Democracy." *Philosophy & Social Criticism* 44 (2018): 353–359.

Sartori, Andrew. "The British Empire and Its Liberal Mission." *The Journal of Modern History* 78, no. 3 (2006): 623–642.

Liberalism in Empire: An Alternative History. Berkeley: University of California Press, 2014.

Schott, Robin May. "Feminism and Kant: Antipathy or Sympathy?" In *Autonomy and Community: Readings in Contemporary Kantian Social Philosophy*, eds. Jane Kneller and Sidney Axinn, 87–100. New York: State University of New York Press, 1998.

Schröder, Hannelore, "Kant's Patriarchal Order." In *Feminist Interpretations of Immanuel Kant*, ed. Robin May Schott, 275–296. University Park: Pennsylvania State University Press, 1997.

Schultz, Bart. "Mill and Sidgwick, Imperialism and Racism." *Utilitas* 19 (2007): 104–130.

Schultz, Bart, and Georgios Varouxakis, eds. *Utilitarianism and Empire*. Lanham: Lexington Book, 2005.

Scott, David. *Refashioning Futures: Criticism After Postcoloniality*. Princeton: Princeton University Press, 1999.

Conscripts of Modernity: The Tragedy of Colonial Enlightenment. Durham: Duke University Press, 2004.

"The Social Construction of Postcolonial Studies." In *Postcolonial Studies and Beyond*, eds. Ania Loomba, Suvir Kaul, Matti Bunzl and Antoinette Burton, 385–400. Durham: Duke University Press, 2005.

"The Traditions of Historical Others." *Symposia on Gender, Race and Philosophy* 8, no. 1 (2012): 1–8.

Sedgwick, Sally. "Can Kant's Ethics Survive Feminist Critique?" In *Feminist Interpretations of Immanuel Kant*, ed. Robin May Schott, 77–100. University Park: Pennsylvania State University Press, 1997.

Semmel, Bernard. *John Stuart Mill and the Pursuit of Virtue*. New Haven: Yale University Press, 1984.

The Liberal Ideal and Demons of Empire: Theories of Empire from Adam Smith to Lenin. Baltimore: Johns Hopkins University Press, 1993.

Sen, Amartya. *Commodities and Capabilities*. Amsterdam: North-Holland, 1985.

Development as Freedom. New York: Knopf, 1999.

Shell, Susan Meld. "Kant's 'True Economy of Human Nature': Rousseau, Count Verri, and the Problem of Happiness." In *Essays on Kant's Anthropology*, eds. Brian Jacobs and Patrick Kain, 194–229. Cambridge: Cambridge University Press, 2003.

Sherman, Nancy. "Kantian Virtue: Priggish or Passional?" In *Reclaiming the History of Ethics: Essays for John Rawls*, eds. Barbara Herman and Christine Korsgaard, 270–296. Cambridge: Cambridge University Press, 1997.

Making a Necessity of Virtue: Aristotle and Kant on Virtue. Cambridge: Cambridge University Press, 1997.

Shklar, Judith. *The Faces of Injustice*. New Haven: Yale University Press, 1990.

Singh, Jakeet. "Colonial Pasts, Decolonial Futures: Allen's _The End of Progress._" _Theory & Event_ 19, no. 4 (2016).

Skinner, Quentin. "Meaning and Understanding in the History of Ideas." _History and Theory_ 8, no. 1 (1969): 3–53.

Skorupski, John. _John Stuart Mill._ London: Routledge, 1991.

Skorupski, John, ed. _The Cambridge Companion to Mill._ Cambridge: Cambridge University Press, 1998.

Sleat, Matt. "Bernard Williams and the Possibility of a Realist Political Theory." _European Journal of Political Theory_ 9, no. 4 (2010): 485–503.

Sloan, Phillip R. "Buffon, German Biology, and the Historical Interpretation of Biological Species." _The British Journal for the History of Science_ 12, no. 2 (1979): 109–153.

"Performing the Categories: Eighteenth-Century Generation Theory and the Biological Roots of Kant's _A Priori._" _Journal of the History of Philosophy_ 40, no. 2 (2002): 229–253.

"Kant on the History of Nature: The Ambiguous Heritage of the Critical Philosophy for Natural History." _Studies in History and Philosophy of Biological and Biomedical Sciences_ 27 (2006): 627–648.

Spencer, Herbert. _Social Statics: Or, the Conditions Essential to Human Happiness Specified, and the First of them Developed._ London: John Chapman, 1860.

Facts and Comments. New York: D. Appleton and Co., 1902.

Spivak, Gayatri Chakravorty. _A Critique of Post-Colonial Reason: Toward a History of the Vanishing Present._ Cambridge: Harvard University Press, 1999.

Stam, Robert, and Ella Shohat. "Travelling Multiculturalism." In _Postcolonial Studies and Beyond_, eds. Ania Loomba, Suvir Kaul, Matti Bunzl and Antoinette Burton, 293–316. Durham: Duke University Press, 2005.

Stratton-Lake, Philip. "Moral Motivation in Kant." In _A Companion to Kant_, ed. Graham Bird, 322–334. Malden: Blackwell, 2006.

Stephen, Leslie. _The English Utilitarians._ London: Duckworth and Co., 1900.

Stewart, Robert Scott. "Art for Argument's Sake: Saving John Stuart Mill from the Fallacy of Composition." _The Journal of Value Inquiry_ 27, nos. 3/4 (1993): 443–453.

Stokes, Eric. _The English Utilitarians and India._ Delhi: Oxford University Press, 1989.

Storey, Ian. "Empire and Natural Order in Kant's 'Second Thoughts' on Race." _History of Political Thought_ 36, no. 4 (2015): 670–699.

Strauss, Leo. "Persecution and the Art of Writing." _Social Research_ 8, no. 4 (1941): 488–504.

Sullivan, Eileen. "Liberalism and Imperialism: J. S. Mill's Defense of the British Empire." _Journal of the History of Ideas_ 44 (1983): 599–617.

Swift, Adam. "The Value of Philosophy in Nonideal Circumstances." _Social Theory and Practice_ 34, no. 3 (2008).

Taylor, Charles. _Multiculturalism and the Politics of Recognition._ Princeton: Princeton University Press, 1992.

Ten, C. L. "Democracy, Socialism, and the Working Classes." In _The Cambridge Companion to Mill_, ed. John Skorupski, 372–395. Cambridge: Cambridge University Press, 1998.

"Mill's Defence of Liberty." In *J. S. Mill's On Liberty in Focus*, eds. John Gray and G. W. Smith, 212–238. London: Routledge, 2015.

ed. *Mill's On Liberty: A Critical Guide*. Cambridge: Cambridge University Press, 2008.

Thompson, Dennis F. *John Stuart Mill and Representative Government*. Princeton: Princeton University Press, 1976.

Tully, James. *An Approach to Political Philosophy: Locke in Contexts*. Cambridge: Cambridge University Press, 1993.

Public Philosophy in a New Key: Volume 2, Imperialism and Civic Freedom. Cambridge: Cambridge University Press, 2008.

"Lineages of Contemporary Imperialism." In *Lineages of Empire: The Historical Roots of British Imperial Thought*, ed. Duncan Kelly, 3–29. Oxford: Oxford University Press, 2009.

On Global Citizenship: James Tully in Dialogue. London: Bloomsbury Academic, 2014.

Tunick, Mark. "Tolerant Imperialism: J. S. Mill's Defense of British Rule in India." *Review of Politics* 68, no. 4 (2006): 586–611.

Turner, Jack. "Thinking Historically." *Theory & Event* 19, no. 1 (2016).

Urbinati, Nadia. *Mill on Democracy: From the Athenian Polis to Representative Government*. Chicago, University of Chicago Press, 2002.

"The Many Heads of the Hydra: J. S. Mill on Despotism." In *J. S. Mill's Political Thought: A Bicentennial Reassessment*, eds. Nadia Urbinati and Alex Zakaras, 66–97. Cambridge: Cambridge University Press, 2007.

"An Alternative Modernity: Mill on Capitalism and the Quality of Life." In *John Stuart Mill and the Art of Life*, eds. Ben Eggleston, Dale E. Miller and David Weinstein, 236–265. Oxford: Oxford University Press, 2011.

Urbinati, Nadia, and Alex Zakaras. *J. S. Mill's Political Thought: A Bicentennial Reassessment*. Cambridge: Cambridge University Press, 2007.

Valdez, Inés. "It's Not about Race: Good Wars, Bad Wars, and the Origins of Kant's Anti-Colonialism." *American Political Science Review* 111, no. 4 (2017): 819–834.

Varouxakis, Georgios. "Guizot's Historical Works and J.S. Mill's Reception of Tocqueville." *History of Political Thought* 20, no. 2 (1999): 292–312.

Mill on Nationality. London: Routledge, 2002.

Liberty Abroad: J. S. Mill on International Relations. Cambridge: Cambridge University Press, 2013.

"Empire, Race, Euro-Centrism: John Stuart Mill and His Critics." In *Utilitarianism and Empire*, eds. Bart Schultz and Georgios Varouxakis, 137–154. Lanham: Lexington Books, 2005.

"The Godfather of 'Occidentality': Auguste Comte and the Idea of 'the West'." *Modern Intellectual History* (2017), doi: 10.1017/S1479244317000415.

Valls, Andrew. "Self-Development and the Liberal State: The Cases of John Stuart Mill and Wilhelm von Humboldt." *The Review of Politics* 61, no. 2 (1999): 251–274.

Villa, Dana. *Public Freedom*. Princeton: Princeton University Press, 2008.

Waldron, Jeremy. "Theoretical Foundations of Liberalism." *The Philosophical Quarterly* 37, no. 147 (1987): 127–150.

"What Plato Would Allow." *Nomos* 37 (1995): 138–178.

"Mill and Multiculturalism." In *Mill's On Liberty: A Critical Guide*, ed. C. L. Ten, 165–184. Cambridge: Cambridge University Press, 2008.

Walzer, Michael. "Mill's 'A Few Words on Non-Intervention': A Commentary." In *J. S. Mill's Political Thought: A Bicentennial Reassessment*, eds. Nadia Urbinati and Alex Zakaras, 347–356. Cambridge: Cambridge University Press, 2007.

Watkins, Eric. "Introduction to *Lectures on Physical Geography.*" In *Natural Science*, ed. Eric Watkins, 434–438. Cambridge: Cambridge University Press, 2012.

Weinrib, Ernest J. "Poverty and Property in Kant's System of Rights." *Notre Dame Law Review* 78, no. 3 (2003): 795–828.

"Kant on Citizenship and Universal Independence." *Australian Journal of Legal Philosophy* 33 (2008): 1–25.

White, Richard. "Liberalism and Multiculturalism: The Case of Mill." *Journal of Value Inquiry* 37, no. 2 (2003): 205–216.

White, Steven K. *The Ethos of a Late-Modern Citizen*. Cambridge MA: Harvard University Press, 2009.

A Democratic Bearing: Admirable Citizens, Uneven Justice, and Critical Theory. Cambridge: Cambridge University Press, 2017.

Williams, Howard. *Kant's Political Philosophy*. New York: St. Martin's Press, 1983.

Williams, Patrick and Laura Chrisman, eds. *Colonial Discourse and Post-Colonial Theory: A Reader*. New York: Columbia University Press, 1994.

Wilson, Catherine. "Kant on Civilization, Culture and Moralisation." In *Kant's Lectures on Anthropology: A Critical Guide*, ed. A. Cohen, 191–210. Cambridge: Cambridge University Press, 2014.

Wilson, Fred. "Psychology and the Moral Sciences." In *The Cambridge Companion to Mill*, ed. John Skorupski, 203–222. Cambridge: Cambridge University Press, 1998.

Wilson, Holly L. "Kant's Evolutionary Theory of Marriage." In *Autonomy and Community: Readings in Contemporary Kantian Social Philosophy*, eds. Jane Kneller and Sidney Axinn, 283–306. Albany State University of New York Press, 1998.

Kant's Pragmatic Anthropology: Its Origin, Meaning and Critical Significance. Albany: State University of New York Press, 2006.

Wood, Allen W. *Kant's Ethical Thought*. Cambridge: Cambridge University Press, 1999.

"Kant and the Problem of Human Nature." In *Essays on Kant's Anthropology*, eds. Brian Jacobs and Patrick Kain, 38–59. Cambridge: Cambridge University Press, 2003.

Young, Iris Marion. *Inclusion and Democracy*. Oxford: Oxford University Press, 2002.

Justice and the Politics of Difference. Princeton: Princeton University Press, 2011.

Yovel, Yirmiyahu. *Kant and the Philosophy of History*. Princeton: Princeton University Press, 1980.

Ypi, Lea. "*Natura Daedala Rerum*? On the Justification of Historical Progress in Kant's 'Guarantee of Perpetual Peace'." *Kantian Review* 14, no. 2 (2010): 118–148.

"Commerce and Colonialism in Kant's Philosophy of History." In *Kant and Colonialism*, eds. Katrin Flikschuh and Lea Ypi, 99–126. Oxford: Oxford University Press, 2014.

Zammito, John. *Kant, Herder, and the Birth of Anthropology*. Chicago: University of Chicago Press, 2002.

"Kant and the Concept of Race: Late Eighteenth-Century Writings." *Notre Dame Philosophical Reviews: An Electronic Journal*, January 10, 2014, http://ndpr

.nd.edu/news/45502-kant-and-the-concept-of-race-late-eighteenth-century-writings/.

"What a Young Man Needs for His Venture into the World: The Function and Evolution of the 'Characteristics'." In *Kant's Lectures on Anthropology: A Critical Guide*, ed. A. Cohen, 230–248. Cambridge: Cambridge University Press, 2014.

Zakaras, Alex. "John Stuart Mill, Individuality, and Participatory Democracy." In *J. S. Mill's Political Thought: A Bicentennial Reassessment*, eds. Nadia Urbinati and Alex Zakaras, 200–220. Cambridge: Cambridge University Press, 2007.

Zastoupil, Lynn. *John Stuart Mill and India*. Stanford: Stanford University Press, 1994.

"India, Mill, and 'Western' Culture." In *J. S. Mill's Encounter with India*, eds. Martin I. Moir, Douglas M. Peers and Lynn Zastoupil, 111–148. Toronto: University of Toronto Press, 1999.

Index